THE PSYCHOLOGY
OF POLITICS

Transaction Books by Hans Eysenck

Dimensions of Personality

Intelligence

The Psychology of Politics

Rebel with a Cause

HANS J. EYSENCK

THE PSYCHOLOGY OF POLITICS

with a new introduction by the author

Transaction Publishers
New Brunswick (U.S.A.) and London (U.K.)

New material this edition copyright © 1999 by Transaction Publishers, New Brunswick, New Jersey. Originally published in 1954 by Routledge & Kegan Paul Ltd.

Library of Congress Catalog Number: 98–24888
ISBN: 0–7658–0430–1
Printed in the United States of America

Library of Congress Cataloging-in-Publication Data

Eysenck, H. J. (Hans Jurgen), 1916–
    The psychology of politics / Hans Eysenck ; with a new introduction by the author.
        p.   cm.
    Originally published: London : Routledge and K. Paul, 1954.
    Includes bibliographical references and index.
    ISBN 0–7658–0430–1 (pbk. : alk. paper)
    1. Political psychology. 2. Attitude (Psychology) I. Title.
JA74.5.E97   1998
320'.01'9—dc21   98–24888
                                                                          CIP

TO GARY

*in the hope that he will grow up
in a society
more interested in psychology
than politics*

'I have no faith in anything short of
actual measurement and rule of three.'

CHARLES DARWIN

'Die Politik ist keine exakte Wissenchaft.'

OTTO VON BISMARCK

CONTENTS

INTRODUCTION TO THE TRANSACTION EDITION   XV

ACKNOWLEDGMENTS   XXV

INTRODUCTION   1

I VOTING, ATTITUDES, AND SOCIAL CLASS   7

II PUBLIC OPINION POLLS   38

III OPINION AND ATTITUDE MEASUREMENT   71

IV THE ORGANIZATION OF SOCIAL ATTITUDES   107

V ATTITUDES, VALUES, AND INTERESTS   143

VI IDEOLOGY AND TEMPERAMENT   170

VII AGGRESSIVENESS, DOMINANCE AND RIGIDITY   199

VIII A THEORY OF POLITICAL ACTION   237

IX SUMMARY AND CONCLUSIONS   265

TECHNICAL NOTES   269

BIBLIOGRAPHY   285

INDEX   312

LIST OF TABLES

  i British Institute of Public Opinion Forecasts and *page* 15
    Actual Votes of Parties in Three Post-War Elections

  ii Relationship Between Social Status and Political 17
    Attitude

  iii Relationship Between Social Class and Political Attitude 15

  iv Relationship Between Social Status and Social Class 19

  v Relationship Between Education and Political Attitude 20

  vi Relationship Between Religious Affiliation and Political Attitude 21

  vii Relationship Between Sex and Voting Intention 23

  viii Intercorrelations Between Six Attitude Questions 25
    and Correlations with Total Score and Voting Intention

  ix The Derivation of Centers's Stratification Score from 27
    Occupation, Power, and Economic Status Indices

  x Intercorrelations of Three Status Scores and Correlations 27
    with Stratification, Class, Conservatism, and
    Voting

  xi Possible Discrepancies Between Number of People
    in Various Cross-Sections of the Population and of a
    Sample Selected to Give the Same Overall Proportions 43

  xii Number in Sample Required to Give Desired Degree
    of Accuracy for Various Divisions of Opinion 48

  xiii 1 Reliability of Assessing Economic Status by the
    Same Interviewer 73

  xiii 2 Reliability of Assessing Economic Status by Independent Interviewers 73

xi

xiv Relationship Between Vote Intention and Actual Vote   74

xv Results of Bogardus Social Distance Scale for Ten Groups as Obtained from an American Population   83

xvi Degree of Anti-Semitism, Reproducibility, and Correlation with Radicalism of Twenty-four Items in Anti-Semitism Scale   94

xvii A Simple Form of Scalogram   96

xviii Inventory of Social Attitudes   122

xix Composition of Experimental Group in Terms of Sex, Age, and Education   126

xx Proportion of 'Yes' Answers of Conservatives, Liberals, and Socialists to Forty Social Attitude Questions, As Well As Factor Saturations of These Questions   129

xxi Detailed Scores on Radicalism and Tough-Mindedness for Various Sub-Groups   134

xxii Reliabilities of R and T Scales for Various Sub-Groups   135

xxiii Comparison of R and T Scores for Middle-Class and Working-Class Voters   138

xxiv Authoritarianism Scale   149

xxv Fascism Scale   157

xxvi Correlations of Dominance and Aggression with Radicalism, Tender-Mindedness and Rigidity   210

xxvii Rigidity Scale   222

xxviii Intolerence of Ambiguity Scale   224

xxix Correlations Between Rigidity Tests, Radicalism, and Tender-Mindedness   226

xxx Stimulus Words Classified by Value Area and Frequency of Occurrence   248

LIST OF FIGURES

1 Diagrammatic Representation of Intervening Variable   *page* 13
2 Increase in Conservative Voting Intention with Increasing Age in Four Economic Groups   22
3 Percentage of Persons in Several Attitude Categories who Voted Republican in 1944   26
4 Relation of Occupational Stratification and Education to Class Identification and Conservatism-Radicalism   28
5 Relation of Occupational Stratification and Age to Class Identification and Conservatism-Radicalism   29
6 Per cent of Different Status Groups Voting Republican or Democrat Sub-Divided According to Class Affiliation   30
7 Per cent of Different Status Groups Voting Republican or Democrat Sub-Divided According to Religious Affiliation   31
8 Number in Sample Required to Reach Desired Degree of Accuracy for Three Different Divisions of Opinion   49
9 Distribution of Height of 8585 Adult Males   81
10 Results from Application of Bogardus Social Distance Scale to British Sample   85
11 Comparison Between Radical and Conservative Scores on Social Distance Scale for Anglo-Saxon and North-European Groups   86
12 Comparison Between Radical and Conservative Scores on Social Distance Scale for South- and East-European and Coloured Groups   87
13 Distribution of Anti-Semitism Scores   93
14 Distribution of Attitude Scores Towards Negroes for Three Populations   102
15 Diagram Illustrating Two-Dimensional Description of Nylons   109
16 Diagram Illustrating Three Hypotheses Regarding Relative Position of Five Main Political Groups   111
17 Diagram Illustrating Relation Between Opinion, Attitude, and Ideology   112
18 Diagram Illustrating Geometrical Representation of Correlation Coefficients   114
19 Dimensionality as a Function of Angles and Correlations   115

20 Diagram Showing Correlations Between Six Attitudes   116
in Terms of a Two-Dimensional Pattern
21 Diagram Showing Invariance of Attitudes with Change   117
of Reference Axes
22 Distribution of 22,208 Votes on a 7-Point Attitude Scale   121
23 Distribution of Attitudes with Respect to Tough-   130
Mindedness and Radicalism
24 Distribution of Scores on Radicalism Factor for Three   136
Political Parties
25 Comparison of Middle-Class and Working-Class Groups   137
with Respect to Tender-Mindedness and Radicalism
26 Tough-Mindedness Scores and Scores of Radicalism-   141
Conservatism of Communists, Fascists, and Neutral
Group
27 Distribution of Attitudes with Respect to Humanitari-   147
anism and Religionism
28 Picture of Directive Leadership, Form for Male Respon-   155
dents
29 Position of Various Guilford Questionnaires with Re-   177
spect to Neuroticism and Extraversion
30 Diagram Showing the Relation Between Radicalism,   178
Tough-Mindedness, Social Values, and Extraversion
Measures
31 Examples of Simple and Complex Drawings Used as   183
Measures of Personality
32 Picture Used to Elicit Aggressive and Non-Aggressive   201
Responses
33 Scores of Fascists, Communists, and Neutral Group with   205
Respect to Direct and Indirect Aggression
34 Scores of Fascists, Communists, and Neutral Group with   206
Respect to Direct and Indirect Dominance
35 Scores of Fascists, Communists, and Neutral Group with   207
Respect to Dominance and Aggression
36 Aggression Scores of Communists, Fascists, and Neutral   212
Group Plotted Against Radicalism-Conservatism
37 Dominance Scores of Communists, Fascists, and Neutral   214
Group Plotted Against Radicalism-Conservatism
38 Water Jar Test of Rigidity   220
39 Maps Test of Rigidity   221
40 Dog-Cat Test of Intolerance of Ambiguity   223
41 The Percentage of Comprehensive, Isolated, and Nar-   230
row Organizations Given by Subjects in Ethnocentrism
Quartiles 1, 2, 3, and 4
42 Stereotyped Estimates and Actual Mean Scores in Intel-   243
ligence Tests of People living in Eight Austrian Counties
43 sE_R or Action Potential as a Function of sH_R (Habit)   251
and D (Drive)
44 Speed of Conditioning in Extraverts and Introverts   262

INTRODUCTION TO THE TRANSACTION EDITION

I N 1954 I published *The Psychology of Politics* (Eysenck, 1954), a book I consider one of my most original, but sadly also one of the least successful. It followed the publication of *The Authoritarian Personality* (Adorno et al., 1950). My theoretical orientation had already found expression in the publication of some early experiments ten years earlier (Eysenck, 1944). My general approach, like that of Adorno and his fellow workers, was based on my experiences in Nazi Germany, and my need to come to grips with the appearance of a dictatorship that did not fit into the common picture of a single left-right continuum from socialism through liberalism to capitalism. Adorno et al. postulated an authoritarian personality that was very largely right-wing; they added certain Freudian notions that are no longer taken seriously, and will not be discussed. My own research and earlier experiences in Germany led me to believe that authoritarianism (tough-mindedness) could appear equally well on the left as on the right, and I saw Stalin as equally authoritarian as Hitler, communism as equally totalitarian as nazism. The book contains the evidence I collected, and the arguments I used.

Unfortunately the Zeitgeist was very much opposed to my thesis. "Uncle Joe" was a great favorite among the pinkish-leftish intelligentsia that had no stomach for the factual account of Stalin's murderous regime that had slaughtered some 50 million innocent people (or whatever the true number was; I don't suppose we shall ever know). This was the time when socialism was victorious in Britain, with its Labour government, and the London School of Economics, founded by the Webbs, who had visited the USSR and returned saying they had seen the future "and its work." All shied away in horror from someone who dared to equate communism with fascism! I was shunned, and never ceased to be persona non-grata in British academic circles. American academics were no different (Christie, 1956; Rokeach & Hanley, 1956). My replies (Eysenck, 1956a, b) went largely unheard; the emotional aspects of the criticisms won the day.

Oddly enough, both Christie (Christie & Geis, 1970) and Rokeach (1973) later advanced theories that resembled very closely those they had so vociferously condemned. Rokeach (1960) advanced the concept of *dogmatism*, which is one personality attitude of the tough-minded type; he also advanced (Rokeach, 1973) a conceptual scheme of human values, which as he himself admits, "most closely resembles Eysenck's (1954) hypothesis" (p.186). In this scheme, the two major, orthogonal value systems are those of *equality* (related to radicalism) and *freedom* (related to tender-mindedness). Christie and Lehman (1970) advanced the concept of *Machiavellianism*, which is closely related to another personality attitude of the tough-mindedness type. Both of these concepts are of much interest in social psychology, and both serve to broaden the notion of tough-mindedness in important directions.

This is not the place to fight again the battles of long ago. The weakness, errors, and absurdities of the Authoritarian Personality are too well-known to require restatement (Stowe, Lederer & Christie, 1993), and reality has redressed the vacuity of the Zeitgeist of those happy days. Americans still are little interested in studies like mine, done in a different country; with different parties and different political problems; the notion of psychology as an international science is still not accepted widely, or with good grace. A more recent book, *The Psychological Basis of Ideology* (Eysenck & Wilson, 1978) brought together a large number of articles published since *The Psychology of Politics*, but did not even get a review in the United States, in spite of the fact that these papers gave massive support to my original thesis, from a large number of workers in many different countries. Wilson's (1973) independent and rather novel approach also gave strong support, but failed to revive interest in my theories. Once a theory misses the boat (or is prevented from even approaching it!), it can seldom be revived. Even the fact that in Russia authoritarianism is clearly linked with communist sympathies (McFarland,

Ageyer & Djintcharadze, 1996; McFarland, Ageyer & Abalabina-Paap, 1992) does not seem to have persuaded people of the existence of a left-wing authoritarianism, an oxymoron if ever there was one for the Adorno group.

Several articles published after *The Psychology of Politics* (Eysenck, 1961, 1971, 1975, 1976; Hewitt, Eysenck & Eaves, 1977) replicated and extended previous findings, but the most important paper undoubtedly was one by Eysenck and Coulter (1972), in which we looked at the attitudes and personalities of members of the communist and fascist parties of Great Britain. (Thelma Coulter had to join both parties, at considerable danger to her life, in order to persuade members to co-operate in the study.) Her results leave little doubt about the great similarity of the two groups as far as aggressiveness and other personality traits are concerned. I feel that this study makes the existence of left-wing fascism as certain as anything in social psychology.

These are extensions of previous research; the most dramatic new finding (which has not yet found its way into the textbooks!) was the discovery that social attitudes are determined in the main not by environmental and familial factors, as had been taken for granted by generations of social psychologists, but by genetic determinants (Eaves & Eysenck, 1974). This finding was so dramatic that it had to be replicated, and final results of the replication were published fifteen years later (Eaves, Eysenck & Martin, 1989). Again heredity was found to play an important part, and the revolutionary consequences of this finding will undoubtedly have an important influence on our future thinking about the factors causing the observed differences in social attitudes that are so very apparent to any careful observer. There are now several further replications to make the facts incontestable (e.g., Martin et al., 1986; Posner et al., 1996; Tesser, 1993; Truett et al., 1992).

This, of course, does not mean that social attitudes cannot be changed. Neuroticism, too, is largely genetically determined (Eaves, Eysenck & Martin, 1989), but specific neurotic symptoms can certainly be eliminated (Giles, 1993). Grossarth-Maticek and Eysenck (1985) have shown that prejudice is a very general factor on the tough-minded side of the equation, based on a neurotic type of temperament leading to a failure to cope appropriately with stress, and that behavior therapy addressing this

underlying trait could produce quite marked changes in atti
tude. Figures I.1 and I.2 show the increase in "without prejudice" people in the treatment group, as compared with non-
treated controls, and the clearance of anti-Semitic sentiment in
the treatment group, as compared with non-treated controls. In
view of the great social importance of racial and national prejudice in this world, evidence that it can be changed is vitally important; genetic influence is often taken as evidence of thera-
peutic nihilism, but that is a complete misunderstanding of the
situation. It would be untrue even if heritability happened to be
up in the nineties, but with h2 only between 50 and 60 percent,
there clearly is ample room for behavioral intervention.

The attempts to disprove the notion of left-wing
authoritarianism draw attention away from other important findings. Thouless (1935) published a paper demonstrating that
religious beliefs followed his "principle of certainty," that is,
people tended either to be believers or atheists, few acknowl-
edged that where there are extreme beliefs, pulling in opposite
directions, a middle (agnostic) position may be more reasonable. I tried to extend this principle to social attitudes and beliefs generally, and found strong support for a general law in
this unpromising field. I thought that in a discipline notoriously
lacking in general laws or principles, a well-supported generalization like this would attract attention, and would be submitted
to extended scrutiny. In spite of the possible importance of such
a principle for an understanding of party politics, social policy
debates, and religious fragmentation, it has hardly ever been
mentioned, and never replicated. This seems to me a great pity;
if true, the principle can powerfully aid an understanding of
social action.

Looking back after forty years on the debates centering on
The Psychology of Politics, it seems to me that while critics were not
necessarily wrong in pointing out weaknesses in the methodology of the research, they concentrated on minor faults and for-
got the larger picture. Is there evidence in the book to contra-
dict the widespread belief that authoritarianism was always and
exclusively on the right (conservatism) side, or was there an
equally strong left-wing authoritarianism? Were communists and
fascists essentially united by a common personality type, and a
common belief in an essentially authoritarian ethos, rejecting

xviii

FIGURE I.1

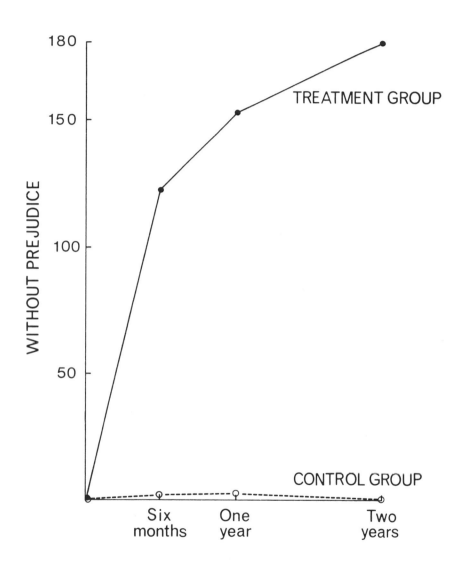

Increase in Number of "Without Prejudice" Subjects in Treated Group
(Grossarth-Maticek, Eysenck & Vetter, 1989)

FIGURE I.2

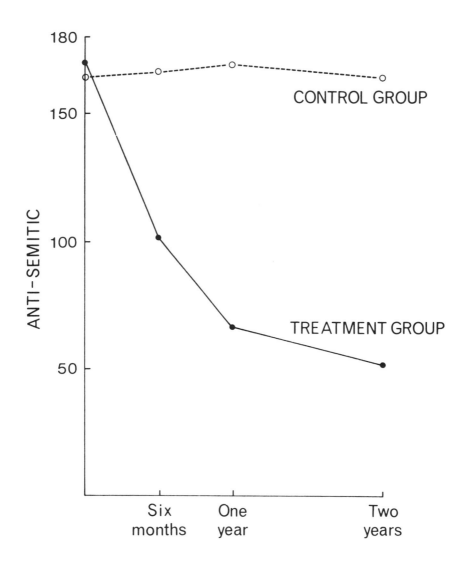

Decline in Number of Anti-Semites After Treatment
(Grossarth-Maticek, Eysenck & Vetter, 1989)

democratic methods and aims? Major social questions like these cannot be decided in the laboratory, but demand empirical studies in which the experimenter does not always have as much choice in the matter of samples, tests, and methodology as he might wish. Similarly, attitudes are not always structured as statistics based on normal distribution would prefer. New problems arise that cannot always be solved in traditional ways. Simple structure does not guarantee psychologically meaningful rotations. Too much concern with minor problems of reliability and too little attention to major questions of validity have been persistent dilemmas in psychology. Small and unimportant problems are best suited to excellent methodology and complex statistics; complex and important problems present difficulties in the way of perfect solutions, and often we have to do the best we can, in the hope that our successors will do better. Drawing upon the social experience of the past forty years, as well as upon the many empirical studies published since 1954, I would confidently say that my major thesis is hardly any longer in doubt, with even the major critics coming up with similar solutions. But even now the Zeitgeist of political correctness makes acknowledgment of the facts difficult, reluctant, and grudging. Perhaps after *The Psychology of Politics*, I should write another book on the politics of psychology; the history of my book furnishes an interesting introduction to such a volume!

REFERENCES

Adorno, T. W., Frenkel-Brunswick, E., Levinson, D. J., & Sanford, R. N. 1950. *The Authoritarian Personality.* New York: Harper & Row.

Christie, R. 1956. Eysenck's treatment of the personality of communists. *Psychological Bulletin, 53,* 411–430.

Christie, R., & Geis, F. 1970. *Studies in Machiavellianism.* London: Academic Press.

Christie, R., & Lehman, S. 1970. The structure of Machiavellian orientation. In Christie & Geis, *Studies in Machiavellianism,* 359–387.

Eaves, L., & Eysenck, H. J. 1974. Genetics and the development of social attitudes. *Nature, 249,* 288–289.

Eaves, L. J., Eysenck, H. J., & Martin, N. G. 1989. *Genes, Culture and Personality.* London: Academic Press.

Eysenck, H. J. 1941. Social attitude and social class. *British Journal of Social and Clinical Psychology,* 10, 210–214.

————. 1944. General social attitudes. *Journal of Social Attitudes,* 19, 207–227.

————. 1954. *The Psychology of Politics.* London: Routledge & Kegan Paul.

————. 1956a. The psychology of politics: A reply. *Psychological Bulletin,* 53, 177–182.

————. 1956b. The psychology of politics and the personality similarities between fascists and communists. *Psychological Bulletin,* 53, 431–438.

————. 1961. Personality and social attitudes. *Journal of Social Psychology,* 53, 243–248.

————. 1971. Social attitude and social class. *British Journal of Social and Clinical Psychology,* 10, 210–214.

————. 1975. The measurement of emotions: Psychological parameters and methods. In L. Lee (Ed.), *Emotions—Their Parameters and Measurement,* 435–467. New York: Raven Press.

————. 1976. Structure of social attitudes. *Psychological Reports,* 39, 463–466.

————. 1979. The structure of social attitudes. *British Journal of Social and Clinical Psychology,* 14, 323–331.

Eysenck, H. J., & Coulter, T. 1972. The personality and attitudes of working-class British Communists and Fascists. *Journal of Social Psychology,* 87, 59–73.

Eysenck, H. J., & Wilson, G. D. (Eds.) 1978. *The Psychological Basis of Ideology.* Lancaster: MTP Press.

Giles, T. R. (Ed.) 1993. *Handbook of Effective Psychology.* New York: Plenum.

Grossarth-Maticek, R., Bastiaans, J., & Kanazir, D.T. 1985. Psychological factors as strong predictors of mortality from cancer, ischaemic heart disease and stroke: The Yugoslav Prospective Study. *Journal of Psychosomatic Research,* 29, 167–176.

Grossarth-Maticek, R., Eysenck, H. J., & Vetter, H. 1989. The causes and cures of prejudice: An empirical study of the frustration-aggression hypothesis. *Personality and Individual Differences,* 10, 547–558.

Hewitt, J. K., Eysenck, H. J., & Eaves, L. J. 1977. Structure of social attitudes after twenty-five years: A replication. *Psychological Reports,* 30, 182–188.

Martin, N. G., Eaves, L. J., Heath, A. C., Jardine, R., Feingold, L. M., & Eysenck, H. J. 1986. Transmission of social attitudes. *Proceedings of the National Academy of Science,* 83, 4364–4368.

McFarland, S., Ageyer, P., & Abalabina-Paap, M. 1992. Authoritarianism in the former Soviet Union. *Journal of Personality and Social Psychology,* 63, 1004–1010.

McFarland, S., Agcyer, V., & Djintcharadze, N. 1996. Russian Authoritarianism two years after communism. *Personality and Social Psychology Bulletin,* 22, 210–217.

Posner, S. F., Barker, L., Heath, A., & Martin, N. G. 1996. Social contact, social attitudes, and twin similarity. *Behaviour Genetics,* 20, 123–133.

Rokeach, M. 1960. *The Open and Closed Mind.* New York: The Free Press.

———. 1973. *The Nature of Human Values.* New York: The Free Press.

Rokeach, M., & Hanley, E. 1956. Eysenck's tender-minded dimension: A critique. *Psychological Bulletin,* 53, 169–176.

Stowe, W. F., Lederer, L. D., & Christie, R. (Eds.) 1993. *Strengths and Weaknesses: The Authoritarian Personality Today.* New York: Springer Verlag.

Tesser, A. 1993. On the importance of heritability in psychological research. The case of attitudes. *Psychological Review,* 100, 129–142.

Thouless, R. H. 1935. The tendency to certainty in religious beliefs. *British Journal of Psychology,* 26, 16–31.

Truett, K. R., Eaves, L. J., Meyer, J. M., Heath, A. C., & Martin, N. G. 1992. Religion and education as mediators of attitudes: A multivariate analysis. *Behaviour Genetics,* 22, 433–62.

Wilson, G. D. (Ed.) 1973. *The Psychology of Conservatism.* London: Academic Press.

ACKNOWLEDGMENTS

ACKNOWLEDGMENT is due to the following authors and publishers for permission to quote and reproduce tables and figures from copy-righted works in this volume:

American Psychological Association and the *Journal of Abnormal and Social Psychology* for excerpts from E. L. Cowen and G. G. Thompson (1951); F. Barron and G. S. Welsh (1953); G. Lindzey (1950); and M. Rokeach (1948).

Appleton-Century-Crofts, Inc., for excerpts and Figures 1 and 43 from *Principles of Behaviour* by C. L. Hull (1943).

Child Development Publications and D. B. Harris, H. C. Gough and W. E. Martin for excerpts from Child Development Publications (1950).

Columbia University Press and P. F. Lazarsfeld, B. Berelson and H. Gaudet for excerpts, Table 14, Figure 8, and Figure 9 from *The People's Choice* (1948).

Harper & Bros., for excerpts from E. Frenkel-Brunswik's chapter and Table 24 from *The Authoritarian Personality* by T. W. Adorno *et al.* (1950); *Appraising Vocational Fitness* by D. E. Super (1949); and *Groups in Harmony and Tension* by M. Sherif and C. W. Sherif (1953).

Heath & Company and S. E. Bogardus for excerpts and Table 15 from *The Measurement of Social Distance* (1928).

Institute for Research in Human Relations and F. H. Sanford for excerpts from *Authoritarianism and Leadership* (1950).

W. Braumueller (Editor) and P. R. Hofstaetter for excerpts and Figure 42 from *Die Psychologie der Oeffentlichen Meinung*, Wien, 1949.

ACKNOWLEDGMENTS

Journal of Personality for excerpts and Figure 41 from M. Rokeach (1951).

Journal of Social Psychology for excerpts from W. A. Lurie (1937); excerpts and Figure 14 from V. M. Sims and J. R. Patrick (1936); excerpts and Tables 27 and 28 from H. C. Gough (1951); and excerpts and Table 25 from R. Stagner (1944).

McGraw Hill Book Company and R. B. Cattell for Figures 18 and 19 from *Personality* (1950).

Prentice Hall, Inc., and S. E. Asch for excerpts from *Social Psychology* (1952).

INTRODUCTION

I N this book I have tried to do two things—with the inevitable result of falling between two stools. In the first place, I have tried to write a book about modern developments in the field of attitude study; a book which would be intelligible to the layman without any special training in psychology or statistics, and which would be of service in the important task of keeping citizens of a democratic country in touch with scientific developments which are likely to have considerable repercussions on their lives, and on those of their children. Science now has something to say about such problems as anti-Semitism, the origin and growth of Fascist and Communist ideologies, the causal determinants of voting behaviour, the structure of opinions and attitudes, and the relationship between politics and personality; it seemed desirable that these factual findings should be rescued from the obscurity of technical journals, often inaccessible, and research reports, often unobtainable, and be presented in a readily intelligible form. The difficulty of doing this is more apparent to me now than it was at the beginning; technical jargon, the shorthand symbolism of statistics, and well-worn abbreviations all too easily slip into one's writing, and are difficult to exorcise.

My second aim has been to write a book which would integrate into one consistent theoretical system a large number of contributions from different fields. In the first place, our research was directed toward finding the main principles of organization or structure in the field of attitudes; these principles were then found to account in a remarkably complete and detailed manner for the systems of political organization found in this country, i.e. the Conservative, Liberal, and Socialist parties, and the Communist and Fascist groups. Next, an attempt was made to relate these prin-

I

ciples to the system of personality structure which has formed the main focus of research activity at the Institute of Psychiatry, and which has been described in detail in *Dimensions of Personality*, *The Scientific Study of Personality*, and *The Structure of Human Personality*. This attempt was successful, and this success was particularly gratifying to me because it suggests that I was justified in the belief which inspired the whole series of attitude studies reported here, viz. that *opinions and attitudes are an integral part of personality*, and deserve serious study by students of personality. As a last step, then, I attempted to integrate attitude research with modern learning theory, probably the most advanced part of psychology, and while this attempt was made on the theoretical level only, I believe it holds exciting promise for future experimental work.

The attempt to achieve two such divergent aims has necessitated recourse to the rather clumsy device of relegating to a series of *Technical Notes* (on pages 269 to 287, referred to by superior figures in the text) the detailed discussion of various points, the citation of references, and the presentation of statistics not immediately necessary to the argument. This has the advantage of making available to the reader the main body of data on which the conclusions are based; if he is interested in the results more than in the proof, he will miss nothing by disregarding these terminal Notes. If he has doubts on any point, however, then he may find the detailed documentation and the list of references contained therein useful.

It hardly requires emphasis that this book is not in any sense an apologia for any political party or system, and that its contents are unlikely to please adherents of one party or group more than those of another. Indeed, my purpose has been to *understand* and *explain*, not to *persuade* and *condemn*. However much some of the attitudes studied may be anathema to me personally, such feelings are irrelevant and must be prevented from contaminating a purely factual and objective study. As Thurstone points out, 'perhaps the principal reason why social psychology has very low prestige is that many authors in that field reveal that they have an axe to grind. It is doubtful whether one can be a propagandist and a scientist in the same field and at the same time.' For the same reason I have kept away from any suggestion as to the possible uses of the findings reported here. As a citizen, I have strong views on this point; as a scientist, I recognize that these views are value-judgments, and that they have no place in this account.

INTRODUCTION

To those who argue that political phenomena cannot be attacked by traditional scientific methods, the proper answer is again provided by Thurstone. 'The excuse is often made that social phenomena are so complex that the relatively simple methods of the older sciences do not apply. This argument is probably false. The analytical study of social phenomena is probably not so difficult as is commonly believed. The principal difficulty is that the experts in social studies are frequently hostile to science. They try to describe the totality of a situation, and their orientation is often to the market place or the election next week. They do not understand the thrill of discovering an invariance of some kind which never covers the totality of any situation. Social studies will not become science until students of social phenomena learn to appreciate this essential aspect of science.' It would more than repay my trouble in writing this book if I could succeed in making the reader feel this thrill on discovering some of the invariances dealt with.

Approximately half the material discussed in the main body of the book derives from published and unpublished reports of work carried out in this country, much of it in the Psychological Department here at the Institute of Psychiatry; the other half derives from various sources, mainly American. It is fortunate indeed, in view of the undoubted leadership of American psychologists in this field, that conditions in our two countries are sufficiently similar to make cross-comparisons fruitful. There is ample experimental work to prove this point, and some of it is mentioned in the text. I have repeated some of our English studies in other countries, and results from Germany and Sweden, as well as from the U.S.A., make it seem likely that the main conclusions drawn here would apply equally well there; it would not be wise, however, to generalize too far. Repetition of at least some of these studies in France, Greece, Italy, Mexico, Egypt, some of the South-American countries, and in Africa and Asia, would add immeasurably to our knowledge. Financial considerations make it unlikely that such studies will be carried out in the near future, and it will be safest at the moment to consider our conclusions to apply to the British Isles and the United States only.

This is particularly important when considering the personality structure of members of groups such as the Fascist and Communist parties. In our culture, these are minority groups; it is unlikely that conclusions based on members of such groups could be transferred without change to members of the Communist Party in the U.S.S.R., or to members of the former N.S.D.A.P. in Germany. When we talk about Communists and Fascists, therefore, it is about British Communists and Fascists we are talking, not about their foreign prototypes. At times the reader will undoubtedly be tempted to generalize beyond this restriction; if he does, he does so at his own peril.

I owe a debt of gratitude to several former research students and colleagues in the Department whose patient, careful, and highly skilled research work has contributed a good portion of the data to be discussed. In particular, I should like to mention the work of Dr. S. Crown on the construction of attitude scales, of Dr. T. Coulter on attitudes and personality characteristics of Fascists and Communists; of Dr. D. Melvin on the measurement of the main dimensions in the attitude field; of Dr. E. I. George on the relation between these dimensions, personality, and values; and of Dr. M. B. Shapiro on the relation between social attitudes and opinions on child upbringing. I am further indebted to the students in one of my Seminars at the University of Pennsylvania during my tenure there of a Visiting Professorship for carrying through a repetition of one of our English studies on an American audience.

Dr. H. Durant, President of the British Institute of Public Opinion, gave me permission to reanalyse and quote at some length some of the extremely interesting surveys conducted by his organization. I particularly appreciate this kindness as I have in the past been somewhat critical of certain aspects of opinion polling, and indeed still have certain reservations which are discussed in full in the text. It is fortunate that in science factual disagreements need not interfere with personal relationships.

I have had the opportunity of meeting several of the people whose work has done much to throw light on the problems discussed in this book. Dr. G. Allport, Dr. S. Asch, Dr. F. Barron, Dr. R. B. Cattell, Dr. L. Festinger, Dr. E. Frenkel-Brunswik, Dr. D. J. Levinson, Dr. R. Likert, Dr. D. W. MacKinnon, Dr. P. E. Meehl, Dr. O. H. Mowrer, Dr. T. M. Newcomb, Dr. M. Rokeach, Dr. N. Sanford, and Dr. L. L. Thurstone are some of those whose stimulating views have contributed to my formulation of hypotheses and experiments. I owe a special debt to Dr. J. Flugel, who was in part responsible for my interest in the field of social atti-

4

tudes. As the story of how this came about may be of interest in demonstrating the irrational, unscientific way in which even highly intelligent people look upon factual studies in the social field, I shall tell it here briefly.

Flugel and Hopkins had been conducting an attitude survey of certain minority groups—vegetarians, sunbathers, anti-smokers, and so forth—in the course of which they sent out questionnaires asking for their opinions on a variety of subjects ranging from anti-vivisection to Esperanto, and from super-tax to psycho-analysis. Before even half the intended number of questionnaires had been distributed, leading articles appeared in the national press complaining about the 'Bolshevisation of our youth', and demanding that this foul piece of propaganda be stopped. The Provost of the University College at which both men were teaching at the time demanded that the offending questionnaires and all the results be burned immediately. When it was pointed out to him that such burning of books was quite fashionable elsewhere at the time, he did not press the point, but demanded that neither of the investigators should in any way continue with the research. The material collected was therefore handed over to me by Flugel and Hopkins, and a detailed analysis of the responses collected suggested to me an hypothesis regarding certain invariant features of social attitudes which has since been amply substantiated by further research, and which is presented in Chapter Four.

This incident happened before the second World War, but there is little evidence to suggest that obstacles to research in this field are any less serious now than they were then. During my stay in Philadelphia, for instance, one member of my Seminar spent a night in gaol because he had interviewed a number of people in the poorer districts of the town concerning their views about Negroes. Suspicious, they telephoned the police, certain that he was a Communist agitator, a view shared by the police who failed to recognize the difference between canvassing for propaganda purposes and interviewing in order to obtain information. Not a very terrible thing to happen, I agree, but enough to make many students, less intrepid than this particular one, feel that perhaps their work was not really being appreciated by society.

However, direct discouragement of this kind is certainly very much rarer and less violent than it would be in non-democratic countries; indeed, it is doubtful if any kind of scientific work on social problems could be carried out at all in dictatorship countries. Much more prevalent is indirect discouragement, which shows itself in the failure to create University and research posts (to give but one example, there is no Chair of Social Psychology in this country), failure to make use of the knowledge and the skill of social scientists, and failure to provide the conditions under which proper scientific research in the social field can be carried out. If the reader is somewhat disappointed after reading this book, and feels that there are very many questions to which it fails to return an answer, let him consider the difficulties and disadvantages under which social psychology is labouring at the moment, and forbear to condemn those who have devoted their lives not only to the solution of extremely difficult problems, but also to a struggle with obscurantism, neglect, irrational hostility, and vested interests of one kind or another.

One last point. The reader will undoubtedly find that some of the results reported bear out common-sense observation and everyday knowledge. This fact has occasionally been used to argue that scientific study is unnecessary where common-sense may arrive at similar conclusions. Several fallacies are involved in this argument. In the first place, common-sense is sometimes right and sometimes wrong; it requires properly conducted experiments to show where it is right and where it is wrong. In the second place, there is a world of difference between a common-sense statement and a scientific one in so far as accuracy and implications are concerned. To take a simple example, Newton's law of gravitation was indeed preceded by common-sense observation to the effect that unsupported objects tend to fall to the ground. Yet it would be very foolish indeed to criticize physics for merely giving elaborate proof of what common-sense knew already. Admittedly, work in the social sciences is of a much lower level of accuracy and implication than was Newton's; none the less, the difference between the approach of common-sense and that of science is still sufficiently distinct to make the differentiation important.

H. J. EYSENCK

Institute of Psychiatry
(*Maudsley Hospital*),
University of London.
30 *September* 1953

Chapter One

VOTING, ATTITUDES, AND SOCIAL CLASS

POLITICS is often defined as the science of government. It clearly is not a science in the way that physics or chemistry are sciences; in so far as it is scientific at all, it is so because it applies and uses principles established by disciplines such as history, sociology, anthropology, economics, psychology, and the other so-called 'social sciences'. As long as these disciplines themselves remain in an immature state of pre-scientific development, politics itself must remain in the frustrating position of being the application of a science which does not yet exist.

This dilemma does not, of course, worry those who take a somewhat romantic view of politics, and would regard the intrusion of scientific methodology with ill-concealed horror. Nor would it worry those who have already given their conscience into the safe keeping of one of the established parties, and who are thereby saved from having to consider anew the problems which arise from day to day. Yet even the romantics and the party stalwarts may occasionally reflect on the disproportion between the success of science in dealing with those problems to which it has been applied, and the abysmal failure of artistic intuition and dogmatic certitude in the political and social fields.

Such worrying thoughts are usually dismissed by reference to one or other of the following two fallacies. The first one is that *human behaviour is not subject to scientific laws*, and that consequently all attempts to apply the method of science to politics and social behaviour generally are doomed to failure; the second one is that *science has already been applied to these problems, and has failed* to provide answers superior to those of common sense and party doctrine.

The first of these two arguments is one which will be recognized easily by historians of science; every application of scientific method to new fields has been greeted in the same way, by a simple denial that the starry heavens, or the circulation of the blood, or the evolution of species, or the inheritance of mental and physical characteristics, are subject to factual scrutiny and scientific study. Even in the complex field of human behaviour there is already sufficient evidence to make impossible any similar assertion; only ignorance, or wilful ignoring of the evidence, can support the claim that here at last is a field forever beyond the ken of science.

The second of these two arguments also is not in accord with fact. The social sciences are very young, and the answers which they give to questions of social policy cannot pretend to the same authority as those given by the physicist to questions of physical provenance. Yet, whether right or wrong, they most certainly differ from the answers given by common sense, and equally certainly they have hardly ever been applied to the solution of practical problems by politicians and other civic leaders. Some small-scale examples of such application, however, do exist, and the triumphant success of the scientific method as compared with the usual political trial-and-error, hit-and-miss procedures has been described in some detail in *Uses and Abuses of Psychology*.

The present book, however, is not concerned with social science as a whole; such an undertaking would be quite outside the competence of the writer. We shall be concerned exclusively with *psychological factors*. It is fully realized that most of the problems discussed must ultimately be seen in their historical, economic, sociological, and perhaps even anthropological context, but little is to be gained at the present time by complicating the picture too much. The scientist always begins by simplifying his problem; having thus acquired some knowledge of the laws which describe the phenomena with which he is dealing, he is then ready to study them in a more complex setting. Our general setting will be the contemporary social scene in this country, in the U.S.A., and in the democratic countries of the European continent; wherever possible, the experimental evidence will be drawn from research carried out in the United Kingdom. The reader will do well to keep this restriction in mind; it is possible that the results reached will be transferable to other cultures, but further evidence would be required before such a transfer can be usefully made. Nor can it be assumed that our results would necessarily be as true in an-

8

other century as they are at the present time; extrapolation in time would be as dangerous as in space. Such restrictions are regrettable but inevitable; large-scale premature generalizations on the basis of insufficient evidence are the mark of the prophet, not the scientist.

To most readers the statement that we shall be concerned with the psychology of politics will not be a very illuminating one. There is an ambiguity about the term 'psychology' in the minds of many people, an ambiguity which is due largely to the fact that there are two types of psychology. There is on the one hand what we may perhaps call popular 'understanding', psychoanalytic, artistic-literary psychology; a psychology which eschews the rigorous amassing of detailed facts and the construction of empirically verifiable, consistent theories, and which instead indulges in interpretation of dreams, artistic productions, and political actions in accordance with rules and canons which are speculative and unverifiable. It is possible that psychologists of this type are right in claiming, as some of them have done, that miners' absenteeism is due to psychological conflicts aroused by hacking away at a symbolic 'Mother Earth', or that social attitudes towards kings and presidents are nothing but reactivated childhood feelings towards the father; possible, but unlikely, and in any case unproven.

On the other hand we have what may be called academic, 'explaining', scientific psychology; a type of psychology much less widely known than the popular, psychoanalytic variety. The reasons for this relative obscurity are not far to seek.

The setting up of hypotheses and the deduction and testing of verifiable consequences, careful control of many relevant variables, rigorous proof and mathematical treatment of data—these features of scientific methodology are not as appealing as unbridled speculation, the promise of panaceas, and the excitement of all-embracing theories. Nevertheless, it is the less spectacular but more systematic type of psychology with which we shall here be concerned; it is here and here alone that the hope of a truly scientific understanding of political problems lies.

Psychology so conceived has one advantage over other disciplines which makes it of particular interest and importance. Political actions are actions of human beings; the study of the direct causes of these actions is the field of study of psychology. All other social sciences deal with variables which affect political action indirectly.

9

Economics, for instance, does not deal with human behaviour directly, but is forced to make assumptions about the reactions of human beings to economic facts; it uses a (largely unrealistic and unsound) psychology of its own as an intermediary between economic fact and social behaviour. The psychologist has no need of such intermediaries; he is in direct contact with the central link in the chain of causation between antecedent condition and resultant action. This central link, in a very general sort of way, is, of course, the human being, but this is far too vague and general a statement to be of any scientific usefulness, and we must look for something more definite and more specific in terms of which we can frame our theories.

Psychology for a long time was handicapped by the absence of a concept which could be used in this connection. Taking over from Tetens and Kant the general division of mental life into willing, feeling, and thinking, or conation, affection, and cognition in more technical language, it failed to account for the facts of social life which inevitably demand an integration of all three elements. Associationist philosophers attempted to solve the problem by concentrating exclusively on cognition and thus rendered their accounts almost entirely in terms of a wraith-like 'rational man' whose actions were determined by reason alone. 'Economic man' is a direct successor of 'rational man', equally wraith-like and equally absurd. Psychoanalysts, on the other hand, attempted to dethrone reason completely and posited 'irrational man', a creature wildly driven by impulses and emotions which he did not understand, and using reason merely to rationalize his actions *ex post facto*.

Clearly, these are both simplifications which are of little use in a scientific account of political behaviour. Human beings do not always act in a completely rational, philosophical manner, debating the ultimate causes and consequences of actions and deciding on the basis of pure ratiocination; neither are they merely the playthings of emotional surges dating back to and deriving their strength from events in their far-distant childhood. What is needed is a concept which will serve to integrate all these divergent ingredients. This concept was introduced into science by that great trio of British psychologists, G. F. Stout, A. F. Shand, and W. McDougall. Using the term 'sentiment' which had earlier been proposed by Shaftesbury, Adam Smith, Herbert Spencer and Alexander Bain, Shand defined this term as denoting systems of character which organize and direct the various primary emotions and impulses. These systems, as Stout had pointed out earlier, are not actual feelings but *dispositions*; they dispose a person to have certain feelings when presented with the object around which the sentiment has grown. Such sentiments are not innate but acquired; as Stout points out, 'an object which has been connected with agreeable or disagreeable activities, which has given rise to manifold emotions, which has been the source of various satisfactions or dissatisfactions, becomes valued or the opposite in and for itself'. A sentiment so acquired has dynamic properties because 'although a sentiment is only an organization of a part of the character, it is in a dynamical relation to the rest and gives a peculiar orientation to the whole'.

These adumbrations of a consistent theory were transformed into the basis of a systematic social psychology by McDougall, whose *Introduction to Social Psychology* first appeared in 1908 and may be said to mark the beginning of that branch of study. Defining sentiment as 'an organized system of emotional dispositions centred about the idea of some object', McDougall also stresses the importance of learning in the development of sentiments. 'Each sentiment has a life history like every other vital organization. It is gradually built up, increasing in complexity and strength, and may continue to grow indefinitely, or may enter upon a period of decline and may decay slowly or rapidly, partially or completely.'

McDougall adds the idea that in the course of development all the sentiments of an individual will tend to build themselves into a hierarchical system at the apex of which is usually placed what McDougall calls the sentiment of self-regard. To him, sentiments and their organization are the building stones of character; . . . 'the development of integrated character consists in the growth of a harmonious system of the sentiments, a hierarchical system in which the working of the sentiments for the more concrete objects is regulated and controlled by the sentiments for general and more abstract and ideal objects, such as devotion to the family, the clan, the occupational or civic group, the nation, or mankind, the love of justice, humanity, liberty, equality, fraternity; and by hatred for cruelty, for injustice, for oppression, for slavery. And volition in the full and higher sense implies that this hierarchy of sentiments culminates in and is presided over by a sentiment of self-regard which, by incorporating in its system these higher abstract sentiments has become an ideal of self, an ideal of character and of conduct to which our daily actions must conform and with which our long range motivations, our ambition and personal loyalties, must harmonize.'

We may briefly summarize now the nature of a sentiment. In the first place it is an organization of conative, affective, and cognitive parts of the mind; in the second place, it is dynamic in the sense that it determines to some degree the behaviour of the organism; in the third place, it is a disposition, a set to react in a certain way once it is aroused; in the fourth place, it is learned rather than innate; and in the fifth place it combines with other sentiments to form a larger structure.

In spite of the great usefulness of this theory, and in spite of the fact that it fulfils an obvious need, it did not live up to its promise. For one thing, it remained theoretical and failed to seek substantiation in large-scale experimental studies. In the second place, it was linked too closely with McDougall's doctrine of instincts, which proved unacceptable to later workers. It was too necessary a concept, however, to be completely forgotten, and consequently it suffered a sea-change; while sentiment as a concept was retained, the term itself was dropped and a large variety of others substituted. The most widely accepted of these terms was that of attitude, but in psychoanalytic circles the term 'complex' also has frequently been used. It would not be profitable to enter into the long history of discussion of definitions beginning with the symposium on the relations between complex and sentiment held shortly after World War I by the British Psychological Society. It is sufficient to say that there is little agreement between psychologists on the differential use or meaning of these terms, except that complexes tend to be regarded as morbid, symptom-producing sentiments, and that the main distinctions between sentiments and attitudes appear to be that sentiments are more lasting and more highly organized than attitudes, and that the objects of attitudes are usually more abstract than the objects of sentiments. This would agree with popular usage; we tend to refer to *personal* sentiments but to *social* attitudes, and there is little doubt that our personal feelings on the whole are more highly organized and less abstract than our social ones.[1]

Be that as it may, we shall here use the term 'attitude' very much in the way in which it has been defined by G. W. Allport:

'An attitude is a mental and neural state of readiness organized through experience, exerting a directive or dynamic influence upon the individual's response to all objects and situations with which it is related.' As so defined, attitude is clearly a hypothetical construct, or an intervening variable; it cannot be directly observed, but has to be deduced from other events which are directly observable. It is, therefore, in the same position as such concepts as electrons, protons, positrons, etc., in the physical field, or as drive and habit in the psychological field. Such concepts can be extremely dangerous unless firm limits are set to speculation, and it is important to realize what the conditions are under which such concepts are acceptable to science.

Hull has set down the rules for acceptance in admirable brevity:

'Despite the great value of logical constructs or intervening variables in scientific theory, their use is attended with certain difficulties and even hazards. At bottom this is because the presence

FIGURE I

Diagrammatic representation of a relatively simple case of an intervening variable (X) not directly observable but functionally related (f) to the antecedent event (A) and to the consequent event (B), both A and B being directly observable. When an intervening variable is thus securely anchored to observables on both sides it can be safely employed in scientific theory.

$$A \text{---} f \rightarrow (X) \rightarrow f \rightarrow B$$

and amount of such hypothetical factors must always be determined indirectly. But once (1) the dynamic relationship existing between the amount of the hypothetical entity (X) and some antecedent determining condition (A) which can be directly observed, and (2) the dynamic relationship of the hypothetical entity to some third consequent phenomenon or event (B) which also can be directly observed, become fairly well known, the scientific hazard largely disappears. The situation in question is represented in Figure I. When a hypothetical dynamic entity, or even a chain of such entities each functionally related to the one logically preceding and following it, is thus securely anchored on both sides to observable and measurable conditions or events (A and B), the main theoretical danger vanishes. This at bottom is because under the assumed circumstances no ambiguity can exist as to when, and how much of, B should follow A.'

Much of this book will be concerned with finding the functional relationships obtaining between attitudes such as Conservatism, Radicalism, anti-Semitism, and so forth, and the antecedent conditions such as income, age, sex, personality, education, and upbringing. We shall also be greatly concerned with some of the consequent events, such as voting, verbal and non-verbal behaviour, and other types of activity, clearly dependent on previous attitudes. It is only through experimental studies of this type, firmly anchoring the concept of attitude in both directions, that we can avoid the fate which has befallen the concept of sentiment.[2]

The discussion up to this point has been entirely theoretical, and it may be worth while to illustrate what has been said by reference to certain empirical studies. In doing so, we shall take extremely simple examples; qualifications and complexities involved will be discussed in later chapters. The attitude chosen for our example is that of Conservatism-Radicalism. In terms of our diagram we must first of all decide on a suitable measure of what has there been called 'the consequent condition'. The most obvious choice would be voting behaviour, on the hypothesis that people whose attitudes are Conservative will tend to vote for the Conservative Party, while people whose attitudes are Radical will tend to vote for the Labour Party. We cannot, of course, use actual election data for this purpose as the election is secret; we shall have to use instead answers given by a sample of the population questioned by interviewers of the British Institute of Public Opinion. There is little doubt that this will involve a small error, but the evidence is fairly conclusive that the size of this error would not affect the results to any appreciable degree. Table I sets out the actual percentage vote cast for the various parties in 1945, 1950, and 1951, as well as the British Institute of Public Opinion prediction based on their poll results. It will be seen that the greatest error is only 1·4 per cent. The average is less than 1 per cent. We can thus accept the polling figures collected during these years with considerable confidence.

As regards antecedent conditions, we have a wide choice. For the purpose of this analysis we may perhaps begin by relating attitude to social class and social status. By social class we shall in this book mean something entirely subjective, namely *the belief which the individual holds concerning his own position in the social class system*. By status, we shall mean something entirely objective, namely *his relative position in the social class system as determined by certain external criteria*, of which income, education, and type of job are perhaps the most obvious. Class and status may agree, i.e. an individual's conception of his own class may be identical with his objective status, or they may disagree, an individual believing himself to belong to a different class to that in which he is placed by objective criteria. This use of the terms 'class' and 'status' is relatively arbitrary. As in the case of the concepts of attitude, sentiment, and complex, there is no universal agreement.

The kind of hypothesis which would link class and status to attitude is a rather obvious one. Centers has discussed the evolution of this hypothesis from early Greek and Roman writers, to Marx and Engels, Sombart, Pareto, Mosca, Veblen, Bukharin, and many

TABLE I

British Institute of Public Opinion Forecasts and Actual Votes of Parties in Three Post-War Elections

Party	1945		1950		1951	
	Fore-cast	Actual Vote	Fore-cast	Actual Vote	Fore-cast	Actual Vote
	per cent	per cent	per cent	per cent	per cent	per cent
Conservatives	41·0	39·4	43·5	43·4	49·5	48·1
Labour	47·0	48·8	45·9	46·1	47·0	48·7
Liberal	10·5	9·2	10·5	9·2	3·0	2·5
Other	1·5	2·6	1·0	1·3	·5	·7
	per cent		per cent		per cent	
Average Error	1·4		0·7		0·9	

others, and has also pointed out the confusion caused by the failure of some of these writers to distinguish between status and class. He himself quite clearly distinguishes between the two: 'Stratification is something objective; it derives . . . primarily from the economic system that happens to prevail in a given culture. The process of getting a living imposes upon people certain functions, statuses and roles. That is, by virtue of the patterning demanded by a particular technological development, people come to have different occupations and roles, to have different amounts of wealth, and different amounts of economic and political power. Social and economic groupings and categories of people distinguished on the basis of occupation, power, income, standard of living, education, function, intelligence, or other criteria are easily and properly denoted by the terms stratum and strata.'

15

'*But these strata . . . are not necessarily classes.* Classes are psycho-social groupings, something that is essentially subjective in character dependent upon class consciousness (i.e. a feeling of group membership), and class lines of cleavage may or may not conform to what seem to social scientists to be logical lines of cleavage in the objective or stratification sense. Class, as distinguished from stratum, can well be regarded as a *psychological* phenomenon in the fullest sense of the term.' Centers has brought together the concepts of status, class and attitude in a general hypothesis which reads as follows. 'A person's status and role with respect to the economic processes of society imposes upon him certain attitudes, values, and interests relating to his role and status in the political and economic sphere . . . . The status and role of the individual in relation to the means of production and exchange of goods and services gives rise in him to a consciousness of membership in some social class which shares those attitudes, values, and interests.' In accordance with this theory we thus have two antecedent conditions which we may expect to be linked with conservative and radical attitudes, i.e. those of *social class* and those of *social status*.'[3]

Let us enquire first of all into the relationship between attitude and status. The figures given relate to a sample of almost 9,000 men and women constituting a representative sample of the population of Great Britain. These were interviewed by members of the British Institute of Public Opinion and divided into four status groups:

AV +: Well-to-do; Men (or their wives), working in the higher professions, e.g. wealthier chartered accountants, lawyers, clergymen, doctors, professors, or in higher ranks of business, e.g. owners, directors, senior members of large businesses. Almost invariably they will have a telephone, car and some domestic help.

AV: Middle and upper middle class; Professional workers not in the top category. Salaried clerical workers such as bank clerks: qualified teachers: owners and managers of large shops: supervisory grades in factories who are not manual workers: farmers, unless their farm is very big when they will be AV +. Many will have a telephone, a car, or employ a 'char'. A person having none of these should not be regarded as AV +.

AV −: Lower middle and working class; by far the biggest group. Manual workers, shop assistants, cinema attendants, clerks, agents.

Group D: Very poor; People without regular jobs or unskilled labourers or living solely on Old Age Pension(s). Housing will be poor. They can only afford necessities. You cannot go too low in the social scale to find them.

Interviewers are instructed in addition to classify retired persons according to former occupation, wives according to husband's occupation, and students according to their home background. They are also told to go as high as possible in the social scale for their AV + and to go as low as possible for Group D. Table II gives the total numbers of people interviewed belonging to each of the four status groups, the total number of people indicating party preferences, as well as the percentages in each of these status groups voting for each of the parties. It will be seen that while 77 per cent of the higher status group voted Conservative, only 8 per cent voted

TABLE II

Relationship Between Social Status and Political Attitude

Status	Conservative per cent	Labour per cent	Liberal per cent	Other per cent	Don't Know per cent	Total Number
Av. +	77	8	11	—	3	447
Av.	63	16	12	1	10	1,855
Av. —	32	47	9	1	11	4,988
Very Poor	20	52	9	1	18	1,621
Total Number	3,411	3,545	894	60	1,001	8,911

Labour; conversely, of the lower status group 20 per cent voted Conservative, but 52 per cent voted Labour. Table II shows the relative decline of Conservative votes with decline in status, and the increase in Labour votes with decline in status in a graphical manner; it also shows the relative independence of Liberal sentiment of considerations of social status.

The relationship between social class and social attitude is indicated in Table III. Respondents were asked to say which of the following social classes they considered themselves to belong to: upper, upper-middle, middle, lower middle, and working class. It will be seen that 79 per cent of those who considered themselves to be upper or upper-middle class voted Conservative, but that only 20 per cent of those who considered themselves to be working-class

17

did so. Conversely, 60 per cent of those who considered themselves working-class voted Labour, whereas only 5 per cent of the self-styled upper-class did so. Again, the relationships have been presented in Table III, showing the close relationship between social class and attitudes as far as Conservative and Radical attitudes are concerned, and the relative independence of class as far as Liberal attitudes are concerned.

TABLE III

Relationship Between Social Class and Political Attitude

	Conservative per cent	Labour per cent	Liberal per cent	Other per cent	Don't Know per cent	Total Number
Social Self-Rating						
Upper class	79	5	10	–	6	63
Upper middle class	79	7	11	–	3	400
Middle class	60	18	12	5	9	2,503
Lower middle class	43	31	15	1	10	1,200
Working class	20	60	7	1	12	4,323
Don't know	30	27	10·5	–	32·5	401

8,911*

* In Tables III, IV and V a few people who failed to reply to the question regarding social class, education and religious evaluation, had to be omitted; this accounts for the fact that the numbers given do not agree exactly with the total size of the sample as shown below the line.

While class and status are clearly both related to attitude, they are obviously not independent and the question arises as to the determination of the one by the other. Table IV shows the dependence of class consciousness on status; of those in the higher status group, 93 per cent considered themselves upper, upper-middle, or middle-class; of those in the lower status group, only 7 per cent did so. The actual degree of dependence of class on status is indicated by a tetrachoric correlation coefficient of ·76; this means that of all the factors determining class-consciousness status contributes something like 58 per cent.[4] (See Technical Note 4 for an explanation of the concept of correlation.)

We may also seek for a more direct numerical expression of the relationship between class and status on the one hand and attitude on the other. Taking only Conservative and Labour votes we can express the relationship in terms of tetrachoric coefficients of correlations. When we do so we find that the correlation between class and attitude is ·67; that between status and attitudes ·53. These figures should not be taken too seriously as it is doubtful whether the mathematical conditions requisite for the calculation of a tetrachoric correlation coefficient are fulfilled to more than an approximate degree. However, they may be taken quite broadly to indicate that of all the conditions which determine radical-conservative attitudes, status and class contribute something like 40 per cent.[5]

These estimates concerning the degree of relationship between voting behaviour, status, and class are probably underestimates of the true relationships. This is due to the fact that we are correlating available estimates of these variables, not true scores. Thus, for example, our correlation of ·55 between status and vote is not between the *true status* of the people in our sample and their *true votes*,

TABLE IV

Relationship Between Social Status and Social Class

Status	Class				
	Upper and upper middle per cent	Middle per cent	Lower middle per cent	Working per cent	Don't know per cent
Av. +	57	36	4	3	–
Av.	16	58	13	10	3
Av. –	2	20	20	55	3
Very Poor	–	7	8	76	11

but between the interviewer's *estimate* of their status and their own verbal *assertion* as to what their vote would be. There is a margin of error in both these estimates, and this margin of error decreases the true correlation which we might expect to find between these variables.

It is possible to correct statistically for some, at least, of the errors which we know to be present by means of what is called 'correction for attenuation'. In order to do this we must know the reliability of our various measures, i.e., the degree to which one interviewer's estimate would agree with that of another interviewer made independently at a slightly later date. Figures of this kind are available for the estimation of economic status and it will be shown in Chapter Three that the correlation between two interviewers' ratings of the economic status of a group of respondents is only ·63, thus indicating that a considerable amount of error enters into the estimation of status. If we use this estimate of reliability to correct the figures given before, we find that the correlation between status and class rises from ·76 to ·95, suggesting that social class estimates are determined almost completely by social status. The correlation between status and vote rises from ·53 to ·66, which is a somewhat less dramatic increase. No similar correction can be made for the correlation between class and vote as the degree of reliability of these two variables is unknown, but corrections here are unlikely to be anything like as important as they are in the case of status estimation.

Before turning to a comparison of these data with those reported on American groups by Centers, we may briefly consider a few other antecedent conditions, some of which are more or less independent of class and status. Education, which is the first factor to be considered, is of course so closely related to status that the results are almost a foregone conclusion. Nevertheless, they are presented in Table V; the results are fully in line with expectation.

TABLE V

Relationship Between Education and Political Attitude

School attended	Conservative per cent	Labour per cent	Liberal per cent	Other per cent	Don't Know per cent	Total Number
Elementary	28	50	9	1	12	5,471
Secondary	53	24	13	1	9	2,179
Technical-commercial	50	27	12	–	11	460
Other	60	19	11	1	9	746
						8,911

Religious affiliation, while not independent of status and class, is nevertheless much less closely related to these two variables than is education, and predictions here would be very much more difficult than those of other variables. Results given in Table VI indicate certain general conclusions. Conservative attitudes are found most frequently in the Established Church, least frequently among atheists, and non-conformists; Radical beliefs, on the other hand, are found most frequently among non-conformists and

20

atheists, least frequently in the Established Church. Liberal sentiments are found least frequently in atheists, Established Church members, and Roman Catholics. The picture is a reasonable one and will be shown later to fit very well into the general picture of attitude structure in this country.

Age is, by common consent, believed to be related to Conservative opinions, and youth to Radical opinions. Figure 2 shows the increase in Conservative voting with increasing age for the four status groups separately. It will be seen that in each case there is a regular progression towards greater Conservatism with increasing age, with only one very slight reversal in the highest status group where, however, the number of cases involved is too small to lend

TABLE VI

Relationship Between Religious Affiliation and Political Attitude

Religion	Conservative per cent	Labour per cent	Liberal per cent	Other per cent	Don't Know per cent	Total Number
Church of England	45	37	8	–	10	4,850
Non-conformist	27·5	40·5	18	1	13	1,257
Roman Catholic	33	51	6	–	10	961
Scottish Church	43·5	37	7·5	1	11	586
Other	33	35·5	15	1·5	15	459
None	17	54	6	5	18	612
						8,911

it any significance. The progression for the total group shows no inversions of any kind and is indeed an almost straight line. It should be noted that for the purpose of this diagram, Liberals, Don't Know's and voters for other parties have been disregarded. Their inclusion would have complicated the diagram without changing it in any material way.

Sex appears to play relatively little part in the genesis of political opinions. Table VII shows that women tend to vote Labour slightly less frequently than men and that they have a larger proportion of Don't Know's among them. The differences are too small to be of any great practical importance.

We may briefly summarize this survey of some antecedent conditions of attitude by saying that attitudes are determined by a person's objective social status; by his private opinion as to what his social class is; by his education, which, of course, in turn is dependent on his status and class, by his religious affiliation, and by his age. Taking all these conditions together and paying regard to their mutual inter-relationships we may say that a person's Conservative or Radical attitude, as measured in terms of his voting

FIGURE 2

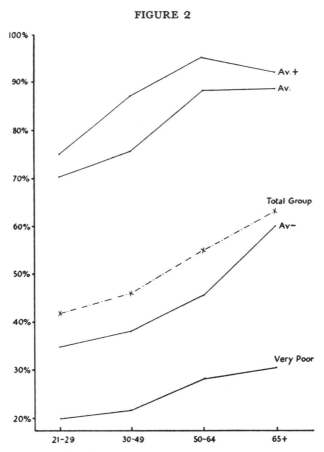

Increase in Conservative Voting Intention with Increasing Age in Four Economic Groups

intention, is determined by these factors to the extent of about 60–70 per cent.

Are these results peculiar to this country, or could they be generalized to other countries as well? From an enquiry carried out by R. Centers on a representative sample of some 1,100 people in the United States, the conclusion seems to emerge that what is true in this country appears to be equally true on the other side of the Atlantic. With a few obvious changes—for Conservatives read Republicans, for Labour Party read Democrats, and neglecting Liberals—the similarity is indeed striking. Before we turn to the actual figures, however, we must note a difference in the procedure which Centers adopted. In the results so far quoted the concept of attitude has not been broken down or clarified in any way; it has merely served as an intervening variable between antecedent condition and voting behaviour. Centers has attempted to approach this intervening variable more directly, and has attempted to measure it by means of procedures which we shall encounter again later on. He drew up a battery of questions in which he endeavoured 'to obtain a more comprehensive, more valid, and more reliable index to the basic politico-economic attitudes or orienta-

TABLE VII

Relationship Between Sex and Voting Intention

	Conservative	Labour	Liberal	Other	Don't Know	Total Number
Men	38	42	10	1	9	4,520
Women	39	37	10	1	14	4,391
						8,911

tions commonly believed to be manifestations of class interests and values . . . Each item provided an opportunity for the respondent to indicate his orientation or disposition in either a conservative or a radical direction.' The six items used by him are given below; it will be obvious in each case what is the 'radical' and what the 'conservative' prediction of the answer.

1. 'Do you agree or disagree that America is truly a land of opportunity and that people get pretty much what's coming to them in this country?'
2. 'Would you agree that everybody would be happier, more secure and more prosperous if the working people were given more power and influence in government, or would you say that we would all be better off if the working people had no more power than they have now?'

3. 'As you know, during this war many private businesses and industries have been taken over by the government. Do you think wages and salaries would be fairer, jobs more steady, and that we would have fewer people out of work if the government took over and ran our mines, factories and industries in the future, or do you think things would be better under private ownership?'

4. 'Which one of these statements do you most agree with? (1) The most important job for the government is to make it certain that there are good opportunities for each person to get ahead on his own. (2) The most important job for the government is to guarantee every person a decent and steady job and standard of living.'

5. 'In strikes and disputes between working people and employers do you usually side with the workers or with the employers?'

6. 'Do you think working people are usually fairly and squarely treated by their employers, or that employers sometimes take advantage of them?'

If Centers's hypothesis is correct we should expect two things. We would expect, in the first place, that Republican voters should differ from Democratic voters in the sense of giving fewer Radical and more Conservative answers; in other words, we should expect each question to correlate with the Republican-Democrat dichotomy.

In the second place, as all the questions are supposed to measure the same general attitude of Radicalism-Conservatism, we would expect all the questions to intercorrelate together in a positive way so that a person who gives a Conservative reply on one question would be expected to give a Conservative reply on all the others. Both these expectations are borne out as is shown in Table VIII. All the intercorrelations between the six questions will be seen to be positive and, as shown in Column Seven, each question correlates positively with the total score on the questionnaire which is made up by simply summing the Radical answers to the questions. Similarly, as shown in Column Eight, which gives the correlations of each question with the criterion, i.e. the voting behaviour of the respondents, each question correlates positively with voting for the Democratic Party, the total score on the questionnaire correlating ·58 with voting behaviour. It will also be noted that there is a tendency for those questions which correlate relatively little with the other questions and therefore with the total score, e.g. questions

1 and 5, also to have low correlations with voting behaviour, while questions correlating highly with total score, e.g. question 4, correlate highly with the external criterion, i.e. voting behaviour.

When respondents are put in five groups (ultra-Conservative, Conservative, Intermediate, Radical, and ultra-Radical) in accordance with their scores on the questionnaires, it can be seen in Figure 3 that the percentage of persons who voted Republican declines from those having an ultra-Conservative score on the questionnaire to those having an ultra-Radical one, there being no inversions on the curve. We thus see that Centers's attitude questionnaire may, by and large, be accepted as equivalent to the use of voting made in previous parts of this chapter.

TABLE VIII

Intercorrelations Between Six Attitude Questions and Correlations with Total Score and Voting Intention

	2	3	4	5	6	7	8
1. Land of opportunity	·14	·41	·35	·12	·39	·49	·16
2. Working people's power	—	·44	·51	·41	·33	·77	·41
3. Government ownership		—	·68	·24	·29	·75	·53
4. Collectivism			—	·37	·39	·88	·56
5. Workers v. Employers				—	·31	·61	·24
6 Treatment of workers					—	·72	·28
7. Total Score						—	·58
8. Democrat v. Republican Vote							—

Having thus clarified the concept of attitude, Centers goes on to clarify the concept of status, again using a somewhat more complex method than the one adopted previously in this chapter. He bases himself on three indices of status, which together give him what he calls a 'stratification score'. These three indices are *occupation*, ranging from large business and professional at the one end, to semi-skilled and unskilled workers at the other; *power*, which ranges from employer and manager at one end to tenant and employee at the other; and *economic status*, which ranges from wealthy to poor. The exact derivation of this score is not very important, but the way in which the three scales are made up may be of interest and is therefore quoted in Table IX.

The three indices of status used by Centers are not independent; he finds, for instance, that occupational and economic status correlate ·70; occupational and power status ·79; and economic and power status ·65. These intercorrelations, together with those of the three indices with total stratification score, self-rated social class status, score on the Conservative-Radical questionnaire, and voting behaviour, are all given in Table X. It will be seen that the correlation between class and status is slightly lower than in the case of the British sample, being ·67 instead of ·76. The correlation between status and voting is ·43; that between class evaluation and voting ·36. Both of these again are lower than was found to be the

FIGURE 3

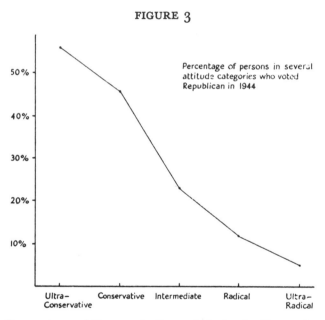

Percentage of persons in several attitude categories who voted Republican in 1944

Percentage of Persons in Several Attitude Categories who Voted Republican in 1944

case in our British sample. These differences, however, are slight, and quite clearly the same general pattern is found in the sample studied by Centers as was found in this country.

These similarities apply equally to the other variables discussed, i.e. age, sex, education, and religion. Education correlates ·56 with middle-class identification and ·38 with Conservatism-Radicalism, and a very interesting Figure given by Centers (Figure 4) enables us to compare the effects of status and education separately,

TABLE IX

The Derivation of Centers's Stratification Score from Occupation, Power, and Economic Status Indices

Scale Value:	Occupation:	Scale Value:	Power:	Scale Value:	Economic Status:
8	Large business	8	Employer	8	Wealthy
7	Professional	7		7	
6	Small business	6	Manager	6	Average+
5	White collar workers	5		5	
4	Farm owners and managers	4	Independent	4	Average
3	Skilled workers and foremen	3		3	
2	Farm tenants	2	Tenant	2	Poor +
1	Semi-skilled workers	1		1	
0	Unskilled and farm labour	0	Employee	0	Poor

showing that while status is the more important variable, nevertheless education also has an independent contribution to make. Centers comments, 'It is noticeable . . . that educational differences seem to produce more stable and consistent variations in class identification than in conservatism, yet, as a rule, people of higher educational attainments not only tend to identify more frequently with the upper and middle classes, but more often to be conservative in attitude as well. This is true of persons in both occupational strata. A difference of substantial magnitude exists between persons of the same education but of different occupation, however, and hence there is no question that occupation is an important index independently of education.'

Centers's correlations of age with class identification (·11) and

TABLE X

Intercorrelations of Three Status Scores and Correlations with Stratification, Class, Conservatism, and Voting

	2	3	4	5	6	7
1. Stratification	·93	·90	·92	·67	·61	·43
2. Occupational Status	—	·76	·79	·69	·56	·37
3. Economic Status		—	·65	·65	·51	·45
4. Power Status			—	·47	·57	·31
5. Class Affiliation				—	·49	·36
6. Conservatism					—	·57
7. Voting						—

with conservatism (00) are in the same direction as ours, but considerably lower. As will be seen in Figure 5, in his sample there is a consistent tendency for class identification and Conservatism to vary with age in the upper occupational stratum, while for the lower occupational stratum there is no consistent relationship. Centers ascribes this greater degree of radicalism of those between 40 and 49 years to the occurrence of the Great Depression, just at the time when these people were 'hitting their stride'. Failure

FIGURE 4

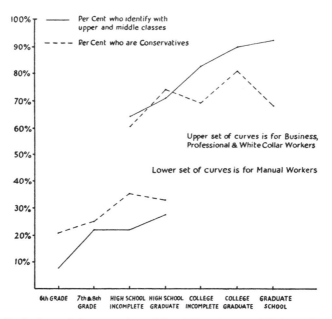

Relation of Occupational Stratification and Education
to Class Identification and Conservatism-Radicalism

of the English sample to show any similar tendency although they were hit equally badly by the slump would seem to throw some doubt on that explanation; rather it would appear that where the total sample is relatively small, as in Centers's case, breakdown into many groups may easily render the number of cases in each group so small that accidental variations may pose artificial problems.

As far as religion goes, Centers finds both that Church Membership and Protestantism correlates significantly both with class identification (·22 and ·19) and with Conservatism (·18 and ·36).

Another investigation which demonstrates similarity of predisposing conditions in attitude formation between England and America is contained in Lazarsfeld's book *The People's Choice*. He studied intensively voting behaviour in Erie County during the 1940 presidential election campaign. In relating Republican voting intention to socio-economic status, he found, as had Centers,

FIGURE 5

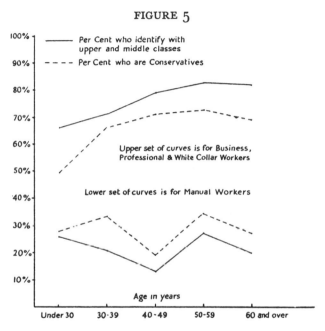

Relation of Occupational Stratification and Age to
Class Identification and Conservatism-Radicalism

that there was a regular decline in the Republican vote from those high as compared with those low in status. With status held equal he found that class identification affected voting to some extent, as shown in Figure 6. The comparison was carried out by asking voters whether they considered themselves as belonging to 'business' or 'labour'. It will be seen that quite marked differences due to 'class' appear in this way, even when respondents are equated for status.

29

Similarly, religious affiliation was shown to play an important part, even when status was held constant in the same manner as before. Results are shown in Figure 7.

Lazarsfeld made up an index of political predisposition combining several factors of the type discussed, and found that this index correlated ·5 with voting behaviour. The correlation between this index and voting appears to be of the same order as correlations found by Centers, and definitely lower than correlations found in this country and reported above. Lazarsfeld sums up his finding by saying: 'There is a familiar adage in American folklore to the effect that a person is only what he thinks he is, an adage which reflects the typically American notion of unlimited opport-

FIGURE 6

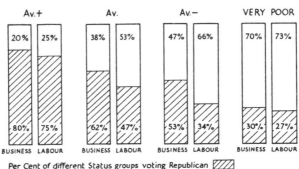

Per Cent of different Status groups voting Republican ▨ or Democrat ☐, subdivided according to Class affiliation (Business or Labour)

unity, the tendency toward self-betterment, etc. Now we find that the reverse of the adage is true: a person thinks, politically, as he is, socially. Social characteristics determine political preference.' To a certain extent, no doubt, it is true that social characteristics determine political preference. However, with a correlation no higher than ·5 it is difficult to regard the statement made by Lazarsfeld as being quite accurate. A correlation of ·5 means that only about 25 per cent of the factors determining voting behaviour are accounted for; this still leaves 75 per cent of these factors to be discovered. It might be more accurate to reword Lazarsfeld's last sentence to read- 'In the U.S.A., social characteristics account for one quarter of all the factors which determine political preference.'[6]

Having thus shown that there is considerable similarity between

American and British conditions, we may now return to a further discussion of attitudes as related to precedent and consequent conditions. The question will have occurred to the reader why intervening variables like attitudes or sentiments are really necessary when it could be so much easier to write a functional equation between antecedent and consequent condition directly. Why, it may be said do we not rest content with relating social class or status directly to voting behaviour? Why is it necessary to introduce a hypothetical construct like attitude, which itself is not observable, and which causes a great deal of trouble in definition and measurement? The full answer to these questions must be postponed until later, but we may note here already the fact that something obviously medi-

FIGURE 7

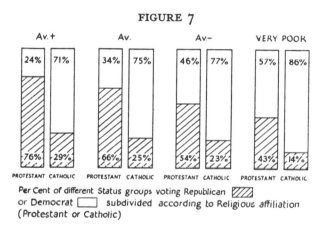

Per Cent of different Status groups voting Republican ▨
or Democrat ☐ subdivided according to Religious affiliation
(Protestant or Catholic)

ates between a person's social status and his voting behaviour. If we do not postulate an attitude there is a gap in the causal chain which makes further analysis impossible, and thus deprives us of the most elementary condition of scientific advance. We have already seen in Centers's scale of Conservatism-Radicalism that further analysis of this central concept is possible, and, indeed, much of this book will be devoted to it.

Before we turn in that direction, however, we may note a few additional results in which various opinions are related to some of the antecedent and consequent conditions to which we have attempted to anchor our concept of attitudes. The particular questions chosen from many hundreds reported by the B.I.P.O. are important in so far as they set a general problem, namely, that of the organisation of attitudes, and at the same time give us some information which will help us in orienting ourselves in this field. In the form in which they are reported they are inevitably scrappy, unorganized, and isolated bits of information; it will be the task of a later chapter to show how easily they fall into place when related to a general picture of attitude organization. All the results quoted were obtained by the British Institute of Public Opinion, from samples of approximately 1,500 people representing a cross section of the adult population of this country.

As our first question, let us take one asked on the 10 August 1948: 'The L.C.C. are now allowing sex hygiene to be taught in public elementary schools. Do you approve or disapprove?' There was a distinct tendency in the answers for the young to approve and for the older respondents to disapprove, the percentage of approval falling from 82 per cent among the 21–29 year olds through 75 per cent and 65 per cent to 42 per cent for those over 65. Remembering that the old are more Conservative, we might have predicted that the higher status groups, who are also more Conservative, would also be opposed to this measure; however, we find that the opposite is the case. For the three higher status groups over 70 per cent are in favour; for the lower status groups only 50 per cent. Thus, we perceive immediately an indication that attitude structure is more complex than has been expressed so far in terms of concepts of Conservatism and Radicalism; the more Radical age group agrees with the more Conservative status group as against the Conservative age group which agrees with the Radical status group.

The opposite effect is found in another question asked on the 18 December 1946, namely: 'Should boys and girls over 11 years of age be taught separately or should they be taught together?' Older groups are in favour of keeping boys and girls separate, while the younger ones would prefer to have them kept together; 38 per cent of those under 50 but 49 per cent of those over 50 voted in favour of separation. When results are grouped according to economic status, higher groups prefer separation, lower groups do not. Figures range from 55 per cent for the highest status group, 41 per cent for the lowest. Here age and economic group appear to go in the same direction as far as Conservatism is concerned. In another question, asked on the 16 April 1952, however, we again find a discrepancy. The question was: 'In some countries medical certificates must be produced showing that neither party to a marriage has V.D. Would you agree or disagree with this being made a requirement here?' Young groups tended to agree (72 per cent for the 21–29 year old group) while older age groups tended to agree only in 61 per cent of the cases. When divided according to status, however, 70 per cent of the upper status groups agreed but only 58 per cent of the lower status groups. Again, therefore, we find a contradiction, the upper status group behaving in a Radical direction but the low status group behaving in a Conservative direction.

The same contradiction appears in another question asked on the 11 January 1949, where respondents who said they had heard or read about artificial insemination were asked whether they approved or disapproved. With increasing age the percentage of approval dropped from 30 per cent through 28 per cent and 17 per cent to 8 per cent; on the other hand, the upper status groups approved in 26 per cent of the cases, while the lowest status group only approved in 8 per cent of the cases.

A rather different type of question was asked in February 1947. 'Do you think that religion has a mission to fulfil in Britain to-day?' Quite marked differences were found between men and women, 51 per cent of the men saying 'Yes' as compared to 58 per cent of the women. Age groups, as expected, show an increasing appreciation of religion from the youngest (48 per cent) to those over 50 (59 per cent). Of the economic groups, appreciation was highest in those of above average incomes (68 per cent) and lowest among the poor (49 per cent). Here we find then that age and status go in the same direction, but sex, which is not connected with Radicalism-Conservatism to any extent, also gives rise to considerable differences.

A similar result is found with another question, asked on the 15 December 1947: 'Do you believe in any form of life after death?' Women shared this belief in 54 per cent of the cases, men only in 49 per cent. The young people (46 per cent) did so less than the old (52 per cent) and the highest income groups (55 per cent) more than the low income groups (45 per cent).

A question relating to Sunday observance again gave somewhat discrepant findings. The question asked on 24 January 1943, ran as follows: 'Would you approve or disapprove of theatres being allowed to open on Sundays, just as they do on other days?' There were no differences between men and women or between economic groups, but the young (75 per cent) approved very much more than the old (49 per cent).

More in line with expectation are the results of another investigation where, on 1 July 1947, the question was asked: 'Do you approve or disapprove of paying women the same wages as men if doing the same work?' Women, as one might have expected, approved of this to a greater extent than men (70 per cent versus 51 per cent); the young (68 per cent) approved more than the old (56 per cent); Liberals (67 per cent) were more in agreement than Labour supporters (60 per cent) or Conservatives (52 per cent).

Corporal punishment is another subject frequently canvassed. On 7 March 1949, the question was asked: 'Do you agree to teachers being able to inflict corporal punishment?' Men approved more strongly than women (49 per cent as compared with 40 per cent) and the old as compared with the young (50 per cent versus 40 per cent). Higher economic groups approved more than lower economic groups, the percentages for the four groups being 53, 49, 42 and 48 per cent. On a similar question posed on 7 July 1939, it was asked: 'A bill now before Parliament proposes to abolish flogging and birching except for offences committed in prison. Do you approve or disapprove?' Women approved more than men (48 per cent versus 41 per cent); Labour supporters more than Conservatives (43 per cent versus 30 per cent); the young more than the old (47 per cent); and the lower economic groups more than the higher economic groups (48 per cent versus 30 per cent).

Another question yet, also dealing with punishment, was asked on 10 May 1948: 'Parliament has decided to try the effect of not hanging anyone for murder for five years. Do you approve or disapprove of this trial period?' Again, the young approved more than the old (30 per cent versus 21 per cent); Labour supporters agreed to the extent of 35 per cent, Liberals to the extent of 26 per cent, Conservatives to the extent of 16 per cent. And on the general question asked on 24 August 1949: 'Do you think that murderers should or should not be hanged?' those with little education thought they should in 57 per cent of all cases; those who had some education thought so in 45 per cent of the cases; and those who had gone to University, only in 41 per cent of the cases. High economic groups thought so less frequently than the very poor, percentages rising from the highest to the lowest economic group (49, 50, 55, 57 per cent).

The question of nationalization produced answers probably much in line with expectation. When the question was asked on 19 October 1950: 'Do you think that nationalization has been good or bad in the case of the Medical Services?', the young approved of the measure slightly more than the old (74 per cent versus 70 per cent) and Socialists (93 per cent) more than Liberals (66 per cent) or Conservatives (48 per cent). Conversely, when asked on 16 October 1946: 'Do you think that the Government should or should not nationalize (A) gas and electricity undertakings; (B) road transport as well as railways?', the young were more in favour than the old (60 per cent and 48 per cent as opposed to 45 per cent and 34 per cent respectively). Socialists were in favour (72 per cent and 61 per cent respectively); Liberals (42 per cent and 21 per cent); and Conservatives (24 per cent and 14 per cent) were not. To the question asked on 7 September 1952: 'Do you approve or disapprove of the Government's proposals about steel?' Conservatives answered 'Approve' in 66 per cent of the cases, Liberals in 40 per cent and Socialists in 10 per cent of the cases. To the question asked on 12 January 1948: 'Do you think that so far nationalization of the coal mines has been a success or a failure?' the young thought of it as a success more frequently than the old (54 per cent versus 47 per cent) and the high economic groups more frequently as a failure than the low economic groups (38 per cent versus 15 per cent). Socialists considered it a success (68 per cent); Liberals did so only in 34 per cent of the cases; and Conservatives only in 24 per cent of the cases.

International affairs also show marked differences. When the question was asked in January 1951: 'Should a war come, do you think it is likely to arise from America, Russia, or in some other way?' 25 per cent of Socialists named America, 51 per cent named Russia, whereas among Conservatives, 8 per cent named America and 78 per cent named Russia. On the same occasion, the question was asked: 'If we became involved in a war against Russia, do you think that the British people would be more willing or less willing to fight than they were against the Nazis?' Differences between Conservatives and Socialists were surprisingly small, 17 per cent of the former and 13 per cent of the latter thinking the British people would be more willing; 30 per cent of the former and 38 per cent of the latter thinking they would be less willing. Again, in the same questionnaire, the question was asked: 'Some people say that Russia's *aim* is to make certain of her security; others say that it is imperialistic aggression. What do you think?' Conservatives answered 'Security' in 17 per cent of the cases, Socialists in 24 per cent. Imperialistic aggression was named by Conservatives in 63 per cent, by Socialists in 47 per cent. There was a considerable proportion of 'Don't Know's'.

Relating to another point of international politics, the question was asked on 26 April 1948: 'Do you think that our Navy, Army, and Air Force are too big, too small, or just right?' Men considered it too small much more frequently than women (in 46 and 31 per cent respectively); and higher economic groups more than lower ones, the percentages for the four groups being 49, 45, 37, and 29 per cent. Similar results appeared when a question was asked on 23 March 1946: 'Do you approve or disapprove of compulsory military service for men in peace-time?' Men approved more than women (62 per cent versus 49 per cent); higher economic groups more than lower (64 per cent versus 52 per cent); and Conservatives (68 per cent) more than Socialists (52 per cent) or Liberals (49 per cent).

A question relating to the atom bomb was put on 26 March 1952: 'Do you approve or disapprove of Great Britain making an atom bomb?' Men approved far more than women (70 per cent versus 50 per cent); the young more than the old (63 per cent versus 44 per cent); higher income groups more than lower income groups (80 per cent versus 32 per cent); and Conservatives (72 per cent) more than Liberals (58 per cent) or Socialists (51 per cent).

Divorce is a subject on which some rather unexpected results are found. The question was asked on 2 April 1950: 'Would you approve or disapprove if it were made possible to get a divorce by agreement between the two parties?' High income groups approved much more than low income groups, percentages being 42, 36, 35, and 20 per cent respectively. Similarly, on the question asked on 27 April 1946: 'Do you think that steps should be taken to make the hearing of divorce speedier or is it a good thing that it takes a long time before the case is heard in the Courts?' high income groups (62 per cent) were more in favour of speed than low income groups (46 per cent); the young were more in favour of speeding hearings up than the old (50 per cent versus 44 per cent); and men more than women (53 per cent versus 45 per cent). On a related topic, the question was asked on the 16 April 1952: 'Would you approve or disapprove of everyone having to see someone like a Marriage Guidance Council to try and mend matters before going to Divorce Courts?', women were more in favour than men (66 per cent versus 61 per cent); the young more than the old (64 per cent versus 58 per cent); and the rich more than the poor (76 per cent versus 53 per cent).

The results from these various polls are obviously related to the concept of attitude structure, but the reader will find it very difficult, if not impossible, to integrate them into any kind of consistent scheme. He may also ask himself a number of questions regarding the degree of reliance which can be placed on the answers. He may begin to query the way in which some of the questions are worded; he may wonder about the truthfulness with which they have been answered; he may wish to know a little more about the way in which the respondents were selected; and he may wonder, somewhat uneasily, about the relationship between simple percentages, such as those reported, and true scientific measurement. All these questions and doubts are fully justified, and an attempt will be made in the next chapters to deal with some of the pitfalls which beset the task of the investigator. Later on, then, an attempt will be made to integrate all the results we have got so far into a general conceptual scheme of attitude organization.

Chapter Two

PUBLIC OPINION POLLS

THE man in the street, when wishing to know someone else's opinion, would under normal circumstances simply proceed to ask him a direct question and, by and large, this is precisely what attitude measurement consists of. However, there are certain awkward problems to be settled before we can have any confidence in our results. The first question is 'Whom should we ask?'; the second problem is 'How should we word our question?'; the third problem is 'Who should ask the question?' and the fourth problem is 'How do we know that the answer obtained is a true one?' To these four problems of sampling, wording, interviewing, and validity, a further one must be added, namely, that of scale construction, i.e. of transforming simple 'Yes' and 'No' answers into a proper scale of measurement. In this chapter, we shall be considering experiments which have a bearing on the first three of these problems.[7]

(a) SAMPLING

Before we can attempt to measure opinions or attitudes, we must, in Mrs. Beeton's immortal phrase, 'catch our hare'. This is a very much more complicated matter than it might appear at first. If we want to know the opinion of a given group of people, say, all persons of British nationality entitled to vote, our best plan obviously would be to ask our questions of every one of them. For reasons of expense, time, and practicability, this is nearly always beyond the resources of a private investigator, and even the Goverment undertake a complete census only very rarely, and almost never with respect to the measurement of people's opinions and attitudes.

38

If, then, we cannot interview everyone in the whole population in which we are interested, we must pick a very much smaller group which we have reason to believe will give answers similar to those which we would have obtained had we, in fact, interviewed every one in the whole population. Such a small group which is investigated because it is believed to represent a much larger population is called a *sample*, and much ingenuity has gone into devising methods for selecting such samples, and mathematical formulae for assessing the degree of accuracy to be expected from samples of varying sizes.

There are three main methods of sampling which are called, respectively, accidental sampling, random sampling, and stratified sampling.

Accidental sampling has been widely used but has nothing whatsoever to recommend it. It consists simply in the accidental choice of individuals who happen to be available, or who can be easily reached because their names are registered in a telephone book, or some other type of directory. Accidental sampling may occasionally give useful answers, but more usually it will not. Perhaps the most famous example of the disaster which may befall users of this method of sampling is the prediction made by the *Literary Digest* at the time of the 1936 Presidential Election. A brief review of the history leading up to this disaster may be useful.

Americans have always been interested in methods of ascertaining public opinion, and as early as 1824 the *Harrisburg Pennsylvanian* printed a report of a *straw vote*, i.e. a kind of public opinion poll, on the chances of the four men who were contesting the Presidential Election. Other newspapers throughout the years undertook similar small-scale polls, and by the turn of the century, polls were conducted by a great number of different papers. Occasionally, polls dealt with general issues of attitude as well as with election forecasts, a famous example being the poll conducted by Lundeen on the question of whether or not America should enter the First World War.

Of all these polls, however, the only one to achieve nation-wide attention was that conducted by the *Literary Digest*, a magazine with a very large circulation which entered the polling field around 1916. Polls were conducted by distributing ballots by mail to readers, to residential telephone subscribers, and to registered automobile owners. The number of polls distributed was quite

39

phenomenal. Thus, in the Presidential Election of 1928 some 18 million ballots were distributed. Victory for Herbert Hoover was predicted with 63·2 per cent of the total vote, the actual superiority in the election turning out to be 58·8 per cent. In 1932, with 20 million ballots distributed, Franklin D. Roosevelt's victory was predicted with an error of only 1·4 per cent.

In 1936 the *Digest* again put forward its prediction, giving Landon 57 per cent of the major party vote. In actual fact, Franklin D. Roosevelt polled 62·5 per cent of the major party vote. This disastrous failure was the end of the *Literary Digest* as an opinion polling organization; it also marked the advent of the Gallup Poll which had not only succeeded in predicting Roosevelt's success with an error of less than 5 per cent but had also predicted that the *Digest's* methods would come to grief, and had indeed predicted within 1 per cent the exact error which would be made by the *Literary Digest*! This was possible because the Gallup and other polls had rejected the accidental sample methods and had used more appropriate techniques which enabled them to put their finger on the vital weakness in the *Digest's* method of ascertaining public opinion by polling in the main people who could afford to run motor cars and own telephones, and who were interested enough in the election to answer questionnaires sent to them by mail. In the 1926 and 1932 elections, when there had been no particular tendency for one of the main parties to be identified with any social class, this had worked reasonably well because car and telephone owners were found as frequently among the Democratic as among the Republican voters. With the advent of Roosevelt, however, this changed, and the Democratic party became more and more identified with the interests of the working class and the Republican party with the interests of the middle class. Under those conditions, the poll, because of the accidental methods of choice involved, obtained mainly middle-class respondents whose responses over-predicted the Republican votes and under-predicted the Democratic votes.

Thus, the history of the *Literary Digest* points two very important morals. The first, that accidental sampling cannot be relied upon to produce accurate results; the second, that even a history of several correct predictions does not guarantee, in the absence of a sound methodology, success in future predictions. Gallup's success in predicting not only the outcome of the election but also the error likely to be committed by the *Literary Digest*, illustrates the superiority of his sampling method; this superiority, however, is proved not by what might have been an accidental success but rather by the theory underlying the methods of sampling used by him, i.e. those of random and representative sampling. To these we must now turn.

In the method of random sampling every individual in the population has an equal chance of being selected, and the process of selection is entirely determined by chance. If, for instance, we took a list from the electoral registers of all men and women in the British Isles entitled to vote in the next election, arranged the names in alphabetical order, and then took every ten thousandth name to make up our sample we should obtain a true random sample of the population. This method presupposes the existence of a complete enumeration of the population in which we are interested and a method of selecting from that population. In this pure form it is hardly ever practicable for any large population as the requisite lists do not usually exist, or, if they existed, would not be accessible to the investigator. In any case, even if they were available the time and money required to prepare a master list, choose names from it at random, and then interview people who might live as far apart as Land's End and John O'Groats, would make this scheme quite impossible of execution.

In the stratified method, the population is first divided into a number of strata (different income groups, different age groups, sex groups, rural-urban groups, and so forth), the number in each stratum of the sample being proportional to the population number in the stratum. The proportions of people in the total population belonging to each stratum must, of course, be known for this purpose; fortunately, this is usually so in civilized countries where accurate registers are kept. It is obviously also necessary that there should be some way of recognizing whether a given individual belongs into one or other of the strata as otherwise we could not allocate him appropriately; this process of recognition and allocation is easy with respect to sex, more difficult with respect to age, and most difficult of all perhaps with respect to income level. Nevertheless, this method is, from the practicable point of view, the easiest to use, and practically all the work done on opinion and attitude measurement is carried out by means of stratified sampling. The exact methods adopted we shall describe later on in this chapter.

The two main methods in actual use at the moment are known as the *quota sampling* and the *area sampling* methods, respectively. The quota method is used by the Gallup Poll and most other similar organizations. Essentially it works as follows: on the basis of the most up-to-date knowledge, a decision is made as to the number of men and women, people of various age groups, people of various income groups, and people from various residential areas who are to be included in the survey. Detailed instructions are then sent to interviewers who are spread all over the country, telling them in exact detail what type of people they should interview. To take one example with which the reader will already be familiar, the socio-economic quotas used by the British Institute of Public Opinion specify that 5 per cent of the sample should be in the Average Plus group, 21 per cent in the Average group, 59 per cent in the Average Minus group, and 15 per cent in Group D, i.e. the very poor. (Descriptions of these groups have been given on Page 16.) Each interviewer has a quota of 10–15 interviews; the total number of people interviewed usually varies from 1,500 to 3,000. The actual bases of stratification used by the British Institute of Public Opinion in their national surveys are as follows:

(a) Regional—the country is divided into 14 geographical areas;
(b) Rural and urban—in the proportion of 20 to 80;
(c) Size of town—four divisions are used: large, medium large, medium small and small;
(d) Political party of sitting member in the constituency;
(e) Sex of person interviewed;
(f) Age group—20–29, 30–49, 50–64, 65 and over.
(g) Socio-economic grouping; four divisions are used.

The method of quota sampling has come in for a good deal of criticism, largely because of the difficulties of being certain of the stratum to which a given person belongs—what should an interviewer do with a middle aged woman who claims to be in the 20–29 year old group, or when a shabbily dressed person pushing a wheelbarrow claims to be in the Average-Plus socio-economic group? Another difficulty is the differential availability of different groups. Interviewers find it particularly difficult to get hold of people in the highest and lowest groups respectively. As the latter are proportionately much more numerous in the population, this error has led in the United States to a constant bias in polling forecasts in favour of the Republican Party, and an under-estimate of the Democratic vote.

One of the main difficulties which arises is that although proportions for each of the strata are equal to the national average, the sub-groups into which the sample is divided may be quite unrepresentative. For example, the number of people in the sample from each of the four age groups may be proportional to the number in the total population; similarly the number of people in the sample belonging to each of the four socio-economic groups may be proportional to that in the total population. Yet most of the people in the highest age group may have come from the lowest income group and most of the young people from the highest income

TABLE XI

Possible Discrepancies Between Number of People in Various Cross-Sections of the Population and of a Sample Selected to Give the Same Overall Proportions

			Age			
		20–29	30–49	50–64	65+	
						Per Cent
Av.+	1	1m (4)	1m (0)	1m (0)	1m (0)	4
Av.	2	5m (20)	5m (0)	5m (0)	5m (0)	20
Av.—	3	15m (1)	15m (25)	15m (25)	15m (9)	60
D	4	4m (0)	4m (0)	4m (0)	4m (16)	16
		—	—	—	—	
	Per Cent	25	25	25	25	

group. As a quite artificial example, let us suppose we are dealing with a population of 100 million of whom 4 per cent are in the Average Plus income group, 20 per cent in the Average group, 60 per cent in the Average Minus group and 16 per cent in Group D, the very poor. Let us also assume that 25 per cent of the population fall into each of the four age groups 20–29, 30–49, 50–64, and 65 and over, and let us further assume that the distribution of people is as indicated in Table XI, i.e. there are one million in the Average Plus group aged 20–29, four million in the very poor group aged 65 and over, and so forth.

Let us now assume that we select a sample of 100 people in such a way that the percentages in the four age groups are, again, 25 for each, and that the percentages in the status groups are also identi-

43

cal with those for the total population. The sample might then be made up as indicated by the figures given in parentheses in Table XI. Thus, all the members of the sample aged 65+ might come from the very poor and the Average Minus group, none of the very poor might come from the three age groups covering the years from 20–64, and all the people of Average and Average Plus status might be in the youngest group. Clearly, such a distribution within the sub-groups would make any conclusions to be derived from the total sample very misleading; nevertheless, stratification according to age and income group would be quite exact.

It might be argued that this is not likely to happen in an actual sample, and undoubtedly such extreme distributions are indeed unlikely to occur. But if we take for example, the actual distribution by age and income group of the British Institute of Public Opinion sample quoted in Chapter One, we find that in the Average Plus group, old people of 65 and above make up 9·4 per cent of the total; in the Average group they make up 5·3 per cent; in the Average Minus group they make up 4·9 per cent of the total; but in the D group, i.e. among the very poor they make up 49·4 per cent.[8] Such a distribution almost certainly is out of line with the proper sub-sample distributions and indicates that the danger mentioned above is not a purely fanciful one. The fact that such faulty distribution within the total group does occur makes a little doubtful any deductions based on the figures which are usually published only in percentage form. Relationships found may be entirely due to incorrect sampling, and therefore have little validity. This is an important criticism, which can be overcome in two different ways. Sampling could be conducted in such a way that members in different sub-groups are specified as well as marginal totals, or, alternately, faulty sampling can be corrected statistically by a suitable system of weighting.

The method of area sampling, sometimes also called the method of specific assignment, does not leave the problem of deciding on the choice of interviewee to the interviewer, but specifies the exact person to be interviewed. The first step in the procedure is to select primary sampling areas which are usually chosen by reference to conveniently accessible government units, like counties and boroughs. The second step is to choose from the very large group of primary sampling areas those in which the interviews are to be conducted. To do this all the sample areas are grouped into strata, usually on the basis of some attribute like population density, or extent of urbanization. Primary sampling areas are then selected at random from each of the strata as a third step, and as a fourth step the primary sampling area chosen is itself sub-stratified into smaller units (streets or city blocks), and then a sub-sampling area chosen from each of the sub-strata at random.

Having obtained this last and smallest sampling unit it becomes necessary to specify the particular persons within it to be interviewed. This is done by random sampling. The names of all the people living in the street or city block are written down in alphabetical order and every nth name taken and specified to the interviewer, so that nothing is left to his choice or judgment; he must find his respondent exactly in accordance with instructions. It may, of course, be necessary for him to call back if the interviewee is not at home, and, in fact, with some people frequent call-backs are necessary before they are found at home. This is necessary because people who are at home a great deal differ in many important ways from those who are out a lot, and consequently it would be a mistake to substitute someone else for the person who is difficult to reach. As an example of the distortion that might arise in this way, we may quote an investigation by Kiser, who found that the sample obtained on first calling contained only 19·4 per cent of people where the number in the household was two, as compared with 26·8 per cent given in the national census. At the other extreme 2·2 per cent of the sample belonged to households of nine and over, whereas only 1·3 per cent did so according to the census. Thus, members of small households would be under-estimated, numbers of large households over-estimated, if substitutions were allowed.

The method of area sampling is clearly superior to that of quota sampling in usually giving a proper sample of the total population within each sub-classification. Its disadvantages are that it is laborious, lengthy, and expensive. There is a considerable amount of controversy in the literature between those favouring quota sampling and those favouring area sampling. The resolution of this conflict appears to lie in the recognition that different investigators have different purposes and aims, and that the method of sampling used should follow from these. For the purpose of predicting the outcome of an election, quota sampling would almost certainly be the method of choice because of the speed with which it can be conducted, and its responsiveness to last-minute trends in public opinion. For purposes where great exactness is required, not only for the total sample, but also for sub-samples, and where time and expense are of little importance, area sampling would probably be the method of choice. A great deal, of course, depends on data to which the investigator has access; accurate street maps, accurate census data, comprehensive lists of inhabitants, and so forth, are indispensable for area sampling, but much less so for quota sampling. It is probably an error to regard these two methods as opposed to each other; they are complementary and either may be used in appropriate circumstances.

Granted that the sample with which we may be dealing has been selected in line with the best possible method suitable for this purpose, there still remain two questions. One is how large should our sample be, the other, what degree of accuracy can we hope to attain? These two questions are interrelated, but before we discuss them we must define somewhat more precisely what we mean by accuracy. Let us suppose that we are dealing with a prediction requiring us to assess a simple percentage, such as the percentage of the total vote which will go to a particular candidate. However large our sample may be, it will still constitute only a very small proportion of the total number of people voting for or against this candidate, and consequently our forecast will always contain a certain amount of error. Let us define the degree of accuracy obtained in terms of the percentage difference between the prediction and the actual vote. To take an actual example, in the 1936 election the *Literary Digest* predicted that Franklin D. Roosevelt would obtain 43 per cent of the major party votes, whereas in actual fact he obtained 62·5 per cent, an error of 19·5 per cent. This figure of 19·5 per cent would, then, represent the degree of accuracy obtained by the *Literary Digest* poll on that occasion.

If we assume now that a certain poll, given to a certain number of people, operates on the average with an accuracy of 3 per cent, we should nevertheless find that on some occasions the forecasts would be more accurate than suggested by this figure, and on other occasions they would be less accurate. This can be predicted on a mathematical sampling theory and is indeed observable in actual polling practice. An *average* error of 3 per cent is not identical with the statement 'no error greater than 3 per cent'. Even with an *average* error of 3 per cent, one prediction out of a very large number of predictions might show a considerably greater error, such as 10 per cent. Thus, we can never be *certain* that our predictions will be accurate within any given range. However, we can be *reasonably certain* of the degree of accuracy which we shall have obtained. This concept of *reasonably certain* requires more accurate statement, and it is usually taken to mean that our prediction would be borne out in 997 cases out of 1,000 and falsified only three times out of 1,000. In other words, the odds against would only be three in a 1,000.

If we now accept this definition of 'reasonably certain' then we can relate the degree of accuracy of which we can be reasonably certain to two factors which, between them, completely determine the amount of chance error to be found from a random sample. The first of these two factors, as might be expected, is the number of cases in the sample. We should expect accuracy to increase as the number of cases in the sample increases; a poll taken of 100 people would be regarded as less likely to be accurate than a poll taken of 10,000. Unfortunately, the accuracy does not increase directly with the size of the sample but only as the square root of the size of the sample; in other words, to double our accuracy we must quadruple the size of the sample. Thus, there is a distinct law of diminishing returns as far as sample size is concerned, and very little is usually to be gained by increasing samples beyond 3,000 or thereabouts.

The second factor which determines the degree of accuracy of our prediction is the actual size of the percentage which we are trying to predict. Percentages in the neighbourhood of 50 are more difficult to predict, i.e. are predicted less accurately, than percentages deviating from 50 in either direction. In other words, a percentage of 80 is easier to predict than one of 70, a percentage of 30 easier than one of 40, and a percentage of 10 or 90 easier than any of the others mentioned. These facts are usually summarized in a formula giving the standard error of a proportion under conditions of completely random sampling. The formula is:

$$S.E._p = \sqrt{\frac{p \times q}{n}}$$

where p is the percentage to be predicted, q is $100 - p$, and n is the number of cases in the sample. Table XII will indicate what this formula means in terms of our two questions. The body of the

47

table contains the number of cases required in order to be reasonably certain of a given degree of accuracy when the division of opinion is 80/20, 70/30, 60/40, or 50/50. Supposing we wish to predict a percentage in the neighbourhood of 50; if the accuracy required is only 10 per cent we could be reasonably certain of attaining this with a sample of 225 cases. To double the accuracy, i.e. to reach one of 5 per cent, we must quadruple this number, i.e. we must use 900 interviews. To reach an accuracy of 1 per cent we need 22,500 interviews. Similarly, when the percentage we wish to predict is 80 (or 20) we should need only 144 interviews where the accuracy required was only 10 per cent, 576 interviews where the accuracy required was 5 per cent, and 14,400 interviews for an accuracy of 1 per cent. Figure 8 shows in diagrammatic form the number of cases required for any degree of accuracy for three different divisions of opinion (50/50, 70/30, and 80/20). Even the use

TABLE XII

Number in Sample Required to Give Desired Degree of Accuracy for Various Divisions of Opinion

Division of Opinion	10%	9%	8%	7%	6%	5%	4%	3%	2%	1%
80/20	144	178	225	294	400	576	900	1,600	3,600	14,400
70/30	189	233	295	386	525	756	1,181	2,100	4,725	18,400
60/40	216	267	338	441	600	864	1,350	2,400	5,400	21,600
50/50	225	278	352	459	625	900	1,406	2,500	5,625	22,500

of logarithmetic paper cannot hide the very rapid increase in numbers needed as the accuracy required approaches 1 per cent.

It must be remembered in consulting this table that the accuracy referred to is stated in terms of what is reasonably certain; in other words, this is not the average accuracy which could be expected from a given number of cases in the sample, but the accuracy which could be relied upon to be reached with reasonable certainty. The average accuracy with these various numbers of cases would in each case be considerably greater. As an example, let us take a sample 2,500, which with a 50/50 break would give us an accuracy of 3 per cent with reasonable certainty, i.e. in 997 cases out of 1,000. The average degree of accuracy obtainable with such a sample, and assuming a break of 50/50, however, would not be 3 per cent but less than 1 per cent.

It will also be remembered that these figures apply to conditions of purely random sampling. Stratified sampling requires certain

FIGURE 8

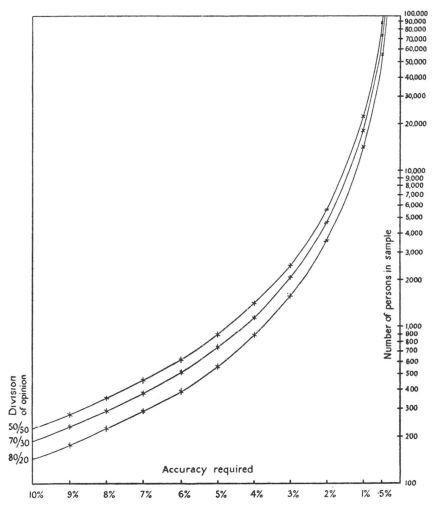

Number in Sample Required to Reach Desired Degree of Accuracy
for Three Different Divisions of Opinion

changes in the formula to take into account degree of success of stratification. Another slight correction is also required in order to take into account the total size of the universe which is being sampled. These formulae can be found in the standard texts and there would be little point in giving them in a book of this type; in any case the actual predictive errors made in polling are so much larger than those predicted on the basis of sampling theory that slight changes in predicted proportions would make very little difference to the observed results. Sampling theory is a highly technical branch of study but its basic principles, as outlined above are easily intelligible and ought to be known far more widely than they are.[9]

(b) WORDING OF QUESTIONS

Having selected our sample and decided on the number of interviews required to give us a given degree of accuracy, we must next decide on the questions to be asked. There are three main types of questions which have been widely used. There are the *two-way*, the *multiple-choice*, and the *open-end* type of question. The open-end type of question allows the interviewee to state the answer in his own words, to introduce any qualifications he may wish, and to make his answer as specific or as general as he pleases. The multiple-choice type of question allows him to choose one of several different answers provided by the interviewer, whereas the two-way type of question restricts the answer essentially to a simple 'Yes' or 'No', with the possible third answer 'Don't Know'.

The advantages and disadvantages of these various forms have been fairly obvious from the very beginning. The open-end type of question permits the respondent to express himself as he pleases, but may make it extremely difficult to interpret what he has to say in any meaningful way, or to categorize the answers of different people in such a way that they can be treated statistically and compared with each other. The two-way type of question may be regarded as being too restrictive and as not presenting the particular alternative which the respondent would most readily endorse. It is a kind of Procrustean method which forces all opinions into a preconceived mould. The multiple-choice type of question may err in the same direction, though to a lesser extent. It also has disadvantages of its own; thus, people tend to forget some of the alternatives presented and more frequently choose those listed first or last rather than those given in between.

As in the case of the quota versus area sampling dispute, so here also it is impossible to say that any of these three methods is superior to the others under all circumstances. Everything depends on the type of issue involved, the people to be polled, and other circumstances which can only be evaluated by the expert experienced in the field. However, even granted that the most appropriate type of question is used there still arise many problems concerned with the precise way of wording the question and avoiding the introduction of bias into it. A list of the main difficulties arising in the forming of questions will be given below, together with examples of polls where these difficulties have not been overcome successfully.

1. *Understanding of words*

A well known story deals with the surprise experienced by an American Government Agency when it was found that among Southern Negroes only a very small proportion voted in favour of levying tax on profits. An investigation on the spot indicated that these Negroes, whose only reading had been the Bible, could find no justification therein for taxing prophets! In case we should feel superior we may remember a question asked in another survey, which went: 'When you speak of profits, are you thinking of profit on the amount of sales, on the amount of money invested in the business, on year-end inventory, or what?' According to Payne, the results indicated that only 12 per cent of the respondents could be assumed to understand the proper meaning of the term 'profit'! He also points out, as further illustrations of popular ignorance, that in various polls it had been found that 25 per cent of the American public said they did not know what a 'lobbyist' in Washington was; 41 per cent said they did not know what the phrase 'socialized medicine' meant; 46 per cent could not describe what 'filibuster' was, and 88 per cent either said they did not know or gave incorrect descriptions of 'jurisdictional strike'.

In another experiment, Cantril and Fried took as their starting point a question asked by the *Fortune* poll. 'Which—C.I.O. or A.F. of L.—do you feel has the lower initiation fees?', and 'Which—C.I.O. or A.F. of L.—do you feel has the stricter entrance requirements as regards the skill of its members?' They then queried a small sample on their understanding of such terms as 'Initiation fees' and 'entrance requirements' and found that at least half of the people who answered the original question did not know precisely what they were talking about. Very great care must therefore be taken to make certain that the terms used in the questions

51

are clearly intelligible even to people with little education; and pre-testing, i.e. the administration of questions to small samples before the actual survey is taken, in order to obtain their reactions to these questions, may be necessary to eliminate words giving rise to misunderstanding.

2. *Ignorance of Issues*

Even though a question may be properly worded, answers may be misleading because the issue to which the question refers has no reality in the minds of the respondents. The question was asked, for instance, by a British polling organization a few years ago: 'Do you think King George of Greece ought to be allowed to go back to his country, or should a referendum be held on the question of his return?' 56 per cent favoured his return, 15 per cent opposed it, and 29 per cent answered 'Don't Know'. These answers do not indicate that the majority of respondents favoured the Conservative side in the Greek political struggle for power. The majority vote was merely an expression of ignorance coupled with a natural view, 'If he is Greek, why shouldn't he go back to Greece?' That this is the right interpretation was shown in a subsequent poll, asking the question: 'Have you ever heard of King George of Greece?' in which only 29 per cent said they had ever heard of the Greek king.

This obtaining of views on pseudo-issues has been illustrated most amusingly by Gill, who got 70 per cent of a population sample to approve or disapprove of a completely fictitious 'Metallic Metals Act', and to say whether this should be enacted nationally or left to the States. He even managed to get substantial proportions in his sample to approve of incest!

This possibility of artificially creating an expression of opinion where really there is no public opinion at all is an ever present one in opinion polls. It can be counteracted by ascertaining, in the first place, whether people in the sample had ever heard of the people or issues involved, whether they had any accurate knowledge about them, and whether they had any strong feelings one way or another. An alternative method would be the use of a formula suggested by Hofstaetter, in which he defines the 'actuality' of a question (A) in terms of the fraction:

$$A = \frac{\sqrt{P_+ \times P_-}}{P_0}$$

In this expression, P_+ and P_- refer to the percentage of the population approving and disapproving of the issue, whereas P_0 refers to the 'Don't Knows'. In the example given above of King George of Greece's return, this would work out as:

$$A = \frac{\sqrt{56 \times 15}}{29} = 1 \cdot 00$$

which indicates a relatively low degree of actuality as compared with a question such as the following one, which had a considerable degree of actuality at the time: 'Would you approve or disapprove of theatres being allowed to open on Sundays just as they do on other days?' 58 per cent of the sample approved, 33 per cent disapproved, 9 per cent had no opinion. Under these conditions:

$$A = \frac{\sqrt{58 \times 33}}{9} = 4 \cdot 9$$

Finally, as an example of a question of the very highest degree of actuality, we may take the following one asked by the British Institute of Public Opinion in June 1953, just before the Government were due to announce their decision on sponsored television, and after a considerable amount of publicity had been given to this question in the national press:

'Which of these alternatives do you prefer as regards T.V. programmes: (A) to leave them as they are, completely in the hands of the B.B.C., or (B) to have commercial stations competing with the B.B.C.?' 60 per cent preferred the B.B.C. only; 36 per cent preferred to have commercial stations competing with the B.B.C.; 4 per cent answered 'Don't Know'. This gives us a coefficient of 11·7.

These values may be compared with others found by Hofstaetter in a survey of 428 polls:

Actuality	A	Frequency in 428 Poll Questions per cent
Low	1·00	8·7
Average	1·00–2·49	43·2
Considerable	2·50–4·99	25·7
High	5·00–10·00	15·2
Very High	10·01+	7·2

Thus low values must be regarded as a danger signal and as suggestive of the possibility that opinions may have been created by the question.

Another method of detecting whether or not an opinion has really crystallized or is just being created by the question is suggested by Gallup. He writes: 'When an opinion is deeply held, when it is a question on which people have formed convictions, the wording of the question is of relatively minor importance.' He goes on to suggest the use of the so-called split ballot vote technique in this connection, i.e. the use of questions worded in a slightly different way on different samples of the population; if results from different wordings show high agreement he would regard this as evidence that opinions had sufficiently crystallized. As an example, he quotes three questions asked by his organization immediately before the outbreak of war in Europe:

	Yes	No
	per cent	
A. Would you like to see England, France, and Poland agree to Germany's demands regarding Danzig?	12	88
B. Do you think Hitler's claims to Danzig are justified?	13	87
C. Do you think Hitler's claims to the Polish Corridor are justified?	14	86

This view that consistency of replies indicates crystallization of opinion is a reasonable one, but it should be noted that there is no direct experimental evidence in its favour; Gallup's claim is simply that 'Certain generalizations have stood the test of polling experience'. While experience is a good guide for setting up hypotheses, it cannot be used to prove them, and experimental proof of this hypothesis would seem desirable.

3. *Vague and Obscure Questions*

Some questions are so vague and obscure that answers cannot be taken to have very much meaning. Cantril and Fried take as an example a question asked by the *Fortune* poll: 'After the war is over, do you think people will have to work harder, about the same, or not so hard as before?' A sample of 40 people was interviewed specifically to gain some insight into their understanding of the meaning of the terms used. It was found that to slightly more than half of the group, the 'people' meant everybody; that it meant a particular class to a third of the group; and that one tenth of the respondents just did not know what they meant by the word 'people'. The word 'harder' turned out to mean higher quality to some, more competition to others, and longer hours to the rest, whereas the phrase 'as before' meant before the war started to one half of the group, and after the war started to the rest of the group. 'On the basis of this analysis it would then be difficult to interpret percentage results obtained from this particular question in any reliable fashion.'

A similar analysis was carried out on a question asked by the Office of Public Opinion Research: 'If the German army overthrew Hitler and then offered to stop the war and discuss peace terms with the Allies, would you favour or oppose accepting the offer of the German army?' Only 11 out of 40 people understood the question in the sense which had been intended. Seven of the forty could not say precisely what the question meant to them, while the meaning most uniformly accepted by the remainder revealed an obvious confusion in that respondents identified the German people with the German army. 'It is significant to see that of those who opposed peace the great majority understood the meaning of the question whereas of those who favoured peace the majority identified the German army with the German people. The simple percentage answers to our original question, then, do not mean at all what they would appear to mean without further probing.'

The danger of such vague and obscure questions, which are frequently to be found, is that they can be interpreted in so many different ways and that results, while appearing to be definite and exact, really are of no value from the point of view of the student of politics.

4. *Loaded Questions*

A loaded question is one which prejudges the issue and does not give a fair chance to people having views different from those of the person writing the question. The accusation that polling organizations are partisan has, of course, frequently been made, usually by those whose party or candidate was predicted to lose an electoral or presidential race. However, there has never been any proof of intentional bias, and the fact that a polling organization's economic future depends on the accuracy of its forecasts makes such bias

55

extremely unlikely. Bias is found much more frequently in questionnaires produced by special organizations for an *ad hoc* purpose. Payne quotes some questions contained in a questionnaire sent to 'trade and industry associations, chambers of commerce, and other small business organizations and to individual businessmen in 48 States'. This questionnaire 'was inspired by Bill S.1913 to create a Small Business Corporation with a billion dollars capital to succeed the much smaller Smaller War Plants Corporation'. Here are some of the questions:

'Does small business need a government wet nurse in all its daily activities?'

'No'—97 per cent

'Would it be healthy for small business, or for the national economy, to have government loans available to all those who wish to engage in business, or enlarge their business, with the implied taxpayers' loss in case of their failure?'

'No'—95 per cent

'Should not the sponsorship for the representation of, and the source of information for and about small business be embodied in a permanent, existing agency like the Department of Commerce?'

'Yes'—84 per cent

The effects of loading questions is shown in an experiment conducted by Roper (1941). He asked three questions of different samples of the populations regarding the right of labour in defence industries to strike about working conditions. The unbiased question was: 'Do you think that the government should or should not forbid labour in defence industries the right to strike about working conditions?' The answer was:

'Should'—59 per cent; 'Should Not'—29 per cent;
'Don't Know'—12 per cent.

The pro-union question read: 'Because every man is entitled to safe and healthy working conditions, labour (in defence industries) should be allowed to strike for them.'

'Disagree'—45 per cent; 'Agree'—45 per cent;
'Don't Know'—10 per cent

The anti-union question ran: 'Because working conditions in this country are the best in the world labour (in defence industries) should not be allowed to strike against them.'

'Agree'—74 per cent; 'Disagree'—17 per cent;
'Don't Know'—9 per cent.

The original question had a fair degree of actuality (A=8), yet the percentage of people disputing the right of labour to strike could be depressed from 59 to 45 per cent, or raised to 74 per cent by slight changes in the wording of the question. Fortunately, it is usually easy to detect biassed wording by simple inspection, and where necessary the existence of bias can be proved by means of the split ballot technique described above.

5. *Use of Stereotypes*

As Payne points out, 'One of the most spectacular forms of loading, and one which has been discussed rather frequently is the influence of stereotypes, the tendency to vote for motherhood and against sin. The name of an organization, or a political party, or an individual becomes heavily charged with emotional reactions. If this name is interjected into a question, some people may react to the name instead of to the issue. It is like waving the red flag in front of the bull, for example, to introduce an issue with a statement explaining how Communists feel about it. Many respondents will vote against whichever side the Communists are said to espouse.'

As an example of stereotyped opinion, we may quote some polls conducted by the American Institute of Public Opinion and the Office of Public Opinion Research.

AIPO (11/40)

Do you believe in freedom of speech?
'Yes'—97 per cent; 'No'—1 per cent; 'Don't know'—2 per cent.
If 'Yes': Do you believe in it to the extent of allowing Fascists and Communists to hold meetings and express their views in this community?
'No'—72 per cent; 'Yes'—23 per cent; 'No Opinion'—5 per cent.

OPOR (7/41)

Do you think that in America anybody should be allowed to speak on any subject he wants to, or do you think there are times when free speech should be prohibited?
'Allowed at all times'—44 per cent; 'Prohibit sometimes'—53 per cent; 'No Opinion'—3 per cent.

If 'Allow at all times': Do you believe in free speech to the extent of allowing Fascists and Communists to hold meetings and express their views in this community?

'No'—60 per cent; 'Yes'—37 per cent; 'No Opinion'—3 per cent.

Cantril, who quotes these figures, comments that they 'clearly show that although practically everyone in the United States says he is in favour of free speech, such freedom seems based on the assumption that it is freedom for only certain types of people'. Stereotypes are so all-pervasive in their influence on the formation of social attitudes and political ideologies that we shall deal with them in much greater detail later and will, therefore, leave this point without any detailed discussion.

6. *Personalization*

A well known Spanish proverb, freely translated, asks for 'justice, but not for my house'. In other words, we may regard a certain policy or mode of action as a good thing in general but reject it for ourselves. This tendency is shown up quite frequently when questions in a split-ballot are asked about a policy in general, i.e. in the abstract, and when the same question is asked as applied to the person concerned. Payne (1946) asked the following questions:

'If you could get some insurance for which you paid a certain amount each month to cover any hospital care you might need in the future, would you rather do that or would you rather pay the hospital what it charges you each time?'

66 per cent preferred to pay insurance; 28 per cent preferred to pay each time; 6 per cent had no opinion.

In the impersonalized version the following question was asked:

'Some people have a kind of insurance for which they pay a certain amount each month to cover any hospital care they or their families may have in the future. Do you think this is a good idea or a bad idea?'

92 per cent thought it was a good idea; 4 per cent thought it was a bad idea; and 4 per cent had no opinion. Payne comments 'by changing from a personalized speak-for-yourself-John question to a general one which allows respondents to answer more altruistically or with less consideration of personal consequences, approval

of prepayment hospital insurance is increased by 26 percentage points'.

As another example, we may quote a question asked by the American Institute of Public Opinion in 1940. In the impersonal manner of statement this read: 'Should the United States increase our army further, even if it means more taxes?', whereas in the personal form it read: 'Should the United States increase our army further, even if you have to pay a special tax?' Approval dropped from 88 to 79 per cent as the personal form was substituted for the impersonal one.

7. *Social Approval*

In any society which has certain generally approved standards and ways of acting, there will almost undoubtedly be a tendency for people to be biassed in their replies to questions dealing with these standards in the direction of claiming to be in accord with them to a greater extent than is actually true. This desire for social approval comes out very clearly in a question asked by the American Institute of Public Opinion during the war: 'Is your regular job in any way connected with the war?' 213 persons who said their work was either directly or indirectly connected with the war were questioned closely by Cantril and his associates as to what they actually did. He found that 31 per cent were in actual defence work; 27 per cent were doing something which really seemed closely connected with the war; 28 per cent had a very indirect connection, even when their work was very liberally judged from the point of view of its relation to the war, and 14 per cent were clearly rationalizing their positions. As examples of rationalization, Cantril quotes a street-cleaner who thought his job was 'necessary to health'; a jeweller who said, 'If we don't pay taxes we can't win wars;' a minister who said he was helping to, 'keep up morale of my people'; a clerk in a store selling orthopaedic shoes who said, 'People are on their feet more now with defence and all that, and need care of their feet'.

Another phenomenon illustrating the desire of respondents to be 'in the swim', i.e. to be thought of well by the interviewer is what election pollsters call the 'past-preference build-up'. When people are questioned after an election as to the candidate for whom they voted, more people claim to have voted than did in actual fact vote (voting being a socially approved mode of behaviour), and more people claim to have voted for the winning candidate than actually did.

Social approval also attaches to the having of opinions on a variety of public issues, and this is probably responsible for the fact that many people express opinions on issues to which in reality they have never given a thought and on which they cannot really be said to have any kind of crystallized opinion at all. As Payne points out, 'In their desire to appear well informed, some people affect to have more knowledge than they actually possess, hence the high proportions who are willing to give opinions on the administration of a fictitious Metallic Metals Act.'

There are, of course, ways of overcoming the desire of respondents to acquire approval in the sight of the interviewer. Instead of asking, for instance, 'Do you own a car?' which although it is a straightforward question, nevertheless has considerable social prestige implications in the eyes of questioner and respondent alike, one might put the question in a slightly different way and ask, 'Are you planning to buy a car in the near future?' Thus, people who would like to be thought of as sufficiently high in the social hierarchy to be capable of car ownership could answer this question in the prestige-giving direction and then admit, with fewer feelings of inferiority, to not owning a car at present.

In the matter of people claiming to have opinions when really they have none, some tests, such as the split-ballot and the A-coefficient have already been mentioned as useful indicators; another possible method is to follow up the original question with others designed to test knowledge of the issue in question and intensity of feeling regarding it.

8. *The Use of Alternatives*

In answering questions, people do not always visualize the exact consequences of their answers and do not always consider possible alternatives unless these are explicitly stated. As an example of this, Rugg quotes the following two questions, which pose apparently exactly the same issue: 'Do you think the United States should allow public speeches against democracy?'; 'Do you think the United States should forbid public speeches against democracy?' The results were as follows:

First Question		Second Question	
	per cent		*per cent*
Should allow	21	Should Not Forbid	39
Should not allow	62	Should Forbid	46
No opinion	17	No opinion	15

Apparently, respondents are quite ready to say that something should not be allowed, but when they realize that the alternative would be to forbid it they become distinctly less enthusiastic. The use of this term brings home to them the dangers to democratic practices implied in deliberately and by governmental action curtailing freedom of speech. Another example comes from the American Institute of Public Opinion, which in May 1941 asked the following split-ballot questions:

(A form)

'If you were asked to vote to-day on the question of the United States entering the war against Germany and Italy, how would you vote—to go into the war, or to stay out of the war?'
Go in 29 per cent; Stay out 66 per cent; No Opinion 5 per cent.

(B form)

'Please tell me which of these policies you think the United States should follow at the present time.' (Interviewer hands card to respondent containing the following statements.)

	per cent
A. Go to war at once against Germany and Italy	6
B. Supply Britain with all war materials we can and also use our navy to convoy ships carrying these materials to Britain	36
C. Supply Britain with all war materials we can, but do *not* use our navy to convoy these materials	46
D. Stop all further aid to Britain	7
E. Other replies	1
No Opinion	4

It will be seen that the choice of intermediate courses between 'going in' and 'staying out' resulted in a considerable drop in the percentage of people willing to go to war. As Cantril comments, 'Where several distinct alternatives existed with regard to inter-

vention, the B form undoubtedly provided a more realistic presentation of the problem. But if an actual war referendum were in
the offing the B form would tend to underestimate the percentage
of those voting for outright war.'

Another example is also given by Cantril. It deals with the attitude of people toward the post-war world.

Post War-Ballot
Which of these things do you think the U.S. should try to do when
the war is over:

	per cent
Stay out of world affairs as much as we can, or	21
Take an active part in world affairs?	68
Don't know or unable to choose	11

If 'Stay Out' ask respondent:
If it should happen that there is trouble and other nations get
ready again for war, do you think we should stay out of world
affairs then?

	per cent
Yes	61
No	25
Couldn't happen	1
Don't Know	10
Other	3

Suppose our standard of living is reduced when we try to get along
on what we grow and produce at home; would you still think that
it would be best to stay out of world affairs?

	per cent
Yes	66
No	14
Couldn't happen	6
Don't Know	13
Other	1

If 'Take Active Part' ask respondent:
Have you ever considered the possibility that we might have to
keep up a large army, navy and air force at great expense to help
police the world if we want to take an active part in world affairs?

	per cent
Yes	94
No	6

If 'Yes' ask:
Do you think this expense would be justified?

	per cent
Yes	97
No	1
Don't Know	2

If our trade with other countries after the war gets us involved in entangling alliances and power politics, as Europe always has been, would you still think it would be best to take an active part in world affairs?

	per cent
Yes	82
No	11
Don't know	7

He derives the following conclusions: 'One-third of the population admitted it had not thought at all about U.S. post-war problems —it was possible to shift the opinion of about 20 per cent who said originally that we should stay out of world affairs, by presenting certain contingencies that might arise if their point of view became official policy. On the side advocating "taking an active part in world affairs" opinion was not so flexible, although here again there was considerable change when certain contingencies were mentioned. It is noteworthy, though naturally to be expected, that persons who said they had not given any thought to the problem proved more suggestible than the rest of the population.'

It is probably safe to say that on most issues the single question can be very misleading unless alternatives are carefully considered and presented. Opportunities for biasing replies by appropriate choice of alternatives is an ever-present danger, as is also the creation of opinion by means of alternatives which respondents had never really considered before they were suggested by the investigator.

9. *Placement on Ballot*

Respondents' views may be influenced in a subtle way by the actual placement of the particular question under investigation in relation to other questions which may establish a certain set, draw attention to certain consequences or alternatives, and generally determine the thought processes of the interviewee. As an example, we may take a question asked by the American Institute of Public Opinion on 9 January 1939, in which one half of the sample was given the A form, the other the B form:

'(A form) Should the United States permit its citizens to join the French and British Armies?

Should the United States permit its citizens to join the German army?

(B form) Should the United States permit its citizens to join the German army?

Should the United States permit its citizens to join the British and French armies?'

		British and French	German
A form	Yes	45	31
	No	46	61
	Don't know	9	8
B form	Yes	40	22
	No	54	74
	Don't know	6	4

On the A form, after endorsing enlistments in the armies of the Allies, people evidently felt obliged to extend the same privilege to those wishing to join the German army (this question was asked at the outbreak of the war in Spetember 1939, when America was primarily interested in remaining strictly neutral). When the question of joining the German army came first (B form), however, fewer people were willing to grant this right to American citizens.

The fact that the context in which a question appears quite decisively influences the reactions to it is illustrated by many other poll results, and again shows the vital necessity of the use of split-ballot techniques, and also the desirability of publishing results not for single questions only but also to publish all other questions

asked in the same interview. Only in this way is it possible to check on the possible after effects of previously asked questions.[10]

(c) PROBLEMS OF INTERVIEWING

Most public opinion polls make use of interviewers who obtain answers by direct questioning of respondents. This method has certain obvious advantages over the use of questionnaires or mail ballots, but it also gives rise to difficulties and distortions of its own. Among these are the facts that answers to questions put by the interviewer are not secret, i.e. at least one person, namely the interviewer, knows what the respondent has said; it may give rise to distortion through the bias of the interviewer, which may be communicated to the respondent; another source of bias may arise through failure of the interviewer to establish rapport with the respondent because of differences in social class, age, or sex between the two of them. Lastly, refusals may complicate the picture in that a majority of those who refuse to be interviewed may hold certain minority points of view which they do not wish to make public and which may, therefore, be under-represented in the total sample. There is ample experimental evidence on all these points which shows that these misgivings are by no means unjustified.

1. *Secrecy of Polling*

It is possible to assess the importance of the factor of secrecy by using a split-ballot technique in which one half of the respondents are interviewed in the ordinary way, while the other half fill in a secret ballot. This was done, for instance, by the American Institute of Public Opinion, who found that in the secret ballot there was a marked decrease in the number of undecided votes as compared with those recorded in the non-secret ballot. This suggests that a good many people not wishing to disclose their voting intentions in a personal interview simply say, 'Don't Know', although their minds may be quite made up.

A more experimental study has been described by Turnbull who used ten questions on 612 respondents, 300 of whom were questioned by means of the conventional interview technique, the others by means of the secret ballot. For the latter purpose, interviewers 'carried a padlocked ballot-box with "SECRET BALLOT" printed ostentatiously on one side. When the secret ballot

form was to be used, the box was prominently exhibited, the printing being made obvious to the respondent, who was assured that he would be allowed to fold his own ballot and drop it into the box himself. He was then given the ballot and asked to mark it privately. When the respondent was to be interviewed, the box was set down inconspicuously near the door, and was ostensibly just a container for used ballot forms.' Approximately the same percentages of refusals were obtained with both forms, and there was close similarity between the groups with respect to sex, colour, income, religious and political affiliation, and age. Marked differences were found, however, in answers to questions on which there was a considerable social pressure to give one answer rather than another. The largest difference was found on the question: 'Do you think the English will try to get us to do most of the fighting for them in this war, or do you think they will do their fair share of the fighting?' At the interview, 57 per cent thought the English would do their fair share of the fighting; on the secret ballot, only 42 per cent. This difference of 15 per cent indicates the influence of the desire to make the socially accepted response when interviewed as compared with expressing one's true opinion in the secret ballot.

Similarly, on the question: 'Do you think the Jews have too much power and influence in this country?' 56 per cent said 'Yes' in the interview, but 66 per cent answered 'Yes' in the secret ballot, a difference of 10 per cent. Here again, the secret ballot appears to give the more correct figure, i.e. one in which the pressure of public opinion plays less part.

Turnbull concludes from his study of these and other results of his experiments 'that the methods of the interview and the secret ballot do produce marked differences in answers under certain conditions. These differences cast some doubt on the validity of the results obtained by the interview method when the subject feels that his answer, if known, would affect his prestige. The discrepancy is probably great enough to warrant the use of the secret ballot whenever questions which have acquired high social prestige are involved, particularly when the questions are of a highly controversial nature, and of deep personal or social significance.'

2. *Interviewer Bias*

The possibility that the personal opinion of the interviewer may influence the responses given by the interviewee cannot be ruled

out. Cantril presents some results which indicate beyond reasonable doubt that such influences cannot be disregarded. He reports that each of the, approximately, 200 interviewers used at the time by the American Institute of Public Opinion was sent an interviewer's ballot, identical with that used on the National Survey, and filled in by the interviewer himself as an expression of his own personal opinions. The following figures are taken from a survey carried out in 1940, the question asked being: 'Which of these two things do you think is more important for the United States to try to do—to keep out of war ourselves, or to help England win, even at the risk of getting into the war?' Those interviewers who favoured helping England reported that 60 per cent of their respondents favoured helping England, while 40 per cent favoured keeping out. Those interviewers who favoured keeping out reported 44 per cent of their respondents being in favour of helping England, while 56 per cent were in favour of keeping out. Cantril concludes: 'The 16 per cent difference in results between these two groups has a critical ratio of 13·9. This difference is so great for the size of the sample used that the possiblility of this difference occurring by chance is almost incalculably small.'

A closer scrutiny of the figures obtained in relation to the size of town in which interviewing occurred showed that 'in large cities interviewers' opinions are not effectively correlated with the opinions of their respondents . . . In the small towns and rural farm areas, on the contrary, the difference is large.' Cantril suggests that this may be due to the fact that in small towns and country areas, interviewers' opinions may often be known to respondents, who will try to express opinions in agreement with those of the interviewer. In large cities, however, interviewers are less likely to interview people with whom they have had previous acquaintance. His suggestion, therefore, is that 'interviewing in small towns and rural areas should be handled by people who are not local residents, but who may, for example, be sent from large cities in the area'.

3. *Interviewer Rapport*

Interviewers of most polling organizations are middle-class people whose class membership might influence both the selection of respondents and also the opinions which respondents are willing to express to them. This problem has been experimentally investigated by Katz, who gave similar assignments to nine middle-class interviewers and eleven specially trained working-class interviewers. The interviews were held in working-class areas in Pittsburgh and the ballot included questions on labour issues, the war, and government ownership of industry.

There was a slight tendency for working-class interviewers to select respondents higher in socio-economic status than respondents selected by middle-class interviewers; this is explained by Katz on the grounds of inexperience, the middle-class interviewers having been accustomed to going very low in the socio-economic scale in order to get a true cross-section of the population, while many of the working-class group, being new to the whole procedure, interviewed an undue number of middle-class people.

In spite of this fact, opinions reported by working-class interviewers were consistently more radical than those reported by middle-class interviewers. As an example, we may take the question on whether or not union-members favoured a law against sitdown strikes. Middle-class interviewers reported 59 per cent in favour of such a law; working-class interviewers reported 44 per cent in favour. This large difference is almost certainly not due to chance, and Katz believes that the findings of the working-class interviewers are more likely to be representative of the true state of opinion among this particular group of respondents. He bases himself on two facts: (1) that the opinions reported by the experienced middle-class interviewers agreed more with working-class interviewers' results than did the results of the inexperienced middle-class interviewers; and (2) because the comments reported by working-class interviewers showed that they had better rapport with their respondents than had middle-class interviewers.

Of similar importance to social class in establishing rapport is probably colour. In an experiment undertaken by the National Opinion Research Centre in 1942 white and negro interviewers, respectively, carried out some 500 interviews of Negroes in a large southern city. Among the questions asked were: 'Would Negroes be treated better or worse here if the Nazis conquered the U.S.A.?' Negro interviewers reported the answer 'Worse' in 25 per cent of the cases, white interviewers in 45 per cent of the cases. On the question: 'Do you think it is more important to concentrate on beating the Axis, or to make democracy work better here at home,' 62 per cent of the negroes answered 'Beat Axis' to white interviewers, but only 39 per cent gave this answer to Negro interviewers.

There is little doubt that rapport is more easily gained when interviewer and respondent are of a similar social-class and of the same ethnic sub-group. It is probable, although no direct evidence exists, that a middle-class Londoner would be less likely to obtain true answers from a Welsh miner, a Cornish fisherman, or a Scottish gillie, than someone coming from the same region and being of a similar socio-economic status. This is an important problem to which polling organization have probably given insufficient attention.

4. *The Problem of Refusals*

It is clear that refusals to be interviewed could have a highly important influence on the accuracy of the poll. It is well-known that the very poor tend to vote Labour in this country and are in favour of the Democratic Party in America. If it could be shown that the very poor also tend to refuse to be interviewed more frequently than do other socio-economic groups, bias could easily be introduced into the poll, which might lead to erroneous opinions. That this is not idle speculation is shown by an experiment reported by Harding, who, in 1942, instructed interviewers in two surveys made by the Office of Public Opinion Research to keep a complete record of all people they approached who, for any reason whatever, refused to be interviewed, or who discontinued an interview that had been started. In both samples, 14 per cent of the people approached for interviews either refused or failed to complete the interview. Such refusals were most frequent among poor people, women, and in large cities. Refusals were also more common among older people. Harding compared opinions given by respondents who refused to continue the interview but who did answer the first question on the ballot paper, and found that on this question there was no very great difference but that 'the opinions of people who refuse to be interviewed are often more superficial and unstable than those of more co-operative respondents. Even the differences found on this question, however, are not large enough to have much practical significance; inclusion of the incompleted interviews in the cross-section would on neither the March nor the July ballot change the proportion of any by more than 1 per cent.' Harding concludes from these data 'that refusals do not greatly affect the extent to which the sample secured by poll interviewers is a representative cross-section of the population . . . . It is extremely doubtful that the bias introduced into poll results by the refusal of some people to be interviewed can compare in size with the bias resulting from the tendency of interviewers to select their respondents in an unrandom fashion, or the bias introduced by the divergence of respondents' answers from their true opinions.' Much more work would seem to be called for on this question than has been done hitherto to justify such optimism. In any case, the fact that greater distortions in the final vote are produced by other factors than refusal hardly entitles us to take this problem lightly.[11]

Chapter Three

OPINION AND ATTITUDE MEASUREMENT

THE previous chapter will have shown the many difficulties involved in opinion polling, and will also have demonstrated the fact that professional workers in the field are alive to many of these pitfalls. However, to be alive to difficulties is not the same as to succeed in overcoming them, and it is clearly necessary to take a somewhat closer view at the success with which opinion measurement is being carried out at the moment.

When we try to determine the success with which a certain measurement is being undertaken we generally evaluate it by reference to the concepts of *reliability* and *validity*. Reliability is often defined as the degree of accuracy with which a given test or other instrument measures whatever it is measuring; validity refers to the degree of success with which a test or other instrument is measuring what it is supposed to be measuring. The two are not identical because, although we may be measuring very accurately a certain ability or attitude, we may in fact be measuring something quite different from what we think we are measuring. To take a simple example, in the early years of the century, psychologists thought that they could use the concept of reflex action as a measure of intelligence. Now reflex action, as for instance in the case of the knee jerk or patellar tendon reflex, can be measured extremely reliably and accurately, but it has no validity whatsoever; in other words, it does not correlate at all with intelligence. Thus, this measure is highly reliable but completely lacking in validity.

While a measure may thus be reliable but not valid, the opposite is impossible. If a measure is unreliable it cannot be valid. This will be self-evident without any extended statistical argument; if the numerical values which we assume for the things we are measuring differ from one occasion to another in a haphazard way, then clearly we are not performing any reasonable kind of 'measurement', and cannot hope that the results which we obtain will have any validity at all. In order to attempt to find out whether opinion polling really deserves the title of scientific *measurement*, we must therefore go into the question of whether it is reliable and, if it should prove to be reliable, whether it is valid; if we should find a complete lack of reliability, of course, we should not need to go on, as this would necessarily imply lack of validity.

The concept of reliability is a relatively complex one, reliability being a generic term referring to many different types of evidence. The first and most widely used measure of reliability we may call *the coefficient of internal consistency*. It has some similarities to the split-ballot technique, and, in the case of opinion polling, would amount to asking two differently worded questions on the same issue of the same group of people, and then ascertaining to what degree their answers to the two questions were congruent. As an example of this type of work we may quote Hayes, who found that the coefficient of internal consistency was in the region of ·65 for two questions regarding armaments and war debts; it was in the region of ·5 for questions concerned with government ownership, taxes on risks, tariffs, unemployment relief, and veterans relief. For five other current issues, the coefficients ranged from ·3 to ·1. These figures are possibly slight under-estimates of the true reliability involved as Hayes worded one of the two questions in each case in a positive, the other in a negative way; this difference in type of wording may lower the consistency of responses. However, it is difficult to view the figures quoted with complacency as all of them are well below the limit of ·8 to ·9, usually regarded as requisite for this type of reliability.

The second type of reliability is one in which the same group of persons is tested, and again retested after an intervening period of time. The index of reliability arrived at in this way is called a *coefficient of stability* and it will be obvious that unless opinions are stable in this sense over at least a short interval of time, their measurement will be relatively meaningless. It will also be obvious that the interval between test and retest should not be too long as otherwise genuine changes in opinion may take place; if we were to give the tests to-day and the retests in twenty years' time, the fact that changes had occurred would not necessarily throw doubt on the accuracy of our measuring instrument.

Some evidence on reliability of opinions and of interviewers' ratings is given by Mosteller. He showed that with an interval of three weeks, estimations of economic status given by the same interviewer correlated to the extent of ·79, 77 per cent of classifications being identical. When, however, in another experiment different interviewers gave the ratings, the correlations sank to ·63 and identical classifications were made in only 54 per cent of the cases. The actual figures for this experiment are given in Table XIII.[12]

TABLE XIII, (1)

Reliability of Assessing Economic Status by the Same Interviewer

Classification at First Interview	Classification at Second Interview					
	W	Av.+	Av.	P	OR	Total
W	8	1				9
Av.+	2	39	23			64
Av.		13	111	10		134
P			10	56	1	67
OR		1	1	1	1	4
Total	10	54	145	67	2	278

r = ·79, Identical Classifications 77 per cent

TABLE XIII, (2)

Reliability of Assessing Economic Status by Independent Interviewers

Classification by First Interviewer	Classification by Second Interviewer					
	W	Av.+	Av.	P	OR	Total
W	3	3	4			10
Av.+	4	20	21			45
Av.	2	24	74	5		105
P.	1	2	57	59	6	125
OR			8	9	9	26
Total	10	49	164	73	15	311

r = ·63, Identical Classifications 54 per cent

With respect to the estimation of age, too, it was found that when the same interviewers gave two ratings, the correlation was higher (·97) than when different interviewers were employed (·91). These high correlations are presumably due largely to the fact that interviewers' judgments were based in most cases on the statement by the respondent of his age; if respondents persistently over- or under-

73

stated their own age, this would make the results highly reliable but, of course, affect the validity adversely.

Even under such favourable conditions there is a good deal of change; thus some people, who by the first interviewer were put in the 30–39 year-old group, were put in the 60–69 year-old group by the second interviewer. Only 71 per cent altogether were classified by both in the same 10–year interval.

One might have expected that purely factual information, such as answers to questions about car ownership or telephone ownership would give almost perfect reliability, but this is by no means so. 14 per cent and 13 per cent of respondents, respectively, change their answers from one interview to the next.

When it comes to an actual opinion question, reliability is not very much inferior to that found with factual questions. Answers were solicited in two interviews, separated by a period of three weeks, to the question, 'Do you think Roosevelt is doing a good job, only a fair job, or a bad job in running the country?' 79 per cent of respondents gave identical answers when both interviews were conducted by the same interviewer; 87 per cent gave identical answers when the two interviews were conducted by different interviewers. The difference between the two percentages is probably due to chance as it is unlikely that different interviewers would show higher agreement than the same interviewer.

Also relevant in this connection is a study reported by Lazarsfeld in which a sample of 483 people was interviewed shortly before the Presidential Election, and immediately after the election. Thus, he knew how these people intended to vote shortly before the election, and also for whom they actually voted. The results were as follows:

TABLE XIV

Relationship Between Vote Intention and Actual Vote

Actual Vote	Rep.	Dem.	Don't Know	Don't Expect to Vote	Total
Republican	215	7	4	6	232
Democrat	4	144	12	0	160
Didn't vote	10	16	6	59	91
Total persons	229	167	22	65	483

As Lazarsfeld points out, '418 out of 483 respondents did what they intended to do; 13 per cent changed their minds one way or another. This 13 per cent represents the *turnover* which took place in the few weeks before the election.' The percentage of identical responses given by Lazarsfeld's subjects will be seen to be very similar to that given in Mosteller's article.

As a third study we may quote one by Vaughn and Reynolds who conducted original and repeat interviews with two groups, one composed of 888 adults in Des Moines, the other of 430 adults in Springfield. Product moment correlations for these two samples were ·85 and ·80 for age; ·82 and ·67 for education; and ·61 and ·42 for socio-economic level. These are similar to those reported by Mosteller, and, indicate moderately reasonable reliability for age and education, but definitely insufficient reliability for socio-economic level.

Altogether, the evidence considered so far suggests that information obtained by opinion polls is rather less reliable than one might have thought on *a priori* grounds with questions of a purely factual nature (age, education, etc.), and is very unreliable with respect to another factual point, namely, socio-economic status. The reliability of answers dealing with voting intentions and political preferences, however, appears to be as high as that of questions on car and telephone ownership. It is surprising that more effort has not been made to obtain information on this vitally important subject; in the main, opinion polls have passed by the subject of reliability with scarcely an acknowledgement of its existence. This is not a satisfactory state of affairs, and we would seem to be justified in asking for further proof of the reliability of opinion statements before accepting the results of attitude polls.

One reply is open to those who wish to defend the present practice of the polls, however. If their work can be shown to be valid, then it must, *eo ipso*, be reliable and it might fairly be argued that as reliability is of interest only in the service of validity it is more important to prove that the polls are valid than that they are reliable. We must turn, therefore, to a discussion of the validity of opinion measurement.

Unfortunately, the concept of validity is a rather complex and difficult one and may be understood in many different ways. Possibly the most widely used meaning is that of *agreement with an outside criterion*, in which the score given by the measuring instrument is compared with the true score on a given trait, ability, or attitude.

75

Thus, if we were attempting to validate a test for the selection of bottom scourers we would correlate the scores on the tests under consideration with the actual performance of the candidates in scouring bottoms; the latter would constitute the criterion, and the degree of agreement with the criterion of each test would constitute its validity. Some attempts have been made to establish and validate opinion measurement by comparing results with outside criteria, and these must now be discussed in some detail.

Perhaps the most widely used proof in this connection is the agreement between poll prediction and voting behaviour. We have already noted in an earlier chapter the smallness of the error made by the British Institute of Public Opinion in predicting voting behaviour during three elections in this country. In America, Gallup has reported that the average error of prediction from 1935–47 was four percentage points; this average relates to over 300 election predictions in the United States. If we look only at presidential elections, Mosteller gives a table showing that the errors of prediction in percentage points for the 1936, 1940, 1944, and 1948 elections were 6·5, 3·0, 2·3, and 5·3 per cent, giving an average of 4·3. This may sound reasonable, but before we can estimate the success of forecasting which is implied by an average error of a given magnitude, we need a base line against which to compare the results. Such a base line is furnished by what is called *persistence forecasting*. This method, taken over from weather forecasting, is a simple routine method in which the forecast for the next occasion is simply made in terms of what happened last time. In weather forecasting one would simply predict that to-morrow will be exactly like to-day. In election forecasting, it would mean predicting that each state will have the same Democratic percentage of the major party vote that it had in the previous presidential election year. This 'persistence' method is quite mechanical, requires no new investigation, and may thus serve as a useful base line in terms of which we can estimate the accuracy of the polls.

Mosteller presents a table of the errors in persistence forecasting as compared with errors in the forecasts made by Gallup and Crossley, and concludes that 'taken as a whole, it cannot be said that the polling forecasts in the past four presidental elections have a very distinguished record compared to persistence forecasts, which were as good or better in three out of four elections. The implication here is not that polling is no better, or not much better, than persistence forecasting but rather that polling has not yet proved its superiority in election forecasting under the conditions obtaining during the last four presidential elections.'

Figures in this country are very much more favourable to the polls, a fact which is due equally to the greater accuracy of British polls and to the larger amount of error found in persistence forecasts. It is difficult to know why there should be these national differences, and although many reasonable suggestions could be made the answer to this question is, in fact, not known.

The stress which has been laid on election forecasting in the attempt to prove the validity of opinion polling is somewhat unfortunate. The reasons for this belief are two-fold. In the first place, even if election forecasting were completely successful and involved errors no larger than those expected on the basis of sampling theory this would, none the less, prove nothing whatsoever about the reliability and validity of other types of questions. It might be perfectly possible for people to answer truthfully and accurately questions about their voting intentions, and yet to give quite misleading answers to questions regarding their opinions on other issues. Evidence in favour of this view has been given in the last chapter.

Conversely, it may be said that although poll prediction might be extremely inaccurate this would not necessarily prove that opinion polling on other issues would not be useful and valid. It is not always realized that a great deal more is involved in predicting the winner of an electoral contest than simply opinion measurement. A minute's thought, however, will clearly show that attitudes and opinions are only one element which will determine the election of one or other of the candidates involved. We shall list a few of the additional difficulties which arise.

In the first place, the theory of sampling states that we should select a random or stratified sample of people from a known universe. However, in election predicting there is no known universe. The people whose opinions we want to consult are those voting in the election. However, it is not known at the time of polling, i.e. one or two weeks before election at the latest, who is going to vote. In other words, we are trying to sample a population which, as yet, does not exist. We can make reasonable forecasts in the sense of saying that few Southern Negroes will vote in the United States, or that a larger proportion of men than women will vote in this country, but such forecasts are hazardous and involve a great additional element of possible error. Our measurement of opinion might be quite accurate, but if our prediction as to who might vote were to be falsified, our electoral prediction would be very far out.

It might, of course, be said that intention to vote or not to vote is itself a psychological variable and should, therefore, be measurable. Up to a point this is true, but there are many outside factors which influence a person's actual behaviour. Thus, it is known that very fine, sunny weather, and very poor, rainy weather both tend to lower the poll. A hurricane in Florida or a blizzard in Minnesota may change the percentage of people voting in those States by 50 or more per cent. Even in this country, where the weather tends to be less extreme, its influence cannot be gainsaid. Unless opinion polling institutes set up in the field of weather forecasting as well, they are labouring under the obvious handicap of having to make a prediction without having all those facts available which will influence the behaviour of people for whom the prediction is made.

Another difficulty which is not always realized is that although the polling agency might be correct in saying that candidate A would win 55 per cent of the popular vote, nevertheless, due to the oddities of the English and American election systems the minority candidate might very well win the election. This has happened before in both countries and is an unavoidable feature of any system which does not make use of proportional representation. If this were to happen, then the polls would reflect popular attitude correctly, and the election result incorrectly, and we should end up by coming to the conclusion that the criterion was inferior to the measure which we were trying to validate against it.

Nor are these the only defects. Electors might wish to vote for a given candidate but erroneously put their X in the wrong box, or invalidate their paper, or get entangled in the complexities of the machines provided by American States for the purpose of recording votes. People may declare in good faith that they are going to vote for a given candidate, only to find that they have not fulfilled the necessary residence qualifications when the time comes to vote. Votes, even after they have been cast, may be miscounted by the Returning Officer; it may even be possible that elections are not honestly conducted and that people long since dead appear on the electoral register and actually cast their votes. This again is more likely in the United States than in this country; the reader may like to consult Gallup's account of the notorious Louisiana elections.

The factors just mentioned are just a few of the complications which may make election forecasting difficult and inaccurate, although the measurement of opinion toward the candidates may be quite valid and reliable. This fact should be borne in mind when estimating such events, for instance, as the widely publicized failure of the polls to predict the winning candidate in the 1948 election. A great deal has been written on the subject and a selection of the most useful references is given in Technical Note 12. Here we will draw attention only to one interesting fact. In the 1936 election which established Gallup's fame, and where his forecasts were hailed by the papers as 'uncannily accurate', the actual democratic percentage of the two party vote was 62·2 per cent with a prediction of 55·7 per cent. Thus, Gallup predicted the right candidate within an error of 6·5 per cent. In 1948 the actual percentage of the two-party vote for the democratic candidate was 49·8 per cent, and Gallup's prediction 44·5 per cent. Thus, Gallup predicted the wrong candidate with an error of 5·3 per cent and the papers decried his forecasts as useless and the methods as unscientific. This is clearly absurd. Scientifically our interest lies in the size of the error, which was less in 1948 than in 1936. The public and the papers, of course, are interested not in the size of the error but in getting the right prediction, but this, as we have seen, is quite a different matter and one which depends on many other conditions than those taken into account by opinion polling. Unfortunately, Gallup and the other pollsters themselves have played into the hands of their detractors by emphasizing the journalistic aspects of forecasting the winning candidate rather than stressing the scientific aspects of reducing the percentage error. Nevertheless, it is the latter which is important and which has, in fact been reduced from 1936 to 1948.

It will be clear from what has been said so far that election prediction does not provide us with the required evidence either for or against the validity of opinion measurement. Yet, curiously enough there is very little evidence from other sources which could give us the required information. We have shown in the previous chapter that it is easy to change responses to opinion questions in a large variety of ways. This fact, combined with the lack of data on validity, has led Quinn McNemar, one of the most astute writers on the subject, to remark that 'so much is known about the variations which can be produced and so little is known about which variation is most nearly correct that one is apt to become pessimistic concerning the possibility of a single poll ever contributing scientifically useful data.' With this view the present writer would agree.[13] The question arises: What alternative is there? There appear to be two main answers. One would be to change from the use of a single question to ascertain attitudes to the use of an attitude scale; the other would be the adoption of a more refined notion of the concept of validity in science. Let us take the question of scaling first.

A simple example may make clear the reluctance of most psychologists, as distinguished from opinion polling agencies, to regard single question opinion measurement as being of great scientific value. Let us assume that we wish to ascertain the average height of English males over the age of 21. The procedure we would adopt is, of course, a very obvious one. We should pick out a random or stratified sample of the population, measure their height in inches to any desired degree of accuracy, and then average the values obtained so as to get the mean height. We should also seek to obtain from our data some measure of the distribution of heights around this mean, i.e. the measure of the tendency in the population either for everyone to be pretty near average or else for some to be very tall, others very short, and so on. Such a measure we might find in what is called the standard deviation or the variance. Lastly, we might seek to give an impression of the actual shape of the distribution by plotting it, as has been done in Figure 9, where different heights are plotted on the abcissa and different numbers of people having these various height measures along the ordinate. This very simple procedure would give us a satisfactory answer to our question, provided that all the steps had been taken with professional efficiency.

Now let us imagine what the procedure would be like if we were to follow the technique of the opinion polling agencies. We should issue all our interviewers with a stick of a given height (corresponding to the uniform question asked by them); we should then ask them to apply this stick to a sample of the population and report for each person whether he was taller than the stick, smaller than the stick, or about equal in height to the stick. (These three categories would correspond to people saying 'Yes', 'No', and

'Don't Know' in response to a given question.) In the office these values would be transformed into percentages, and in summary we should read in our morning newspaper that 22 per cent of the population were tall, 70 per cent were small, and 8 per cent did not know whether they were tall or small.

This may sound like a parody of public opinion polling, but in actual fact this method still flatters the polling agencies because,

FIGURE 9

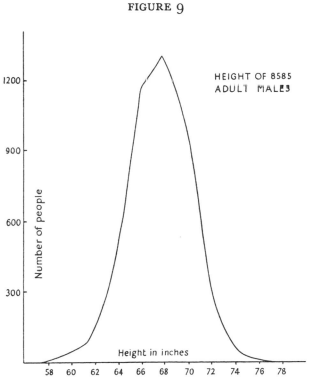

Distribution of Height of 8585 Adult Males

as we know the height of the stick, we can from the percentage results deduce a great deal about the true height of the population. This, however, is an item of information which is not usually available to the opinion polls. Let us take as an example a study by Eysenck and Crown on anti-Semitism. Of the population interviewed, 38 per cent agreed with the proposition 'The Jews have too much power and influence in this country'. This might lead us to say that 38 per cent are anti-Semitic. However, only 24 per cent agreed with the statment 'Jews will stoop to any kind of deceit in order to gain their own ends'. Only 4 per cent agreed with the proposition 'The Jews are the most despicable form of mankind which crawls on this earth'. On the other hand, 84 per cent believed that 'The dislike of many people for the Jews is based on prejudice, but is nevertheless not without a certain justification'. All these four percentages could be taken as estimates of the degree of anti-Semitic prejudice in the population, which would thus vary according to the height of the yardstick taken, from 4 to 84 per cent. Clearly, such results are meaningless unless we know something about the exact height of the yardstick; in other words, unless we know something about the degree of anti-Semitism shown by each particular question. But in order to know that we must possess the kind of information which makes the yardstick so useful an instrument of measurement. In other words, we must have a true zero point and equal units of measurement. If we have those, and if we can assign an exact point on the resulting scale to our questions, then, and only then, can we interpret opinion polls of social attitudes with the same degree of meaningfulness as the results of our hypothetical 'stick' estimation of the nation's average height. As none of these conditions are fulfilled in actual fact, however, it is difficult to escape the conclusion that public opinion polling by single questions is of very doubtful value indeed for the ascertaining of social attitudes. Our only escape from this unsatisfactory position is to construct scales of measurement which possess, as will be shown later, many additional advantages, such as those of greater reliability, more easily ascertainable validity, and known dimensionality.

An example of one of the earliest scales to be constructed is the Bogardus Social Distance Scale. Arguing that a person's attitude towards a national or racial group might best be described in terms of the 'social distance' at which he would keep members of that group, Bogardus made up the following scale, which can be applied to any racial or national group whatsoever. The instructions are as follows:

'According to my first feeling reactions, I would willingly admit members of each race (as a class, and not the best I have known, nor the worst members) to the classifications which I have encircled.' The classifications are:

1. Would admit to close kinship by marriage.
2. Would admit to my club as personal chums.
3. Would admit to my street as neighbours.
4. Would admit to employment in my occupation.
5. Would admit to citizenship in my country.
6. Would admit as visitors only to my country.
7. Would exclude from my country.

It will be seen that these seven steps indicate different degrees of 'social distance'—obviously someone whom we would admit to close kinship by marriage or to our club as a personal friend elicits more positive feelings than someone whom we would admit as a visitor only, or whom we would exclude completely from our

TABLE XV

Results of Bogardus Social Distance Scale for Ten Groups as Obtained from an American Population

Nationality	1	2	3	4	5	6	7
English	94	97	97	95	96	98	100
Irish	70	83	86	90	91	96	99
French	68	85	88	90	93	96	99
German	54	67	79	83	87	93	97
Italian	28	50	55	58	82	92	98
Spanish	15	26	35	55	71	86	95
Poles	11	12	28	44	58	80	95
Turks	1	9	12	39	57	82	87
Negroes	1	10	12	19	25	58	77
Indians	1	7	13	21	24	53	81

country. Table XV gives some results obtained from 1725 Americans in 1928 by Bogardus. The nationalities have been grouped into four main groups:

1. The Anglo-Saxon.
2. The North-European.
3. The Southern and Eastern Europeans.
4. The Coloured groups.

One change has been made from the usual way of presenting data; it will have been noted that a positive answer to the first five questions indicates a favourable attitude to the national group in question, while a 'Yes' answer to the last two questions indicates a negative attitude. For the purpose of tabulation, therefore, the percentage of 'Yes' answers given to our questions six and seven have been subtracted from 100, so that the figures given in Table XV really apply to questions six and seven in reverse, i.e. 'Would *not* admit as visitors only to my country' and 'Would *not* exclude from my country'. Two points will be obvious from the table. One is that preferences for nationalities decrease as we go from the Anglo-Saxon, through the North European, to the South and East European and the Coloured groups, i.e. as we descend vertically down the table. The other is that percentages increase as we go horizontally across the table, i.e. as we go from the items indicating little social distance to those indicating greater social distance. It will also be apparent, however, that the steps on Bogardus's seven point scale are not by any means equal.

Similar investigations conducted in this country by the present writer have given relatively similar results. One main difference, however, should be mentioned, and that is a disagreement regarding the degree of social distance indicated by the seven steps. Figure 10 gives results for a representative group of 100 British adults; it will be seen that there is no regular ascent from left to right, but that the lines sag in the middle. In other words, to us, admission to citizenship and to employment indicate a greater degree of acceptance than do admission to street as neighbours or to club as personal friends. This is perhaps a reflection of the much greater laxity of employment and naturalization rules in the United States as compared with this country. However this might be, it indicates that the Bogardus Scale in its original form cannot usefully be applied in this country.

For the purpose of obtaining valid results for this country, the scale has been curtailed and made into a four point scale, in which (1) is measured by the 'marriage' item, (2) by the average of the 'employment', 'club', and 'citizenship' items, (3) by the 'neighbour' item, and (4) by the 'visitors' and 'exclusion' items. When this was done and the populations split into a Conservative and Radical group, the clear-cut results presented in Figures 11 and 12 were obtained. It will be seen that in every case, the Anglo-Saxon group, i.e. the Americans and Irish, were most preferred; the North European group, i.e. the French and Germans, a little less; the South and Eastern European group (Italians, Spaniards, Poles), a good deal less still; and the Coloured groups (Turks, Indians, Negroes), least of all. These results are in good agreement with the American work. It would also be noted that in each case Conservatives tended to put more social distance between themselves and each of the four groups than did the Radicals. Thus, ethnocentrism or the tendency to prefer one's own immediate in-group and to look down upon and dislike all types of out-groups, appears to be correlated with Conservatism.

The advantages of a scale of this type over single question polling are obvious, yet this scale is by no means satisfactory. As Adcock has shown, it is lacking in one important feature, which should characterize any scale, in that it is not uni-dimensional. By that,

FIGURE 10

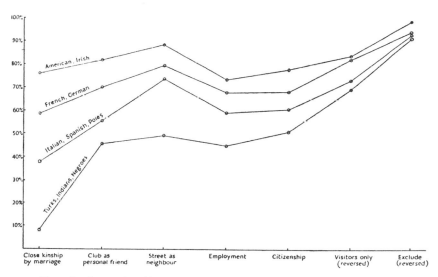

Results from Application of Bogardus Social Distance Scale to
British Sample

we mean that the different questions contained in it do not measure the same variable but tend to measure different variables in different combinations. To take but one example, refusal to let a person of another ethnic group marry into one's family may indeed be a reflection of prejudice; it may also be an indication rather of concern for the offspring and the ostracism that children of mixed parentage are likely to experience. In other words, endorsement of this item might indicate prejudice; it might also indicate instead a realistic appreciation of social forces outside one's control. We must seek, then, to find a way of ensuring uni-dimen-

85

FIGURE I I

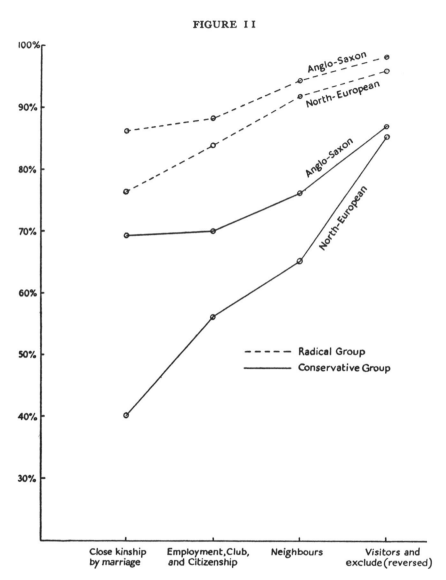

Comparison Between Radical and Conservative Scores on Social
Distance Scale for Anglo-Saxon and North- European Groups

FIGURE 12

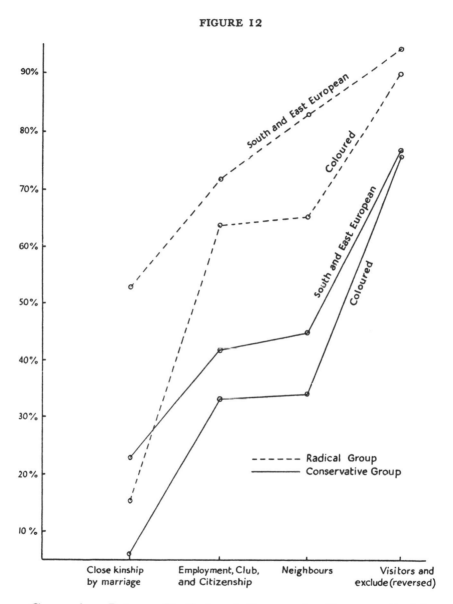

Comparison Between Radical and Conservative Scores on Social
Distance Scale for South- and East-European and Coloured Groups

sionality, i.e. of making certain that all the questions in our scale really measure one and the same underlying attitude.[14]

As an example of the use of more modern methods of scale construction, we may follow through the preparation of a scale for the measurement of anti-Semitism. The first step consists in the selection of a large number of attitude statements chosen on the basis of written and spoken comments about the Jews, collected from books, periodicals, and scientific statements made by various groups interviewed by the open-end technique. 150 items were collected in this way after over-lapping, unclear, and ambiguous items had been excluded.

As a second step, these 150 items, each typed on a separate slip of paper, were submitted individually to 80 judges, who were asked to judge the degree of anti-Semitism shown by each item and to put each in one of 11 piles, the most anti-Semitic on the first, the most pro-Semitic on the 11th, and neutral items on the central pile. By averaging the position given to each item by the 80 judges it was then possible to calculate its average position with respect to the degree of anti-Semitism shown. That this rating of the items is a purely cognitive task and is not affected by the attitudes held by the judges is shown by the fact that there was almost perfect agreement between the anti- and the pro-Semitic judges.

As a third step, all items were discarded which showed considerable disagreement between the judges as to the exact scale position of that item. This helps to weed out items the meaning of which is doubtful, as it would clearly be useless to have in the questionnaire items which could be interpreted as being either favourable or unfavourable to the Jews. Items retained are clearly and unambiguously regarded by all the judges as indicating a given degree of anti-Semitism.

The fourth step then consisted in selecting items which would cover the whole range from very strongly anti-Semitic, through neutral, to strongly pro-Semitic. As far as possible, one would attempt to make the intervals between items of degree of anti-Semitism equal, so that one would end up with what Thurstone has called an 'equal-appearing interval scale'.

As the fifth step, the 24 items would be printed in random order, and each supplied with five different possible answers, i.e. strongly agree, agree, uncertain, disagree, strongly disagree. The printed scale is given below. In brackets, after each item is given the scale position of that item from 1, the most pro-Semitic, to 11, the most anti-Semitic.

OPINIONS ON THE JEWS

In this questionnaire you will find 24 different opinions on the Jews. We want to know in each case whether you agree or disagree with the view expressed. Underneath the statement of each opinion you will find five alternative reactions:

strongly agree; agree; uncertain; disagree; strongly disagree.
Underline whichever alternative gives the most correct picture of your own view. PLEASE DO NOT LEAVE OUT ANY STATE-MENTS even when you find it difficult to make up your mind. Your views will remain quite anonymous; you are asked not to sign your name.

Thank you for your co-operation.

1. Dislike of the Jews comes mainly from misunderstanding (4·7):
   strongly agree; agree; uncertain; disagree; strongly disagree
       (3)   (3)   (4)   (5)   (5)

2. Jews monopolize everything to the detriment of the English (8·8):
   strongly agree; agree; uncertain; disagree; strongly disagree
       (7)   (5)   (4)   (3)   (1)

3. The Jews are an isolated group in society because of their religion (5·9):
   strongly agree; agree; uncertain; disagree; strongly disagree
       (3)   (4)   (4)   (4)   (5)

4. Jews will stoop to any kind of deceit in order to gain their own ends (9·5):
   strongly agree; agree; uncertain; disagree; strongly disagree
       (7)   (6)   (4)   (2)   (1)

5. Jews are as valuable, honest and public spirited citizens as any other group (2·3):
   strongly agree; agree; uncertain; disagree; strongly disagree
       (1)   (2)   (4)   (6)   (7)

6. There are both 'good' and 'bad' Jews, as there are both kinds of Englishmen, and there is not much to choose between them on the whole (3·0):
   strongly agree; agree; uncertain; disagree; strongly disagree
       (1)   (3)   (4)   (5)   (7)

7. The Jews as a whole cannot be held responsible for the mis-
   deeds of a minority who run foul of the laws and customs of
   this country (5·6):
   strongly agree; agree; uncertain; disagree; strongly disagree
        (3)   (4)   (4)   (4)   (5)

8. Jews corrupt everything with which they come into contact
   (10·2):
   strongly agree; agree; uncertain; disagree; strongly disagree
        (8) (6)   (4)   (2)   (0)

9. There is no reason to believe that innately the Jews are less
   honest and good than anyone else (3·9):
   strongly agree; agree; uncertain; disagree; strongly disagree
        (2) (3)   (4)   (5)   (6)

10. The dislike of many people for the Jews is based on prejudice,
    but is nevertheless not without a certain justification (7·2):
    strongly agree; agree; uncertain; disagree; strongly disagree
         (5) (5)   (4)   (3)   (3)

11. The Jews are mentally and morally superior to most other
    people (1·5):
    strongly agree; agree; uncertain; disagree; strongly disagree
         (0) (2)   (4)   (6)   (8)

12. The Jews have too much power and influence in this country
    (7·9):
    strongly agree; agree; uncertain; disagree; strongly disagree
         (6) (5)   (4)   (3)   (2)

13. The Jews have a stranglehold on this country (8·3):
    strongly agree; agree; uncertain; disagree; strongly disagree
         (6) (5)   (4)   (3)   (2)

14. The Jews have survived persecution because of the many ad-
    mirable qualities they show (2·0):
    strongly agree; agree; uncertain; disagree; strongly disagree
         (0) (2)   (4)   (6)   (8)

15. Jews in their dealings with others are an absolute menace,
    money-grabbing and unscrupulous (9·1):
    strongly agree; agree; uncertain; disagree; strongly disagree
         (7) (5)   (4)   (3)   (1)

16. Jews are just as loyal to the country in which they live as any
    other citizens (2·7):
    strongly agree; agree; uncertain; disagree; strongly disagree
         (1) (2)   (4)   (6)   (7)

17. Jews lack physical courage (7·5):
    strongly agree; agree; uncertain; disagree; strongly disagree
        (5)   (5)   (4)   (3)   (3)
18. The Jews are a menace to any nation and to any country in
    which they happen to live (9·9):
    strongly agree; agree; uncertain; disagree; strongly disagree
        (7)   (6)   (4)   (2)   (1)
19. The Jews are a decent set of people on the whole (3·5):
    strongly agree; agree; uncertain; disagree; strongly disagree
        (1)   (3)   (4)   (5)   (7)
20. The Jews should give up their separate customs and become
    average citizens of this country (6·3):
    strongly agree; agree; uncertain; disagree; strongly disagree
        (5)   (4)   (4)   (4)   (3)
21. There are too many Jews in the highly-paid professions (6·7):
    strongly agree; agree; uncertain; disagree; strongly disagree
        (5)   (4)   (4)   (4)   (3)
22. Jews can't be expected to behave any better towards the rest of
    the world than the rest of the world behaves towards them
    (4·4):
    strongly agree; agree; uncertain; disagree; strongly disagree
        (2)   (3)   (4)   (5)   (6)
23. The Jews are the most despicable form of mankind which
    crawls on this earth (10·7):
    strongly agree; agree; uncertain; disagree; strongly disagree
        (8)   (6)   (4)   (2)   (0)
24. The Jewish menace has been much exaggerated (5·1):
    strongly agree; agree; uncertain; disagree; strongly disagree
        (3)   (3)   (4)   (5)   (5)

The sixth step deals with the adoption of a scoring system. The scale product method appears to be the most reliable one to be used. It makes use of two items of information—the first is the 'extremeness' of the statement, as indicated by the fact that its scale position deviates in either direction from 6, which is the neutral point; the second item of information is the degree of *emphasis* with which the answer is made. Thus, a person who *strongly agrees* with an anti-Semitic item may be judged more anti-Semitic than one who only *agrees*. These two sources of information can be combined by weighting the responses strongly agree, agree, uncertain, disagree, and strongly disagree, 1, 2, 3, 4, 5, or 5, 4, 3, 2, 1, respectively, depending on the direction of the statement, i.e. whether it is anti-Semitic or pro-Semitic, and multiplying this by the scale position of the item. As an example, let us take two items, both of which are answered 'strongly agree', and would therefore score five points. One of these items, say, is mildly anti-Semitic, the other extremely so; their relative scale positions might be 7 and 11, where 6 denotes neutrality. Clearly the endorsement of the second item is a much stronger indication of anti-Semitism than the endorsement of the first, and should consequently be weighted much more heavily. This weighting is accomplished automatically by multiplying the weight (5) by the scale position (7 and 11 respectively), so that the respective weights would be 35 and 55. Scores thus derived are usually rather high and unwieldy and can often be improved by dividing and rounding off. Final scores thus derived are printed in brackets underneath the responses to the 24 questions on pages 89–91.

The seventh and eighth steps are concerned with finding the reliability and the distribution of the trait under investigation. A group of 200 students was given the scale, which was found to have a split-half reliability of ·94, which is relatively high for scales of this type. The distribution of scores is given in Figure 13. The mean value of the subjects tested, as indicated by an arrow in the diagram, lies at a score of 107. The neutral zone, i.e. the zone of scores which are neither pro- nor anti-Semitic is indicated by shading and lies between 81 and 90. It will be seen that there is a tendency for the majority of respondents to be anti-Semitic and for a minority to be pro-Semitic.

The ninth step in the preparation of the scale would be a demonstration of its validity. While a more thorough discussion of validity will be given later on, an indication may be given here of one method of making at least a preliminary study of this vital factor. Fifty students in the writer's extra-mural evening classes were given the task, as part of their training in social psychology, to administer the scale to five friends whose attitudes and opinions they knew reasonably well. They were also asked to write brief essays on the actual views held by these friends on a variety of questions, including ethnocentrism, anti-Semitism, and so forth. They were particularly asked to pay attention to behavioural manifestations of attitudes, such as going to Fascist or Communist meetings, overt acts of anti-Semitism, and so forth.

By and large, agreement between raters and questionnaire was surprisingly close; in only one case did the rater seriously question the accuracy of the questionnaire return. In 14 cases the rater admitted that he did not know enough about the respondent's views to give any judgment; all of these 14 respondents scored near the neutral point. In the remaining 235 cases, the raters agreed that the respondents had answered the questions honestly and in accordance with their known views. Often, actual items of behaviour were quoted in support of this information.

A few examples of students' remarks on respondents, together

FIGURE 13

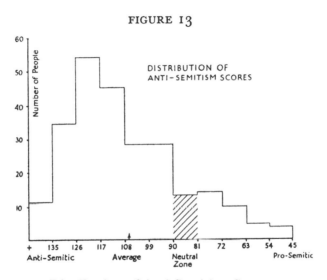

Distribution of Anti-Semitism Scores

with the actual scores of respondents on the anti-Semitism scale, may help to show the reader the kind of correspondence which leads us to believe that the questionnaire has a certain amount of validity. Scores on the questionnaire range from the highest possible anti-Semitic score of 152, through a neutral 96, to the most pro-Semitic score possible of 40. Of respondent A, whose score is 136, it is said that ' . . . she possesses all the current prejudices against Jews and is in fact violently anti-Semitic—even to the point of contributing financially to the cause of Fascism'. Respondent B, who scores 52, ' . . . . has only been observed to lose his temper on one occasion and this was caused through a chance remark of an

93

anti-Semitic nature—the iron obviously enters into his soul on this particular subject because although subject is a Gentile he propounds his views in defence of the Jewish people with great sincerity and feeling'. Respondent C, with a score of 127, 'is particularly anti-Semitic. . . . Judging from his many remarks on the subject I think it not improbable that he is jealous of the brilliance of the Jewish race in all fields of human activity.'

The tenth step would consist in the provision of population norms, i.e. figures for a representative sample of the population, broken down with respect to such variables as age, sex, social class, political affiliation, and so on.

The eleventh step required for the proper construction of a scale is a demonstration that the scale is actually uni-dimensional. In other words, that all the items are measuring the same underlying attitude. There are two main methods which can provide such a proof. One is the method of factor analysis; the other is the method of scalogram analysis. Only a brief indication will be given of the logical basis of these two methods, as a detailed discussion would be too technical for a book of this type.

The factor analytic proof of uni-dimensionality is based on the following argument. If all the items in the scale measure one and the same attitude, then a person who is anti-Semitic should answer all the anti-Semitic items in the positive direction and all the pro-Semitic items in the negative direction. Conversely, a person who was pro-Semitic should answer all the anti-Semitic answers in a negative direction and all the pro-Semitic items in a positive direction. If this were so, we should expect different items to correlate with each other over a large group of people, containing anti-Semites as well as pro-Semites. These correlations would not be expected to be extremely high because a moderate anti-Semite might disagree with an extremely anti-Semitic item as much as with a mildly pro-Semitic one, thus lowering the correlation, but, by and large, we should expect to find a certain pattern of correlations the properties of which can be predicted and ascertained with considerable accuracy. When the correlations between the various items in the questionnaire were calculated, it was found that most of them were high, and all in the expected direction. We can, from these correlations, make calculations as to the degree to which each item correlates with the hypothetical attitude of anti-Semitism; these correlations are given in Table XVI in the first column.

It will be seen that some items have much higher correlations than others, and are thus much better measures; thus, item 9, 'There is no reason to believe that innately the Jews are less honest and good than anyone else' is an extremely good item, correlating ·91 with anti-Semitism. Item 11, 'The Jews are mentally and morally superior to most other people' is a very poor item, correlating only

TABLE XVI

Degree of Anti-Semitism, Reproducibility, and Correlation with Radicalism of Twenty-four Items in Anti-Semitism Scale

Item	Anti-Semitism Factor Saturation	Reproducibility	Correlation with Radicalism
1	·75	94	·45
2	—.89	93	—·43
3	.18	69	·14
4	—·86	88	—·42
5	·84	96	·43
6	·74	88	·23
7	·85	87	·34
8	—·91	93	—·42
9	·91	94	·44
10	—·29	85	—·19
11	·04	73	—·05
12	—·78	92	—·48
13	—·72	85	—·33
14	·48	73	·15
15	—·86	86	—·53
16	·71	83	·32
17	—·64	75	—·43
18	—·89	89	—·41
19	·85	92	·42
20	—·30	70	—·15
21	—·73	81	—·42
22	·22	74	—·12
23	—·79	80	—·44
24	·82	90	·30

·04 with anti-Semitism. When the influence of this factor of anti-Semitism is separated from the intercorrelations, the residual correlations are so small that they can reasonably be disregarded. According to this method, then, we have some proof that each scale is reasonably uni-dimensional.

Scalogram analysis starts out from a different proposition. It posits that items in a scale must have a special cumulative property. Stouffer gives us an example of a hypothetical scale of stature made up of responses to three items:

1. Are you over 6 feet tall?   ....Yes   ....No
2. Are you over 5 feet 6 inches tall?   ....Yes   ....No
3. Are you over 5 feet tall?   ....Yes   ....No

If a person checks item 1 'Yes', he must, unless he is careless, also check items 2 and 3 'Yes'. If he checks item 1 'No' and item 2 'Yes' he must also check item 3 'Yes'. Hence, if we give a score of 2 to a man who has endorsed two items we know exactly *which two items* he endorsed. He could not say 'Yes' to item 1, 'No' to item 2, and 'Yes' to item 3. The four admissible response patterns to the three items are shown below:

TABLE XVII

A Simple Form of Scalogram

Rank order of respondents	Score	Says yes to item			Says no to item		
		1	2	3	1	2	3
1	3	X	X	X			
2	2		X	X	X		
3	1			X	X	X	
4	0				X	X	X

This simple diagram is called a scalogram—hence the name scalogram analysis for the procedure.

It will be seen that the X's on the Table form a definite pattern, and it will also be clear that if an X were to appear outside this pattern it would indicate a wrong answer to a question by one of the people responding. We know that because we know that a scale of measurement for height has uni-dimensional properties. However, we can invert the argument for another scale about whose uni-dimensionality we are not certain, and say that if the pattern of responses deviates to any considerable extent from the regular pattern indicated in Table XVII, then this scale is not uni-dimensional. The degree of departure from uni-dimensionality is often indicated in terms of reproducibility. The scale illustrated in Table XVII is perfectly reproducible because, by knowing the score of a person, we could reproduce exactly the way that score was arrived at, i.e. we should know which items he had endorsed.

Unfortunately, perfect reproducibility is never found in attitude measurement because of the intrusion of error, and reproducibilities of 85–90 per cent are all that can be expected of scales which are reasonably uni-dimensional. The reproducibility of each of our 24 anti-Semitism items is given in Table XVI, and it will be seen that the overall reproducibility of the scale is 85 per cent. It will also be seen that items having high factor saturations also tend to be items having high reproducibility, while items having low factor saturations tend to be items having low reproducibility. Thus, these two methods agree not only in showing that the scale is relatively uni-dimensional, but also in showing which items contribute the greatest amount of error, and are, therefore, the least useful measures of the trait in question. It seems likely from this analysis that the total scale could be reduced to 12 items, without lowering its reliability or its validity.

The twelfth and last point in the proper construction of the scale concerns the relationship of the attitude under investigation to other attitudes, or, to put it more precisely, its position in the multi-dimensional attitude universe. We have already seen, for instance, that ethnocentrism is related to conservatism; it seems likely that anti-Semitism too is so related. Table XVI gives in the last column the correlation between each of the 24 items and a measure of Conservatism, which will be described in detail in a later chapter. It will be seen that our hypothesis is strongly supported. As this whole question of this relationship between different attitudes and the structure of the whole attitude universe is a somewhat complex one, and as it is of very great importance indeed, we will not discuss it in detail now, but postpone consideration until a later chapter.

It will be clear to anyone who has followed the rationale of the twelve steps which are implied in the construction of an attitude scale that here we have an instrument of measurement very much superior in every way to the single question favoured by opinion polls. This superiority manifests itself in the following ways. In the first place, it allows us to perform a more quantitative type of measurement than is possible with the single question. All that the single question enables us to do is to put everyone in the population into one or other of two categories, those in favour and those against a particular policy, or those agreeing with and those opposed to a given attitude: it is impossible to measure the degree of favour towards the given issue and inevitably many people differing widely among themselves will be classified together under the very wide headings of *pro* and *con*. In addition, the line of demarcation between the two is quite arbitrary and depends to a very large extent on the exact form of the question asked.

The attitude scale, on the other hand, makes it possible for us to perform measurement of a much more refined character. It allows us to sub-divide a whole population into as many classes as we wish, or as are required by our research design. The classes themselves are much more homogeneous—in fact, the degree of homogeneity is merely a function of the number of questions included.[15]

These are very real advantages, yet we should be careful not to over-state the case. The type of measurement which attitude scales permit us to undertake is not identical with that made possible by, say, the yard-stick. Attitude measurement is an *ordinal* measurement, i.e. it enables us to rank people in order of size for the given trait or attitude involved, but it does not furnish us with an absolute zero point, and it does not give us equal units of measurement, as does the tape-measure, which is an example of *cardinal* measurement. In other words, when we apply our anti-Semitism scale, we can be reasonably certain that a person with a score of 90 would be more anti-Semitic than a person with a score of 70, and also that a person with a score of 60 would be more anti-Semitic than a person with a score of 40. We cannot say, however, that the person with a score of 90 would be as much more anti-Semitic than a person with a score of 70, as a person with a score of 60 would be more anti-Semitic than a person with a score of 40. Nor can we say that a person with a score of 80 is twice as anti-Semitic as a person with a score of 40. Some psychologists believe erroneously that it is, at the moment, possible to construct cardinal scales of measurement which possess these virtues, but it is difficult to discover sound reasons for such a belief, nor is it essential for most purposes that our scales should be cardinal scales of measurement. Even in such a highly developed science as physics, ordinal scales are frequently employed, as, for instance, in the measurement of hardness. As long as we realize the limitations of our scales and do not use them for purposes for which they are not adequate, scale construction must be judged to have been an important step forward in the measurement of attitudes.

The second advantage possessed by scales is that they get away from the notion of absolute values implied in single questions, and from statements of results in terms of percentages. By allowing us to plot the distribution of scores, scales give us a frame of reference against which to evaluate a given score, whereas the single question fails entirely to provide us with such a frame of reference. By knowing which is the highest possible anti-Semitic score which can be reached, and which is the lowest possible pro-Semitic score which can be made, we immediately are enabled to give a rough judgment of the meaning of any given score which is found experimentally. When we add to this a knowledge of the zone of neutral opinion, and a knowledge of typical scores made by groups whose views and actions are known (Fascists, Communists, Jews themselves, etc.), we build up a whole system which endows a particular score with ascertainable meaning. All this is impossible with a single question, which, therefore, must inevitably remain at the lowest level of measurement.

The third advantage which scales have over questions lies in the ease with which measures of reliability can be calculated. While it is only in exceptional circumstances that anything is known about the reliability of single questions, attitude scales are hardly ever published without some information regarding their reliability. When it is realized how necessary for measurement high reliabilities are, the importance of this point will be appreciated. It will also be realized that high reliabilities are very much more easily reached by means of scales than by single questions. The reason for this advantage is a very simple one. The single question performs one measuring operation; a scale of 24 questions performs 24 measuring operations, and thus gives chance errors an opportunity of cancelling out. The principle involved here is the same which leads the physicist to make several independent determinations of the same variable when a high degree of accuracy is required.

A fourth point of superiority for the scale lies in its uni-dimensional nature, and more particularly in the fact that evidence can be produced experimentally with regard to this very vexed and difficult problem. In the case of the single question, the assumption is usually made that it is uni-dimensional, but this assumption is not necessarily justified and in any case cannot be proved or disproved directly. The difficulties involved will be seen if we consider as a single question one item from the Bogardus Social Distance Scale, namely: 'Would you admit a Negro to close kinship by marriage?'. As pointed out before, a negative answer may be indicative of anti-Negro prejudice, but it may also be an indication rather of an appreciation of practical difficulties and likely trouble and unhappiness, coupled with a genuine regard for and liking of Negroes as a whole. In other words, this item does not measure only one dimension, but at least two, and we cannot tell in a given case whether a negative answer can be taken as a sign of prejudice or not. Nor can we tell whether such a theor-tical analysis of possible reasons for different kinds of answers is justified or not; we simply have to take the results on trust and interpret them in any way we may think fit. It is only when such a question is made part of a scale that we can prove or disprove hypotheses regarding its uni-dimensionality, and when this is done, as mentioned before, this particular question turns out to be unsatisfactory.

With scales, on the other hand, there is no insuperable difficulty in ascertaining whether or not they are uni-dimensional, and if not, which are the items which must be excluded. Even where a scale turns out to be multi-dimensional, the method of factor analysis enables us to obtain a reasonably pure measurement of all the dimensions involved, as well as enabling us to identify the number of dimensions and their meaning. These are very great advantages indeed, both from the point of view of measurement, and also from that of theory.

The fifth and last point of superiority relates to the problem of validity. Here, there is relatively little to choose between scales and single questions, as most of the methods of validity determination are applicable as easily to the one as to the other. Yet, historically, studies of validity have always been carried out in connection with scales rather than with single questions, so that far more is known about the validity of scales. It may be useful to set down in detail the main methods of experimentation which have been used to determine the validity of scales, and to classify them according to the criteria involved. The discussion will deal entirely with scales, simply because there are hardly any reports in the literature of validation of single questions; however, it will be clear that very little change would be involved in order to make these methods applicable to single questions also. The first method of validation of scales to be discussed is that of *agreement with ratings based on personal knowledge.*

One example of this method has already been given above, in connection with our description of the design of the anti-Semitism scale. The advantages and disadvantages of this method will be too obvious to require lengthy discussion. Strongly held opinions for and against a given issue will almost certainly be known to one's friends and intimate acquaintances, who should be able to judge, from opinions voiced over a long period and from actions observed, the exact state of a person's attitudes. On the other hand, lay judges and lay raters are untrained and may often be extremely imperceptive and lacking in insight into a person's motivation, and the very complex structure of attitudes and opinions which determine his words and actions. By and large, however, we should be justified in feeling very doubtful about the validity of a scale which did not show considerable agreement with ratings so obtained.

The second method of validation may be called *the method of agreement with self-ratings*. An example of this method may be found in the work of Stouffer, who had 238 students fill in an attitude scale dealing with prohibition. Each student also wrote an anonymous account of his experiences, feelings, and opinions with respect to prohibition laws and to the drinking of spirits. The resulting case histories were rated independently by four judges as to the degree of favourable or unfavourable attitude towards prohibition laws which they indicated. The judges agreed very highly with each other, and their average ratings showed considerable agreement also with the results of the attitude scale, a validity coefficient of ·86 being obtained. The students were also asked to rate their own attitudes toward prohibition laws on a graphic scale and these ratings also were found to agree with the attitude scale to a considerable extent, the validity coefficient being ·80.

Again, the strengths and weaknesses of this method will be obvious. The weakness is that we are comparing one item of verbal assessment (the attitude scale) with another (the case history as written by the student himself.) If there were intention to deceive, it would be easy to make both congruent, yet there is no reason to think that any deceit was intended or could reasonably be expected in these anonymous case histories, and again it will be agreed that if the case histories had shown little agreement with the attitude scale we should have felt rather doubtful about the validity of the latter.

The third method of ascertaining validity is *the method of agreement with known fact.* Thus, it is known that Northerners and Southerners in the United States differ in their attitude towards Negroes. Several writers, such as, for instance, Likert and Johnson have shown that such differences are mirrored in attitude scales administered to comparable groups of students in Northern and Southern colleges. The most impressive in this connection, perhaps, is a study by Sims and Patrick, who applied a scale for the measurement of attitudes towards the Negro to three groups, consisting of Northern students, Southern students, and Northern

FIGURE 14

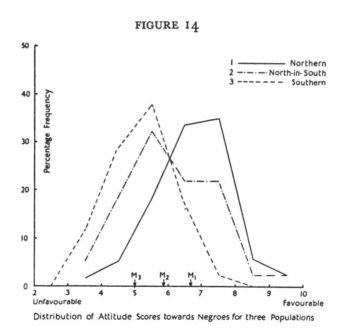

Distribution of Attitude Scores towards Negroes for three Populations

students living in the South. Results of this study are given in Figure 14, and it will be seen that, as expected, the Northern group is the most favourable, the Southern group the most unfavourable, and the group of Northerners living in the South is almost exactly intermediate between the other two.

The outstanding advantage of this method is that it enables us to start out with a clear-cut hypothesis, which can be disproved or supported by the data of the experiment. Its disadvantage may lie in the fact that there may be disagreements as to what constitutes 'known fact'. Southerners have been known to argue that they are no more anti-negro in their attitudes than are Northerners, and they might consequently be willing to dispute the major premise of the experiment. However, this objection is probably purely academic, and in many cases there will be no reasonable doubt about the results which would be expected from the administration of a valid scale.

Our fourth method might be called *the method of agreement with reasonable expectation*. It is known, for instance, that there is a stronger prejudice against orientals in the Western United States as compared with the Eastern seaboard. We might expect Filipino students enrolled in American colleges and universities to react to this prejudice by showing more negative attitudes towards America when enrolled in Western universities than when enrolled in Eastern universities. That this is indeed so has been shown by Nystrom (1933).

Again, it is known that the Tennessee Valley Administration (the T.V.A.) benefited inhabitants of the Southern States more than the inhabitants of the Northern States. Consequently, we should expect Southerners to be more favourable towards the project than Northerners. Similarly, it is known that the T.V.A. was bitterly opposed by commercial electricity companies, whereas it was approved by people who had a direct interest in the project. When a specially developed scale for measuring attitude towards the T.V.A. was applied to various groups, Sims showed that stockholders in a privately owned electric power company had an average score of 68, while employees of another electric company averaged 75. At the other end, government employees had an average score of 23, applicants for T.V.A. jobs one of 28, and merchants in the T.V.A. region had an average score of 34. A group of Northerners averaged 48 points, a group of Southerners 36 points. Thus, all the results are in accordance with reasonable expectation.

In essence, this method is similar to the one mentioned before, except that the criterion cannot be regarded as definitely and certainly established, but forms itself part of the hypothesis. In other words, if the results had been negative in these studies we should not have known whether this failure to support the hypothesis was due to inadequacy of the measuring instrument, or to an erroneous hypothesis regarding the criterion. This is a very important difference as it affects both the design of the experiment and the interpretation, and we shall discuss it again later on in connection with experiments on the hypothesis that Fascists are more aggressive than the average population.

Our fifth method might be called *the method of agreement with measured behaviour*. As an illustration, we may take Neumann's study of international attitudes. He applied a scale to 40 people definitely identified with movements or activities of an international character, such as, for instance, members of the Communist party, leaders of an international religious movement, and so forth. He not only found that attitude scores agreed with overt behaviour as determined by these evaluations, but succeeded in showing that there was not a single exception to this agreement with prediction. Similarly, Porter applied a scale for the measurement of opinion on war to 100 people who had taken an overt stand on this issue. He found that a group of adult reserve officers made a very high militaristic score, while a group of conscientious objectors and student pacifist leaders made a definitely pacifist score. Similarly, he found denominational colleges to make a slightly pacifist score on the average, while a University O.T.C. group made a slightly militaristic score.

One further experiment that is worthy of mention in this connection is Telford's study of religious attitudes. He compared the frequency of church attendance with the mean scores of his subjects on an attitude scale for the measurement of religious attitudes, and found a regular increase in scores as frequencies of church attendance fell from regularly (mean score 1·91), through frequently (mean score 2·48), occasionally (mean score 3·50) and seldom (mean score 4·95) to never (mean score 6·75).

The sixth method of estimating the validity of attitude scales may be called *the method of agreement with experimental determination*. As an example, we may quote Corey's work on cheating. He constructed a highly reliable scale to measure attitudes towards cheating, and then set up an experimental situation which permitted his subjects to cheat in such a way that they thought they could do so without being found out, while yet their behaviour was under close experimental control. He found a quite negligible correlation of ·02 between attitude and behaviour in the experiment.

Another example may be taken from an experiment predicated on the hypothesis that subjects would be less suggestible to members of minority groups towards which they held negative attitudes.

This experiment used the well-known autokinetic movement, i.e. the fact that when a very small dim light is held in a stationary position in a dark room, it seems to move around in space when viewed for a minute or so. This phenomenon is largely subjective and has been shown by Sherif to be subject to group pressure and suggestion. The experimenter chose subjects who made anti-Semitic or anti-Negro scores on an attitude scale and had them judge the apparent movement of the light together with a member of the disliked minority group, the hypothesis being that the subjects would be less easily influenced by the minority members' suggestions as to the movement of the light than they would be by similar remarks made in a control experiment by a member of their own ethnic group. In actual fact, exactly the opposite happened and it was found that the subjects were more suggestible to the opinion of members of disliked minority groups.

These two experiments will serve not only as examples of the method, but also to indicate some of the defects and dangers attending it. Cheating behaviour, as Hartshorne and May have shown, is relatively specific and requires a large number of different situations for its accurate measurement; thus, the criterion chosen by Corey is of doubtful validity and reliability and hardly any conclusions can be drawn from his study. In the autokinetic phenomenon experiment the hypothesis was put forward on the basis of a simple hunch and it is difficult to know whether the negative outcome of the experiment can be used to discredit the validity of the attitude measurement. It is much more likely to be the result of our ignorance of the factors which determine the person's reactions in the rather unusual experimental situation, and until these are clarified, such experiments cannot be taken too seriously. Ideally, of course, this method of agreement with experimental determination is superior to all the others because it allows us to manipulate the variables in the situation; in practice it is the most complex, difficult, and time-consuming of all the methods considered and is not likely to give acceptable and valid results unless the many complex conditions determining the outcome of the experiment are carefully controlled and measured.

All the methods concerned so far share one feature in common in that they all depend on agreement with an external criterion. This is at once their strength and their weakness. Comparison with an external criterion makes the task of validation relatively simple because all that is required is calculation of a correlation coefficient between scale and criterion. The weakness of the method derives from the fact that our criteria are often of very doubtful standing and themselves require a criterion of selection. In other words, some criteria may be presumed to be good and valid, others are clearly poor, invalid, and unreliable. We must have a criterion to distinguish between good and bad criteria, and in this we are apparently driven to an infinite regress in which we constantly have to find criteria to determine the adequacy of other criteria. This logical impasse leads us to our seventh and last method of validation, which to the present writer appears the most useful and valid of all.

This may be called *the method of agreement with systematic prediction.* It comes closest to the traditional scientific methods of physics and chemistry and demands essentially the construction of a hypothetico-deductive system which allows one to make predictions and to test these predictions by actual experiment. Such a system does not treat criteria and attitude scales as being in any way differentiated; instead it tries to integrate all available data. It is easier to demonstrate the use of this method than to explain it in detail, and in any case the interested reader will find lengthy discussions of logical and philosophical desiderata in current books on logic and scientific method. It should not be argued, of course, that this method of agreement with systematic prediction is an alternative to the other six methods outlined; they all find their rightful place within it and derive a more secure logical basis from it. The remainder of the book will deal with an attempt to construct the first approximation to such a system within the field of attitude measurement and political behaviour.

Chapter Four

THE ORGANIZATION OF
SOCIAL ATTITUDES

THERE can be no doubt whatever that attitudes do not occur in splendid isolation but are closely linked with other attitudes in some kind of pattern or structure. Indeed, the very existence of parties and political labels implies as much; to say that a person is a Socialist or a Conservative immediately suggests that he holds not just one particular opinion on one particular issue, but rather that his views and opinions on a large number of different issues will form a definite pattern.

This common-sense view is strongly supported by empirical evidence. We have already shown in the first chapter that Conservatives and Socialists do, in fact, differ from each other on a variety of different points, and an experiment by Centers has been quoted in Chapter One to illustrate the pattern of correlations which exists among different attitudes.

However, results so far mentioned merely indicate the existence of the problem; they do not tell us very much about the nature of the patterns which do exist, or about the method by means of which we can discover these patterns; nor do they give us any information about the most crucial point of all, namely the question of measurement. Even assuming that patterns exist, how can they be subjected to scientific measurement? These are the questions this chapter will be dealing with. Essentially, we shall throughout remain at the descriptive level—in other words, we seek merely to describe and measure what actually is found in a cross-section of the population of this and other countries. We shall postpone consideration of how these patterns originated and what are the forces which contributed to form them to a later chapter.

Before going into this problem, however, there are certain preliminary steps we must take. In the first place, we must try and indicate the method of representation which we shall choose for our patterns; in the second place, we must elaborate some kind of formal model within which to incorporate our results. Let us take up these two points in that order.

The most usual method of describing large numbers of heterogeneous objects in science is by means of some kind of dimensional system in which the dimensions are chosen in such a way that each of them corresponds to one of the principles of heterogeneity present. A homely example may illustrate the point. If we take a random selection of nylon stockings, we shall find that their texture differs considerably, but that all the variability observed can be reduced to two fundamental dimensions. These are, respectively, called *denier*, or the thickness of the thread, which may very from 15 to 45, and *gauge*, which refers to the closeness of the knit. It is measured in terms of the number of stitches across $1\frac{1}{2}$ inches. This may vary from 45 to 66. Figure 15 will indicate the resulting two-dimensional system, and I have also included examples of four very commonly found combinations of *denier* and *gauge*, namely, the 15/51, 15/66, 30/45, and 30/54 stockings. It will be noted that this method of representation is very convenient because it is graphical; in other words, we can see at a glance where any particular stocking may lie with respect to these two dimensions. The two axes representing gauge and denier have been drawn at right angles, which is the customary way of indicating that these two are quite independent of each other; theoretically, at least, you could have any combination between denier and gauge, although in actual practice, of course, some of these are not used.

Another point will be noted. By allocating a given stocking to a certain point on this diagram we have not described it completely. Colour, for instance, is another important variable which is used to characterize the stocking, and if we wanted to include that in our diagram we should have to have a third axis or dimension at right angles to both the other two, i.e. sticking out from the plane of the paper. Even that, of course, would not completely describe the stocking. We should need at least one other dimension, namely, that of size. This dimension again would be at right angles to the other three, but, as we have by now run out of dimensions in physical space, we could not illustrate this four-dimensional model in any sort of graphical or representative way; it would remain a purely mathematical construction in multi-dimensional space.

How can we apply this conception to politics? Let us start with a

FIGURE 15

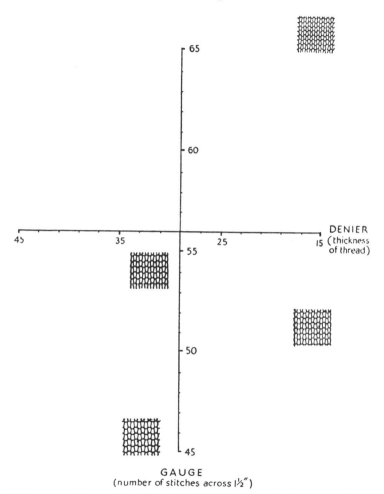

DENIER
(thickness of thread)

GAUGE
(number of stitches across ½″)

Diagram Illustrating Two-Dimension Description of Nylons

purely common-sense source of evaluation. It is often said that in the political spectrum Socialists are to the left of Liberals, Liberals to the left of Conservatives, with Communists and Fascists, respectively, constituting the extreme left and the extreme right. In terms of dimensions, therefore, we might represent the position somewhat as in Figure 16A, with one dimension being thought sufficient to represent political parties.

On the other hand, it is also sometimes said that there is a considerable similarity between Fascists and Communists; so much so, indeed, that there is very little to choose between them. Both, on this reckoning, are opposed to the democratic parties, i.e. the Socialist, Conservative, and Liberal parties, and some observers (usually Liberals) would add that both the Conservatives and Socialist parties have advanced some way towards the Communist-Fascist outlook, leaving the Liberals, as it were, at the other end of this continuum, which might therefore look something like that indicated in Figure 16B.

Much might be said in favour of both these hypotheses, but clearly they cannot both be true *as long as we restrict ourselves to a one-dimensional system.* They could easily be reconciled if we accepted a two-dimensional system, as illustrated in Figure 16C, where our abscissa represents our left-right continuum, and our ordinate represents our democratic versus autocratic continuum, as we may provisionally call it. It should be noted, of course, that we are presenting this two-dimensional pattern merely as an heuristic hypothesis, not as a definite fact; it is inserted to indicate the kind of descriptive result which we might obtain from a dimensional study of the structure of opinions and attitudes. So far it merely pictures in diagrammatic form commonly held opinions regarding the relationships between the attitudes characterizing members of these five parties.

So far we have thus given a rough common-sense sort of answer to the question of how we shall describe the structuring of attitudes. We must do so in terms of dimensions which are preferably independent of each other, and which can be measured. Can we integrate this demand with the information we have already unearthed in previous chapters, and achieve some kind of model which will help us to translate this projected system into an empirical reality? We can do this by taking note of the fact that attitudes appear to be arranged in some kind of hierarchical system. This was already noted by McDougall, and some of the other writers we quoted in our first chapter, and this notion of hierarchical structure or arrangement will provide us with the necessary hypothesis regarding the model we wish to construct.

Roughly speaking, we can discriminate four different degrees of organization or structure. Right at the bottom we have opinions which are not related in any way to other opinions, which are not in any way characteristic of a person who makes them, and which are not reproducible in the sense that if the same or a similar question were asked again under different circumstances, the

FIGURE 16

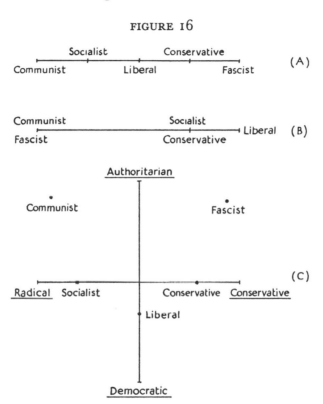

Diagram Illustrating Three Hypotheses Regarding
Relative Position of Five Main Political Groups

answer might be different. Such purely ephemeral opinions are of no great interest or value; they do not go beyond themselves and they do not throw any light either on the personality or on the ideologies of the people holding them.

A higher level is reached when we come to opinions which are reproducible and which form a relatively constant part of an individual's make-up. In other words, these are opinions which are voiced in the same or a similar manner on different occasions, and which are not subject to sudden arbitrary changes, such as are opinions at the lowest level. In terms of the statistical concepts we mentioned earlier, these opinions are *reliable* in the sense of being *stable*.

At the third level, we have what we may call attitudes. Here we find not only that an individual holds a particular opinion with regard to a particular issue with a certain degree of stability; we

FIGURE 17

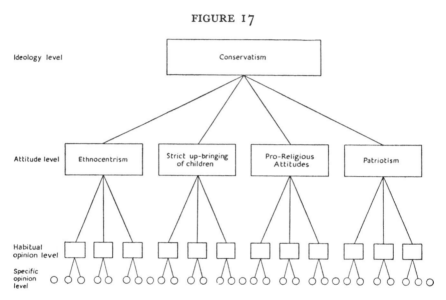

Diagram Illustrating Relation Between Opinion, Attitude, and Ideology

also find that he holds concurrently a large number of other opinions on the same issue which in combination define his attitude towards that issue. As an example of such an attitude, we might think of anti-Semitism and the large number of opinions which went to make up the questionnaire on anti-Semitism given in the previous chapter. Anti-Semitism as an attitude is demonstrated not so much by the fact that any given opinion out of the twenty-four is endorsed by a subject, but by the fact that the whole set of opinions is interrelated and gives rise to a uni-dimensional attitude of anti-Semitism, which can be measured. At this level, in other words, we have the first indication of structure. Opinions do not occur in isolation any more; they are closely related to other opinions on the same issue and thus give rise to our third level.

But even attitudes of this kind are not independent. As we shall see later, a person who is anti-Semitic will also tend to be religious, in favour of flogging and the death penalty, hold strict views on the upbringing of children, be patriotic, and ethnocentric. In other words, attitudes themselves are correlated and give rise to what we might call super-attitudes or ideologies. A particular ideology which is defined by the various beliefs outlined above would be the Conservative ideology; as will be shown later, all the views mentioned above tend to be held more frequently by Conservatives than by Liberals and Socialists, and they all correlate together to define this concept of conservatism.

Figure 17 sets out in diagrammatic form the model we have constructed. Its hierarchical nature will be obvious, going as it does from the very large number of unrelated specific opinions through the smaller number of habitual opinions, and the relatively small number of structured attitudes, to the highest level of ideology, a level at which, as we shall see, only very few concepts will be found.

This model has two advantages. In the first place, as we shall see later, it corresponds well with the known facts and helps to systematize them. In the second place, it indicates to us an empirical way of studying the interrelationships of opinions and attitudes and of verifying hypothesis such as those embodied in Figure 16.

Before we turn to this question of empirical verification, a word should be said about terminology. It will be noticed that we have used the term *opinion* for the lowest two levels, the term *attitude* for the third level, and the term *ideology* for the highest level. This is a convenient distinction and from now onwards, the terms will be used with these precise implications. This usage links up conveniently with the various distinctions in opinion and attitude measurement to which we have drawn attention before. Public opinion polls are practically always at the level of single opinion statements, i.e. at the lowest levels; attitude measurements by means of uni-dimensional scales are concerned with the third level; factor analysis and the more complex statistical procedures are mostly concerned with the ideological level. Thus our levels are differentiated not only with respect to their status in the hierarchy, but also with respect to the most frequently used methods of investigation.

It will have been noticed that the definition of our levels, as well as proof for their existence, depends entirely on the empirical fact of correlation. When we find that a specific opinion as voiced on one occasion is also voiced on another, i.e. when the two correlate, then we speak of opinion measurement proper. When we find that certain opinions are inter-correlated in a certain way, we speak of attitudes, and when we find that certain attitudes are inter-correlated in a certain way, we speak of ideologies. Thus, the concept of correlation is quite fundamental for our system. It is equally fundamental that such correlations should be signs of empirical

FIGURE 18

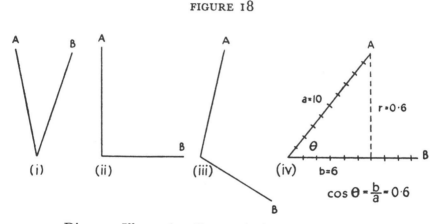

Diagram Illustrating Geometrical Representation of
Correlation Coefficients

rather than logical implication. In other words, if one attitude logically implies another, then to find that the two are in fact related is of comparatively little interest. There is no logical relationship between, say, anti-Semitism, strict child-rearing practices, and religious attitudes; it is precisely because of this lack of logical implication that the factual, empirically observed correlations between these attitudes are of interest.

However, one obvious difficulty appears to arise; correlations are arithmetical and algebraic in nature; the kind of dimensional pattern which we sketched out in Figure 16 is geometrical. How can we go from one to the other? The answer lies in the fact that a correlation can be translated into a geometrical relationship, as indicated in Figure 18.* When two attitudes, A and B, are highly correlated as in (I) they will appear close together, separated by only a small angle. If they are quite uncorrelated, as in (II), they will be at right angles, as in the diagram. When the correlation is negative, A and B will be separated by an obtuse angle, as in (III). Quite generally, the convention is that the cosine of the angle between the two attitudes is exactly equal to the given correlation coefficient, as shown in (IV). This convention enables us to transform abstract concepts, like correlation coefficients, into observable features like angles and lines.

FIGURE 19

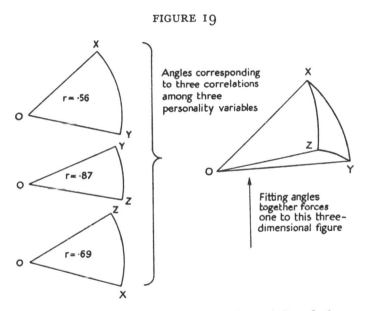

Dimensionality as a Function of Angles and Correlations

Now, from knowing the correlations between certain variables, or in other words from knowing the angles between them, we can immediately tell something about the number of dimensions required to represent these correlations or angles respectively. This is indicated in Figure 19,* where we have plotted on the left side correlations between three variables, X, Y, and Z, in terms of the angles they make with each other. Y and Z correlating together to the point of ·87 have the narrowest angular separation; X and Y

* This diagram is quoted by permission from R. B. Cattell's book, *Personality*.

correlating only ·56 have the widest. If we now try and fit together these three angles, it will be seen that this cannot be done
on the plane of the paper; as shown at the right of Figure 19, we
require one more dimension. Thus, it is possible to indicate the
number of dimensions required for any given set of correlations.

Supposing now that we have a very large number of attitudes
and that we have intercorrelated each of these with each of the

FIGURE 20

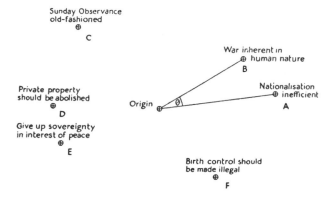

Diagram Showing Correlations Between Six Attitudes
in Terms of a Two-Dimensional Pattern

others, thus obtaining an even larger number of intercorrelations.
If, for instance, we intercorrelated 40 items we would have

$$\frac{40 \times 39}{2}$$

=780 correlations. Let us further suppose that we could fit all these
intercorrelations and all the angles they represent into a two-
dimensional pattern. We should then have 40 dots scattered about
the origin in the plane of the paper in such a way that the angle
formed by connecting any two dots to the origin would represent
the correlation between the attitudes presented by the dots. It is
clear that this would enormously simplify our task of description
as we should have reduced a quite unmanageable table of 780 correlations to a simple two-dimensional diagram which could be in-
spected without difficulty. (Cf. Figure 20 for a small scale example).

However, we would wish to take one further step. In the case of our nylon diagram, we could refer the four patterns illustrated there to the two axes and describe each pattern in terms of the exact denier and the exact gauge number which it represented. Can we find such reference axes in the cases of our correlational diagram also? The answer to this question is 'Yes'. It can be done in every case, but the meaningfulness of the resulting axes or dimensions cannot always be guaranteed. Figure 21 shows a plot of

FIGURE 21

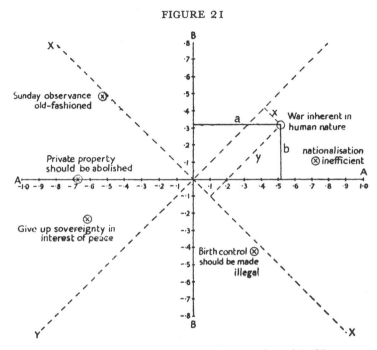

Diagram Showing Invariance of Attitudes with Change
of Reference Axes

points each representing an attitude taken from an actual research described later in this chapter in more detail. We can obviously draw a pair of axes at right angles to each other, practically anywhere, and refer our points to these axes; for the purpose of the argument, two such pairs of axes (A–B and X–Y) have been drawn in. But this very multiplicity of positions makes it clear that the position of these axes is quite arbitrary and that we must look for some kind of criterion which will enable us to find a unique position which is the most meaningful.

This problem, of course, is not unique to psychology; it arises to the same extent in other sciences. For instance, in the case of our nylon diagram (Figure 15, page 109), we have chosen to characterize stockings by reference to the two factors of denier and gauge, but this is not the characterization which most women would employ. They would talk rather in terms of a dimension of 'sheerness', which is a combination of gauge and denier. A sheer stocking is one having a low denier number and a high gauge number and would, therefore, be located in the fourth quadrant in our diagram, i.e. in the right bottom corner. There is no reason why we should not discuss stockings in terms of sheerness rather than in terms of denier and gauge. These are alternate ways of description which may be useful for different purposes. The physicist and the lady of leisure are not forced to use the same concepts, but are quite at liberty to choose those which are most relevant to their particular purposes. Similarly, in psychology we are at liberty to choose the position of our axes with reference to various criteria, and we will have something more to say about the most useful principles to be employed there.

When we turn to the empirical findings which have used this approach, we appear at first to encounter a great variety of apparently divergent solutions.[16] However, a closer study soon reveals a considerable degree of agreement and it appears that all the results so far reported in this country, the United States, Germany, Sweden, and elsewhere, can be integrated into one consistent scheme. That this was so was first suggested by the writer in 1944 in a paper in which he reanalysed results reported by various previous writers, all of them American, and also reported on the analysis of intercorrelations between attitude measures taken in this country on various groups. It was found that all these data and the intercorrelations between the attitudes and opinions measured could be represented in terms of two axes, dimensions, or factors. The first of these two factors appeared in every way to bear a close similarity to the Conservative ideology as opposed to the Radical ideology. At the Conservative end of it were found favourable attitudes towards patriotism, Sunday observance, capital punishment, the church, harsh treatment of criminals, a belief in the inevitability of war, and in the reality of God. At the other extreme were found a cluster of radical beliefs favouring Communism, Pacifism, birth control, divorce reform, sexual freedom, and a belief in evolution. These results are in line with common-sense and might have been predicted by anyone having even a limited degree of insight into our current ideological patterns. Even so, it should be noted that while the fact of the clustering of these attitudes in opposing corners is objective, the interpretation of these clusterings, in terms of Radicalism-Conservatism, is essentially a subjective judgment and will later on require a definite proof. Until such a proof is discussed on a later page, we shall merely regard the outcome of this experiment as suggestive.

One dimension was not found sufficient to account for all the intercorrelations, and the second dimension at right angles to the first had to be posited. Here we immediately ran into difficulties because, while Radical and Conservative are terms very frequently used in everyday talk, nothing was found either in the literature of psychology or that of politics to correspond to this second dimension. An idea of its meaning can probably be obtained from a consideration of those attitudes which most strongly characterize the two extremes. At the one end, we have attitudes favourable to capital punishment, divorce reform, harsh treatment of criminals, sexual freedom, eugenics and birth control, belief in the inevitability of war, and in evolution. At the opposite end we have attitudes favourable to Sunday observance and the church, to Pacifism, abstemiousness, prohibition, and a belief in the reality of God. The following interpretation was offered at the time as a suggestion: 'The interpretation of this second factor is rather more difficult, although the underlying character of the dichotomy indicated by it is perhaps clear enough. Thus, on the one side we have the practical, materialistic, extraverted person, who deals with the environment either by force (soldier) or by manipulation (scientist). On the other side we have the theoretical, idealistic, introverted person, who deals with problems either by thinking (philosopher) or by believing (priest). The best way of describing this factor is perhaps by stressing the *practical-theoretical* dichotomy . . . this factor also seems to be connected closely with temperamental factors. The *practical* attitude is that of James's 'tough-minded' man, of the extravert; the *theoretical* attitude is that of the 'tender-minded' introvert.'

It should be noted, as in the case of the first dimension found in this study, that while the clustering of attitudes is an observable fact, the interpretation of the factor is entirely subjective and will require proof before it can be accepted. We may note, though, as a suggestive possibility that this practical-theoretical factor may be identical with the second dimension previously suggested in Figure 16 where we labelled it authoritarian; authoritarians often regard their régime as more 'practical', and tend to look down on the pre-occupations of democracies with theoretical, legal, and religious problems and scruples. The very term 'Realpolitik' was originally coined to convey this impression of political behaviour unhampered by extraneous considerations of a theoretical or philosophical ethico-religious character. Again, this suggestion is merely intended as an heuristic hypothesis to be proved later on, not as constituting proof in itself.

One further point in this research is of interest as the principle underlying it will come up again in our later discussion. This concerns the confirmation and extension of the 'principle of certainty' first enunciated by Thouless. He enounced it in the following way: 'When, in a group of persons, there are influences acting both in the direction of acceptance and of rejection of a belief, the result is not to make the majority adopt a lower degree of conviction, but to make some hold the belief with a high degree of conviction, while others reject it also with a high degree of conviction.' In the experimental investigation reported in these papers, subjects were asked to indicate their agreement or disagreement with each proposition on a seven point scale ranging from 'I strongly approve of the proposition' (+ 3 points) through 'I am on the whole in favour of this proposition' (+ 2 points) and 'I am uncertain, but if forced would probably vote for the proposition' (+ 1 point) to 'I am uncertain, but if forced would probably vote against the proposition' (− 1 point), 'I am on the whole against the proposition' (− 2 points), and 'I strongly disapprove of the proposition' (− 3 points).

More than 22,000 statements of attitude contained in this study were plotted diagrammatically and the results are shown in Figure 22. It will be seen that there is a distinct tendency for extreme values (+ 3 and − 3) to be more frequent than intermediate values. It was also found that when the different groups who had taken part in the study were compared there was a marked tendency for the more *extreme* groups to be more *certain* of their opinions. This characteristic we shall find again in our discussion of Communist and Fascist ideologies.

The findings of this first study suggested a more carefully designed repetition, and the results of the second experiment were published in 1947. Great care was taken in the selection of questions to be included. The method used took account of previous work, both factorial and non-factorial, to discover in its broadest outline the total universe of social attitude questions as defined by

FIGURE 22

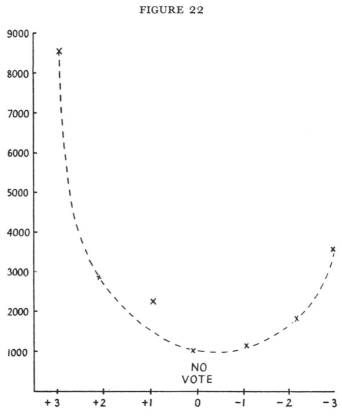

Distribution of 22,208 votes on a 7-point attitude scale

social psychologists, sociologists, and statisticians active in this field. From a total of some 500 items, all those were selected which had been shown to be of importance or relevance in any previous research. When pruned of duplications, it was found that these items did not suffice to make up the mininum number considered requisite, and others were added by random selection until 40 items altogether had been chosen. These items, their wording changed appropriately to suit English conditions where necessary, were then put together in the form of a test and given to various pre-testing groups who were encouraged to make comments and criticisms. Several changes were made in the wording of some of the items to meet the more general criticisms. The resulting questionnaire is presented as Table XVIII, together with a list of questions of personal details included at the time. (The item referring to political party affiliation was universally understood to refer to voting preference in the 1945 election.)

TABLE XVIII

Inventory of Social Attitudes

Below are given 40 statements which represent widely-held opinions on various social questions, selected from speeches, books, newspapers, etc. They were chosen in such a way that most people are likely to agree with some, and to disagree with others. After each statement, you are requested to record your personal opinion regarding it. If you strongly approve, put two crosses after it —like this: + +. If you approve on the whole, put one cross after the statement. If you can't decide for or against, or if you think the question is worded in such a way that you can't give an answer, put a zero—like this: O. If you disapprove on the whole, put a minus sign. And if you strongly disapprove, put two minus signs, like this: ——. Be sure not to omit any questions.

Attitude Statements	*Your opinion*
1. Coloured people are innately inferior to white people.	....
2. Present laws favour the rich as against the poor.	....
3. War is inherent in human nature.	....
4. The marriage bar on female teachers should be removed.	....
5. Persons with serious hereditary defects and diseases should be compulsorily sterilized.	....
6. Our treatment of criminals is too harsh; we should try to cure, not to punish them.	....
7. Our present difficulties are due rather to moral than to economic causes.	....
8. In the interests of peace, we must give up part of our national sovereignty.	....
9. Sunday-observance is old-fashioned, and should cease to govern our behaviour.	....
10. It is wrong that men should be permitted greater sexual freedom than women by society.	....
11. Unrestricted freedom of discussion on every topic is desirable in the press, in literature, on the stage, etc.	....
12. Ultimately, private property should be abolished, and complete socialism introduced.	....

Attitude Statements   *Your opinion*

13. Conscientious objectors are traitors to their country, and should be treated accordingly. ....

14. A certain amount of sex education should be given at school to all boys and girls. ....

15. The laws against abortion should be abolished. ....

16. Only by going back to religion can civilization hope to survive. ....

17. Marriages between white and coloured people should be strongly discouraged. ....

18. Jews are as valuable, honest, and public-spirited citizens as any other group. ....

19. Major questions of national policy should be decided by reference to majority opinion (e.g. by referendum). ....

20. There should be far more controversial and political discussion over the radio. ....

21. The present licensing laws should be altered, so as to remove restrictions on hours of opening. ....

22. All human beings are born with the same potentialities. ....

23. Divorce laws should be altered to make divorce easier. ....

24. Patriotism in the modern world is a force which works against peace. ....

25. Modern life is too much concentrated in cities; the government should take steps to encourage a 'return to the country'. ....

26. Crimes of violence should be punished by flogging. ....

27. The nationalization of the great industries is likely to lead to inefficiency, bureaucracy, and stagnation. ....

28. It is right and proper that religious education in schools should be compulsory. ....

29. Men and women have the right to find out whether they are sexually suited before marriage (e.g. by companionate marriage). ....

30. The principle 'Spare the rod and spoil the child' has much truth in it, and should govern our methods of bringing up children. ....

31. Women are not the equals of men in intelligence, organizing ability, etc. ....

32. Experiments on living animals should be forbidden. ....

33. The Jews have too much power and influence in this country. ....

34. Differences in pay between men and women doing the same work should be abolished. ....

35. Birth control, except when medically indicated, should be made illegal. ....

36. The death penalty is barbaric, and should be abolished. ....

37. There will be another war in 25 years. ....

38. Scientists should take no part in politics. ....

39. The Japanese are by nature a cruel people. ....

Attitude Statements   *Your opinion*

40. Only people with a definite minimum of intelligence and
education should be allowed to vote.   ....

Personal Details. It would be appreciated if you would fill in the following
details.

41. Age.......... 42. Sex.......... 43. Weekly income (self or husband): £.......

44. Profession (in detail, e.g. Maths. teacher at secondary school)...................
....

45. Are you happy in your present job? ....
46. Are you satisfied with your prospects? ....
47. Put a cross after the group in which you would include yourself:
    1. Conservative, Nat. Lib., Nat. Lab., Unionist, etc.   ....
    2. Liberal.   ....
    3. Labour, Socialist, Commonwealth, I.L.P., etc.   ....
    4. Completely unpolitical, wouldn't vote at all.   ....
48. At what age did your full-time education finish? ....
49. Underline the type of school you went to: Primary. Secondary. Grammar.
    Senior. Central. Technical. Public. University. (Underline as many as may
    apply.)

The questionnaires were administered by students of the writer
in University classes, University extension classes, and W.E.A.
classes to friends of theirs whose views on political and social questions they knew sufficiently well enough to be able to judge the
accuracy of the replies. This task formed part of the standard
course given to these students on attitude measurement, construction of attitude scales, sampling, and so forth. Before these matters
were dealt with the students were told that they would soon be
given lectures on the measurement of attitudes and this discussion
would gain in meaningfulness to them if they could carry out some
sample investigations of their own. They were then given from
5–15 inventories and told to give them to friends and acquaintances of theirs, to have them filled in, to discuss the reactions of
their subjects with them, and to write a report on their findings,
stressing particularly any disagreement between subjects' attitudes
as written down, and attitudes known to be held. They were also
told particularly to note down any criticisms which might be made
of wording, construction, or meaning of the test-items. In addition,
they were to give a personality sketch of the subjects, and try to
discover by interview some of the causes which led them to hold
these particular views.

During the lectures which followed, they were told about the difficulties which arise in the measurement of attitudes, and the criticisms which have been made of this branch of psychology. With these in mind, they were encouraged to criticize, on the basis of their own experience in giving the questionnaire, its construction, its validity, and its wording. These criticisms formed the last section of their completed papers, which were then collected by the writer.

Analysis of the detailed reports proved that attitude surveys like this one show extremely close agreement with attitude as rated by friends and acquaintances of the persons filling in the questionnaires. Although warned against the possible dangers of questionnaire studies, and sensitized to the falsifications which may be introduced through conscious or unconscious factors, the students reported that in 98 per cent of the cases they studied they thought the respondent had given a picture of his attitudes which agreed well with the pattern of opinions he was known to hold. It will be noted that with 98 per cent agreement, there appeared 2 per cent of the attitude statements which failed to show agreement. In actual fact, this failure is more apparent than real. In many cases the respondents complained that the questionnaire forced them to record complex attitudes as simple dichotomies; many said they 'could write a book' on each of the statements. However, to the outside observer the questionnaire answer appeared usually to give a very close approximation to the 'total' attitude which the respondent complained he could not put down. In the 2 per cent 'disagreements' the student had usually taken his cue from the respondent and reported, not that the respondent's answer differed from what was known about his attitudes, but that the respondent himself did not think that the questionnaire gave an accurate picture of his attitudes. It is likely, therefore, that the figure of 2 per cent gives an exaggerated impression of the lack of validity of the answers to the questionnaire. In a number of cases, the writer himself discussed questionnaire answers with respondents who had said that they considered the questionnaire did not give an accurate picture of their views. When asked to amplify their answers, either in writing or verbally, the response was very scant; the elaborations put forward certainly did not justify the claims of the respondents. Nor would they, in the writer's view, have altered the position on the attitude scale marked by the respondents. Often remarks were frankly irrelevant; sometimes they merely restated in a slightly bombastic fashion what the questionnaire statement said more simply; frequently they consisted of unimportant quibbles regarding wording. It would seem on the whole that very few people who claim that a statement of the kind included in the questionnaire is too simple, and that they have thought so deeply about the issue that they 'could write a book on it' can add even a single phrase which would extend the coverage of the item, or alter its meaning in a useful fashion.

Of the large number of questionnaires returned, those of 750 middle-class subjects were chosen in such a way that 250 were supporters of the Conservative party, 250 supporters of the Liberal party, and 250 supporters of the Labour or Socialist party. These

TABLE XIX

Composition of Experimental Group in Terms of Sex, Age, and Education

Group	Conservative	Liberal	Socialist
MOU	25	23	23
MON	29	26	26
MYU	37	42	42
MYN	22	22	22
FOU	11	14	14
FON	26	23	23
FYU	64	69	69
FYN	36	31	31
	250	250	250

three parties will in future be referred to by the letters C, L and S. The actual composition of this total group with respect to three other variables, age, education, and sex, is given in Table XIX. In this table are given the numbers of persons over 30-years old (denoted by O), under 30-years old (Y); persons who have had a university education (U), who have not (N); males and females (M and F). It will be seen that the three political groups are closely matched for sex, age, and education.

The decision to make the numbers of subjects for each of the three political groupings equal was taken, in spite of the fact that at the time the survey was done only 25 per cent of the middle class group would be Socialists and 13 per cent Liberals, while 61 per cent would be Conservatives. The main reason for this decision was a very simple one. Our interest lay not in obtaining a representative cross-section of the population but in comparing different political groups. This can best be done by having the groups of equal size, thus reducing sampling errors to a minimum. If mean values are wanted for the total population, then mean values for the selected groups can be multiplied by the proportions these groups form of the total population, thus giving an adequate indication of population values.

Correlations were worked out between all the items for the total group of 750, and two main factors or dimensions discovered. The items which defined the first of these dimensions were clearly grouped into two opposing sets. On the one hand, we find a belief that private property should be abolished, that the death penalty ought to go, that Sunday observance is old fashioned, that Jews are valuable citizens, that the divorce laws ought to be altered, that we should give up part of our sovereignty, that we should abolish abortion laws, that we should cure criminals rather than punish them, that laws favour the rich, that companionate marriage should be allowed, and that patriotism is a force that works against peace. On the other hand, we have a belief that nationalization is inefficient, that compulsory religious education is desirable, that the Japanese are cruel by nature, that we should go back to religion, that Jews are too powerful in this country, that flogging should be retained as a deterrent, that war is inherent in human nature, that conscientious objectors are traitors, that birth control should be made illegal, and that coloured peoples are inferior. We shall take up the interpretation of this factor in a minute.

Regarding the second factor, we again find two sets of items defining its two poles. On the one hand, we find a belief that we must go back to religion, that birth control should be illegal, that the double standard of morality is bad, that religious education should be made compulsory, that our troubles have moral causes, that we should give up our sovereignty, abolish the death penalty, and attempt to cure criminals rather than punish them. The opposing set of beliefs approves of companionate marriage, wants to alter divorce, licensing, and abortion laws, considers the Japanese cruel by nature, the Jews too powerful, war inherent in human nature, Sunday observance old fashioned, compulsory sterilization desirable, women and coloured peoples inferior, and conscientious objectors traitors to their country.

The detailed results given in Table XX. This records the proportion of 'Yes' answers given by supporters of the three political parties to each question, the difference between the percentages of the Conservative and Socialist voters respectively (under 'D'), as well as the correlations of each of the 40 opinions statements with our two dimensions under the heading I and II respectively. (Item 14 had to be omitted here as agreement on this item was too high to make possible the calculation of correlation coefficients).

It may help the reader in visualizing the two factors concerned to have a diagrammatic, two-dimensional picture, and accordingly Figure 23 is presented below.* Apart from those features of Figure 23 which aid in the interpretation of the meaning of the two factors there are several curious aspects of the distribution of opinions and attitudes in the two-dimensional space generated by our two factors which may repay attention. We shall come back, therefore, to a more detailed consideration of this Figure in a later chapter.

We must now turn to the interpretation of our two factors or dimensions. When we turn to the items defining the extremes of our first dimension the possibility will immediately suggest itself that here we are again dealing with a factor of Radicalism-Conservatism. Fortunately, we have a possibility now of proving the validity of this interpretation. An item having a high positive correlation with this factor would on our interpretation be a Conservative item, i.e. an item which should be endorsed much more frequently by Conservatives than by Socialists. Conversely, an item having high negative correlation with this factor should be a Radical item, i.e. one much more likely to be endorsed by Socialists than by Conservatives. Items having very low correlations with this dimension should be neither Conservative nor Radical in import and should, therefore, be endorsed with approximately equal frequency by supporters of these two parties.

We can verify this deduction by reference to Table XX. It will be quite clear in comparing column D with the column giving the correlations of the items with the first factor that this deduction is indeed verified. In practically every case, items which are endorsed much more frequently by one group than by the other have high correlations with the factor, and in every case the direction of the

* This figure is based on the results of the study summarized in Table XX and of several similar researches carried out since on altogether some 3,000 subjects.

TABLE XX

Proportion of 'Yes' Answers of Conservatives, Liberals, and Socialists to Forty Social Attitudes Questions, As Well As Factor Saturations of These Questions

Question	Proportion of 'Yes' answers, three parties			Factor Saturations		'D'
	C	L	S	I	II	
1	42	27	19	·47	·32	23
2	27	37	65	—·33	·15	—38
3	67	57	34	·51	·32	33
4	76	86	91	—·41	·03	—15
5	69	59	63	·20	·28	06
6	39	58	72	—·57	—·22	—33
7	54	49	42	·25	—·38	12
8	32	60	76	—·62	—·23	—44
9	36	44	68	—·53	·49	—32
10	66	71	80	—·13	—·27	—14
11	75	79	79	—·22	·20	—04
12	03	15	56	—·68	·01	—53
13	28	16	09	·45	·39	19
14	92	96	99	—	—	(07)
15	28	40	53	—·45	·33	—25
16	65	56	36	·46	—·65	29
17	77	66	49	·50	·17	28
18	40	58	67	—·55	—·14	—27
19	52	54	53	·07	·14	—01
20	67	71	84	—·30	—·09	—17
21	42	42	54	—·26	·33	—12
22	12	10	14	·08	·03	—02
23	33	42	61	—·46	·47	—28
24	34	49	60	—·39	—·06	—26
25	72	65	62	·35	—·03	10
26	65	49	28	·65	·28	37
27	86	58	16	·72	·11	70
28	66	55	32	·57	—·34	34
29	35	40	62	—·53	·56	—27
30	56	49	38	·41	·16	18
31	40	30	28	·23	·25	12
32	19	28	27	·06	—·01	—08
33	68	52	39	·55	·23	29
34	68	77	83	—·29	—·03	—15
35	22	22	08	·36	—·42	14
36	30	42	64	—·60	—·20	—34
37	34	33	22	·24	·23	12
38	32	28	20	·35	·17	12
39	58	37	19	·65	·29	39
40	55	47	39	·21	·07	16

discrepancy agrees with the sign of the correlation. In practically every case where there is little difference between the endorsement given by members of the two parties, the correlations with the factor are low. Agreement is not far short of perfection, and we may therefore reasonably argue that the evidence strongly supports the interpretation of this first factor as one of Conservative as

FIGURE 23

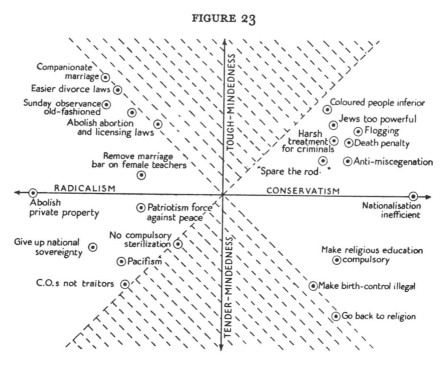

Distribution of Attitudes with Respect to Tough-Mindedness
and Radicalism

opposed to Radical ideology. We shall in future refer to this factor as one of Radicalism, or, more briefly, as the R factor.

When we turn to our second factor we notice that it closely resembles the theoretical-practical dimension described in connection with the previous research. A better name for this dimension might perhaps be a set of terms taken from a book by W. James, where he refers to two opposed types of temperament leading to opposed philosophical beliefs as the 'tender-minded' and the 'tough-minded' respectively. As we shall make much use of this dichotomy, a brief quotation from James will make its meaning clearer. James starts his discussion on pragmatism by pointing out that philosophical systems are often influenced or determined by the temperament of their authors. He goes on to say that 'the particular difference of temperament that I have in mind . . . is one that has counted in literature, art, government, and manners as well as in philosophy. In manners we find formalists and free-and-easy persons. In government, authoritarians and anarchists. In literature, purists or academicals, and realists. In art, classics and romantics. You recognize these contrasts as familiar; well, in philosophy we have a very similar contrast expressed in the pair of terms "rationalist" and "empiricist", "empiricist" meaning your lover of facts in all their crude variety, "rationalist" meaning your devotee to abstract and eternal principles.' James then goes on to a brief discussion of some of these differences and finally gives a table of these: 'I will write these traits down in two columns. I think you will practically recognize the two types of mental-make up that I mean if I head the columns by the titles "tender-minded" and "tough-minded" respectively.

The tender-minded	*The tough-minded*
Rationalistic (going by "principles")	Empiricist (going by "facts"),
Intellectualistic	Sensationalistic
Idealistic	Materialistic
Optimistic	Pessimistic
Religious	Irreligious
Free-willist	Fatalistic
Monistic	Pluralistic
Dogmatical.	Sceptical.'

James then goes on to discuss the antagonism between these types of temperament which 'has formed in all ages a part of the philosophic atmosphere of the time. It forms a part of the philosophic atmosphere to-day. The tough think of the tender as sentimentalists and soft-heads. The tender feel the tough to be unrefined, callous, or brutal.' Modern science, he believes, has tended to favour the tough-minded. 'Ideals appear as inert by-products of physiology; what is higher is explained by what is lower and treated forever as a case of "nothing but"—nothing but something else of a quite inferior sort. You get, in short, a materialistic universe in which only the tough-minded find themselves congenially at home.'

We may perhaps accept for the time being James's term and call this dimension tender-mindedness versus tough-mindedness, or, more simply, the T-factor. The intrinsic meaningfulness of this factor will become more apparent as we discuss further evidence; for the moment let us merely note that the tender-minded set of opinions appears to be dominated by ethical, moralistic, super-ego, altruistic values, while the tough-minded set of opinions is dominated by realistic, worldly, egotistic values, and it may be noted that Koestler's book, *The Yogi and the Commissar*, seems to drive at much the same division as indicated by this factor, a division which clearly cuts across party lines. On the left we have the 'tender-minded' (Lansbury, I.L.P., the Pacifist group, the religious leftists, etc.) as well as the 'tough-minded' (Communists, Trotskyites, etc.). Similarly, on the right there are the 'tender-minded' religious groups as well as the 'tough-minded' semi-fascist combinations. Indeed, in practice this division is well recognized by parties of the right as well as of the left, but no term has been suggested to point out what is common to the adherents of either the 'tough' or the 'tender' line in both parties.

While the interpretation and discussion so far appears to follow from the experimental results it seemed desirable to see whether similar results could be obtained with different populations and with different items. As regards the former, it has been shown that when the 40 items in Table XVIII are administered to American, German, and Swedish groups very similar results are obtained to those found in English groups and reported in this chapter. It appears, therefore, that results are not specific to this country, but may be generalized to these other national groupings as well.

The question of invariance of factors under change of items was taken up by Melvin, who also attempted to improve the reliability and validity of the R and T scales by increasing the number of items and improving their selection. Using 38 new items, as well as scores on the R and T scales, he obtained intercorrelations for 650 subjects and factor analysed the resulting table of intercorrelations. The results showed that our original results could be reproduced with an entirely different set of items.*

* Melvin was also successful in improving the R and T scales, and the new scales, together with scoring instructions, are reproduced in technical note 17. They are of interest as many of the results reported later in the book were obtained through the use of these improved scales.

If we wish now to formulate hypotheses regarding our two dimensions, and particularly if we wish to verify deductions made from these hypotheses, then we must obviously construct measuring instruments for R and T respectively. Two scales were accordingly constructed by combining the items most highly correlated with the two factors respectively, each scale consisting of 14 items. The possible range of scores on R is from O, the highest Conservative score, to 14, the highest Radical score. Similarly, T scores range from zero, the most tough-minded, to 14, the most tender-minded score. Mean values of scores for various combinations of party, sex, age, and education are given in Table XXI. Reliabilities of the scales and correlations between R and T for various groups are given in Table XXII.

There is a clear differentiation between the three political parties with respect to their R scores, as shown in Figure 24. The Conservatives and Socialists are at opposite extremes of this dimension, with Liberals in the middle. It will be noted that there is a considerable amount of overlap, some Conservatives holding attitudes which put them well to the left of the average Socialist, and some Socialist voters holding views which put them well to the right of the average Conservative. This finding will not surprise anyone who knows about the complexity of the factors determining voting behaviour, and the fact that Radical-Conservative attitudes as defined here play an important part, but not an exclusive part, in this determination. There are no significant differences between the political parties with respect to the T factor.

Age and sex appear to have exerted little influence on R, but the university trained subjects are more radical than the non-university trained subjects. With respect to T, age and education again appear to have exerted little influence, but as one might have expected, women are more tender-minded than men, a finding which has found support in several later studies.

The reliabilities of the scales may be used to give us some information on the degree of structuring obtaining within the various groups. Males are found to show a more definite structure of attitudes than do females; university educated subjects show a more definite structure than non-university educated subjects; and the old show a more definite structure than the young. These findings are true for both factors R and T and are probably in line with expectation.

If our interpretation of the T factor were correct, we should be able to make certain predictions which could be tested by empirical procedures. One such prediction might relate the T factor to social

TABLE XXI

Detailed Scores on Radicalism and Tough-Mindedness for Various Sub-Groups

PRIMARY SOCIAL ATTITUDES: R

				C	L	S
Y	M	U	1	6·1±2·3	7·3±3·0	10·9±2·5
		N	2	4·0±2·5	6·0±2·0	8·4±3·1
	F	U	3	5·1±2·4	7·1±2·6	9·8±3·0
		N	4	4·4±1·9	5·7±2·2	8·0±3·3
O	M	U	5	4·2±2·3	6·9±2·8	9·0±3·2
		N	6	3·8±2·1	6·0±3·0	9·8±2·5
	F	U	7	5·5±2·6	6·7±2·8	10·4±2·7
		N	8	3·7±2·2	4·6±2·7	8·9±2·9

AVERAGES:
C = 4·6±2·37   M = 6·9±2·36   Y = 6·9±2·58   U = 7·4±2·69
L = 6·3±2·80   F = 6·7±2·59   O = 6·7±2·64   N = 6·1±2·54
S = 9·4±3·04

PRIMARY SOCIAL ATTITUDES: T

				C	L	S
Y	M	U	1	6·2±2·7	7·8±2·3	7·4±2·0
		N	2	7·4±2·6	7·1±2·4	7·5±2·2
	F	U	2	8·2±2·5	8·9±2·1	8·3±2·1
		N	4	7·9±2·7	7·0±2·7	8·4±1·9
O	M	U	5	7·3±2·6	6·7±2·0	9·2±2·8
		N	6	7·2±2·2	8·6±2·4	7·0±2·5
	F	U	7	8·3±2·0	9·9±2·3	8·3±1·7
		N	8	8·2±2·1	7·3±2·3	8·0±2·7

AVERAGES:
C = 7·6±2·60   O = 8·0±2·29   M = 7·4±2·4   U = 8·0±2·4
L = 7·9±2·50   Y = 7·7±2·31   F = 8·2±2·2   N = 7·6±2·2
S = 8·0±2·32

class. If indeed the tender-minded are more concerned with ethical and theoretical issues, the tough-minded more with the direct satisfaction of hedonistic impulses, then we should expect working-class subjects as a whole to be more tough-minded than the middle-

class subjects. In part, at least, this prediction is derived from the extensive studies of Allison Davis in the United States, and Himmelweit in this country, showing the greater degree of 'socialization' of middle-class children as compared to working class children.

The other prediction which may be made on the basis of our analysis has already been mentioned before. If we can identify tough-mindedness with the authoritarian factor, which hypothetically divides the Communist and Fascist parties at the one end from

TABLE XXII

Reliabilities of R and T Scales for Various Sub-Groups

	Reliability Scale R	Reliability Scale T	Correlation R v. T
Conservatives	·63	·55	—·20±·05
Liberals	·66	·58	—·19±·05
Socialists	·73	·63	—·19±·05
Total Group	·81	·64	—·12±·03
Males	·88	·66	—·14±·05
Females	·74	·63	—·12±·05
University	·80	·63	—·17±·05
Non-University	·74	·53	—·11±·05
Old	·83	·58	—·24±·05
Young	·78	·57	—·16±·05
Validity	·90	·80	————

the Democratic parties, and particularly the Liberal party, at the other, then we should predict that the scores of Communist party members could be found in the tough-minded, Radical quadrant, and that the scores of Fascists would be found in the tough-minded, Conservative quadrant; Socialists and Conservatives would be found to be neither particularly tough-minded nor particularly tender-minded; Liberals would be the most tender-minded group of all, while intermediate on the Radicalism-Conservatism continuum.

A preliminary verification of both these hypotheses was furnished by the writer in 1951. In addition to the three middle-clas

FIGURE 24

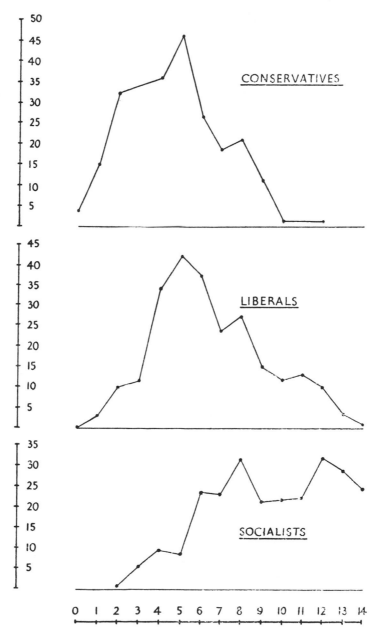

Distribution of Scores on Radicalism Factor for Three Political Parties

groups mentioned already, 50 middle-class Communists, 96 working-class Communists, 65 working-class Conservatives, 27 working-class Liberals, and 45 working-class Socialists, as well as 7 members of the Fascist party were tested. A comparison of the scores of all these groups, except the very small Fascist group is given in Table XXIII; the average scores of the Fascists were 5·2 for the R factor and 4·7 for the T factor. Figure 25 shows the results in

FIGURE 25

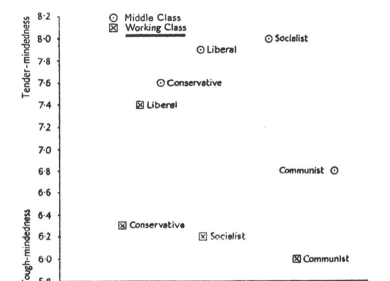

Comparison of Middle-Class and Working-Class Groups with regard to Tender-Mindedness and Radicalism

diagrammatic form. It will be seen that our first prediction is unequivocally borne out. Middle-class Conservatives are more tender-minded than working-class Conservatives; middle-class Liberals more tender-minded than working-class Liberals; middle-class Socialists more tender-minded than working-class Socialists, and even middle-class Communists are more tender-minded than working-class Communists.

When we average the average scores of the groups on the T factor, i.e. without paying attention to the fact that the number of cases is different between groups, we find that the Liberals are the most tender-minded with a score of 7·7; that the Socialists and Conservatives follow next, with a score of 7·0; and that the combined Communist-Fascist group has much the most tough-minded score (5·5). Thus, this prediction also is borne out. The results, therefore, strongly support our identification of the T factor with the hypothetical authoritarian factor, and we find indeed that Communists appear almost without exception in the tough-minded Radical quadrant and that Fascists without exception appear in the tough-minded Conservative quadrant. Because of the small number of Fascists included, this result may be slightly less convincing

TABLE XXIII

Comparison of R and T Scores for Middle-Class and Working-Class Voters

R SCORES

	Middle Class	Working Class
Conservatives	4·6±2·37	2·8±2·03
Liberals	6·3±2·80	3·7±2·34
Socialists	9·4±3·04	6·4±2·90
Communists	12·4±2·02	10·7±2·45

T SCORES

	Middle Class	Working Class
Conservatives	7·6±2·60	6·3±2·24
Liberals	7·9±2·50	7·4±2·51
Socialists	8·0±2·32	6·2±2·50
Communists	6·8±1·50	6·0±1·99

than would be desirable, but we shall see later on that even with much larger numbers, the prediction is still borne out.

One further interesting point will be noted from Figure 25. It will be noted in each case that in comparing working-class and middle-class voters for a given party, there is a distinct and significant tendency for the working-class to be more Conservative than the middle-class group. At first, this may appear contrary to expectation, as we have seen in the earlier chapters that there is a strong correlation between high social class and Conservative voting behaviour. The contradiction, however, is more apparent than real. By only comparing people voting for the same party we have ruled out, as it were, the influence of class on voting, and are therefore left with a residual effect which is independent of voting behaviour.

It will also be noted that this tendency of middle-class people to be more Radical than working-class people has often been observed by political commentators. Almost traditionally, for instance, the trade union votes at the Labour Party Congress are more frequently cast for Conservative policies, while the constituency party votes, with a very much larger middle-class membership, are usually cast for the more Radical policies. Similar observations have been made with respect to the Communist party. It has been impossible to discover comments of a similar nature with respect to either the Conservative or the Liberal party, but the figures clearly show that this trend applies to them also.

We thus find that within a given party, working-class voters tend to be more tough-minded and more Conservative than middle-class voters. It may be of interest to list those items on which class differences are largest for all four parties. The differences on these 13 items are all in the same direction for the four parties, and show that working-class people as opposed to middle-class people share the following beliefs: in favour of compulsory sterilization; in favour of harsh treatment of criminals; in favour of unrestricted freedom of discussion; opposed to conscientious objectors; against miscegenation; opposed to changes in the licensing laws; agreeing that human beings are all born with the same potentialities; that modern life is too much concentrated in the cities; that flogging is good in cases of violence; that Jews are too powerful; that the Japanese are by nature a cruel people; that the death penalty should not be abolished; and 'spare the rod and spoil the child'. Another eight differences show agreement between three parties, with the fourth showing a very small difference in the opposite direction, or no difference at all. According to these eight statements, working-class people believe that war is inherent in human nature; that we must not give up our national sovereignty; that we should not give up private property (!); that we should not abolish laws against abortion; that Jews are not valuable citizens; that divorce should not be made easier; that wage differences between sexes should not be abolished; and that companionate marriage should not be allowed.

These differences are of particular interest in the light they throw on the Marxian hypothesis of what Centers has called 'the interest group theory of social classes'. The working-class person is shown to be more Conservative than the middle-class person voting for the same party, in spite of his obvious class interests which according to the theory should pull him in the opposite direction. Nor can one maintain the superficially plausible hypothesis that there are two kinds of Conservatism involved, one dealing with economic matters, the other with ideational causes, in such a way that working-class people are economically Radical and ideationally Conservative, while middle-class people are economically Conservative and ideationally Radical. The falsity of this hypothesis is shown by the fact that the item calling for the abolition of private property is actually endorsed much more frequently by middle-class people. It is perhaps surprising that these general tendencies are shared by members of the Communist party to an extent equal to that shown by the other parties; this result greatly strengthens the case for generalizing our findings.

One further interesting finding may be mentioned. Table XXIII shows that the Communist groups tend to have much smaller S.D.s for their R and T scores than do the other groups, either working-class or middle-class. This greater cohesion of Communist groups, again, is hardly unexpected. It appears to go together with a greater tendency to believe *strongly* in the correctness of the attitude held. If we average the $+ +$ and the $- -$ scores, indicating strong approval or disapproval, we find that only 35 per cent of the Socialist, Liberal and Conservative responses have been marked in this fashion, but 54 per cent and 51 per cent respectively of the middle-class and working-class Communist responses. This finding, too, might have been anticipated. There was no appreciable difference in S.D. between the middle-class and the working-class group, although such differences had been expected, on the hypothesis that middle-class groups might be thought to have a more consistent, thought-out philosophy of political and social behaviour. The facts do not support this view.

While the results of this experiment in the main bear out the hypothesis that Communists will be found in the tough-minded Radical quadrant, while Fascists will in the main congregate in the tough-minded Conservative quadrant, the numbers involved were not large enough to make the proof definitive. Further evidence was consequently collected by Coulter, using Melvin's improved form of the R and T questionnaires. She administered

FIGURE 26

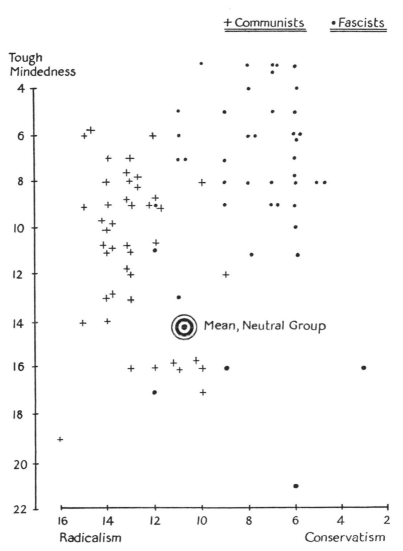

Tough-Mindedness Scores and Scores of Radicalism-Conservatism
of Communists, Fascists, and Neutral Group

these questionnaires to 43 male, working-class Communists, 43 male, working-class Fascists, as well as to a group of 86 soldiers who were neither Communist nor Fascist supporters but constituted a fairly random sample of British working-class males.

Figure 26 shows the outcome of the experiment. It will be seen that with very few exceptions both Fascists and Communists have more 'tough-minded' scores than the average of the soldier group. Similarly, nearly without exception the Fascists are more Conservative, and Communists more Radical, than the average of the soldier group. These results bear out in every detail the results of the previous study, and we may accordingly conclude that our main hypothesis is strongly supported.

Chapter Five

ATTITUDES, VALUES, AND INTERESTS

In the previous chapter we have dealt entirely with researches carried out by members of the Maudsley Laboratory on English populations of various kinds. We have also seen that the results could be used to describe, with equal success, the structuring of attitudes in Germany, Sweden, and the United States. However, the approach outlined in the last chapter is not the only one that has been made in this field, and it will be worth while in this chapter to compare our results with those of a number of American investigators whose method has differed from our own in two important respects. The first point of difference is this. When we wish to arrive, by means of correlational procedures, at the main ideologies in a given culture we do so, as has been explained before, by intercorrelating a number of attitudes, the assumption being that an analysis of these intercorrelations will suggest hypotheses to us, or will help us in deciding between rival hypotheses.

However, in carrying out this work we have two alternatives, both of which have their own advantages and disadvantages. One alternative is to decide on a number of attitudes, such as, for instance, attitudes towards war, towards the church, towards the Jews, etc., construct scales along the lines described in Chapter Three in connection with our anti-Semitism scale, and apply a series of such scales to the experimental population. Scores would then be derived from each scale and intercorrelated. The advantage of this procedure is that we should have a highly reliable measure for each given attitude; the disadvantage would be that a very large number of attitude and opinion questions would be required. If each scale contained 24 items, as is the case, for instance, in our anti-Semitism scale, then to obtain measures on only 30 attitudes we should require 720 statements altogether. Very few subjects would be willing to spend several hours on a task of this kind, and even those who might be willing to do so would probably lose interest after a short while and become inattentive and inaccurate in their marking. To keep the number of statements to a relatively reasonable limit, we should be restricted to investigating only a small number of attitudes, and it is doubtful whether the added reliability of the individual measurements for each attitude would counterbalance the loss in having only a few attitudes available for intercorrelation.

The alternative policy would be to choose only one or two items to represent a given attitude, thus losing the advantage of very high reliabilities, but gaining the advantage of being able to use measures of a relatively large number of attitudes without over-burdening the subject with very long questionnaires.

It is difficult to decide between these two approaches. Ideally one would wish to have as reliable measures as possible for each attitude, and as large a number of different attitudes investigated as possible. In practice, one or the other of these two demands has to be given up and it will be noted that in the work referred to in the last chapter the second alternative has been adopted. The reason for this is essentially that, as is shown in Table XVI, a single item dealing with anti-Semitism may have correlations of ·8 or ·9 with anti-Semitism, as measured by the total scale. Such values may be regarded as indications of the relatively high reliability of the items and suggest that for practical purposes the single item may very well be used instead of the whole scale. (It will be realized, of course, that this is true only for correlational purposes; from the point of view of public opinion polling, where we are interested in means, distributions, and similar details, this argument would not hold.)

However, while a decision was thus made in favour of the second alternative, it must be recognized that the other alternative also possesses advantages, and it is the other alternative which has been adopted by several American investigators, notably Ferguson, who has contributed a whole series of studies on this question of the structure of attitudes. This is doubly fortunate because, as will be shown later, his findings are practically identical with those reported in the previous chapter, and consequently it would appear that our choice between the two alternatives does not prejudice the final result to any considerable extent.

Much the same may be said about the other difference which appears to separate the work of the authors considered in this chapter from our own. This difference is of a somewhat technical nature, and refers to the actual position of the dimensions or factors which were used as reference axes for our various attitudes. The problem may perhaps be clarified by going back to Figure 15 and our nylon example. We have shown that it is possible to describe nylon fabrics in terms of two factors, denier and gauge. This we may call the physical description. It is also possible to describe nylons in terms of sheerness, i.e. in terms of a dimension which combines denier and gauge and, which as it were, can be symbolized by an axis drawn at an angle of 45 degrees to either of the physical ones. This might be called a psychological description because it is arrived at largely by the psychological requirements of nylon users. Up to a point, both descriptions fit the facts equally well as long as we are merely interested in description; the main superiority of the physical system arises in terms of causation. As long as we remain at the descriptive level we may adopt different systems of description without in any way changing the configuration or patterning of whatever it is that we are describing.

Something very much like this has happened in the case of the descriptions of attitude patterning given by different authors. If, for the moment, we may refer to the description given in the last chapter as being similar to the physical description of nylons, then we shall find that the descriptions given by Ferguson and the other writers in this chapter may be regarded as similar to the psychological description, i.e. as rotated through an angle of 45 degrees. As will be shown, this does not in any way affect the underlying structure, and without using further facts other than those of simple intercorrelations between attitudes, it is impossible to choose between these alternate systems of description. Simply in terms of their derivation they are equally useful and can very easily be transformed one into the other by means of a simple mathematical equation. There may, however, be external considerations which favour one system over the other, and this question we shall return to after a consideration of Ferguson's data.

This writer has made a determined effort in a large number of research papers to solve the problem of structure in the attitude field. He used ten carefully constructed scales dealing with evolution, birth control, God, capital punishment, treatment of criminals war, censorship, communism, law, and patriotism, which he administered to various groups of students. We shall not follow the whole course of his very extensive and careful work, in which he showed that his original results could be duplicated on different populations and at different times, but will instead reserve consideration to the main outcome of his analysis. This is shown in Figure 27.* It will be seen that he also finds two main factors in his analysis and that the positions of the various attitude scales in this two dimensional universe are practically identical with those found in our own work. Attitudes favouring capital punishment and the harsh treatment of criminals are found in the tough-minded Conservative quadrant; attitudes favourable to evolution, Communism, and birth control are found in the tough-minded Radical quadrant, anti-war attitudes in the tender-minded Radical quadrant, and attitudes favourable to God, censorship, and the law, in the tender-minded Conservative quadrant. Patriotism appears to lie almost exactly on the Radical-Conservative axis itself. In so far as there is overlap between these attitudes and those measured in our own work, agreement is almost complete.

Ferguson, however, does not use these factors or axes as they stand; he rotates them through 45 degrees, as indicated in Figure 27 and emerges with two factors which he calls Humanitarianism and Religionism. These terms describe with sufficient accuracy the nature of the two dimensions or continua which he believes to underlie the structure of social attitudes, and, as we pointed out before, it is impossible to decide between his choice and ours on the basis of the intercorrelations themselves. Both solutions are equally justifiable statistically and both describe the facts with equal accuracy.

There are two reasons why a solution in terms of Radicalism-Conservatism and Tough-mindedness versus Tender-mindedness appears preferable to a solution in terms of Religionism and Humanitarianism. In the first place, the Radical-Conservative dichotomy is so well established in political life and has found such strong institutional representation, that it seems artificial, to say the least, to try and account for social attitudes in different terms.

In the second place, it appears more reasonable to talk about

* The actual analysis on which Figure 27 is based was carried out by the writer on the basis of figures published by Ferguson. This was necessary as Ferguson has never published the full results of an analysis of all ten measures.

Fascist attitudes as being a mixture of Tough-mindedness and Conservatism, or about Communist attitudes as being a mixture of Tough-mindedness and Radicalism, than to talk about Conservative beliefs as a mixture of Religionism and anti-Humanitarianism and about Radical beliefs as a mixture of Humanitarianism and anti-Religionism. These reasons are largely reasons of Semantic convenience; more convincing would be experimental evidence showing that Tough-mindedness had correlates in other fields, such as, for instance, in the field of personality, which neither

FIGURE 27

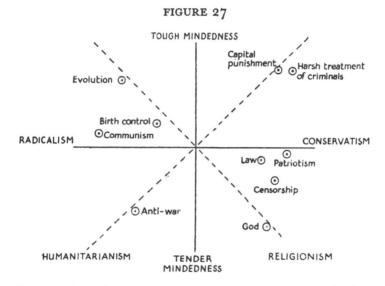

Distribution of Attitudes with Respect to Humanitarianism
and Religionism

Religionism nor Humanitarianism possessed. A proof of this type will be attempted in a later chapter, and the reader is asked to suspend his judgment until then and to accept for the time being a discussion in terms of our own two factors R and T.

Another important set of studies in connection with the problem of attitude organization is contained in a book by Adorno, Frenkel-Brunswik, Levinson and Sanford, called *The Authoritarian Personality*. These authors set out from a rather different point of departure; their interest lay primarily in trying to account for the emergence of anti-Semitism. As a first step they constructed five scales, 'dealing respectively with imagery (opinions) of Jews as personally *offensive* and as socially *threatening*; with attitudes concerning what should be done to or against Jews; and with the opposing views that Jews are too *seclusive* or too *intrusive* (assimilative).'

High correlations were found between these five scales and consequently they were amalgamated into one general anti-Semitism (A-S) scale.

The next step was the construction of an ethnocentric scale, referred to as the 'E' scale. This scale was made up of three sub-scales, dealing respectively with negroes, various other minorities, and patriotism (extra-national groupings). Again, correlations were high between the sub-scales, and anti-Semitism was found to correlate ·8 with the total E scale. Accordingly, these writers conclude that 'Anti-Semitism is best regarded . . . as one aspect of this broader frame of mind; and it is the total ethnocentric ideology rather than prejudice against any single group which requires explanation'.

The third step was the construction of a scale of politico-economic Conservatism (PEC). This was found to correlate with anti-Semitism to the extent of ·43 and with ethnocentrism to the extent of ·59, thus showing quite clearly that the marked relationship between Conservatism and ethnocentrism which we had found in this country obtains also in the United States.

So far, there is nothing very new or original in this work. The writers, starting out with one single item (anti-Semitism) in the tough-minded Conservative quadrant have shown that this item correlates highly with other items (ethnocentrism) in the same quadrant, and also correlates somewhat less highly with Conservatism. These results confirm the previous analysis of Ferguson, Eysenck, and others. However, the next step taken by this group is a distinct advance on previous work and deserves to be described in some detail.

The hypothesis leading to this next step is well set out by the authors of *The Authoritarian Personality* themselves: 'There gradually evolved a plan for constructing a scale that would measure prejudice without appearing to have this aim and without mentioning the name of any minority group. . . . It was clear at the time the new scale was being planned that anti-Semitism (A-S) and ethnocentrism (E) were not merely matters of surface opinion but general tendencies, with sources, in part at least, deep within the structure of the person. Would it not be possible to construct a scale that would approach more directly these deeper, often unconscious forces? If so, and if this scale could be validated by means of later clinical studies, would we not have a better estimate of anti-democratic *potential* than could be obtained from the scales that were more openly ideological?'

It may be of interest to state briefly the hypotheses regarding the nature of this authoritarian-Fascist character which guided Adorno and his co-workers in their selection of items. In their view, authoritarianism was characterized by *conventionalism*, or the rigid adherence to conventional middle-class values; *authoritarian submission*, or a submissive uncritical attitude toward idealized moral authorities of the in-group; *authoritarian aggression*, or the tendency to be on the look-out for and to condemn, reject, and punish people who violate conventional values; *anti-intraception*, or opposition to the subjective, the imaginative, and the tender-minded; *superstition and stereotypy*, the belief in mystical determinants of the individual's fate—the disposition to think in rigid categories; *power and toughness*, preoccupation with the dominance-submission, strong-weak, leader-follower dimension; identification with power figures, exaggerated assertion of strength in attitudes; *destructiveness and cynicism*, generalized hostility, vilification of the human; *projectivity*, the disposition to believe that dangerous things go on in the world, the projection outwards of unconscious emotional impulses; *sex*, exaggerated concern for sexual 'goings-on'.

The items in this scale are reproduced below (Table XXIV). It was entitled the F scale because Adorno *et al.* considered it to be a measure of Fascist potential. This interpretation, however, as we shall very soon see, is in part at least erroneous as we have found Communists to make almost as high scores on this scale as Fascists, and consequently we shall in this book refer to the F-scale rather as the *authoritarianism* scale.

TABLE XXIV

*Authoritarianism Scale**

CONVENTIONALISM: Rigid adherence to conventional, middle-class values.
Obedience and respect for authority are the most important virtues children should learn.
A person who has bad manners, habits, and breeding can hardly expect to get along with decent people.

* Some items are repeated as they fall equally cogently under different headings.

If people would talk less and work more, everybody would be better off. The business man and the manufacturer are much more important to society than the artist and the professor.

AUTHORITARIAN SUBMISSION: Submissive, uncritical attitude toward idealized moral authorities of the in-group.

Obedience and respect for authority are the most important virtues children should learn.

Science has its place, but there are many important things that can never possibly be understood by the human mind.

Every person should have complete faith in some supernatural power whose decisions he obeys without question.

Young people sometimes get rebellious ideas, but as they grow up they ought to get over them and settle down.

What this country needs most, more than laws and political programs, is a few courageous, tireless, devoted leaders in whom the people can put their faith.

No sane, normal, decent person could ever think of hurting a close friend or relative.

Nobody ever learned anything really important except through suffering.

AUTHORITARIAN AGGRESSION: Tendency to be on the lookout for, and to condemn, reject, and punish people who violate conventional values.

A person who has bad manners, habits, and breeding can hardly expect to get along with decent people.

What the youth needs most is strict discipline, rugged determination, and the will to work and fight for family and country.

An insult to our honour should always be punished.

Sex crimes, such as rape and attacks on children, deserve more than mere imprisonment; such criminals ought to be publicly whipped, or worse.

There is hardly anything lower than a person who does not feel a great love, gratitude, and respect for his parents.

Most of our social problems would be solved if we could somehow get rid of the immoral, crooked, and feebleminded people.

If people would talk less and work more, everybody would be better off.

Homosexuals are hardly better than criminals and ought to be severely punished.

ANTI-INTRACEPTION: Opposition to the subjective, the imaginative, the tender-minded.

When a person has a problem or worry, it is best for him not to think about it, but to keep busy with more cheerful things.

Nowadays more and more people are prying into matters that should remain personal and private.

If people would talk less and work more, everybody would be better off.

The businessman and the manufacturer are much more important to society than the artist and the professor.

ATTITUDES, VALUES, AND INTERESTS

SUPERSTITION AND STEREOTYPY: The belief in mystical determinants of the individual's fate; the disposition to think in rigid categories.

Science has its place, but there are many important things that can never possibly be understood by the human mind.

Every person should have complete faith in some supernatural power whose decisions he obeys without question.

Some people are born with an urge to jump from high places.

People can be divided into two distinct classes: the weak and the strong.

Some day it will probably be shown that astrology can explain a lot of things.

Wars and social troubles may someday be ended by an earthquake or flood that will destroy the whole world.

POWER AND 'TOUGHNESS': Preoccupation with the dominance-submission, strong-weak, leader-follower dimension; identification with power figures; overemphasis upon the conventionalized attributes of the ego; exaggerated assertion of strength and toughness.

No weakness or difficulty can hold us back if we have enough will power.

What the youth needs most is strict discipline, rugged determination, and the will to work and fight for family and country.

An insult to our honour should always be punished.

It is best to use some prewar authorities in Germany to keep order and prevent chaos.

What this country needs most, more than laws and political programs, is a few courageous, tireless, devoted leaders in whom the people can put their faith.

People can be divided into two distinct classes: the weak and the strong.

Most people don't realize how much our lives are controlled by plots hatched in secret places.

DESTRUCTIVENESS AND CYNICISM: Generalized hostility, vilification of the human.

Human nature being what it is, there will always be war and conflict.

Familiarity breeds contempt.

PROJECTIVITY: The disposition to believe that wild and dangerous things go on in the world; the projection outwards of unconscious emotional impulses.

Nowadays when so many different kinds of people move around and mix together so much, a person has to protect himself especially carefully against catching an infection or disease from them.

Nowadays more and more people are prying into matters that should remain personal and private.

Wars and social troubles may someday be ended by an earthquake or flood that will destroy the whole world.

The wild sex life of the old Greeks and Romans was tame compared to some of the goings-on in this country, even in places where people might least expect it.

Most people don't realize how much our lives are controlled by plots hatched in secret places.

151

sex: Exaggerated concern with sexual 'goings-on'.
Sex crimes, such as rape and attacks on children, deserve more than mere imprisonment; such criminals ought to be publicly whipped, or worse.
The wild sex life of the old Greeks and Romans was tame compared to some of the goings-on in this country, even in places where people might least expect it.
Homosexuals are hardly better than criminals and ought to be severely punished.

Perusal of this scale will indicate immediately that many of its items are identical with those which characterize the tough-minded end of our second factor. Such items as flogging, the harsh treatment of criminals, the inevitability of war, and others, clearly fit in with this picture.

The majority of items, however, are of rather a different nature, and while we may entertain the hypothesis that the F-scale is essentially a measure of tough-mindedness direct experimental proof of such a belief is required. Before we turn to such a proof, however, we may look for one moment at another problem, namely, that of the internal consistency of the scale. Adorno *et al.* have shown that the reliability of the scale is in the neighbourhood of ·9, so that there is little doubt that the items tend to measure some common variable. The items intercorrelate, the average intercorrelation being ·13. Adorno and his colleagues have not carried out a factor analysis of the items in this scale, but have kindly made their unpublished material available to Dr. Melvin, who performed such an analysis. He found that a very strong general factor ran through all the items, thus confirming the main hypothesis of the Californian group on the basis of which the questionnaire was constructed. He also found a rather slight tendency for materialistic and aggressive items to cluster together and be opposed to a cluster of items dealing with superstition and submissiveness. This tendency of some of the items to form clusters was not strongly enough marked, however, to detract from the essential unitary nature of the F-scale.

Proof for the hypothesis that the F-scale is essentially a measure of tough-mindedness rather than of Fascism comes from the work of Dr. T. Coulter, who gave the F-scale and the R and T scales to a sample of 83 soldiers, who were neither Fascists nor Communists, to 43 male Communists, and to 43 male Fascists. The average score on the F-scale was 75 for the soldier group, 94 for the Communist group, and 159 for the Fascist group; the Communists scored significantly more 'Fascist minded' than did the soldiers. As regards intercorrelations of the scale, the F-scale correlated ·43 with tough-mindedness in the soldier group, ·63 in the Fascist group, and ·62 in the Communist group. Correlations with Radicalism were quite insignificant throughout. Thus, there is strong support in favour of the hypothesis that the F-scale is a measure of tough-mindedness and that it is not restricted to the measurement of *Conservative* authoritarianism.

Work on other correlates of authoritarianism has been carried out by F. H. Sanford, whose main interest was in the concept of leadership and the attitude of followers towards leaders. In his research he administered an eight-item authoritarian scale (similar to but shorter than the F-scale) to about 1,000 people as part of an hour-long interview on various aspects of leadership. In this interview, use was made of a large number of different devices, some of which will be mentioned below.

In one section of the interview, for instance, the following incomplete sentences were read to the interviewees, who had to complete them verbally. The answers were then collected, and coded and related to the authoritarian scores of the interviewees to give some idea of the general ideology of leadership. The questions used were:

1. In a democracy a leader must . . .
2. The President of the United States should be a man who . . .
3. Our country would be better off if our leaders in Washington were more . . .
4. Our military leaders must be men who are . . .
5. If there were a great emergency right around here people would need a leader who . . .
6. In a small neighbourhood group, a leader should be . . .
7. The best boss is one who tells you . . .

Answers to these seven questions showed that those with scores towards the authoritarian end of the scale tended to talk about leaders in stereotyped, moralistic terms. 'They say that leaders in a democracy should be "true Americans" and "men of good character" and that they should work hard and possess common sense. They appear to want leaders who are strong and who are possessed of in-group status. They prefer leaders who are "educated", "brave", and "strong", and they prefer a boss who tells them what to do. There appears, further, an element of "personalness" in the authoritarian's orientation to leaders. He appears not so much concerned with the leader's relation to the job to be done or to *all* the followers as he is concerned with the leader's relation to *him*, the follower. There is the general suggestion that the authoritarian has strong personal psychological needs to be met by the leader and he is concerned more with the leader's ability to meet these personal needs than he is with the leader's ability to meet the social needs inherent in the leadership situation. . . . The equalitarian behaviour in the presence of these stimulus items presents a contrasting picture . . . the equalitarians talk in terms of "fairness" and "kindness" and warmth when he reacts to distant leaders. Instead of power, strength and personal competence, they talk of the leader's personal democracy and responsiveness to people. Instead of emphasizing the leader's relation to the single follower, the equalitarian can think about the leader's orientation to the job to be done. And instead of thinking in terms of vague terms such as "good leader", he thinks in terms of more specific and function-flavoured terms ("quick acting"). The equalitarian does not appear to need strong and directive leadership, but he seems able to accept it when the situation demands it.'

In another part of the interview, the cartoon given on page 155 —(Figure 28) was shown to the interviewees, who had to give the answer implied in the empty balloon. They also had to complete another set of sentence completion items, which ran as follows:

'Followers who disagree with the leader should . . .'

'The leader who is not sure of himself should . . .'

'The leader who is very sure of himself will make people feel . . .'

'The leader who tells people exactly what to do and how to do it will make people feel . . .'

Sanford's interpretation of the results obtained from these devices were as follows:

'The people who score high on the A-E scale tend either definitely to accept strong leadership or definitely to reject it. We have good evidence that for them any directive authority is emotionally charged. Often this authority is immediately accepted. Sometimes it is immediately rejected. There is some support for the general interpretation that authority is rejected if it is perceived as weak or if it seems to go too far beyond conventional bounds of propriety. And then, perhaps, it is rejected most often when there is a safe way—like resigning from the group—to express rejection. The authoritarians appear to perceive with suspicion a leader who is "sure of himself" but to accept a leader who is described as actually doing very directive things—telling people exactly what to do. And their willingness to accept strong leadership may be behind their feeling that followers who disagree with the leader should be suppressed. The data on these functional items give us indications of a strongly ambivalent feeling toward leaders on the part of authoritarians. They accept direct authority but, when given half a chance, react to it with vigorous hostility.

FIGURE 28

Picture of Directive Leadership, Form for Male Respondents

'Equalitarians again demonstrate a relatively rational and relaxed feeling for leaders. In the face of strong authority, they are more inclined to observe calmly what will happen than to fly off immediately into either acceptance or rejection. They are tolerant of signs of weakness in a leader, and they are tolerant of great confidence. But they observe that the leader who tells people exactly what to do will be rejected. In the face of strongly directive leadership they adopt a rational, group-centered position instead of coming down with petulance and maladaptive resentment.'

The last part of the interview dealt with the feelings of the interviewees about women, teachers and the educated as leaders; they were also asked to nominate some great person, living or dead, whom they admired most, and another whom they did not admire. The results were very much as expected. People with high authoritarianism scores predominantly accepted prestigeful figures as leaders and rejected women, while interviewees low in authoritarianism were very unimpressed by mere status and accepted women as leaders. Authoritarians admired those figures who are symbols of power and conventional American values. 'In talking about their heroes they put emphasis on the power and prestige of the man they choose—his personal magnetism, his general but vaguely conceived competence, his statusful social role. And they demonstrate the previously noted bargaining or "what's in it for me?" relation with their heroes. For villains they appear to fix on those who have failed. Equalitarians admire the more humanitarian people. And they admire them for humanitarian reasons, thinking, as in the case of leaders, about the great person's feeling for people and his performance in their behalf. They also demonstrate again the ability to go beyond the narrow confines of egocentrism in demonstrating an interest in the personal history of their heroes and showing a concern for the heroes' political beliefs. They regard as villainous those who are seen as having insulted human rights and interfered with human welfare.'

Typical heroes of the authoritarians are Calvin Coolidge, Harry S. Truman, Herbert Hoover, Theodore Roosevelt and George Washington; typical heroes of the non-authoritarians are Jesus Christ, Dr. Ralph Bunche, Thomas Edison, Eleanor Roosevelt, and Benjamin Franklin.

In addition to discovering these various correlates of authoritarianism, Sanford also presents some data on the relationship between authoritarianism and personality; these will be dealt with in the next chapter.

Another writer who has systematically explored the structure of opinions and attitudes is Ross Stagner. His main concern throughout an important series of papers has been with the Fascist ideology, i.e. with items in our tough-minded Conservative quadrant.

Stagner's work has been guided by hypothesis to a much greater extent than has Ferguson's, and he has also tried to link up his findings with personality variables, such as aggressiveness. These

156

relations with personality will be discussed in some detail in a later chapter. Here we shall only be concerned with the actual structuring of attitudes found by him.

After a series of preliminary studies, Stagner finally drew up a scale of eighteen items, all of which were collected on the basis of a thorough perusal of the theoretical literature, and a considerable

TABLE XXV

Fascism Scale

1. Recovery has been delayed by the large number of strikes.
2. The U.S. should stop immigration to give American workers more jobs.
3. If we buy European made goods, we make the depression in this country last longer.
4. Building a bigger Navy would give men jobs and protect our foreign markets. so that should be done.
5. Most labor trouble happens only because of radical agitators.
6. The people who complain most about the depression wouldn't take a job if you gave it to them.
7. The unemployed should be given military training so our country could be protected in case of war.
8. Any able-bodied man could get a job right now if he tried hard enough.
9. Most people on relief are living in reasonable comfort.
10. We must protect our trade in the Philippines against the Japanese.
11. The government must first balance the budget.
12. CCC camps where the boys learned military discipline and self-control would be a good idea.
13. The president was justified in protecting U.S. interests in Cuba.
14. Labor unions are all right but we can't have strikes.
15. While raising the standard of living we must safeguard property rights as guaranteed by the Constitution.
16. The U.S. should make these European countries pay off their war debts.
17. Unemployment insurance would saddle us with a nation of idlers.
18. These unemployed organizations are just a bunch of chronic complainers.

amoun tof pretesting and item analysis, as relevant to Fascist beliefs. This scale is given above; the reader should bear in mind that it was drawn up in the United States during the great slump and that consequently many of the items are rather dated.

The correlations between these items were almost all positive, and Stagner went on to analyse them further by means of a factor-analytic study which showed three main components of this general Fascist complex. The first of these components he entitled: 'regard for property rights as opposed to human rights'. The questions most clearly delineating this aspect were (1) (Recovery has been delayed by the number of strikes); (9) (Most people on relief are living in reasonable comfort); (13) (The president was justified in protecting U.S. interests in Cuba); (14) (Labour unions are all right but we can't have strikes); and (15) (While raising the standard of living we must safeguard property rights as guaranteed by the constitution).

The second component he identified as 'middle-class consciousness'. It is shown by items such as (6) (The people who complain most about the depression wouldn't take a job if you gave it to them); (8) (Any able-bodied man could get a job right now if he tried hard enough); (17) (Unemployment insurance would saddle us with a nation of idlers); and (18) (These unemployment organizations are just a bunch of chronic complainers).

The third and last component he identified as 'agressive nationalism'; it is shown in items like (4) (Building a bigger navy would give men jobs and protect our foreign markets, so that is what should be done); (7) (The unemployed should be given military training so our country could be protected in case of war); (10) (We must protect our trade in the Phillipines against the Japanese); and (12) (CCC camps where the boys learned military discipline and self-control would be a good idea).

In view of the fact that many of the attitudes in the Fascist scale are somewhat aggressive, Stagner attempted to construct a scale which would indicate attitude towards the use of force in a social situation. Some of the items in this scale were as follows:

'FORCE SCALE'

5. 'The persecuted Jews in Germany should band themselves into a secret society and assassinate Hitler and his henchmen.'

7. 'If a labour union starts a riot, it is only proper to call out the National Guard and suppress this disturbance forcibly.'

10. 'Mussolini's sons claim that it was very good sport to drop bombs on terrified Ethiopians, to see them run like terrified game, to see them blown to unrecognizable bits. These Italian aviators should be tied to stakes in an open field and subjected to bombing from planes overhead.'

This scale was correlated with the Fascism scale as well as with scales measuring attitude towards war, nationalism, intolerance, and capital punishment, the hypothesis being that the tendency towards the aggressive use of force would be found to characterize all these different attitudes. All the correlations were found to be relatively high—correlations between the 'force' scale and the others ranged from ·41 to ·44—and there appears to be little doubt that Stagner's original hypothesis was verified.

Stagner attempted to obtain evidence of the validity of the scales from personal interviews with the subjects and from other special observations and concluded that all of the scales had sufficient value to justify further study. He also compared scores of Radical and Conservative groups and found that in each case the Conservatives had significantly more forceful, aggressive attitudes, which is very much what we should have expected on the basis of our own findings.

Stagner's experiments are of considerable historical importance and have established a number of conclusions which have been confirmed by later work. The main criticism of his studies must be that they were limited to a very small sector of the whole field of attitudes and that in the absence of the larger view, made possible by more extensive sampling of attitudes, his conclusions remain inevitably somewhat restricted.

Hitherto in our discussion of the structure of attitudes, we have only dealt with what are customarily called social attitudes; we have not dealt with certain other concepts which bear some relation to the attitude field, although they customarily go by different names. The two most obvious concepts here are those of *values* and those of *interests*.

Values are often thought of as belonging to philosophy rather than psychology. Their intrusion into the psychological field, particularly the field of personality, is due largely to the German psychologist Spranger, who in his book *Types of Men* tried to classify people in accordance with the main values which they hold and which activate their behaviour.

The first of these values he called *theoretical*, implying a dominant interest in the discovery of truth. The person activated by theoretical values characteristically takes a cognitive attitude, divesting itself of judgments regarding the beauty or utility of objects and seeking only to observe and to reason. Since his main interests are empirical, critical, and rational, the theoretical man is necessarily an intellectualist, frequently a scientist, or a philosopher, whose chief aim in life is to order and systematize his knowledge.* In case this may appear a somewhat exalted method of classification, it should be emphasized that a high degree of talent or attainment is not necessary to qualify a person for classification in this or in any other type. It is not by his achievements but by his interests or intentions that Spranger would classify a person.

The dominant interest of a person with *economic* values is in what is useful. Starting out with the satisfaction of bodily needs his interest in utilities extends to practical affairs of the business world, the production, marketing, and consumption of goods, and the accumulation of wealth. As opposed to the theoretical man, the economic type is eminently practical. His one-sided regard for utility usually leads to a certain opposition to other values. Aesthetic, theoretical, and religious values, for instance, only exist for him in so far as they serve useful ends; their pursuit for their own sake appears to him frivolous, abnormal, introverted, or highbrow.

A person whose values lie in the *aesthetic* field judges experiences from the standpoint of grace, symmetry, or fitness, having highest esteem for form and harmony. Such a person need not himself be a creative artist; it is sufficient that he should find his chief interest in the artistic and aesthetic aspects of life. This general attitude colours his outlook towards other values. Thus, in the field of religion, the aesthetic man is likely to confuse beauty of ceremony with purer religious experience. In the social field this type may be interested in persons, but not in the welfare of people.

In this he is strongly opposed by the *social* type, whose highest value is love of people. The social man prizes other persons as ends and therefore tends to take an altruistic or philanthropic view, being himself kind, sympathetic, and unselfish. He regards love as the only suitable form of human relationship.

A person whose main value is the *political* is also primarily interested in social relations, but for the concept of love he substitutes that of power. Competition and struggle are the ruling concepts in his philosophy and he would tend not only to regard power as the most universal and most fundamental of motives, but also to seek

* A better name for this value might be 'scientific' rather than 'theoretical'; the main interest is in *knowledge* rather than in *speculation*. The German term *Wissenschaft* and its straightforward translation may be somewhat misleading.

for a direct expression of this motive. He is characterized, there-fore, above all by a desire for personal power, and influence.

The *religious* type is probably the easiest to characterize, although it should be mentioned that Spranger in his delineation of this type seeks to go beyond the simple conventionalities of church-going to mystical religious experiences.

These, then, are Spranger's six types of men, each governed by a different value. It will be noted that these values are all some-what exalted and that more lowly sensuous kinds of values are not included in this account. In spite of this obvious limitation, and in spite of the fact that Spranger admits that many people are not pure examples of any of his types but show them in various mix-tures, his set of concepts has become widely known, and has proved useful in both theoretical analysis and practical work. It has achieved positive results largely through the work of Allport and Vernon, who made an early attempt at the construction of a ques-tionnaire which would reveal the dominant value patterns of their subjects. [18]Their 'Study of Values' consists of two parts, in the first of which the subject has to make a choice between two alternatives, each of them implying a separate value, whereas in the second part four alternative answers to each question are provided, one of which has to be chosen by the subject. A few examples of the kind of question which might be used in such an inventory may make the point clearer.

'If you had a choice of reading one or the other of two books, would you prefer one dealing with (a) religion, or (b) economics?'

'At your University, would you prefer to join (a) a political club, or (b) the college orchestra?'

'If you had the choice, would you prefer (a) to read a book set-ting forth the results of recent research on the causes of war, or (b) take an active part in helping the victims of former wars?'

'If you had the choice of reading a biography of one of the fol-lowing, which would you choose?

    (a) Caesar
    (b) Newton
    (c) Lord Nuffield
    (d) Thomas Aquinas.'

(In this last type of question the subject would be required to rank the four in order of preference.)

Altogether, the Study of Values asks the subject to provide 120 answers, 20 of which refer to each of the six values. Reliabilities of the scale are reasonably high, ranging from ·73, for the theoretical value, to ·90 for the religious value, with a mean reliability of ·82.

The reader will have formed some *a priori* views of the relation between these six attitudes and our T and R factors on reading through the description of Spranger's types. It seems fairly obvious that the political and economic values would lie in the tough-minded Conservative quadrant, the theoretical in the tough-minded Radical, the social value in the tender-minded Radical, and the religious in the tender-minded Conservative quadrant. The aesthetic value is difficult to place on *a priori* grounds, although it seems to be opposed to the political and economic values more than to any of the others.

The evidence appears to support such a view. The first attempt to carry out a factor analysis of the Allport-Vernon test was made by Lurie. This author used 24 scores obtained from the various items of the Allport-Vernon test, and found four main factors. 'Factor I is clearly *social* and altruistic, a factor having to do with the valuing of human relations, as such. . . . The second is complex, involving items supposed to correspond to Spranger's economic and political types, and inversely to the aesthetic type; one might call this pattern the *Philistine* type, aggressive, go-getting, utilitarian, anti-cultural. Factor III is plainly *theoretical* . . . number IV is a *religious* type, probably more closely connected with doctrine and practice than the vague mystical unity with the cosmos that Spranger envisaged.' These four types appear to correspond perfectly to the four quadrants of our R-T model, the Philistine being the tough-minded Conservative, the theoretical corresponding to the tough-minded Radical, the social to the tender-minded Radical, and the religious to the tender-minded Conservative.

Lurie had used a number of independently derived scores for his analysis in order to get over a difficulty which arises in connection with the somewhat unusual scoring system of the study of values. As will have been seen from our examples, endorsing one value in any one item automatically makes it impossible to endorse the other values in that item; consequently, there will be a spurious tendency for all values to be negatively correlated. In spite of this difficulty, Duffy and Crissy carried out an analysis of the correlations between the original six value scores and obtained congruent results. Their first factor opposes the economic and political values to the aesthetic and religious values, and is called by them 'Philistine', following Lurie's example. The second factor has high loadings on social and religious values as opposed to theoretical one and is called by them 'social', or interest in people. The last factor has high loadings on theoretical as opposed to political and religious, and is called by them 'theoretical', or interest in science.

More recent and much more convincing than these earlier attempts is a study by Brogden, who intercorrelated 60 items from the scale and factor analysed the results. He obtained a number of primary factors, which were themselves intercorrelated, giving rise to several higher-order factors of which only one, however, was of any considerable importance. This one he entitles 'idealism versus practicality', and it is interesting to note that it appears to correspond very closely indeed to our concept of tough-mindedness versus tender-mindedness. This becomes clear from a consideration of some of the items having highest correlations with this factor, and also from Brogden's discussion of his own interpretation of it. Here are some of the items characterizing the 'idealistic' (tender-minded) as opposed to the 'practical' (tough-minded) person.

'He is more interested in reading accounts of the lives and works of such men as Aristotle, Plato, and Socrates; than of such men as Alexander, Julius Caesar, and Charlemagne.

'If he had unlimited leisure and money, he would prefer to make a collection of fine sculptures or paintings; rather than establish a mental hygiene clinic for taking care of the maladjusted and mentally deficient, aim at a senatorship or a seat in the Cabinet, or enter into banking and high finance.

'Assuming that he had the necessary ability and that the salary for each of the following occupations was the same, he would prefer to be a mathematician, clerygman or politician; rather than a sales manager.

'He would prefer a friend of his own sex who is seriously interested in thinking out his attitude toward life as a whole; rather than one who is efficient, industrious, and of a practical turn of mind, one who possesses qualities of leadership and organizing ability, or one who shows refinement and emotional sensitivity.

'He believes that one should guide one's conduct according to, or develop one's chief loyalties toward, one's ideals of beauty; rather than one's religious faith, one's business organizations and associates, or society as a whole.

'He believes that a man who works in business all week can best spend Sunday in trying to educate himself by reading serious books, going to an orchestral concert, or hearing a really good sermon; rather than by trying to win at golf or racing.

'During his next summer vacation he would prefer to write and publish an original biological essay or article; rather than stay in some secluded part of the country where he could appreciate fine scenery, compete in a local tennis or other athletic tournament, or get experience in some new line of business.

'He believes that good government should aim at more aid for the poor, sick, and old; rather than the development of manufacturing and trade, introduction of more ethical principles into its politics and diplomacy, or the establishing of a position of prestige and respect among nations.

'Florence Nightingale interests and attracts him more than Napoleon, Henry Ford, or Charles Darwin.

'He would prefer to hear a series of lectures on the comparative development of the great religious faiths rather than the comparative merits of the forms of government in Britain and the United States.'

This is what Brogden has to say about his factor: 'In terms of the content of the variables as shown by the Allport-Vernon scoring key for the Test of Values (this) Factor . . . is heavily anti-political and anti-economic. To a somewhat lesser degree content scored as social, aesthetic, and theoretic is evident among the alternatives having positive correlation with (this) Factor. A number of the variables involving alternatives scored as religious have high loading. . . . Persons scoring high . . . may be characterized as idealistic, if the following restricted interpretation of the term is kept in mind. Idealistic, as we will use the term, characterizes individuals who evaluate highly concepts and beliefs which are aimed at the solution of the problem of the ideal social structure, the ideal manner of life, and who evaluate highly those aspects of our present day and of past cultures which they believe to be improvements over the usual, accepted, or conventional set of values. In line with this tendency, the individual high on (this) Factor appears to evaluate contemplation more highly than direct action. This latter tendency is further evidenced in aesthetic preferences that the more practical individual would regard as esoteric, involved, or "high brow".'

'It was indicated in the foregoing discussion that items on the positive pole were, according to the scoring key for the test, aesthetic, social, and theoretic in content. The comments in the preceding paragraph suggest a reasonable hypothesis as to the common component in high evaluation of these apparently different types of content. The first two of these three types of content suggest idealism with respect to cultural development of the individual, and with respect to human relations and the structure of society. Idealism, as we use the term, is logically related to high evaluation of theoretic items, since speculation, contemplation, or theorizing is a necessary activity of individuals who concern themselves with "how things should be" rather than accept "things as they are". There is the further suggestion that individuals scoring high on (this) Factor may evaluate more highly what they have acquired through the schools, through reading, and through contact with what might be termed cultural influences. They appear, in other words, to have been more heavily influenced by such aspects of our present-day culture than by the everyday world of practical affairs.'

'Individuals who are low scoring or on the negative pole . . . are characterized in part by a tendency toward low evaluation of variables with social, aesthetic, and theoretic content. Such individuals appear to be unconcerned with the problem of "how things should be" but accept the "things as they are" and evaluate favourably those things which are related to effective action within the framework of the accepted set of values of the dominant "we group" of our present-day culture. On a somewhat more tenuous basis, the author suggests that the low-scoring individuals, because they accept "things as they are" and are concerned with effective action within this framework, react with antagonism, lack of patience, lack of understanding, or disparagement toward refusal to accept "things as they are".'

So far our evidence linking values with the R-T framework has been based on interpretation of research findings rather than on direct correlation. A more direct proof is provided in the work of George, who has intercorrelated R and T scores with scores on the six Spranger values. Results are in line with prediction; Figure 30 in the next chapter, shows the findings in diagrammatic form, as well as the relationship of factors and values to various temperamental variables. (Cf. p. 178.)

After values, interests. This term is often used in popular opinion as an alternative to the term attitudes. To say, 'I am interested in Socialism or Religion or Conservatism' is almost synonymous with saying, 'I have a positive attitude toward Socialism or Religion or Conservatism'. In the psychological literature, however, the two terms have acquired different meanings, 'attitude' referring to social attitudes largely, whereas 'interests' refers to vocational and occupational interests of one kind or another. It seems reasonable to believe that if our T-factor is as all-embracing and fundamental as we believe it to be, then it should also be found to intercorrelate with certain patterns of interests as defined.

Many different instruments have been used for the measurement of interests, but the only one which has proved its value, both from the theoretical and the practical point of view, is the Strong Vocational Interest Blank. This Blank is a device by means of which patterns of interest characteristic of members of different trades and professions can be determined. It consists of 400 items, to each of which the subject responds by indicating whether he likes, dislikes, or is indifferent to that item. 100 items refer to occupations; the remaining 300 refer to amusements like golf and fishing, to school subjects, and to activities and peculiarities of people. Other parts of the Blank call for an indication of most and least liked activities from a given list; preference judgments between alternate choices; and estimates of one's abilities and characteristics.

In its construction the Strong Inventory resembles earlier attempts at constructing measures which would predict a person's success in a given field, the method being the very simple one of asking him to express a liking or a dislike of various occupations, and then making the predictions in terms of these preference judgments directly. Thus, if a person endorsed 'Like very much' as a reply to the question: 'Would you like to be a book-keeper?', the prediction was made that, given the requisite abilities, he would make a success of this particular job. It was soon found that this procedure was extremely fallible. In the first place, such endorsements were found to possess very low reliabilities, being subject to considerable change, even within a relatively short period. In the second place, it was found that few people knew very much about most of the professions and occupations towards which they endorsed an opinion, and that consequently their endorsements had no real predictive value.

Strong, although using an Inventory constructed on similar principles, altered the scoring system and the interpretation to such an extent that his work bears no real relation to that of the earlier students. Essentially, his argument runs as follows: People who are successfully employed in a given occupation tend to have a certain pattern of interests, i.e. if 500 of them fill in a questionnaire of this type they will tend to distribute their answers in accordance with a certain pattern which will differ from the pattern shown by a group of 500 people in some other occupation. A person's likelihood to be successful and happy in a given occupation will depend, not on his saying that he likes that occupation very much, but on his giving a pattern of answers which resembles closely that given on the average by members of the profession to which he aspires. This was the *a priori* argument put forward by Strong, and there is overwhelming evidence to show that in its essential points his argument is correct. This is not the place to summarize the evidence; suffice it to say that for vocational guidance, no other test has been found more successful in predicting a person's likelihood of success than the Strong Inventory. (We are excepting from this statement all test of ability, of course, as lack of ability is obviously something that cannot be compensated for in any way whatever. The statement applies to all efforts advising candidates possessing the requisite ability as to which of several professions they would be most likely to succeed in.)

The average pattern of interests for some forty occupations has been studied by Strong, who in each case used large enough numbers to make the results relatively stable. It is possible to determine the degree of resemblance between any two patterns by means of correlations, and, as one might have expected, considerable similarities and dissimilarities have been discovered. Indeed, we would expect, on *a priori* grounds, the patterns of the physicist and the chemist, say, to agree with each other, and to disagree with the patterns made by the theologian, or the lawyer, or the businessman. One of the earliest attempts to carry out a factor analysis of such correlations was reported by Thurstone, who discovered four main interest factors, which he labelled 'Interest in Science', 'Interest in Language', 'Interest in People', and 'Interest in Business'. Interest in science characterized most of all chemists, engineers, psychologists, medical people, and architects; the lowest interest in science was evinced by life insurance salesmen, real estate agents and advertising men. Interest in language was evinced most by advertising men, lawyers, preachers, journalists, and artists; the lowest interest in language was shown by farmers, engineers, and purchasing agents. Interest in people characterized preachers, teachers, personnel managers, and Y.M.C.A. secretaries. Interest in business was highest in real estate agents, certified public accountants, lawyers, life insurance salesmen, and purchasing agents. It was lowest in preachers, teachers, and psychologists.

These four factors show some degree of correspondence with our R and T scheme. Interest in business would fall into the tough-minded Conservative quadrant; interest in people in the tender-minded Radical quadrant; and interest in science in the tough-minded Radical quadrant. Interest in language does not seem to find any counterpart in our scheme; it certainly could not be directly identified with the tender-minded Conservative quadrant, although preachers have the highest score in this.

No formal experiment has been done to identify the exact positions of the various interests with respect to the R and T factors, but there is a good deal of evidence relating interests to values. Duffy and Crissy, for instance, in the research mentioned already, found people with interests typical of lawyers to score high on economic and political values, and low on aesthetic and religious values. People with interests similar to those of physicians scored high on theoretical values, people with interests similar to those of authors and writers high on aesthetic and low on economic and social values, whereas people with interests similar to those of a nurse showed the opposite pattern, having high social and low aesthetic values. People with interests like those of office workers had high values on economic and political, and low values on the aesthetic and theoretical scales.

In another study, van Dusen *et al.* found that economic values had a high relation with the interest patterns of office clerks and certified public accountants. Theoretical values were positively related to the interest patterns of schoolteachers and engineers, while in examining the vocational choices of the aesthetic group, seventeen in the highest quartile were found to have chosen an aesthetic vocation as compared with only three in the lowest quartile.

Many other studies have given similar results, and Super has summed them up in the following way: '. . . numerous studies have shown that professional students are differentiated by the Study of Values in accordance with expectation. *Theoretical* values are found in students of education, engineering, medicine, natural science, and social studies. *Economic* values characterize only students of business. *Aesthetic* values are strong in students of drama, education, literature, and the social studies. *Social* values have not so frequently been studied, as the scale is not reliable enough for individual diagnosis; it is adequate for the study of group trends, which show that YWCA secretaries stand high on it, but, surprisingly, that students majoring in the social studies tend to make low scores. *Political* values are significantly high in engineering students, physical education students, and law students. *Religious* values have been found to be high in seminarians and in YWCA secretaries.'

It is not necessary to go further into the hundred or so studies which might be quoted in connection with the Strong Vocational Interest Blank; the evidence is fairly conclusive that values as measured by the Allport-Vernon Scale are closely related to interest patterns and that these interest patterns show a structure well in line with our T factor. Direct evidence on this point for an English population, unfortunately, is not available and until it is forthcoming any further discussion would be merely speculative.

We may summarise this chapter by saying that results obtained by investigators in the United States in the attitude field are remarkably similar to those achieved in this country; that people's values, as measured by the Allport-Vernon Scale, are structured in a manner which is very similar to that indicated by attitude studies; and that vocational interests also agree to a remarkable extent with this pattern. It is possible to conclude, therefore, that the principles of structuring indicated in the previous chapter have a much wider generality than might at first have been supposed, and touch intimately upon features of the personality superficially remote from the field of social attitudes.

Chapter Six

IDEOLOGY AND TEMPERAMENT

In the previous two chapters the reader may have noticed one peculiarity which appears particularly clearly in Figures 23 and 27. It will be seen there that not a single attitude statement can be found which measures the T-factor without any admixture of Radical or Conservative content. This tendency is very striking in both figures; the whole quadrants centring around the T-axis in both its positive and its negative aspects are quite empty of any attitude statement whatever.

Such a phenomenon is certainly strange, particularly as it appears in two quite different sets of investigations, namely those carried out by Ferguson and by workers in the Maudsley laboratories. It might of course be ascribed entirely to chance, but in science it is often rewarding to pay attention to unexpected and unpredicted features of the record, and an explanation might appear to be called for.

The clue to a possible explanation has already been given in our first discussion of the T-factor, and indeed is adumbrated in the very terms 'tough-minded' and 'tender-minded' used to describe this factor. It will be remembered that William James used these terms essentially to denote qualities of character and personality which exert their influence on a person's philosophy and presumably on his social attitudes also. We might therefore frame an hypothesis to the effect that there is in truth only one ideological factor present in the attitude field, namely that of Radicalism-Conservatism. The T-factor itself does not constitute an alternative ideological system but is rather *the projection on to the social attitude field of a set of personality variables.*

Thus, according to this hypothesis individuals would be distributed along the Radicalism-Conservatism continuum in line with their social attitudes; the way in which these social attitudes are expressed, whether in a religious or semi-Fascist way on the right, or in a Pacifist or Communist way on the left, would depend on the temperamental peculiarities of the people holding these views.

It need hardly be said that the data which we have collected so far do not prove this hypothesis; they merely suggest that the rather extraordinary phenomenon noted at the beginning of this chapter might find a common-sense and reasonable explanation along these lines. In this chapter we shall be concerned mainly with an attempt to prove the correctness of this hypothesis and to show in some detail what are the personality variables concerned.

Before we can answer this question, however, it will obviously be essential to decide the terms in which we can phrase such an answer. The description of personality is a very thorny problem in psychology. It has been dealt with in great detail in the author's book *The Structure of Human Personality*, and there is no intention here of repeating the arguments set down there, or quoting the large number of books and papers surveyed. Instead, only a brief dogmatic statement of the main conclusions will be given.

The man in the street, when asked to describe someone's personality, will almost invariably do so in terms of either *traits* or *types*. He may say that his friend is courageous, has a sense of humour, is somewhat rigid and tends to be talkative. He would thus be positing traits of humorousness, rigidity, talkativeness and courage, and he would further assert that his friend had a more than average endowment with respect to these traits.

Alternatively the description might be in terms of types. He might describe his friend as being a sociable type, or a talkative type, and so forth. As used in common parlance then, the words *trait* and *type* would be almost synonymous. Scientists prefer not to waste useful terms in order to denote something already denoted by another term, and consequently in technical psychology the two terms are used in a rather different way. The term trait is used in much the same way as it is in common parlance; the term type, however, is used as denoting a whole system of traits. Thus, for instance, Jung's famous introverted type would be characterized by a *set* of traits such as persistence, subjectivity, shyness, irritability, introspectiveness, and so forth. The term *type*, therefore, is more inclusive than the term *trait*, and indeed it is defined by the observed correlation of a number of traits.

This difference in verbal usage, however, is not the only difference between the way in which psychologists and laymen use these terms. The layman is quite happy to invent new traits to cover any observed behaviour whatever, and feels under no obligation to prove that the hypothetical traits which he is invoking can in any reasonable sense be said to exist. Occasionally the difficulties which arise in this common sense use of the terms becomes obvious, and then finer distinctions may be made. Thus the trait 'courageous' may be split up when it is found that people who are courageous in one situation may not be so in another. The person who shows a great deal of military courage in the field of battle may show very little civil courage in standing up for his democratic rights. The V.C. may faint at the sight of the dentist's drill. These exceptions to the assumed universality of a trait are very serious as they obviously cast doubts on the existence of the traits hypothesized and as they make difficult, if not impossible, any kind of accurate prediction. The term 'courageous' is useful only if it can be taken to mean (a) that the courageous person has always behaved in a certain fashion when confronted with threatening situations, and (b) that the courageous person will continue to behave in this manner when confronted with similar situations. Admit once that he may not always behave in such a fashion, and the whole usefulness of the concept disappears as we can never be sure to what precise situation our predictions will apply.

Much the same must be said about the use of the term type. The concept of type is useful only if it enables us to create some kind of order out of the vast multiplicity of actions in which people indulge; the moment we find that exceptions to such generally consistent behaviour are more frequent than adherence to the rules, the concept begins to lose its value. It is for this reason that psychologists have laid down certain rules which must be fulfilled if the terms trait and type are to be employed in any useful fashion.

The first of these rules is that the conduct in question should be measurable. In the early parts of the century much reliance was placed on ratings in which a given judge would rate a number of people, whom he knew well, with respect to the degree to which they possessed certain traits. It was very soon found, however, that this method possessed many disadvantages. The judges did not always agree on the meaning of the terms employed, for instance. Thus when asked to rate people on their possession of 'sense of humour' some judges might understand this to mean 'ability to make jokes spontaneously'. Others might take it to mean 'ability to understand jokes and laugh in the right place'. Others yet might take it to mean 'being always in a good humour and not minding jokes being played on one'. There is no reason to assume that a person showing one of these qualities would also show the others, and consequently judges apparently judging the same quality might in reality be judging entirely different things. Even when verbal agreement on the meaning of the terms used was insisted on, it was soon found that judges tended to invest the subjects with a 'halo'; in other words, they tended to like some and dislike others, and to attribute all the good qualities to those they liked, and all the bad qualities to those they disliked. These and many other difficulties soon made it clear that human beings are not very good judges of personal qualities, and consequently interest became centred on more objective and reliable methods of measurement.

The second way in which psychologists differ from laymen in their approach is in their insistence on obtaining some numerical estimate of the degree to which people tend to manifest the same trait in different circumstances. As an example let us take the hypothetical trait of 'persistence'. If we wanted to measure this trait we would first of all design a number of objective situations in which our subjects could demonstrate their persistence. Thus as our first test we might ask them to pick up a dumb-bell and hold it out sideways as long as they could, the time being a measure of their degree of persistence. As a second test we might give them a jigsaw puzzle from which some of the pieces had been removed and others substituted, so as to make the task impossible of solution; the length of time during which they continued with this activity would be taken as a measure of their persistence. As a third test we might give them the word 'generations' and ask them to use the letters in this word to make up as many new words as they could, again using the time as a measure of persistence.

When 20 or 30 tests of this type are administered to large groups of subjects it is found that the original hypothesis, namely that all these tests measure the same trait of 'persistence' is indeed verified; all the tests correlate positively with each other, thus showing that a person who is persistent in one test also tends to be persistent in the other tests, and conversely that a person lacking in persistence in one test will also be lacking in persistence in the others.

As a third and last step in our procedure, we should require some evidence of the validity of our particular set of tests. In the case of persistence we should find, for instance, that ratings by teachers, school friends, and others show relatively high correlations with our objective tests; that observations of high scorers and low scorers in live situations involving persistence show their behaviour to be congruent with their test scores; and lastly, that the test scores would enable us to predict with a certain amount of success the ability of our subjects to reach their goals in school and university, even after the influence of intelligence had been eliminated. Without such evidence of validity, few psychologists would regard the alleged trait of persistence as being reasonably well established.*

Similarly, in positing a personality type psychologists look for definite proof that the traits which are supposed to characterize the particular type in question are actually correlated. Thus in our example of the introverted type we would ask for direct evidence that tests of persistence, subjectivity, shyness, irritability, and so on, intercorrelate with each other at a reasonable level. Without such proofs the alleged 'type' remains entirely at a theoretical level and lacks any real proof for its existence.

We are now in a position to state in somewhat more detail the exact hypothesis which we shall be investigating. We shall suggest that 'tough-mindedness' is a projection on to the field of social attitudes of the *extraverted* personality type, while 'tender-mindedness' is a projection of the *introverted* personality type. Before turning to a proof of this hypothesis let us first briefly discuss this concept of extraversion-introversion. Unfortunately these terms have been used so widely by non-psychological writers and by the man in the street that they have lost almost entirely the meaning which they originally carried, and to which we must revert here. The terms *extravert* and *introvert* were used by the psychiatrist Jung to refer to two types of personality which are antithetical to each other and which had in essence been described by several other writers before him, notably by the English psychologist Furneaux Jordan and by the Austrian psychiatrist Otto Gross.

* The concept of 'trait' will be seen to have certain points in common with the concept of 'attitude'. Technical Note 19 discusses the question of their differentiation.

Jordan had posited an antithesis between the *reflective* and the *active* type of person; he went on to point out that the reflective type tended to be more emotional, the active type less emotional. Gross added to this hypothesis a physiological theory of how this distinction might have come about. It was not however until Jung popularized and extended these concepts that they were really widely accepted among psychologists.

Jung states very extensively all the personality traits which characterize the introvert and the extravert respectively; they all derive from the fundamental fact that the extravert has turned his interests and his instinctual energies *outwards*, i.e. towards the world of objective reality, while the introvert has turned his interests and his instinctual energies *inwards*, i.e. towards himself. 'Quite generally one might characterize the introvert point of view by pointing to the constant subjection of the object and objective reality to the ego and the subjective psychological process . . . according to the extraverted point of view the subject is considered as inferior to the object; the importance of the subjective aspect is only secondary.' Apart from this fundamental distinction the extravert emerges as a person who values the outer world both in its material and in its immaterial aspects (possessions, riches, power, prestige), he shows outward physical activity while the introvert's activity is mainly in the mental, intellectual sphere. The extravert is changeable and his emotions are easily aroused, but never very deeply; he is relatively insensitive, impressionable, experimental, materialistic and tough-minded. The differentiation between extravert and introvert according to Jung lies at the basis of the great dichotomy which we find in neurotic illnesses. The extravert is prone to disorders like hysteria and psychopathy, i.e. asocial illnesses in which moral rules tend to be disregarded. The introvert, on the other hand, is more liable to disorders involving manifestations of anxiety, depression and obsessional-compulsive features.

The evidence regarding the Jungian hypothesis has been reviewed in great detail in *The Structure of Human Personality*, and it appears that the great majority of studies carried out in this field supported it strongly. There does appear to exist a concatenation of traits such as is posited in Jung's hypothesis, and it also appears that those situated towards the extraverted end of the continuum tend to develop symptoms of the hysterical, psychopathic type during periods of emotional instability, while those towards the introverted end develop symptoms of anxiety and depression during periods of emotional instability.

Support for this view comes from a variety of sources making use of many different methods of investigation. Thus we have studies made of ratings, of questionnaires and inventories, of objective behaviour, of physique, of physiological measures, and of what are called 'projective techniques', all supporting the Jungian hypothesis. In the experiments to be described now three techniques have been used because of the ease with which the various instruments could be transported and applied outside the confines of the laboratory. The first of these instruments is the questionnaire, or personality inventory.

For many years questionnaires have been constructed, mainly by American authors, for the measurement of 'extraversion-introversion'. These efforts were entirely unsuccessful, largely because of two reasons. In the first place the instruments were constructed on an *a priori* basis rather than on an empirical one; in the second place investigators appear to have misunderstood or rejected Jung's view of introversion, which regards it as something entirely different from and unrelated to emotional instability or neuroticism, and to have accepted rather Freud's view which identifies these two concepts. Consequently questionnaires of introversion were found to measure exactly the same personal qualities as did questionnaires of neuroticism.

This disappointing outcome to the considerable amount of work done in this field has prejudiced many people against the use of questionnaires. However, Guilford succeeded in showing that by the use of a much more critical and analytical method of scale construction he could overcome the difficulties which had been fatal to the early attempts. He succeeded in constructing a number of scales for the measurement of different traits such as those of sociability, ascendancy, masculinity, quarrelsomeness, nervousness, depression and so forth. These traits were themselves found to be intercorrelated and to give rise to two main factors or 'types'. One of these factors was the all-pervasive one called emotional instability or *neuroticism*. The other was extraversion-introversion. The scale which succeeded best in measuring this trait of extraversion Guilford had called 'rhathymia' or carefreeness. The actual inter-relationship of the various scales is shown in Figure 29. It will be seen that Scales D (Depression), C (Instability), and T (Introspectiveness) are good and almost pure measures of neuroticism, while Scale R (Carefreeness) is an almost pure measure of extraversion. Scale S (Sociability) is a measure of both extraversion and lack of neuroticism. Experimental proof of this identification of the two factors has been given by Hildebrand, who showed that scales S, C, and T discriminated between normal and neurotic

FIGURE 29

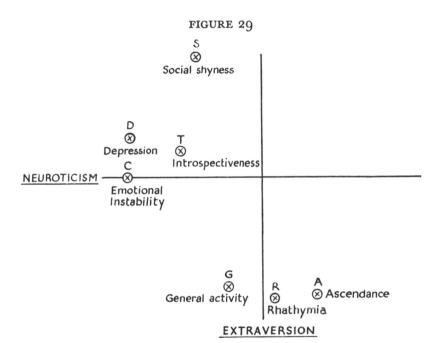

Position of Various Guilford Questionnaires with Respect to Neuroticism and Extraversion

subjects, while the R scale discriminated between hysterics and psychopaths on the one hand, and depressive, anxious, and obsessional patients on the other. The S scale, as predicted, discriminated between all the groups, and may be regarded as a measure of both extraversion and neuroticism.

E. I. George applied the Allport-Vernon Values scales, the R- and T-scales, as well as the Guilford questionnaires S, T, D, C, and R to groups of middle-class male and female Conservatives, Liberals, and Socialists. As it proved difficult to find sufficient

Liberals, males and females were not treated separately; for the other two parties, separate analyses were carried out for the two sexes. The analysis consisted in intercorrelating the scales and factor-analysing the resulting table of correlations. Figure 30 shows the first two factors extracted from an analysis the results of the total group of 500 people.

FIGURE 30

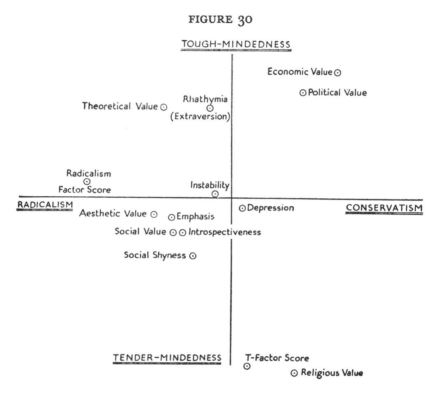

Diagram Showing the Relation Between Radicalism, Tough-Mindedness, Social Values, and Extraversion Measures

It will be seen that the Radical-Conservative axis and the tough-minded—tender-minded axis are uniquely located in terms of the R-scale and the T-scale respectively. The value scores are located in the appropriate quadrants; the economic and political values in the tough-minded Conservative quadrant, the theoretical value in the tough-minded Radical quadrant, the social value in the tender-minded Radical quadrant, and the religious value in the

178

tender-minded Conservative quadrant. These results are borne out by the analysis of the various other groups, and there is little point in reporting them all in detail.

Of particular interest in connection with the main theme of this chapter, however, is the position of the R (rhathymia) and the S (social-shyness) scales. As explained above, in terms of our hypothesis linking tough-mindedness with extraversion and tender-mindedness with introversion, we should expect the rhathymia scale to correlate positively with tough-mindedness, and the social-shyness scale to correlate negatively with tough-mindedness. The results bear out this prediction; rhathymia correlates with tough-mindedness $+\cdot41$, while social shyness correlates with tough-mindedness $-\cdot24$. Results for the other groups investigated are similar. Taking them in the order male Socialist, female Socialist, mixed Liberal, male Conservative, and female Conservative, the correlations between rhathymia and tough-mindedness are $\cdot51$, $\cdot42$, $\cdot56$, $\cdot22$, and $\cdot27$. Between social-shyness and tough-mindedness, the correlations are $-\cdot38$, $-\cdot18$, $-\cdot29$, $-\cdot03$, and $-\cdot15$. All the results, therefore, bear out our prediction, and we may regard the correlation between extraversion-introversion and the T-factor as established.[20]

A rather different approach to the question of the relationship between tough-mindedness and extraversion was followed by Coulter. She made use of a projective device, the so-called Thematic Apperception Test. This test is based on a hypothesis which has found considerable support in the experimental literature and which is stated in Lindzey as follows: 'In completing or structuring an incomplete or unstructured situation the individual may reveal his own strivings and conflicts.' This hypothesis is common to all the so-called projective techniques; it takes a special form when applied to the Thematic Apperception Test in which a somewhat indeterminate picture, i.e. one in which it is impossible to decide objectively on precisely what kind of action is going on, is shown to the subject who has to make up a story about it. In connection with this test the following hypothesis is made: 'In the process of creating a story the story teller ordinarily identifies with one person in the drama, and the wishes, strivings and conflicts of this imaginary person may reflect those of the story teller. It is assumed further that the identification figure can be established through the application of a number of specific criteria, e.g. person appearing first in the story, person doing most of the behaving, person most similar to the story teller, etc. It is also assumed that additional figures in the stories such as father, mother or brother often may be equated to the real life counterparts of the story teller and the behaviour of the hero towards them used as indicative of the story teller's reactions to these persons.'

There is a good deal of evidence in favour of these hypotheses.[21] Consequently a number of pictures were shown to groups of Communists, Fascists, and soldiers not affiliated to either of these two parties, and stories obtained from them in the usual way about the pictures. These stories were then scored for a number of variables characteristic of the extravert and introvert respectively. These scores took into account the following variables: (1) Fundamental interest in outer, objective world, as opposed to interest in the inner, subjective world; (2) interest in materialistic values (power, prestige, possessions) as opposed to idealistic values; (3) interests in persons and things; outgoing social participation; (4) the tendency to go by facts as opposed to going by principles; (5) sensationalistic as opposed to intellectualistic approach. There was good agreement between the experimenter and an independent scorer in the scoring of the stories, the average agreement being 82 per cent.

The extraversion score derived by adding together ratings on these various points correlated, as was suggested, with *tough-mindedness* in all three groups, the correlations being ·301 for the Communists, ·297 for the Fascists, and ·307 for the soldiers. All three values, it will be observed, are almost identical and all are statistically significant as well as being in the expected direction.

It has been shown in a previous chapter that Fascists and Communists are more tough-minded than the soldier group. We should expect on the basis of our hypothesis identifying tough-mindedness with extraversion that Communists and Fascists would show higher extraversion scores on the Thematic Apperception Test than the soldier group. The score of the soldiers was $8\cdot01\pm3\cdot22$, that of the Communists was $8\cdot78\pm2\cdot78$, while that of the Fascists was $9\cdot76\pm 2\cdot19$.

All these results are exactly in line with prediction, and while neither the correlations nor the mean differences are as high as one might have wished, this is not unexpected in view of the known low reliability of the T.A.T. test.

Our first two methods of proof in support of the hypothesis that extraversion is a determining factor in the tough-minded attitude have been fairly direct and straightforward. Our third proof is somewhat more indirect and complex and will show how very wide are the ramifications of this temperamental variable. Historically we may begin with an observation made by the author during an intensive study of aesthetic judgments of a great variety of materials such as landscape paintings, sculptures, photographs, carpets, silverware, poems, odours, polygonal figures, and so forth. Rankings of the objects in each class by the subjects taking part in the experiment were intercorrelated, and it was found that there was considerable agreement between judges on the aesthetic value of the objects judged. It was also found that people who were good judges in one field also tended to be good judges in another field. By the term 'good judges' we mean in this connection nothing more than that they agreed particularly strongly with the average judgments. This use of the term will probably be disputed by aestheticians; however, there is ample evidence to justify its use, even from their own standpoint. (This evidence has been discussed in *Structure of Human Personality* and as it is not relevant to our present purpose we shall not dwell on it here.)

After the influence of this first factor had been eliminated, a very strongly marked second factor appeared which was called the K-factor. It divided subjects with preferences for simple, symmetrical and regular polygons, strong obvious odours, poems with regular rhythms and an obvious type of rhyming scheme, paintings and sculptures in the modern manner, from those whose preferences were for complex, assymetrical polygonal figures, subtle odours, poems with subtle and complex rhythms and highly diversified and non-obvious rhyming schemes, and classical, pre-impressionistic paintings and sculptures.

Futher investigation on relatively small numbers of subjects showed that this complexity/simplicity factor showed important relationships to other personality variables. Thus a significant tendency was found for *introverts* to prefer the *complex*, *extraverts* the *simple* kinds of pictures and objects. Thus, if our identification of extraversion with tough-mindedness be accepted, we should expect a preference for simplicity to go with attitudes in the tough-minded quadrants, and for complex preferences to go with attitudes in the tender-minded quadrants.

No further work was done by the author in this connection, but the topic was taken up independently by Barron and Welsh, whose work lends considerable support to our general hypothesis. The first step taken by these writers was the construction of a scale for the measurement of complexity preferences. This scale consisted of 65 drawings of the kind illustrated in Figure 31. Very stable preferences were found for either the complex or the simple type of drawing and the whole scale had a very high reliability.[22] It was used by the authors in a whole series of investigations, the results of some of which are of considerable interest here.

In the first place it was found that those who preferred the simple figures tended to prefer in their artistic preference judgments themes involving religion, authority, aristocracy and tradition, while those who preferred the complex figures preferred in their artistic judgments those pictures which were radically experimental, esoteric, primitive and naïve. On the personality side simplicity was found related with masculinity and the rejection of soft, gentle and effeminate behaviour. This tendency, which was found both in questionnaires and ratings, fits in well with our hypothetical identification of *simplicity* and the attitudes in the tough-minded quadrant.

At the other end, the preference for complexity was found associated with originality, artistic expressions and excellence of aesthetic judgments. Again these correlations were found both in terms of ratings and of separate tests, and again these results are in line with our hypothesis.

The tendency of preference for complexity to be related to originality would lead one to hypothesize that preference for simplicity would tend to go with rigidity and this was indeed the case. Ratings of rigidity, which was defined as 'inflexibility of thought and manner; stubborn, pedantic, unbending, firm', correlated ·35 with preference for simplicity and a similar correlation was observed when a questionnaire was substituted for the rating.

A trait related to both originality and rigidity is *constriction*, as opposed to *impulsiveness*. A comparatively strong tendency was found for preference for complexity to go with impulsiveness (·50) and for constriction to go with preference for simplicity (·42).

In line with the Jungian hypothesis we should expect a preference for complexity to be found in the anxious and depressed type of patient, and of liking for simplicity to be found among hysterics.

FIGURE 31

SIMPLE DESIGNS COMPLEX DESIGNS

Examples of Simple and Complex Drawings Used as Measures of Personality

Among neurotic subjects such a tendency was in fact observed by Eysenck, and Barron, using questionnaires among university students, corroborated the finding. He showed that preference for simplicity correlated ·30 with a hysteria scale, while complexity correlated ·34 with a measure of anxiety. As Barron points out 'preference for the complex in the psychic life makes for a wider consciousness of impulse while simplicity, when it is preferred, is maintained by a narrowing of that consciousness. . . . To tolerate complexity one must very often be able to tolerate anxiety as well.'

More directly relevant than these findings is the fact that preference for complexity was found to be negatively correlated with ethnocentrism. In addition to these results, which were based on questionnaire answers, staff ratings showed that preference for simplicity correlated ·47 with conformity and ·29 with submissiveness defined as 'deference, willingness to be led, compliance, overready acceptance of authority'. These results directly and strongly support our original hypothesis.

In yet another study Barron and Welsh compared responses to certain attitude questions of a group of students having respectively very high and very low scores on complexity. The following questions were answered 'true' by high scorers on complexity:

1. The unfinished and imperfect often have greater appeal for me than the completed and the polished.

2. I could cut my moorings . . . quit my home, my parents and my friends . . . without suffering great regrets.

3. Politically I am probably something of a radical.

4. I think I take primarily an aesthetic view of experience.

5. I would enjoy the experience of living and working in a foreign country.

6. Many of my friends would probably be considered unconventional by other people.

7. Some of my friends think that my ideas are impractical if not a bit wild.

8. I enjoy discarding the old and accepting the new.

9. When someone talks against certain groups or nationalities I always speak up against such talk, even though it makes me unpopular.

In contrast, the following questions were answered 'true' by low scorers on complexity:

1. I don't like modern art.

2. Disobedience to the government is never justified.

3. Perfect balance is the essence of all good composition.

4. Straightforward reasoning appeals to me more than metaphors and the search for analogies.

5. It is a pretty callous person who does not feel love and gratitude towards his parents.

6. Things seem simpler as you learn more about them.

7. I much prefer symmetry to asymmetry.

8. Kindness and generosity are the most important qualities for a wife to have.

9. When a person has a problem or worry it is best for him not to think about it but to keep busy with more cheerful things.

10. It is a duty of the citizen to support his country, right or wrong.

11. Barring emergencies I have a pretty good idea what I will be doing for the next ten years.

12. I prefer team games to games in which one individual competes against another.

Barron sums up the main results of his work in the following words: 'Preference for simplicity is associated with social conformity, respect for custom and ceremony, friendliness towards tradition, somewhat categorical moral judgments, and undeviating patriotism and suppression of . . . troublesome new forces. . . . This last item is almost prototypical of the simple person's orientation towards repression as a psychic mechanism . . . complexity goes along with artistic interests, unconventionality, political radicalism, strong cathection of creativity as a value and a liking for change.'

'It seems evident that, at its best, preference for simplicity is associated with personal stability and balance, while at its worst it makes for categorical rejection of all that threatens disorder and disequilibrium. In its pathological aspect it produces sterotyped thinking, rigid and compulsive morality, and hatred of instinctual, aggressive and erotic forces which might upset the precariously maintained balance.'

One last experiment links up the work of Barron with that of Asch, and is of particular interest in connection with the hypothesis which we are discussing in this chapter. Before turning to this experiment we must briefly discuss the technique which Asch has elaborated in order to study the influence of group forces on the modification and distortion of judgments. He took his clue from a series of studies carried out several years earlier, in which Sherif had shown the importance of group judgments in creating a frame of reference when none existed before. Sherif in his experiments made use of a well-known perceptual illusion, the so-called autokinetic phenomenon. When in a dark room a pin point of light is exposed there is a strong tendency for most people to see this objectively stationary point as moving about in the room. This phenomenon, the causes of which are not yet well understood, can be subjected to measurement by asking the subject either to report on the direction and extent of the movement observed, or alternatively, to make a drawing of the seen movement on a sheet of paper.

Sherif in his original experiments tested each subject over a period of days and found that their judgments concentrated around a central tendency which remained relatively constant from day to day; further he found that there were consistent differences between the judgments of different observers. Making use of this observation Sherif then planned the second phase of his experiments in which he placed together in the same experimental situation two or three individuals whose respective levels of estimation were known, and who differed substantially from each other.

Under these conditions the judgments of the various individuals began to approach each other, each departing from his previously established judgments, and the subjects tended to converge towards the common level. In subsequent individual sessions the subjects maintained the level they had established in the preceding groups sessions.

These experiments, which showed the importance of group influence on the modification of the individual's frame of reference, made use of a very unstructured and suggestive kind of situation. There is no objective right or wrong about the answers given to the question: 'How far and in what direction did the spot of light move?'—except of course in so far as all answers specifying any kind of movement are objectively wrong. Asch carried this work forward by studying the influence of group judgments in a situation where there was an objectively correct answer. His technique was as follows: 'A group of 7 to 9 individuals ... are gathered in a class-room. The experimenter explains that they will be shown lines differing in length and that their task will be to match lines of equal length. The setting is that of a perceptual test, the experimenter places on the blackboard in front of the room two white cardboards on which are pasted vertical black lines. On the card at the left is a single line, the standard. The card at the right has three lines differing in length, one of which is equal to the standard line at the left. The task is to select from among the three lines the one equal in length to the standard line . . .'

'The lines are vertical and their lower ends are at the same level. Comparison lines are numbered 1, 2, 3. . . . In giving his judgment each subject calls out in accordance with the instruction the number of the comparison line ('one', 'two', 'three') that he judges to be equal to the standard. When all the subjects have stated their judgments the two cards are removed and replaced by a new pair of cards with new standard and comparison lines. There are 12 sets of standard and comparison lines in all.'

'The differences to be discriminated are considerable; most unequal comparison lines are clearly longer or shorter than the standard . . . the comparison lines differ from the standard by varying amounts and no attempt was made to maintain a constant ratio between them. On successive trials the equal line appears in different positions in random order. The two unequal comparison lines vary in their relation to the standard in the different trials: both are longer or both are shorter or one is longer and the other shorter than the standard.'

During the first two trials the experiment proceeds simply and normally. Discriminations are easy, and each individual monotonously calls out the same judgment. At the third trial, however, a single member of the group seated towards the end calls out a different number to that given by all the others. The same event is repeated a number of times during the course of the experiment, the same individual disagreeing again and again with the group. The reason for this peculiar behaviour of the one subject lies in the most crucial feature of the whole experiment. 'The subject whose reactions we have been describing is the only member of the group who is reacting to the situation as it has been described. All the others are without his knowledge co-operating with the experimenter by giving at certain times unanimously wrong judgments by calling two unequal lines equal. . . . Actually the group consists of two parts: the instructed subjects whom we shall call the *majority* and one naïve person whom we shall call the *critical subject* and who is in the position of a *minority of one.*'

The experimenter made a record of the responses of the critical subject but also, in order to throw further light on the subject's reaction, engaged him in discussion at the end of the experiment. In this discussion the whole group would take part, putting questions to the critical subject apparently out of curiosity and interest, and apparently quite spontaneously. 'At first the discussion centred on how to account for the disagreement that had developed. As the critical subject began increasingly to occupy the centre of the scene he was asked to indicate who in his opinion was right—the group or himself. He was asked whether it was likely that the entire group was in error and he alone right, how much confidence he placed in his judgment under the circumstances, and so on.' After all the qualitative and quantitative results had been obtained, the subject was told the nature and purpose of the experiment to allay any anxiety or worry that might have remained.

Results of the experiment showed on the quantitative side that of the responses made by critical subjects two-thirds were correct and independent of the majority trend; the remaining third were errors identical with those of the majority. The errors were not equally distributed among the critical subjects; some remained completely independent, others went with the majority without exception. Asch concluded that 'the experimental condition significantly distorted the reported estimates. There were extreme individual differences in responses to majority pressure, ranging from complete independence to complete yielding.'

The qualitative results reported by Asch further elaborate these conclusions. Among those who did not yield to majority pressure he reports two main types of reaction which he calls 'the independence of confidence' and 'independence without confidence'. These two terms are probably self-explanatory. Among the yielders he observed three main groups. The first he called 'yielding due to distortion of perception'. In this case there apparently occurred an actual visual illusion on the part of the subject due to the majority judgment, so that he actually saw the stimuli differently to what they objectively were. A second type of reaction Asch calls 'yielding due to distortion of judgment'. 'There are those who relatively early in the experimental episode reach a conclusion that may be summarized as "I am wrong, they are right" . . . quickly they

188

transformed their disagreement with the majority into a sign of personal defect. To respond independently acquired for them the meaning of announcing openly their failure to judge correctly. Consequently they felt more strongly the pressure of the majority and the fear of exposing themselves to ridicule.'

A third type of reaction was called by Asch 'yielding due to distortion of action'. Unlike the other subjects whose reactions have been described 'they lose sight of the task and become relatively unconcerned with the question of their correctness. Instead they experience one imperious need: not to appear different. They are dominated by the thought that they are excluded from the group and that this represents a serious reflection upon them. Consequently their concern narrows to a desperate determination to appear like everyone else, to submerge themselves in the group . . . they simply suppress their judgment; in this they act with full awareness of what they are doing. They know that they are not acting properly but they cannot change their course. Unable to reach a solution that would meet with their approval and that of the majority, they take what appears to them the easiest way out.'

We cannot go any further into the fascinating results reported by Asch of the various changes in the experimental situation which he made, as for instance by having a smaller majority, by increasing the number of critical subjects in the group, or by having one confederate only in a naïve group. We must turn instead to the relationship between independence as defined by Asch's test and complexity as defined in terms of the Barron-Welsh aesthetic judgment test. In terms of our hypothetical identification of complexity and tender-mindedness, and in view of the personality correlates of complexity already enumerated, we should expect the person showing *complex preference* to show *independence of judgment* on the Asch test. Barron has reported an experiment in which he compared the complexity preference of 46 non-yielders and 44 yielders on the Asch test. He demonstrated at a very high level of significance that the yielders preferred the simple designs, the non-yielders the complex designs. Thus the results are distinctly in conformity with the hypothesis, and an experimental measure of non-conformity is found to be characteristic of the introvert, tender-minded group while the extravert, tough-minded group is characterized by yielding and submissiveness to group pressure.

We may finish this account of the relationship between complexity and independence of judgment by quoting a summary of views held by independents as opposed to yielders. These views were expressed in an attitude questionnaire, and Barron reports that the following main five points discriminated at a high level of significance between the two groups:

1. Independents value creative work in others and in themselves. They are receptive to new ideas, even apparently impractical ones, and are more interested in the originality or aptness of an idea or theory in describing reality than in its possible practical applications.

2. Independents place particular value on the person as an individual and respond more to the inward integrity of another person than to spuriously pleasant characteristics.

3. Independents are independent. They are not fond of taking orders or integrating with a group or getting along with everyone, and they do not subscribe to the notion that rebellion in youth is to be indulged because after all young people *will* be rebellious before settling down sensibly. They do not particularly value strict discipline, or tireless and devoted leadership as an alternative to law.

4. Independents tend to be in communication with their own inner life and feelings and are intraceptive rather than extraceptive. They have empathy.

5. Independents like some uncertainty and do not respond favourably to polish and perfection. They prefer imperfections and contradictions which challenge the understanding and call for imaginative completion by the observer.

The data reported so far in this chapter are all in agreement with the two general hypotheses stated at the beginning. We may therefore accept provisionally the view that tender-mindedness and tough-mindedness are not in themselves representative of attitude constellations, but rather are the projection of personality variables on to a Radical-Conservative attitude continuum. As such tender-mindedness may be considered as the projection of introverted personality traits, tough-mindedness as the projection of extraverted personality traits. It hardly requires saying, of course, that what we have reported in this chapter are tendencies which are true on the average. There will be very few persons embodying all the traits, tendencies and peculiarities mentioned to any striking degree. None of the correlations reported are anywhere near perfection; indeed if they were we should rightly be suspicious

of the experimental set up. Nevertheless, in spite of only representing tendencies the agreement between so many different investigators working in different countries, and using a variety of different procedures, is too striking to be neglected, and the general
hypothesis discussed here serves to integrate a large body of work
on many different variables.

In view of the importance of the variables described in this
chapter, we must try and formulate an hypothesis which will account for their origin. An attempt to do so has been made by
several writers, all of whom have taken an environmentalist position, i.e. they consider the influences determining social attitudes
to be due to social learning, either in later life or from an early
stage of development. Lasswell, for instance, attempted to show
that attitudes favourable to revolt against established institutional
practices were associated with aggression against the father. Similarly, Krout and Stagner found in their radical subjects more frequent feelings of rejection by their parents and in general more unhappiness in childhood than in a control group. In another study,
Stagner found that a group of active Radicals had reliably less
satisfactory relationships with parents and lower personal morale
(self-satisfaction) than a control group. Within male college populations, there was a consistent tendency, sometimes statistically reliable, for men with good family morale to be more Conservative,
more nationalistic, and more aggressive. In general, men reporting
more antagonism to parents were relatively liberal and interna-
tionalist, but also aggressive as compared to those reporting less
parent antagonism.

Other writers have laid stress rather on direct family influence,
as shown by the correlation of attitude scores between parents and
children, or between brothers and sisters. Kulp and Davidson
found correlations in the neighbourhood of ·3 between siblings;
Newcomb and Svehla found rather higher figures in a similar
study, ranging from ·4 to ·6. Parent-child correlations were found
even higher. As regards attitude towards the church, for instance,
correlations between scores of parents and children, taking the
sexes separately, ranged from ·6 to ·7, while correlations between
mothers and fathers was as high as ·76.

Helfant, in a more recent study, found considerably lower correlations, ranging from ·1 to ·3 only between parents and children,
and between ·3 and ·4 for correlations between parents. There is

some evidence that in lower occuptional levels, correlations between parents and children are higher than they are at higher occupational levels.

These results are of some interest, but can hardly be considered
surprising, except perhaps that the correlations observed are probably rather lower than one might have expected on *a priori*
grounds. They do not, however, throw very much light on the
problem of causation of tough-minded and tender-minded attitudes, and we must turn to rather a different approach and a different type of hypothesis. The theory underlying this approach is
clearly stated by Frenkel-Brunswik, who carried out a study of the
social attitudes of children. She writes, 'There is evidence that
much of the personality structure of the children observed can be
traced to the home situation. Family relationships in the prejudiced homes are commonly based on roles clearly defined in
terms of demand and submission. Execution of obligations rather
than affection is a basis of smooth functioning in such homes.
Furthermore, there is stress on stereotyped behaviour and on adherence to a set of conventional and rigid rules.' Similarly, Harris,
Gough, and Martin, who carried out a similar study, state that
their work is based on an assumption, namely, 'that parental handling, especially in control and affectional relationships with children, has definite repercussions in the child's personality structure.
These repercussions develop not so much directly as indirectly,
through the child's system of organic and social 'needs'. More
specifically for this study, the writers were interested in the hypothesis that authoritarian and disciplinary attitudes of parents concerning child training practices would be related to a greater
incidence of ethnic bias in the children of these parents.'

Parents and children were given a number of questionnaires to
ascertain the degree of prejudice of the children, and also the
favourite methods of child control adopted by the parents. Children with particularly high and low scores, respectively, on the
ethnocentrism questionnaire were chosen, and their parents compared with respect to their answers to the child upbringing questionnaire. Mothers of prejudiced children showed a significantly
greater tendency to agree with the following propositions:

1. 'A child should never be permitted to set his will against that
of his parents.'

2. 'A child should never keep a secret from his parents.'

3. 'Obedience is the most important thing a child can learn.'
4. 'It is wicked for children to disobey their parents.'
5. 'A child ought to be whipped at once for any sassy remark.'
6. 'I prefer a quiet child to one who is noisy.'

These results clearly show a marked difference between the attitudes towards child upbringing of the mothers of prejudiced children as compared with the mothers of non-prejudiced children.

The items quoted above, as well as a number of others which had been found to discriminate at high levels of significance, were put together into an *empirical scale*, a high score on which would reflect the pattern of child-rearing practices and opinions typically held by mothers of markedly prejudiced children. In addition to this scale, five others were constructed on *a priori* grounds and following certain hypotheses about the nature of authoritiarianism. These hypotheses were that the parents of prejudiced children would show:

1. More authoritarian attitudes and practices, such as being strict and firm, punishing children severely, and keeping them quiet.

2. Less permissive attitudes, in the sense of being lenient and broad-minded in handling children, and giving them considerable latitude.

3. Less parent-child integration, defined as 'evidence of a close, effective emotional relationship between parent and child'.

4. More parental rigidity or 'fussiness', defined as 'unwillingness to put up with children's noise, antics, disruption, etc.'.

5. Less good 'judgment', as defined by adherence to what are regarded by psychologists as good practice in modern child rearing.

All these scales were found to differentiate in the expected manner, to intercorrelate in the expected manner, and also to correlate with the children's ethnocentrism scores. There thus appears to be little doubt that the writers have succeeded in proving a relationship between methods of child upbringing and children's tough-mindedness or tender-mindedness respectively.

A closely related problem has been investigated by Shapiro, who framed the hypothesis that the child rearing attitudes held by parents would be related to their general attitude structure. He applied measures of Radicalism and of tender-mindedness to 197 parents, as well as a specially constructed parental opinion inventory, the assumption being that child-rearing practices favoured by Radical parents would differ from those favoured by Conservative parents, and similarly that the child rearing practices of tender-minded parents would differ from those of tough-minded parents.

This expectation was fulfilled. Radical parents endorsed the following items much more frequently than did Conservative parents:

1. I think that punishment does no good to children.
2. I try to spend as much time as possible with my child.
3. I let my child have any children he likes for his friends.
4. A child should have as much say as it is capable of in family affairs.
5. I let my child bring any children he likes into the house, even ones I don't like.
6. A child should be free to handle as many things as possible in the house.

Conversely, Conservative parents agreed more frequently with the following propositions:

1. I want my child always to be neat and clean.
2. I am very strict with my child.
3. Children should always obey their parents without question.
4. I expect my child to be grateful for all its parents have done for it.
5. I believe in the saying, 'Spare the rod and spoil the child'.

Tough-minded parents agreed with the following propositions:

1. I want my child always to be neat and clean.
2. My husband and I never kiss one another in front of the children.
3. A father cannot understand 'mother love'.
4. I believe in the saying, 'Spare the rod and spoil the child'.
5. Women marry more for a home than for love.

Tender-minded parents disagree with all this and in addition believe 'It is best to leave a child to wean itself from the bottle in its own good time'.

We may summarize the results of the various studies discussed. It appears that (1) tough-minded parents adopt different child rearing practices from tender-minded parents; (2) Radical parents adopt different child rearing practices from Conservative parents; (3) tough-minded children tend to have been brought up in a different manner from tender-minded children; and (4) attitudes of children tend to agree with attitudes of parents. Do these findings support the hypothesis we set out to investigate? Up to a point, undoubtedly, they do. We have in fact found the expected correlation between the attitudes of children and the child rearing practices of parents which were hypothesized by Frenkel-Brunswik and some of the other writers mentioned. However, we cannot easily accept the coefficient of correlation as an indication of causality without falling into the ancient logical error of *post hoc ergo procter hoc*. There are several other hypotheses, apart from the one under investigation, which would equally easily explain the experimental findings.

Let us recall exactly what it is that Frenkel-Brunswik and Gough are trying to prove. Their hypothesis is a two-fold one. The first part might be put in this fashion: 'Certain child rearing practices give rise to certain personality structures in children.' The second part of the hypothesis might be put in this way: 'The personality structure resulting from certain child rearing practices causes children to develop ethnocentric and other types of attitudes.' It will be seen that while this hypothesis is not disproved by the data, there is a quite unnecessary link in the chain, namely, the alleged and hypothetical 'personality structure' of the children. One could much more easily put the hypothesis without including the children's personality structure at all, as for instance in the following way: 'Tough-minded parents adopt certain tough-minded child rearing practices. Also, tough-minded parents teach their children to hold attitudes similar to theirs. Consequently, children who have received a tough-minded upbringing will show tough-minded attitudes, not as a result of the upbringing, but as a result of direct indoctrination by their parents.' We have already shown that there is ample evidence for the two propositions involved in this hypothesis, namely, (1) that attitudes of children correlate with the attitudes of parents, and (2) that child-rearing practices of tough-minded parents are different from those of tender-minded parents. The resulting correlation between child-rearing practices and the attitudes of the children would on this hypothesis be regarded not as proof of any causal relationship; it would merely be considered coincidental. On the principle of parsimony, we must, therefore, reject the more complex hypothesis unless some special evidence can be adduced to support it.

It might be thought that such evidence might be forthcoming from a consideration of the data reviewed earlier in this chapter. We have shown that tough-minded attitudes are indeed related to personality structure, and that tough-minded people tend to have extraverted types of temperament. Here, then, we appear to be obliged to account for an additional factor. Frenkel-Brunswik and Gough have plumped for an explanation in environmentalistic terms, i.e. they would account for extraverted traits in children (and for any other temperamental traits that might characterize the tough-minded person, as discussed in the next chapter) in terms of the type of child rearing practices to which they had been subjected. This is, of course, in line with general psychoanalytic theory, which has always laid great stress on early childhood experiences in the genesis of personality traits.

However, again it is necessary to bear in mind possible alternative formulations and hypotheses. We cannot rule out the possibility that a child's extraversion is caused by authoritarian child rearing practices in the parents, but we must also consider the possibility that an extraverted pattern of behaviour is largely based on heredity, so that the true sequence of events would read (1) extraverted parents develop tough-minded attitudes; (2) tough-minded attitudes lead to authoritarian child rearing practices; (3) the children inherit the extraverted personality pattern, which in turn leads them to adopt tough-minded authoritarian attitudes. Thus, here again there would appear a correlation between child rearing practices and children's attitudes which could not be regarded as directly causal but as purely fortuitous. The fact, then, that correlations are found between child rearing practices and children's attitudes does not help us to decide between these different hypotheses; such a correlation could certainly not be accepted as proof of the environmentalist hypotheses.

There is little evidence on this point, and the only direct study which has been carried out on this problem appears to be one by Hugh McLeod, who used the so-called 'twin method'. This method makes use of the fact that some twins are identical, i.e. are produced by the splitting of one fertilized ovum, and have identical heredity, while other (fraternal) twins are produced by the simultaneous fertilization of two different ova and are no more alike than ordinary siblings, i.e. share heredity only to the extent of fifty per cent. Any differences between identical twins, consequently,

196

must be due entirely to the action of the environment. Differences between fraternal twins would be due to the joint action of heredity and environment. It will be seen that if differences between identical twins are just as large as those between fraternal twins, then we have no evidence at all in favour of hereditary determination of the trait under consideration. The more alike identical twins are, however, as compared with fraternal twins, the stronger becomes the evidence in favour of heredity. It is easy to measure the degree of resemblance between twins in terms of correlation coefficients, and it is possible from these correlations to deduce roughly the amount of influence which heredity has had on the trait under investigation.

Making use of this method, McLeod gave a battery of tests, which factor analysis had shown to be measure of extraversion-introversion, to groups of monozygotic and dizygotic twins; a score of extraversion derived from this battery was found to show considerably higher correlations in the group of identical twins, than in the fraternal group. This very marked difference indicates that between 70 per cent and 80 per cent of the total variance of extraversion-introversion in this sample was caused by hereditary factors.

The exact figures are not particularly important as on repetition of the experiment they might easily shift somewhat in an upwards or downwards direction. The experiment does seem to prove conclusively, however, that hereditary factors do determine a person's standing on the introversion-extraversion continuum to a considerable degree. Thus, as far as the available evidence is concerned, we certainly cannot dismiss outright the hereditary hypothesis, as is done so frequently by writers of the psychoanalytic school.

We have laid great stress on the alternative hypotheses, which might account for the observed data, not only because the problem is an important one in itself, but primarily because most writers in the field seem altogether to neglect such alternative hypotheses and to accept a simple observed correlation as proof of the particular view they are holding. This kind of procedure is not justifiable and goes counter to the tenets of scientific psychology, which requires not only that verifiable deductions should be made from a hypothesis, but also that the observed data should not be explicable on any reasonable alternative hypothesis. There is no argument about the observed facts, but there is little doubt that these could be accounted for on many different hypotheses, and they do not, therefore, provide crucial evidence for the correctness of any of these views. Many more careful, detailed, and properly designed experiments will have to be carried out before we can be certain which of the various causal chains considered is the correct one. As far as the evidence goes it would appear that the direct transmission of attitudes from parents to children, through the well known mechanisms of precept and teaching, added to the hereditary determination of temperament, can account for all the facts considered. So little is known however, in this field that this view is presented only very tentatively and with the greatest hesitation.

Chapter Seven

AGGRESSIVENESS, DOMINANCE AND RIGIDITY

HITHERTO we have been concerned with the verification of a rather general hypothesis dealing with the relationship of extraversion and introversion to the T-factor. However, even though this hypothesis be true, it seems unlikely that all the traits constituting extraversion will be equally strongly represented in a group of tough-minded subjects. It seems much more likely that certain traits will be more characteristic of tough-mindedness than others, and it would be worth-while to set up and test certain hypotheses along these lines. The first hypothesis of this kind to be tested will deal with a trait which will come almost inevitably to anyone's mind who contrasts members of the Fascist and Communist groups with their less tough-minded compatriots. This is the trait of aggressiveness.

Aggressiveness is implicit in many of the attitudes which make up the concept of tough-mindedness. Capital punishment, flogging, approval of war—these are only a few of the examples which spring to mind. There is therefore a strong *a priori* probability of a relationship between tough-mindedness and aggressiveness, and particularly of Conservative tough-mindedness, as compared with Radical tough-mindedness.

The first one to make an explicit study of this hypothesis appears to have been Stagner, whose work has already been mentioned earlier. He attempted to obtain some evidence on a theory which originated with William James, and which was reformulated by Freud. James had suggested that a 'moral equivalent for war' might be found in sublimating aggressive urges through physical exercise, the conquest of nature, etc. Writers of the psychoanalytic

199

school took up this notion and suggested that individuals who released their aggressions in their personal relationships would have less hostility and aggressiveness to displace on to 'out-groups'.

Among his other questionnaires, Stagner included a number of questions such as: 'Do you like to play games which require strength and courage such as [American] football? Do you like such activities as public speaking which take you in front of groups? When someone else does something to interfere with you or what you wish, do you express your annoyance openly and directly? On the whole are you successful in getting other people to do what you want them to do?'

Reactions to these questions which were meant to tap openly aggressive behaviour were compared with the scores of the subjects on questionnaires dealing with capital punishment, war, the use of force, and Fascism, the hypothesis being that if sublimation had taken place, then the open expression of aggressiveness in football and other games and in the individual's private life would make him less aggressive with respect to capital punishment, war, and the use of force in general. No support for the hypothesis was found; there was a distinct tendency for individuals who behaved aggressively in their personal relationships and who indulged in aggressive activities also to show attitudes of an aggressive character, i.e. to favour captial punishment, not to be opposed strongly to war, and so forth. Stagner comments: 'Of course this evidence does not dispose of the possibility that both displacement and sublimation may be very important factors in attitudes, but it raises an alternative for serious consideration, viz. that aggressiveness becomes a generalized pattern in both overt and verbal behaviour.' This alternative hypothesis has received considerable support from later studies.

One of these studies was carried out by Sanford and its general design has already been mentioned before. He compared reactions of about 1,000 subjects to a variety of attitude questions and projective devices with their scores on an authoritarianism scale. As one of the variables the picture reproduced in Figure 32 was shown to the respondents, and they were asked to suggest the reply that might go into the empty balloon.

The hypothesis on which Sanford based his predictions was phrased in terms of the concepts of extra-punitiveness, intro-punitiveness and impunitiveness. These terms, which were introduced by Rosenzweig, suggest three ways in which a person might react to frustrating circumstances. If he is extra-punitive he will blame other people for his difficulties; if he is intro-punitive he will blame himself; if he is impunitive he will take a relatively objective view

FIGURE 32

Picture Used to Elicit Aggressive and Non-Aggressive Responses

of the situation without immediately attributing blame to anyone.

Sanford phrases his hypothesis in the following way: 'We expect from theory that authoritarians will generally tend to blame outside forces for their troubles, particularly if the outside force is

unable to fight back. If it is dangerous to blame the outside force—
if it has a mantle of power of authority—we expect the authoritarian to turn intro-punitive. The equalitarian can be expected to
be relatively impunitive, viewing the situation with more objec-
tivity and not immediately falling into a dither about who is to
blame.'

'The results add up to a confirmation of the theory. The authoritarians tend to approach the situation aggressively by saying 'Sez
you' or 'What makes you think so' or they respond immediately in
terms of blame—either yours, mine or partly both. Equalitarians
say with relative neutrality 'It was not my fault' or they take a
calm impunitive stand, saying 'Let's talk this over' or 'Let's find
out the facts here' . . . thus equalitarians clearly tend towards impunitiveness while high scorers go in for blame either of the other
person or of themselves.'

Along similar lines respondents were shown a picture of a man
(or woman) in a restaurant with a waiter bringing his (or her)
food. The waiter says 'I am sorry but the cook did not do this the
way you ordered it.' There is a blank bubble over the customer.
The respondent is asked to state what the customer would say.

People with high authoritarianism scores tended to reject the
food and to be aggressive to the waiter, while low scorers accepted
the food with little or no fuss. The results demonstrated a significant relationship between authoritarianism and aggressiveness in
this study.

Probably the most detailed and most important study of the
relationship between authoritarianism and aggressiveness, however, is an experiment carried out by Coulter. Some of the results
from her study have already been mentioned, and it may be remembered that her subjects consisted of 43 Fascists, 43 Communists and 86 'neutral' subjects, i.e. subjects not belonging to either
of these two Parties but otherwise unselected. All subjects were
working class people of approximately the same age. It has already
been shown in an earlier chapter that Communists and Fascists
were significantly more tough-minded than the members of the
neutral group, and had higher scores also on the F or authoritarianism scale.

An attempt was made to obtain some evidence regarding the
aggressiveness of the members of these various groups by means of
the Thematic Apperception Test which has also been described in

a previous chapter. Stories were elicited on ten different pictures from the subjects of the experiment, and the resulting stories were then scored for the amount of aggression and the amount of dominance shown in them. A distinction was made between overt aggression or dominance on the one hand, and disguised or indirect aggression or dominance on the other. Thus a person knocking down someone else would be overtly aggressive; a person furiously arguing with another in order to convince him would be aggressive in a more disguised sort of way.

A few details regarding the experiment may be of interest. The ten cards used were 4, 6BM, 7BM, 10, 11, 12M, 15, 16, 18BM, and 19 from Murray's set. Seven of these pictures contain one or more male figures which might call forth stories including male identification. Three cards have no human figures; one of these is the 'blank card'. They were selected because of the ambiguity of their content. Verbatim records of the subjects' stories were taken and analyzed. Fifty-eight variables in all were scored, but only the Dominance and Aggression scores were used in this study.

Dominance was defined in line with Murray's original definition in the following way: To try to influence the behaviour, sentiments, or ideas of other people; to work for an executive position; to lead, manage, govern, coerce or restrain. Aggression was defined thus: To hate, fight, or punish an offence. To criticize, blame, accuse, or ridicule maliciously. To injure or kill, or behave cruelly. To fight against legally constituted authorities; to pursue, catch or imprison a criminal or enemy.

The reliability of the scoring was established by having a random set of 82 protocols from the combined groups rescored by a second scorer. Inter-rater agreement was consistently high, ranging from 84 per cent to 91 per cent for each of the stories. In view of the great differences in length of the stories, final scores were multiplied by Murray's correction factor, so that the position of a subject on a variable did not depend on the length of his story more than on its content.

The hypothesis which was suggested by previous work was that the tough-minded groups, i.e. Communists and Fascists, would be more dominant and aggressive than the neutral group; it was also anticipated that the Fascists would be more aggressive than the Communists. Observation of the actual behaviour of Fascist and Communist groups from whom the sample of subjects was taken suggested a further hypothesis, namely that Fascists would be more *openly* aggressive in their behaviour and in their stories while Communists would show a greater tendency to *indirect* aggression.

The results of the study clearly bore out these anticipations. The mean scores of the neutral group with respect to overt aggression was 6·6; that of the Communists 6·7 and that of the Fascists 11·8. For indirect aggression the score of the neutral group was 4·7, that of the Communists 9·3 and that of the Fascists 8·2. Thus Communists and Fascists are more aggressive both directly and indirectly than members of the neutral group, but there is a distinct tendency for the Fascists to be *openly aggressive* and for the Communists to be *indirectly aggressive*.

With respect to direct dominance, the neutral group has a mean score of 6·6, the Communists of 8·7 and the Fascists of 7·1. On indirect dominance the normals have a score of 6·4, the Communists of 6·5 and the Fascists of 10·8. Thus here also the hypothesis is verified and we find the Communists and Fascists are more dominant than are members of the neutral group. It should be noted, however, that here the Communists are more *openly* dominant, while the Fascists show *indirect* or covert dominance. This finding also is in accord with observations made at the time of the study. Communists are well indoctrinated and eager to convert anyone with whom they may be speaking, and because of their greater technical knowledge easily assume a dominant position in the discussion. Fascists are much less well indoctrinated, tend to be more ignorant, and do not display any eagerness to argue and establish dominance in this way. Their dominance rather is of the imaginary indirect kind, i.e. they like to think of themselves as already having won power and of achieving dominance in this fashion.

Figures 33 and 34 show in diagrammatic form the distribution of scores of the Communist and Fascist groups on the Aggression and Dominance variables respectively; in each case the position of the 'neutral' group has also been indicated. Figure 33, showing the results of the Aggression analysis, has been drawn in such a way that scores on indirect aggression are plotted along the ordinate, scores on direct aggression along the abscissa. A diagonal line has been drawn to enable a rough estimate to be made of the number of misclassifications, i.e. of Communists who have higher direct than indirect aggression scores, and of Fascists who have higher indirect than direct aggression scores. There are 6 of the latter and

13 of the former, giving an overall misclassification of 19 out of 86, or just over 20 per cent. A much better discrimination could be obtained by using a second-degree curve as indicated in the Figure; this gives less than 5 per cent misclassifications. The improvement is due to the fact that the correlation between direct and indirect aggression is strikingly different for the two groups; for Com-

FIGURE 33

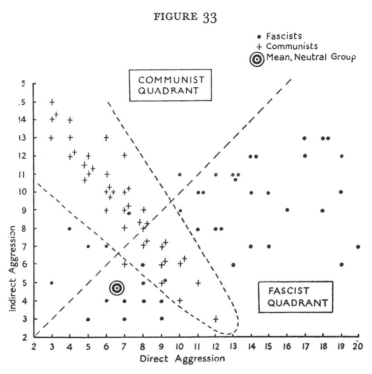

Scores of Fascists, Communists, and Neutral Group with Respect to Direct and Indirect Aggression

munists it is —·94, while for Fascists it is +·61. (In the neutral group it is —·64.) This difference between our two tough-minded groups is highly significant, and we are therefore justified in making use of the observation for the purpose of differentiation.

In Figure 34, direct dominance is plotted along the ordinate and indirect dominance along the abscissa. Again a straight line is included to indicate the amount of misclassification; two Fascists show higher direct than indirect dominance, while eight Communists show higher indirect than direct dominance. Thus the total amount of misclassification is slightly in excess of 10 per cent. No improvement on this figure can be reached by using more complex types of curves; the correlations between the two dominance scores are very similar for the different groups, being ·61 for the Fascists, ·64 for the Communists, and ·78 for the neutral group.

FIGURE 34

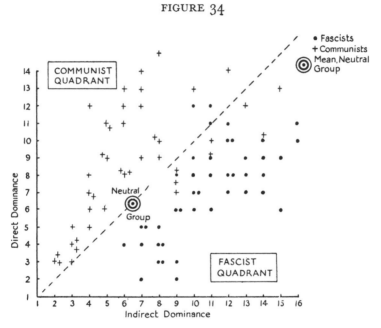

Scores of Fascists, Communists, and Neutral Group with
Respect to Direct and Indirect Dominance

It is possible to combine the aggression scores into one index, to be denoted D_1, by subtracting direct from indirect aggression; similarly we can combine the dominance scores into one index, to be denoted D_2, by subtracting indirect from direct dominance. These two scores are plotted against each other in Figure 35, D_2 being plotted on the ordinate, D_1 on the abscissa. The differentiation again is indicated by a best-fitting straight line, and the amount of misclassification is just in excess of 5 per cent. Little improvement could be expected by any other kind of boundary line, and in any case it would be unreasonable to expect perfect discrimination.

206

These results suggest three alternative hypotheses. It is possible that the differentiation between Communists and Fascists shown by their scores on the aggression and dominance variables is characteristic of Radicals and Conservatives generally, so that Radicals would be found to be directly dominant and indirectly

FIGURE 35

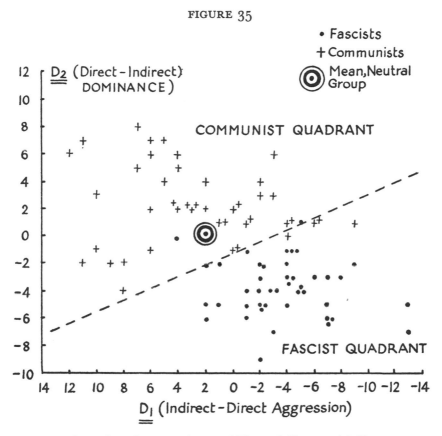

Scores of Fascists, Communists, and Neutral Group with Respect to Dominance and Aggression

aggressive, while Conservatives would be indirectly dominant and directly aggressive. It is possible to test this hypothesis by correlating the R scores of the 84 members of the neutral group with the aggression and dominance scores. The results are not in line with the hypothesis, as none of the correlations are significant. As a further test of the hypothesis, D_1 and D_2 scores were derived for the members of the 'neutral' group in the manner indicated in the last paragraph; these scores were then correlated with R. Correlations again were insignificant. There appears to be little likelihood, therefore, of any determination of Radical or Conservative attitudes through the aggressive-dominant complex of traits.

The second hypothesis would lead one to speculate along the following lines. Parties change in character according to historical circumstances; their membership is determined by economic and political factors which it would be very difficult to disentangle. Nevertheless, it seems reasonable to suppose that if personality factors such as the need for aggression and dominance are responsible to some degree for a person's choice of party, these traits will be shown most clearly by members of the party when it is relatively small and far from the seats of power. At that time, self-seeking and time-serving motives cannot in the nature of things be present, and the membership will therefore be something of a pure culture of these personality traits for which the party policy is attractive. As the party grows in power, other people will be attracted to it for a great variety of reasons, and this process of dilution will make the average member less and less distinctive from the point of view of his personality structure. The Fascist party is so small as to be almost non-existent; consequently we might expect almost all its members to be characterized by certain personality traits. The Communist party is much larger, and consequently we should expect a certain degree of dilution already in the personality picture. This might explain the fact that while both Communists and Fascists show aggressive and dominant traits, as well as rigidity and intolerance of ambiguity (as will be shown later), yet the Fascists show all these traits somewhat more clearly than the Communists.

The difference in size between the two parties may also determine certain aspects of their policy. The Communist party, sufficiently large to have some influence on the political life of the nation, has nothing to gain and everything to lose from displays of open violence and aggression; the Fascist party, on the other hand, has nothing to lose, and may indeed attract attention, by displays of aggression. Thus the emphasis of teaching and indoctrination is towards direct aggression in the Fascist group, towards indirect aggression in the Communist group. A dramatic illustration of this fact is furnished by the discovery that out of the sample of 43 Fascists studied, four had been members of the Communist party who had changed over because they had not found appropriate outlets there.

It would be difficult to prove an hypothesis of this type; indeed, it would be quite impossible to do so in this country. If we postulate politico-economic causes to account for the size and policy of our two parties, then experimental manipulation of these causes is *eo ipso* ruled out. It should not be impossible, however, to repeat studies of this kind in other countries—Germany might be an excellent testing-ground of such hypotheses—where the historical and politico-economic pattern is different. Until such further experiments are carried out, however, it should be emphasized that while the facts reported here are unlikely to be incorrect, their explanation is speculative, and may be altogether along the wrong lines.

A further hypothesis makes use of the concept of intelligence. Although no intelligence test was given to the Communist and Fascist group because of pressure of time, results of some of the tests used, as well as observation and discussion, suggested strongly that the Communists were more intelligent than the Fascists. In this connection, it is of interest to note that in the neutral group, where intelligence tests were applied, the following correlations were found: Direct dominance and intelligence $= \cdot 201$; Indirect dominance and intelligence $= -\cdot 163$; direct aggression and intelligence $= -\cdot 211$; indirect aggression and intelligence $= \cdot 261$. Thus the more intelligent person appears to be characterized by direct dominance and indirect aggression, while the stupid person is characterized by indirect dominance and direct aggression. This picture of the intelligent person's trait-organization thus agrees with that of the Communist, while that of the stupid person agrees with that of the Fascist. Again, in view of the fact that no actual measurement of intelligence was carried out on the two political groups this hypothesis cannot be regarded as proved; replication of the experiment with the addition of an intelligence test appears to be called for.

There is one objection to accepting the facts reported here as being a decisive proof of the hypothesis linking tough-mindedness with aggression and dominance. What we have done, in essence, is to take two minority groups, advocating certain policies which are unorthodox and unusual, and compare them with a neutral or orthodox group. It might be argued, quite reasonably, that possibly all minority groups advocating unorthodox policies would be found to be dominant and aggressive; indeed, many writers have commented on the prevalence of these traits in Pacifists, fundamentalists, and other groups having no connection with Communism or Fascism. Fortunately we have a method of proof which obviates this objection. If the quality of tough-mindedness, which distinguishes both Communists and Fascists, is indeed re-

TABLE XXVI

Correlations of Dominance and Aggression with Radicalism, Tender-Mindedness and Rigidity

	Dom. d.		Dom. i.		Agg. d.		Agg. i.	
Radicalism	—·10		—·19		—·04		·01	
	·24	·13	·27	·23	—·25	—·01	·29	·12
Tender-mindedness	—·67		—·52		—·37		·09	
	—·93	—·55	—·56	—·33	·68	—·32	—·71	—·18
F-Scale	·30		·33		·29		—·11	
	·60	·63	·49	·35	—·50	·28	·52	·31
Rigidity Scale	·45		·32		·28		—·17	
	·50	·41	·37	·17	—·43	·10	·46	·37
Intol. of Ambig.	·22		·03		·25		—·07	
	·24	·03	·12	·17	—·21	·00	·23	—·07
Dom. d.			·78		·32		—·24	
			·64	·68	—·68	·07	·68	—·26
Dom. i.					·31		—·17	
					—·64	·18	·56	·08
Agg. d.							—·64	
							—·94	·61
Agg. i.								

lated to aggression and dominance, then we should expect that in our neutral group the T-score would show correlations with these personality traits. The correlations between dominance and aggression on the one hand, and tough-mindedness on the other, are therefore of crucial importance.

Table XXVI gives the correlations between Radicalism, Tender-mindedness, F-scale, a Rigidity and an Intolerance of Ambiguity scale to be described later, and the direct and indirect Dominance and Aggression scores. Correlations are shown separately for the three groups; the top figure in each case applies to the 'neutral' group, the figure on the left below to the Communist, and the figure on the right below to the Fascist group. The following features of this set of correlations will be noted: (1) There is no consistent relation between Radicalism and Aggression, with the possible exception that Radicals may be slightly less directly aggressive and slightly more indirectly aggressive. A repetition of the study would be required to render this conclusion secure. (2) Tender-mindedness shows a strong negative relationship with both dominance and aggression. There is only one real exception to this trend, viz. the positive correlation between direct aggression and tender-mindedness in the Communist group. Possible causes of this reversal have already been discussed. (3) The pattern of correlations with the F-scale is very similar to that shown by the T-scale, though of course all the correlations have opposite signs. This was expected in virtue of the relatively high negative correlations between the F- and T-scales, reported in Table XXIX. (4) A tendency is found for rigidity and intolerance of ambiguity to correlate with dominance and aggression; these correlations will be discussed after we have introduced these concepts in some detail. (5) Direct and indirect dominance correlate quite highly together for all groups; they also show somewhat lower positive correlations with direct aggression, and variable correlations of doubtful significance with indirect aggression. (6) Direct and indirect aggression show negative correlations for the neutral group and the Communists, but a positive correlation for the Fascists. It almost appears as if the Fascist group were so full of aggression that instead of showing it in *either* of these two ways, as do the other two groups, they must show it in both ways at once.

The result of this study then strongly confirms those predicted on the basis of previous work and of common observation. Tough-mindedness correlates strongly with aggression and with dominance. This tendency can perhaps be seen most clearly in Figure 36 which sets along the abscissa scores on the R-factor and along the ordinate aggressiveness scores derived from combining indirect and direct aggression. It will be seen at a glance that all the Communists have aggressiveness scores higher than the mean of the neutral group, while all but five of the Fascists have scores higher than the mean of the neutral group. Comparison with Figure 26 in which we have plotted in a similar manner the relationship between the three groups along the tough-mindedness axis will show that aggressiveness scores separate out the two tough-minded groups from the neutral group almost as well as does our tough-mindedness scale.

One other feature will be noticed in this diagram. Aggressiveness

FIGURE 36

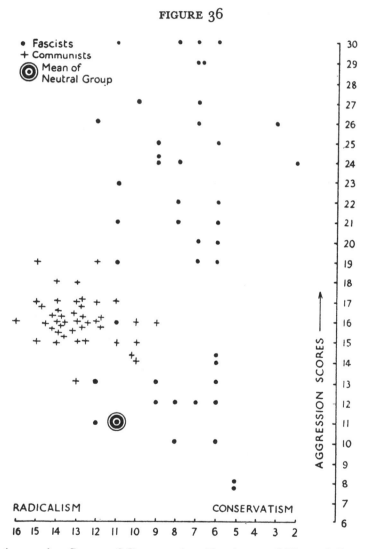

Aggression Scores of Communists, Fascists, and Neutral Group
Plotted Against Radicalism-Conservatism

scores of the Fascists range all the way from 8 to 30, in other words there is a tremendous diversity in the Fascist group going from extreme aggressiveness to comparative unaggressiveness. All the Communists' scores on the other hand lie between 13 and 19. In other words all the Communists in the sample lie within a very narrow range indeed—7 points as compared to 23 for the Fascists!

This tendency of Communist groups to show less scatter had also been observed with other variables, in particular the various attitude scales which they had filled in, and it had seemed likely that this close agreement might be due to the 'party line' and the considerable amount of indoctrination which is known to take place in Communist circles. The results shown in Figure 36 make this hypothesis rather unlikely as it does not seem very probable that Communists receive any kind of indoctrination in responding to selected pictures on the T.A.T. The only other hypothesis which suggests itself is that the Communist Party, having a well known, clearly defined programme and policy, tends to attract people who are rather alike with respect to their attitudes and to their degree of aggressiveness. Even if we accept this hypothesis, however, it is still not clear why the same should not be true of the Fascist Party whose strongly aggressive, anti-Semitic and anti-Socialist policy is also well known and would certainly not be a surprise to those taking the trouble to join the Party.*

Whatever the answer to this question may be, we may conclude that the data summarized in Figure 36 leave little doubt about the essential correctness of our hypothesis regarding aggressiveness. With respect to dominance, Figure 37 shows combined dominance scores as plotted against Radicalism-Conservatism. It will be observed that here differentiation is less successful, although still in line with prediction. The Communist group shows an even greater scatter than does the Fascist group, so that clearly whatever may be the causes responsible for the small scatter of Communist scores on the aggressiveness variable cannot be active in the case of dominance.

We must next turn to a consideration of a theory which has re-

* The fact that Communists and Fascists are tough-minded, aggressive and dominant Radical, and Conservatives respectively should not be inverted to read that all tough-minded, aggressive and dominant Radicals and Conservatives are Communists and Fascists. All policemen are tall, but not all tall people are policemen!

ceived widespread acclamation and which, if true, would account for many features of anti-minority prejudice in terms of aggressiveness. This is the famous scapegoat theory of prejudice.

This theory is intimately linked with another originally sug-

FIGURE 37

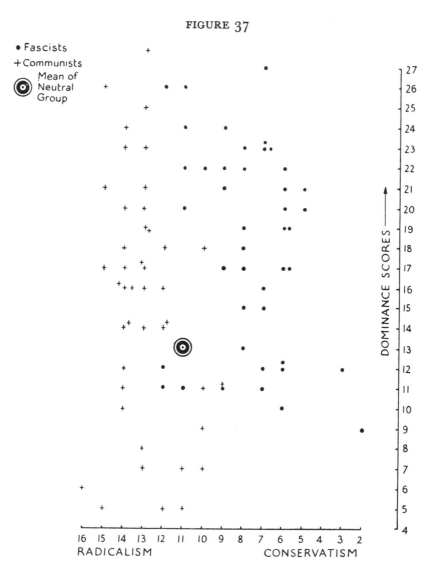

Dominance Scores of Communists, Fascists, and Neutral Group
Plotted Against Radicalism-Conservatism

gested by McDougall and later adopted by Freud. This theory, the so-called frustration-aggression hypothesis, has been developed extensively by the Yale school, particularly by Dollard and Miller; it maintains in essence that aggression is the inevitable consequence of frustration and that all aggression is due to some kind of frustration.[23] The scapegoat theory maintains that the individual high in prejudice has a certain amount of hostility or aggression which he has not been successful in expressing or acting out against the original object of aggression, i.e. the original cause of the frustration which produced the aggression. The theory holds further that the person succeeds in reducing his hostility by displacing or redirecting aggression against the more or less helpless members of minority groups in the form of prejudiced behaviour.

We need not take the frustration-aggression hypothesis in its pure form too seriously. (It has, indeed, been revised by its earlier proponents.) We may admit that frustration may have other consequences than aggression, and we may admit that aggression may have other causes than frustration. Nevertheless, taking the theory in its most general form it cannot be dismissed on any *a priori* grounds and certain experiments indeed speak in its favour. Thus in one study, questionnaires concerned with attitudes towards Mexicans and Japanese were administered before and after a long series of difficult examinations. At the same time that the subjects (boys in a summer camp) filled out these questionnaires they were forced to miss a highly prized social activity. After this experimental frustration there was a significant increase in the amount of unfavourable opinion expressed against the two minority groups. In this study then we appear to find a certain amount of support for the frustration-aggression theory. It should be noted, however, that this experiment fails to provide evidence for one feature which lies at the heart of the scapegoat theory, namely *differential displacement*. In other words the scapegoat theory demands that those who are high in prejudice should be *more* liable to displace aggression than those who are low in prejudice; the experiment merely demonstrates that on the average some displacement takes place under the experimental conditions of frustration.

An experiment to test this additional hypothesis was carried out by Gardner Lindzey. This author attempted to formulate the scapegoat theory in a reasonably rigorous form; he then made a number of predictions from it and proceeded to test them. His main statement of the theory was as follows: 'The high in pre-judice have developed a strong preference for reducing aggressive tendencies by means of displacement to an object other than the original instigator of the aggression, while the low in prejudice have not developed such preference for this means of adjustment.'

As an alternative hypothesis Lindzey proposes the following: 'The high in prejudice differ from the low in prejudice not in tendency toward displacement of aggression but rather in the amount of aggression they must reduce or act out. This possibility may be broken down into three special causes, depending upon the place of origin of this surplus of aggression: (a) the greater amount of aggression is a result of constitutional determinants or early developmental experiences that have left the individual with an enduring aggressive need or trait; (b) the greater amount of ag-gressive tendency is a result of chronic and persistent objective frustrations in the environment of the individual that result in his being exposed to excessive frustration; (c) the greater amount of aggressive tendency is the result of the individual's sensitivity to frustration which results in his being more severely frustrated than the average person in the same objective situation.'

Lindzey tested these hypotheses in the following way. Having selected groups of high and low scorers respectively on an ethno-centrism questionnaire he proceeded to measure their aggressive tendency by means of two tests which we have already encoun-tered. One is the Thematic Apperception Test, the other the Picture Frustration Test which consists essentially of a number of pictures like those shown on pages 155 and 201. These measures of aggressive tendency were administered to the subjects at the begin-ning of the study and readministered immediately following the experimental frustration situation which took place about two months after the initial testing. This frustration experience was designed to evoke the maximum amount of frustration and ag-gression. The subjects were made to go without food for from ten to twelve hours; they were induced to drink from a pint to a quart of water and prevented from urinating for approximately three hours; a blood sample was taken with a sterilized spring lancet in such a way as to cause considerable pain. Finally they were made to fail at an assigned task in a group situation when highly moti-vated to succeed, and when their apparent failure caused them to lose status with the other members of the group, all of whom were accomplices of the experimenter, a circumstance unknown to the subjects of course. This failure in the group situation was the most crucial part of the frustration situation, the earlier physiological assaults being designed chiefly to lower the subject's threshold of annoyance or frustration.

The following deduction made from the hypothesis was confirmed by the data. 'Aggressive tendencies that are denied expression against the object originally serving as instigator will be displaced so that they will be directed against non-instigating objects.' On both the T.A.T. and the Picture Frustration test the subjects showed greater aggressiveness after the frustrating situation than before, thus giving evidence that they had displaced the aggressiveness, which they could not openly show towards their instigator, on to the test material. This result is in line with the study already mentioned. The second deduction from the scapegoat theory, however, was not confirmed. This deduction reads as follows: 'Individuals high in minority group prejudices will show more tendency towards displacement of aggression following frustration than those low in minority group prejudices.' Contrary to this deduction the data actually showed that the high in prejudice displaced *less* than the low in prejudice, although this difference was not large enough to be statistically significant. 'The failure to confirm this proposition suggests that the difference between the high and the low in prejudice must lie elsewhere than in the tendency towards displacement of aggression.'

Lindzey's third deduction is similar in nature to the propositions already discussed and states: 'Individuals high in minority group prejudice will show more evidence of outwardly directed aggressive tendencies than those low in minority group prejudice.' We have quoted a good deal of evidence in favour of this hypothesis and in these data, too, the high in prejudice show more aggression both on the T.A.T. and on the Picture Frustration test than those low in prejudice, although the differences here are not as impressive as they are in our own data.

Lindzey's fourth deduction reads: 'Individuals high in minority group prejudice will show more frustration susceptibility as measured by the extent to which frustration is experienced as subjectively frustrating than those low in minority group prejudice.' Data to confirm this deduction were obtained by interviewing the subjects, from observing their reactions, and in other similar ways.

217

This evidence lends strong support to the hypothesis, so that we may accept the view that those high in prejudice are not only aggressive but also tend to experience frustration more strongly than those low in prejudice, thus setting up a vicious circle of aggressiveness leading to frustration, then to greater aggressiveness, and so forth.

The presented evidence by Lindzey forces us to discard the scapegoat theory of prejudice. There is no evidence that the subjects who showed high prejudice tended to displace aggression more than those who showed low prejudice. Neither was there any evidence in his work or in that of other authors quoted by him to suggest that the frustration-aggression hypothesis fared any better; while more aggressive, the high prejudice individual did not in fact suffer any more objectively frustrating events in his environment than did the person low in prejudice. On the other hand, however, it will be remembered that the high in prejudice showed a distinct tendency to *experience* more strongly those frustrations which they did encounter, so that the major difference between the groups appears to lie in the greater frustration tolerance of the unprejudiced.

The main outcome of this discussion appears to be that aggressiveness and dominance are direct correlates of tough-mindedness and that they account directly for many of the observed characteristics of tough-minded groups. Auxiliary hypotheses, such as the frustration-aggression and the scapegoat theories do not appear to serve a useful purpose, or to have sufficient experimental backing. Much further work is obviously needed in this field but the outlines of a general theory are beginning to appear.

We must next turn to another trait which has often been put forward as characterizing the tough-minded, namely that of rigidity. We have already encountered this trait in connection with the Barron-Welsh studies; we must now consider some direct experimental attacks on this hypothesis. Before describing these studies, however, it should be noted that the possibility cannot be ruled out of there existing more than one trait of 'rigidity'. There has not yet been a study to show that all the various tests used to measure this trait correlate together in such a way as to show them all to be measures of one and the same underlying psychological factor. Strictly speaking then we should be careful not to talk about rigidity as a general trait, but rather about rigidity as measured by this or that test. Doing so, however, would make our account of the experimental work much more difficult to follow, and consequently the reader is asked to bear this warning in mind.[24]

The first set of studies undertaking an objective investigation of the relationship between rigidity and ethnocentrism was carried our by Rokeach who made use of a technique originally suggested by Luchins. This technique is known as the so-called Einstellung experiment, the German word '*Einstellung*' being an equivalent of the English term 'set'. Roughly speaking, these tests are set up in such a way that a special *set* is created in the subject to respond in a certain way. Later on in the experiment he is given a choice according to whether he goes on responding in the same way or adopts a new, more appropriate method. The rigid person, according to this hypothesis, would continue along the lines of his set while the non-rigid person would switch over to the more appropriate new method.

One example is the so-called Water Jar Test. Subjects are asked to solve problems in which required quantities of water are to be obtained by manipulating three jars of given capacities. To establish a set a number of problems are presented which can be solved only by a relatively complicated method. Then follow several critical problems which can be solved both by the complicated method and by a more simple direct one. An example of the first type of problem is given below in Figure 38. Three jars are given with capacities of 31, 61 and 4 quarts respectively. The problem is to obtain exactly 22 quarts of water using these jars. The correct solution is to fill the 61 quart jar, from this to fill the 31 quart jar once and the 4 quart jar twice. There then remains in the 61 quart jar the required 22 quarts of water. If the three jars are called A, B, and C respectively as in Figure 38 the method of solution would be B–A–2C.

After a number of similar problems, all of which are solved by the same series of moves (B –A –2C), there are given a few critical problems which can be solved by a simple method as well as by this more complex one. For example, three jars having capacities of 25, 55 and 5 quarts respectively might be given and the quantity of water required might be 20 quarts. In this example the complicated method of solution is $55 - 25 - 5 - 5 = 20$. The more simple solution is $25 - 5 = 20$. The solution of such a problem by the complicated method is taken as an indication of rigidity.

Rokeach compared 35 students scoring high and 35 students scoring low on an ethnocentrism questionnaire with respect to their rigidity as measured by this test. Significant differences were observed in the expected direction, i.e. the high scorers on ethnocentrism were found to be more rigid than the low scorers. (It may be of interest to know that intelligence did not correlate to any extent with the rigidity scores so that we cannot account for the observed facts in terms of intellectual differences.)

Another test used by Rokeach is the so-called Map Test. In this the subject is presented with five simple maps in booklet form, all identical except for street names. A typical map is shown in Figure 39A. The subject is allowed to study each map for 15 seconds; when this period is over the subject turns to the next page and is asked to: 'Describe in your own words the shortest way to go from the corner of Carter Road and Ady's Road, to the corner of

FIGURE 38

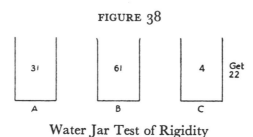

Water Jar Test of Rigidity

Overhill Road and Turner Street.' Different street names are of course used for the different problems but in all problems the starting point is the S.W. corner and the goal is the N.E. corner.

Each of the maps contains a diagonal pathway which is of no help in reaching the goal as it goes in the wrong direction. After the set has been established for disregarding this diagonal pathway there follow five critical map problems identical with the previous maps except that the diagonal pathway is usable as a short cut in reaching the goal. Such a map is illustrated in Figure 39B. The hypothesis is again that the more rigid will tend to persist in the set set up by the original problems and disregard the diagonal pathway even when it could be used as a short cut.

Rokeach presented the tests to groups high and low on ethnocentrism and as demanded by the hypothesis the high in prejudice showed greater rigidity than the low in prejudice. Thus we appear to have here consistent findings in favour of the original hypothesis.

If our hypothesis linking ethnocentrism with tough-mindedness is correct, then we should expect to find Communists and Fascists more rigid than members of the more tender-minded groups. Coulter carried out the experiment, using the Water Jar and the Maps test, and found incongruent results—the Water Jar test failed to give significant results, the Maps test showed the Communists least, the Fascists most rigid. Unfortunately rigidity tests were found to be correlated with lack of intelligence, and it might

FIGURE 39

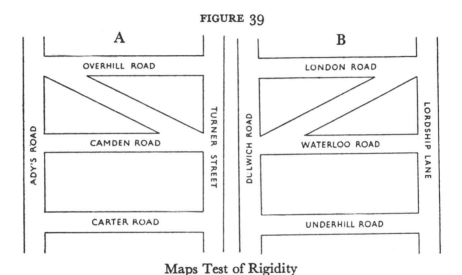

Maps Test of Rigidity

be argued that this factor disturbed the results. She also applied the questionnaire scale of rigidity reproduced below (Table XXVII) which showed the normals least rigid (11·5), the Communists significantly more rigid (13·8) and the Fascists most rigid of all (15·4).

Related to rigidity is the concept of intolerance of ambiguity intoduced by Frenkel-Brunswik. The term is almost self-explanatory. The rigid person attempts to gain security by grouping concepts into rigid categories of black and white, and refuses to admit intermediate shades of grey. The non-rigid, tolerant person can admit these finer grades and is less liable to form rigid dichotomies of good and bad, we and they, in-group and out-group.

TABLE XXVII

Rigidity Scale

Please read each statement carefully and say whether you think it is *true* or *false*. Put your answer in the right-hand column. Answer the questions as truthfully as possible; there are no right or wrong answers.

1. I wish people would be more definite about things. ....
2. I don't like to work on a problem unless there is the possibility of coming out with a clear-cut and unambiguous answer. ....
3. I am in favour of a very strict enforcement of all laws, no matter what the consequences. ....
4. For most questions there is just one right answer once a person is able to get all the facts. ....
5. The trouble with many people is that they don't take things seriously enough. ....
6. It bothers me when something unexpected interrupts my daily routine. ....
7. I often start things I never finish. ....
8. I set a high standard for myself and I feel others should do the the same. ....
9. People who seem unsure and uncertain about things make me feel uncomfortable. ....
10. Most of the arguments or quarrels I get into are over matters of principle. ....
11. I don't like things to be uncertain and unpredictable. ....
12. I think that I am stricter about right and wrong than most people. ....
13. It is annoying to listen to a lecturer who cannot seem to make up his mind as to what he really believes. ....
14. Once I have my mind made up I seldom change it. ....
15. I always see to it that my work is carefully planned and organized. ....
16. Our thinking would be a lot better off if we would just forget about words like 'probably', 'approximately', and 'perhaps'. ....
17. I like to have a place for everything and everything in its place. ....
18. I never make judgments about people until I am sure of the facts. ....
19. I am known as a hard and steady worker. ....
20. I find that a well-ordered mode of life, with regular hours and an established routine, is congenial to my temperament. ....
21. A strong person will be able to make up his mind even on the most difficult questions. ....
22. It is hard for me to sympathize with a person who is always doubting and unsure about things. ....

FIGURE 40

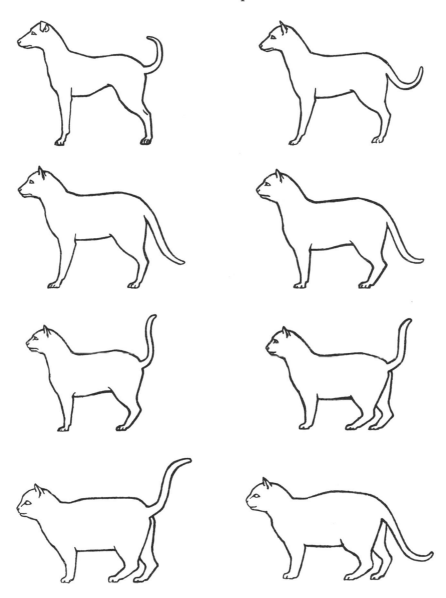

Dog-Cat Test of Intolerance of Ambiguity

Several measures of this tendency have been proposed such as, for instance, the Dog-Cat test used by Coulter. This test, reproduced in Figure 40 shows eight drawings of a dog turning slowly and by degrees into a cat. The hypothesis is that when these drawings are presented seriatim to the subject with the request that he should say what each drawing represents, then the rigid person would continue to cling to the original 'dog' concept long after this concept has objectively failed to account for all the observed details. According to this theory he would be forced into this rigid adherence to the original concept by his intolerance of the ambiguity introduced in the intervening pictures.

Coulter, in giving this test to Fascists, Communists and her neutral group, found highly significant evidence in favour of the hypothesis that Communists and Fascists are more intolerant of ambiguity, mean scores for the neutral group being 5·0, for the Communists 5·8 and for the Fascists 6·2. Similarly on a specially constructed questionnaire dealing with intolerance of ambiguity and reproduced below (Table XXVIII), Communists and Fascists

TABLE XXVIII

Intolerance of Ambiguity Scale

Please read each statement carefully and say whether you think it is *true* or *false*. Put your answer in the right-hand column. Answer the questions as truthfully as possible; there are no right or wrong answers.

1. I always make up an ending for a story when the author leaves me in doubt as to the fate of the hero. ....
2. Parents nearly always know best. ....
3. Most women are either good or bad. ....
4. If I have the choice of two alternatives and I cannot decide, I find it is better to choose either one to get the decision over with. ....
5. I dislike working puzzles to which there seems to be no solution. ....
6. There is only one true religion. ....
7. It makes me feel uncomfortable when someone is speaking about something which I do not understand. ....
8. Women act too much like men nowadays. ....
9. I change my mind easily when someone puts forth a convincing argument. ....
10. I take a philosophical view of life most of the time. ....
11. I make up my mind very rapidly. ....
12. It makes me uncomfortable to do anything unconventional. ....
13. I dislike learning things about which I know absolutely nothing. ....
14. It is always desirable to do the socially acceptable thing. ....

have significantly higher scores than people in the neutral group, mean scores being 7·7 for the neutral group, 8·0 for the Communists and 8·8 for the Fascists.

Again, as in the case of aggression and dominance, we must ask ourselves whether the correlations within each of the groups between the various measures of rigidity and intolerance of ambiguity considered support the hypothesis that these variables are related to tender-mindedness. Table XXIX shows the required correlations; again the figure on the top line refers to the 'neutral' group, the figures in the bottom line to the Communist and Fascist groups, in that order. The following features will be noted: (1) Correlations of all the tests with Radicalism are effectively zero. (2) Correlations of all the rigidity and intolerance of ambiguity tests are negative with tender-mindedness, and positive with the F-scale; the Maps test is the only one to go counter to this rule, and results from the Water Jar test are incongruent for the Communist group. (3) The Dog-Cat test and the Intolerance of Ambiguity questionnaire show a remarkably high positive correlation; the correlations of these two tests with the rigidity tests, although mainly positive, are very low indeed and do not reach the required level of significance. (4) Intercorrelations of the three rigidity tests are positive but rather slight, with the exception of the correlation between the Water Jar and the Maps test, which is surprisingly high. (5) Correlations of all tests with intelligence are slight.

The main conclusions to be drawn from these facts appear to be that while there is good support for the hypothesis that Intolerance of Ambiguity characterizes the tough-minded sort of person, there is little support for the identification of this trait with rigidity, and only tenuous support for the hypothesis linking rigidity with tough-mindedness and authoritarianism as measured by the F-scale. 'Perceptual and conceptual rigidity', as measured by the Water Jar and the Maps test, is therefore rather less promising a correlate of tough-mindedness than had been thought.

A rather different approach to the measures of intolerance of ambiguity was used by Block who made use of the autokinetic phenomenon which we have already explained. It will be remembered that in the ambiguous situation presented by a pin point of light apparently moving about in the room subjects gradually established certain norms which served as a frame of reference for later judgment. There are marked individual differences in the

225

TABLE XXIX

Correlations Between Rigidity Tests, Radicalism, and Tender-Mindedness

	R 1	T 2	F 3	Dog-Cat 4	I.o.A. 5	Rig. 6	Jar 7	Map 8
1. Radicalism	—	·00 —·26 —·07	—·01 ·07 ·15	·09 ·12 —·17	—·06 ·01 ·01	·04 ·16 ·03	·06 —·09 —·37	—·01 —·02 ·08
2. Tender-mindedness		—	—·43 —·63 —·62	—·15 —·30 —·21	—·39 —·36 —·27	—·47 —·58 —·41	—·20 ·10 —·12	·13 ·23 —·25
3. F-Scale			—	·05 ·26 ·21	·23 ·35 ·18	·20 ·71 ·56	·12 —·09 ·15	—·07 —·10 ·45
4. Dog-Cat test				—	·55 ·56 ·46	·12 ·09 ·22	·05 —·21 ·13	·04 —·20 ·03
5. Intolerance of Ambiguity Scale					—	·13 ·31 ·04	·13 —·09 —·04	·04 —·12 ·20
6. Rigidity Scale						—	·21 ·01 ·19	·07 ·02 ·11
7. Jar Problems							—	·43 ·68 ·08
8. Maps test								—
9. Intelligence (Neutral group only)	·231	·198	—·282	—·079	—·130	·168	—·284	·179

number of trials necessary for a subject to establish his own individual norm, some subjects establishing norms quickly while others required a long series of trials.

Block set up the hypothesis that a person intolerant of ambiguity would proceed as quickly as possible to establish a frame of reference within which this subjective phenomenon could be judged, while a person tolerant of ambiguity would take rather longer because for him there was no pressing need to categorize norms. In accordance with this general hypothesis, Block predicted that people high in ethnocentrism would set up norms quickly whereas people low in ethnocentrism would set up norms late or not at all. This prediction was borne out by the results, so that here again we have evidence to show that tough-minded groups are more intolerant of ambiguity than are tender-minded groups.

Another concept related to rigidity is that of concreteness of thinking and reification of thinking. Rokeach again was the first to investigate this problem, his original experiment dealing with certain aspects of the Einstellung tests discussed above. In the water jar test subjects were allowed to use rough paper, and Rokeach hypothesized that there would be a tendency for those more concrete in their mode of thought to make more use of the paper. 'It seemed reasonable to suppose that the use of rough paper might mean that the subject did not really perceive the problem as a whole but rather saw the problem as being composed of several parts which when manipulated in a sterotyped, temporal and positional fashion would automatically and mechanically lead to the "correct" solution.'

Another measure of concreteness of thinking used by him was the verbalization of response. Some subjects gave the answer in arithmetical form while others gave a verbal response. Thus one person might give the answer '61 −31 −4 −4=22' while another might say: 'Fill the 61 quart jar, pour off 31 quarts leaving 30 quarts in the 61 quart jar. Then pour off 4 quarts twice leaving 22 quarts in the big jar.'

Results showed that those high in ethnocentrism showed greater concreteness of thinking as defined by making greater use of rough paper and by tending to verbalize their responses. These preliminary observations led Rokeach to use another rather different approach, in which he asked subjects to define 10 concepts, namely Buddhism, Capitalism, Catholicism, Christianity, Communism,

Democracy, Fascism, Judaism, Protestantism, and Socialism. Definitions were categorized as abstract, reified, concrete or miscellaneous. A concrete definition was defined as one in which the concept was explained in terms of a person or group holding a belief, or in terms of a person being a member of a church or religion, etc., or if the concept was otherwise defined implicitly or explicitly in terms of the subject himself or of another person or people. Such concrete definitions were found significantly more frequently among people high in ethnocentrism, while other types of definitions were found among those low in ethnocentrism and Rokeach concludes that concreteness of thinking characterises the tough-minded.

Another concept also related to rigidity, intolerance of ambiguity and concreteness of thinking is that of 'narrow-mindedness'. Here again Rokeach has provided an experimental method of investigating this trait. Using the same set of 10 concepts mentioned above, five of which are religious in character while the remaining five are political-economic in character, Rokeach gave his subjects the following instructions. 'As you can probably see, the terms . . . refer to important social problems existing in the world to-day. To some extent all of these are related to each other. Here is what I would like you to do next. Write a paragraph in the blank space provided at the bottom of your sheet in which you describe in what way all of these terms might be interrelated with each other. Do not worry about how well organized your paragraph is, because it is not important for the purposes of this experiment. Just tell me in what way these terms are related to each other. If you do not think that *all* of these terms are very much related to each other then just write about those terms which you think *are* related to each other and skip the rest. You have five minutes to do this. Go ahead!'

Rokeach found that answers could be grouped in three categories. In the first place answers might show evidence of *comprehensive organization*. The subject's organization was considered to be comprehensive if it was both broad and integrated, that is if all 10 concepts were clearly present in his description and if he stated specifically the manner in which all 10 concepts were interrelated.

The second form of organization he called *isolated cognitive organization*. In this something less than a complete integration of all 10 concepts was achieved, meaning that all the 10 concepts are present but that they are broken down into two or more sub-groups which are relatively isolated from each other. Although the subject's total organization is broad enough to embrace all objectively present parts there is little or no intercommunication between sub-structures. An example of comprehensive organization might be 'All 10 concepts refer to peoples' faiths or ways of life', while examples of isolated cognitive organization might be 'Five are religious beliefs, the other five are types of government'.

A third type of organization Rokeach called *narrow cognitive organization*. 'Qualitatively different from the non-comprehensive organizations involving isolation or lack of communication are those organizations in which one or more of the objectively present parts is clearly missing from the subject's organization.' An example for instance would be this: 'The only ones that are related are the religious because they all try to teach you there is one God and everyone should believe in him.' (The political-economic concepts are not mentioned in this definition). Rokeach defines 'narrow-mindedness' in terms of the degree to which narrow organization is found in the classifications given by his subjects, while comprehensive organization is indicative of lack of narrow-mindedness.

Following up his establishment of these concepts he went on to hypothesize that narrow-mindedness as so defined would be found more frequently among the tough-minded, ethnocentric types of persons. Dividing his whole group of 144 subjects into four equal quartiles of 36 each on the basis of their ethnocentrism, he obtained the results shown in Figure 41. It can be seen from this Figure that the relative frequencies of the different kinds of organization given by the four groups differ in several important respects. Approximately 70 per cent of the subjects falling into the lowest prejudice quartile had comprehensive organizations. Less than 40 per cent of subjects in the other quartiles showed evidence of such organization. Isolated organizations are most frequent among subjects in the middle range of prejudice where 50 per cent manifested such organizations as contrasted with 20 per cent in quartile 1 and 33 per cent in quartile 4. Lastly, narrow organization is found to increase directly with increase in prejudice, the percentages of such organization found in quartiles 1–4 being 6, 8, 11 and 28 respectively. The number of narrow organizations found in the subjects highest in prejudice is greater than that found for all the subjects in the remaining three groups put together. Again, therefore, we find evidence for distinct differentiation of the tough- and tender-minded in terms of a particular aspect of rigidity, namely that evinced in cognitive structure.

If the tough-minded are rigid, and if tough-mindedness, as we have shown, has many personality correlates, then we should expect to find as the last piece in this jigsaw puzzle that rigidity too would be correlated with various personality traits. A study along

FIGURE 41

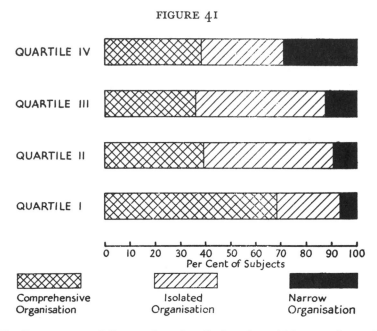

The Percentage of Comprehensive, Isolated, and Narrow Organizations Given by Subjects in Ethnocentrism Quartiles 1, 2, 3, and 4

these lines has been reported by Cowen and Thompson who made use of the Rorschach test as a means of obtaining information regarding the personality of their subjects. While this test is highly subjective, and while evidence in its favour is mainly of a clinical kind, the results achieved by these two investigators in comparing Rorschach responses of rigid and non-rigid subjects agree so well with our general picture that their summary may be worth quoting. 'Based upon an assumed relation between certain Rorschach responses and personality attributes, the personality factors which

230

appear to be related to Einstellung rigidity (as contrasted with flexibility) include: limited productivity and imaginativeness, diminished resourcefulness, inability to perceive complex relationships and to integrate constructively, a generalized suppression of emotional expression with respect to both rich inner creativity and interaction with the outer environmental reality, an inability and hesitancy to enter psychologically new situations . . . a restricted range of interests and narrow sphere of function and a poorer adjustment to society.'

Having now discussed in some detail two traits believed to be related to tough-mindedness, namely rigidity and aggressiveness, we must next consider various other traits which have been studied in less detail. We shall in particular be concerned with two series of studies, one by Gough basing itself on questionnaire responses, while the other by Frankel-Brunswik based itself on interview material and projective techniques. Throughout the studies of these two writers we shall find recurring again and again themes already noted in previous work. Gough in one of his early studies used a variety of instruments such as the Allport-Vernon Scale of Values, The Rosenzweig Picture Frustration Study and the Minnesota Multiphasic Personality Inventory, a very detailed and lengthy questionnaire dealing with a large number of personality traits. Comparing anti-Semitic students with non-prejudiced students he found that the former were on the average 'less liberal in social outlook, less tolerant of other races and groups, less internationally minded, more nationalistic, more cynical concerning the ideals of democracy, less impressed by the record of achievement in securing human rights and privileges in this country, less tolerant and trusting of others in a general way, less magnanimous, less respectful of others' integrity, less able to overlook and ignore minor irritations and frustrations, less concerned with resolving and rectifying problems once they do arise in inter-personal reaction'.

Gough then proceeded to carry out an item analysis in which he compared the reactions to each of the items in the personality questionnaire of ethnocentric and non-ethnocentric students. The following are some of the items to which the ethnocentric subjects replied 'true' more frequently than the non-ethnocentric: 'I think most people would lie to get ahead,' 'Most people are honest chiefly through fear of being caught,' 'Sometimes I feel as if I must injure either myself or someone else,' 'I don't blame anyone for trying to grab everything he can get in this world,' 'Most people make friends because friends are likely to be useful to them,' 'Most people inwardly dislike putting themselves out to help other people,' 'Much of the time I feel as if I have done something wrong or evil,' 'Most people will use somewhat unfair means to gain profit or an advantage rather than to lose it,' 'I commonly wonder what hidden reason another person may have for doing something nice for me,' 'I have strange and peculiar thoughts,' 'It is all right to get around the law if you don't actually break it,' 'When a man is with a woman he is usually thinking about things related to her sex,' 'I feel sure that there is only one true religion.'

These are only some of the items discriminating between the tough and the tender-minded, but they will serve to give the reader a flavour of the difference. Gough then divided all the items into main sections, each of which serves to differentiate the prejudiced from the non-prejudiced. The first of these factors he calls 'anti-intellectuality'; 'The less tolerant subjects do not like poetry and do not like science, and one might infer an antipathy to systematic and logical analysis of human behaviour and a distrust of intellectuals, theorists and "long hairs".' A second cluster of items refers to a prevailing sense of pessimism and lack of hope and confidence in the future; 'The high scorers doubt whether they will be very successful in life, feel that the future is too unsure for making serious plans, and in general appear to be dispirited and dour concerning the future.'

Closely related to this attitude are feelings of cynicism, distrust, doubt and suspicion. 'The high scorers feel that other people cannot be trusted, that others will prey upon them and exploit them and that notions such as rectitude, probity and so forth, are in fact mere facades and fictions. There is a brooding, doubting and apprehensive quality to their conceptions and they are unable to put confidence in others. Tendencies such as these would also suggest a basic lack of self regard and a basic distrust of self integrity. It is as if the high scorers, feeling unable to accept themselves, were unable to credit the motives and behaviour of others.'

'This basically cynical cast seems to carry over furthermore into a diffuse misanthrophy and querulousness. The more prejudiced students not only appear to doubt others but they also appear to resent them and to dislike them. There is a tendency to debunk and discredit the beliefs and achievements of others, to deflate and to disrespect. Another item cluster bespeaks a rather hostile and bitter outlook on the part of the more prejudiced which ramifies into destructiveness as exemplified in the item: 'Sometimes I feel as if I must injure either myself or someone else.' This is a rather transparent expression of aggression and emphasizes the emotional basis of the intolerant person's animosities as opposed to rational or intellectual ones.'

'The seventh cluster of items betokens a repining, grumbling and discontented evaluation of their current status by the more prejudiced students. The high scorers are resentful of the way in which others respond to them and complain of the unfairness and injustice of their difficulties. They state that they have had more than their share of things to worry about, that they have often been punished without cause, that others are jealous of their good ideas, and that most people inwardly dislike putting themselves out to help others.'

Gough was able on the basis of this analysis to construct a scale made up entirely of personality items from the Minnesota Multi-Phasic Inventory which on various samples of high school and university students correlated significantly with measures of ethno-centrism. We may therefore regard his study as another demonstration of the importance of personality factors in the determination of tender- and tough-minded attitudes.

Much of the work described in this chapter found its inspiration in theoretical formulas and experimental studies contributed by Frenkel-Brunswik, some of whose work on the authoritarian personality we have already had occasion to mention. Supplementing the development by her colleagues of the ethnocentrism, anti-Semitism and authoritarianism scales, she carried out an interview study of students respectively high and low on authoritarianism. These interviews, devised on the basis of a definite hypothesis, verified five main sources of differentiation between the authoritarian and the non-authoritarian groups interviewed.

The first of these five variables was labelled 'Repression versus Awareness'. The authoritarian individual showed a failure on the whole to be aware of unacceptable tendencies and impulses in himself. This failure made it difficult if not impossible for him to integrate these tendencies (fear, weakness, passivity, sex impulses and aggressive feelings against authoritarian figures such as the parent) satisfactorily with the conscious image he had of himself and led to their being repressed.

From this repression derived a second main feature of Frenkel-Brunswik's analysis called by her 'Externalization versus Internalization'. As a defence against the repressive tendencies the authoritarian subject has recourse to projection. In other words he attributes to the outer world that which he cannot accept in himself. Part of this process of externalization is a tendency towards avoidance of introspection and of anxiety in general. 'Since the energy of the person is in this case largely devoted either to keeping instinctual tendencies out of consciousness or to striving for external success and status, there appears to be relatively little left for genuine libidinization of one's own personal relationships or of one's work as ends in themselves.'

A third source of differentiation is labelled by Frenkel-Brunswik 'Conventionalism versus Genuineness'. The authoritarian person shows a high degree of conformity; he appears to need external support given by authorities or public opinion in order to find some assurance of what is right and what is wrong. Attitudes towards parents, children and members of the other sex tend to be conventionalized. The unprejudiced person on the other hand is not governed in his attitude by conventional approaches to the same extent and displays more genuine feelings and reactions.

One implication of the factors discussed so far is what Frenkel-Brunswik calls the 'power-orientation' of the authoritarians as opposed to the 'love-orientation' of the non-authoritarians. The prejudiced person is oriented towards a search for power. 'The comparative lack of ability for affectionate and individualized interpersonal relations, together with conception of threatening and dangerous environment, must be seen as underlying the prejudiced person's striving for the attainment of power either directly or by having the powerful on his side.'

The last of Frenkel-Brunswik's distinctions is one we have already noticed in some detail. It is the opposition between rigidity and flexibility. One of the most characteristic aspects of the prejudiced individual, in her view, is his rigidity. 'This must be seen as a consequence of the features discussed so far. In order to keep unacceptable tendencies and impulses out of consciousness, rigid-defences have to be maintained. Any loosening of the absoluteness of these controls involves the danger of a breaking through of the repressed tendencies.'

Frenkel-Brunswik extends this theoretical account of the hypothetical origin of rigidity by pointing out that repression does not cause these impulses to lose their dynamic strength but that quite on the contrary abrupt or unsuccessful repression prevents rather than helps in their control and mastery. An ego thus weakened is all the more in danger of becoming completely overwhelmed by the repressed forces and an ever greater rigidity of defence is needed to cope with such an increased threat. 'In this vicious circle impulses are not prevented from breaking out in uncontrolled ways. Basically unmodified instinctual impulses lurk everywhere beneath the surface, narrowing considerably the content of the ego so that it must be kept constantly on the look out. Rational control extends to a small sector of the personality only.'

It is not necessary to accept the Freudian hypothesis given by Frenkel-Brunswik and her colleagues in explanation of their main findings. Alternative explanations may be found and may in fact be better able to account for the facts. What should be noted rather is the degree to which the facts themselves are in agreement with those discussed in connection with other experiments. Psychology is often accused of producing nothing but contradictory results; in this field at least there is almost overwhelming agreement between the many different writers who have attacked this problem in different countries, using quite divergent methods of exploration. The discovery of such agreement strongly supports the general correctness of the observations here recorded.

This account of Frenkel-Brunswik's work really closes this chapter, but a few words at least must be added about two further variables which can hardly be passed by without mention. These two variables are *intelligence* and emotional instability or *neuroticism*. Politicians habitually accuse their opponents either of stupidity and ignorance, or of lack of emotional stability—apparently on the ancient principle that 'any stigma is good enough to beat a dogma with'. We may therefore briefly consider the question of whether there is any factual evidence to support the view that these variables play an important systematic part in the genesis of social attitudes.

There is ample evidence from numerous studies carried out in the United States that among university students there is a slight but definite correlation between intelligence and Radical opinion.* Contrasted with this tendency we must note the fact that many researchers have shown middle class groups to score higher on intelligence tests than do working class groups and that, as we have shown in the first chapter, middle class groups tend to be conservative, working class groups radical. This would almost certainly mean that over the whole population intelligence would show a slight positive correlation with Conservatism. These two results may appear contradictory but they are not necessarily so. There is no reason to expect that correlations between two variables in the total population should be identical with correlations between these variables taken on very highly selected groups. Neither must it be forgotten that during the period when these studies were carried out the 'intelligentsia' tended to have somewhat left-wing attitudes, and that these were reflected in the writings of the best-known authors of the period.

We would suggest, therefore, that in general no conclusions can be drawn from the large mass of data which has been accumulated. Until studies of this type are carried out in different cultures and in different periods it will be impossible to generalize from data collected in one particular culture in one particular, very narrowly circumscribed, period of time. Certainly the data do not give any comfort to partisans in either camp; highly intelligent people have held beliefs located at any point of the radical-conservative continuum, and the very slight tendencies observed for the more intelligent to hold one view or the other can certainly not be generalized to argue in favour of the correctness of any particular political belief.

Even more definite is the result of considering studies of emotional instability in relation to political attitudes. While occasionally there is a suggestion in American studies that Radical students are less well adjusted than Conservative students, differences are nearly always slight and may simply indicate the difficulty of holding unorthodox opinions in a strongly Conservative society. A study carried out by the writer in this country failed to show any correlation between Radical tendencies and instability, and it is difficult to arrive at any other conclusion but that Radicalism and Conservatism are not in any direct way related to this variable.

* For a brief discussion of this point, see technical note 25. See also the last line in Table XXIX for correlation between Radicalism and intelligence in British working class people.

Chapter Eight

A THEORY OF POLITICAL ACTION

A theory in science has two main functions. In the first place, it serves to organize and structure a variety of apparently unrelated facts, relating them all together in a system the properties of which can be deduced from some more general principle or law. In the second place, it serves to suggest deductions from such principles or laws which may lead to the discovery of new and hitherto unknown facts, and which may be used to support or disprove the original theory. Usually, there is little in the way of verifiable theory to be found in the early stages of a science, and certainly the psychological study of attitudes is no exception to this rule. There are thousands of empirical studies, but very few attempts to relate these together in a coherent scheme; thousands of isolated results, but no general agreement even on the concepts to be used in discussing and ordering these results. We have already seen in an earlier chapter how divergent are the definitions of such widely used terms as 'attitude', 'opinion', and 'ideology'; definitions are almost as numerous as writers on the subject. Such a state of affairs is not compatible with a reasonable rate of advance in knowledge and understanding, and it is not to be wondered that this lack of theory has given rise to many pseudo-problems which befuddle thinking in this field.

One of these pseudo-problems in particular has troubled many writers on the subject of social attitudes, as well as many critics. The problem in question will almost certainly have occurred to the reader early on in our discussion, and he will hardly be satisfied unless an answer is found to the question: 'What is the relation between attitudes and opinions, i.e. verbal expressions of mental states, and actual behaviour as shown in physical action?' It is obvious that there is no one-to-one correspondence between the two, yet it is with the former we have so far been concerned, while it is the latter which the student of politics is interested in; superficially, at least, 'actions speak louder than words', and there is an overwhelmingly strong tendency for most people to regard actions as automatically more 'valid' than words.

One possible answer might be that *neither* words nor actions are invariably accurate reflections of underlying attitudes. If a person's words may be distorted reflections of his attitudes because of his desire to agree with an interviewer, make a favourable impression on his boss, or avoid being sent to a concentration camp, so also may his actions. He may join a party, or take part in a pogrom for precisely the same reasons, and without actually holding the attitudes which might be inferred from his conduct. Thus, instead of saying that actions are better measures of an attitude than are words, we should rather say that both actions and words are indirect measures of the underlying attitudes in which we are interested, and that under certain circumstances both may mislead the unwary investigator.

The whole distinction between actions and words, in fact, is somewhat superficial. Verbal expressions, after all, are physical actions in the same sense that attending a political meeting, or throwing a rotten egg at a speaker, or beating up an opponent are physical actions. In each case, a series of muscles is inervated, and movement of parts of the body results in consequence. To say: 'Off with his head!' is merely a verbal expression, but it may nevertheless have dire consequences. To make a cross on a ballot paper is merely an expression of opinion, just as is the making of a cross on the interviewing schedule of the Public Opinion Interviewer; nevertheless it may cause a government to topple, and another to be put in its place. The distinction so often made, surely, is not between verbal expression and action, but rather between one type of action (verbal, non-violent) and another (non-verbal, involving the larger muscles groups). The whole distinction appears to be without a difference, and is of no fundamental importance.

Such an answer, while not inaccurate, would nevertheless obscure a very real problem. There may be no real theoretical distinction between verbal and non-verbal types of response; nevertheless, there may be crucial differences between responses given in one type of situation and those given in another. The experimental literature furnishes several examples to illustrate this point. One of the best-known is an experiment by LaPiere, who wrote to several hotel managers asking them whether they would be willing to let rooms to coloured people. He then visited those hotels where he had obtained negative replies, taking with him two coloured friends, and found that in almost every case they were put up without difficulty. This experiment has often been quoted to show that attitudes, as expressed by letter in this case, may not be very accurate indices of actions, as expressed in the actual acceptance of coloured visitors.

Along similar lines, Schanck studied opinions on card playing and the use of tobacco and liquor in a small rural community in which the Methodist Church was dominant. On the investigator's first arrival, the inhabitants expressed the approved attitudes of condemnation both orally and in attitude questionnaires. After being accepted by the individuals making up the group, however, he participated with many of them in card games and in drinking sessions, behind locked doors and drawn blinds! Overt verbal disapproval was found together with covert approval and actual participation.

At the level of common-sense, both these studies reveal the importance of the actual situation upon the expression of attitudes verbally or in action. They do not necessarily prove that either method of expression is more valid than the other. The truth appears to be, rather, that *in dealing with behaviour a knowledge of attitudes is not sufficient.* Other factors enter into the problem and no theoretical formulation is possible without some knowledge of these other factors. We must therefore turn to a more thorough investigation of the nature of attitudes, and of the general formula which links them to overt behaviour, whether verbal or non-verbal. In order to do this, we may best start with a feature of attitudes which has often been remarked upon, and which has been the subject of numerous empirical studies. The feature in question is usually labelled 'stereotypy', and indeed for many writers the terms 'attitude' and 'stereotype' are almost synonymous. A study of stereotypes may therefore reveal to us certain properties of attitudes which will lead to the construction of a theory capable of reconciling the apparent contradictions we have noted above.

The term *stereotype* derives from the printer's habit of making paper-pulp moulds of the forme which contains the type and illustrations for the printed page. Molten metal is then poured into these moulds, and the metal plate thus obtained is used for printing. Walter Lippman, the American columnist, applied the term to the field of attitudes and ideas because of the rigid character of the mental processes which mould the material of experience into fixed patterns. As he points out: 'For the most part we do not first see and then define, we define first and then see. In the great blooming, buzzing confusion of the outer world we pick out what our culture has already defined for us and we tend to perceive that which we have picked out in the form stereotyped for us by our culture.'

An early experiment by Sir Charles Goring may be of interest in this connection. He was investigating the well-known theories of Lombroso, who believed that criminals could be recognized by the presence of certain physical characteristics which he called 'stigmata of degeneration'. Goring thought that this belief was based merely on stereotyped thinking and set about to prove his point. He had an artist draw from memory portraits of inmates of a penal institution in London. Using a technique invented by Sir Francis Galton he made a composite photograph of these drawings and found that this approached very closely to Lombroso's view. Then he took actual photographs of the same criminals and had another composite photograph made of these. This showed no evidence of Lombroso's 'criminal type', and bore no resemblance at all to the one based upon the drawings. Lombroso and the artist clearly did not see what was physically there, but had their perception determined by previously acquired attitudes of a stereotyped character.

Such sterotypes, or 'pictures in the head', as Lippman calls them, are connected with almost any group of people we can think of—Communists, Capitalists, Fascists, gangsters, Jews, workers, bureaucrats, brass-hats, gigolos, dancing girls, students, old maids. Each term immediately conjures up a conglomeration of traits which may or may not correspond with reality, and which in any case forms a bed of Procrustes into which we then attempt to fit the actual Communists, Capitalists, Fascists, etc., whom we may meet.

One clear example of the working of stereotypes is seen in preference judgments for different national groups, as shown, for instance, in the Bogardus Social Distance Scale. Hartley demonstrated the non-rational character of such judgments very neatly by including in an experiment with the Bogardus scale the names of three groups which did not exist at all, but which he had made up—the Danireans, the Pireneans, and the Wallonians. The subjects of the experiment expressed definite attitudes towards these non-existent groups and, what is particularly interesting, *these attitudes were congruent with those they expressed towards real groups.* Thus, people who tended to be ethnocentric and to dislike Turks, Negroes, Indians, Southern Europeans, and so forth, also tended to dislike Danireans, Pireneans, and Wallonians; others who had no such prejudices against real groups also were prepared to admit the three imaginary groups to their street, to their clubs, and to their families. Thus, ethnocentric attitudes are based on generalized and stereotyped views of out-groups, not on factual knowledge about members of these groups.

The same is true of political parties. Hartmann, for instance, administered an attitude scale through personal interviews to a group of voters who showed a strong inclination towards a collectivist policy in the sense that they favoured the public ownership of natural resources, industry, insurance, and so forth. However, when issues were put to them in terms of stereotyped concepts with strong emotional associations, their attitudes were contrary in many ways to what they had been before. Thus, 90 per cent of them believed in the efficacy of the protective tariff; 78 per cent were opposed to nationalization of the land, and 65 per cent would refuse a licence to teach in public schools to teachers believing in socialization. As Hartmann concluded, 'These voters want the specific things for which socialism stands, but they do not want to have them labelled that way.' The strong influence of the name as opposed to the actual policy indicates the important influence of stereotyped thinking as opposed to factual thinking.

It is not suggested that stereotypes are infallibly wrong. Undoubtedly they often are, but upon occasion they may embody a true generalization. Two examples may be given to illustrate the existence of a false and a true stereotype, respectively. The first of these derives from a careful study, carried out by LaPiere on attitudes towards Armenian immigrants to Fresno County in California. He found a common attitude to the effect that Armenians were dishonest, lying, and deceitful, but the records of the Immigrants' Association gave them as good a credit rating on the

241

average as any other group. They were described as parasitic, but they applied much less frequently for charity to the County Welfare Bureau than native Americans. They were considered to have an inferior code of social morality and to show evidence of considerable social friction, yet they appeared in fewer legal cases than their numbers would lead one to expect. If anything, therefore, the stereotype of the Armenians is not only irrelevant; it is directly contrary to fact.

Hofstätter reports a different study in which stereotypes were found to give an accurate picture of reality. He reports that there exists in Austria a stereotyped view of the intelligence of the inhabitants of the eight federal States of that country, the inhabitants of Vienna being at the top, those of Salzburg second, those of Lower Austria third, those of Upper Austria fourth, followed by those of the Tyrol, Styria, Carinthia, and Burgenland. During the war it was possible to compare intelligence test results for recruits coming from these various states. The results are shown in Figure 42 and it will be seen that while the differences are not very large, they agree exactly with the stereotyped order, with Vienna at the top and Burgenland at the bottom. Thus, stereotypes need not be incorrect but may have some factual basis.

This brief discussion will have shown the reader why to so many psychologists attitudes are indistinguishable from stereotypes. Like stereotypes, attitudes prejudge the issue by determining our *set*, our way of reacting to new facts and new experiences; like stereotypes, attitudes give us an organized frame of reference which determines what we perceive and how we perceive it; like stereotypes, *attitudes are mental habits* which, if aroused, determine our actions. Here, it may be suggested, we have the analogue we have been looking for in our endeavour to fit attitudes into a comprehensive scheme of psychological knowledge. Much is known about the nature of habits, their origin and their effects. Could this large amount of knowledge accumulated by students of learning be used to throw light on the problem stated at the beginning of this chapter? It is the firm belief of the writer that only by doing so can the study of attitudes be made part and parcel of general psychology. But before making the attempt, a brief account of modern learning theory may not be out of place. In this account we shall follow Hull, who has done more than any one man to create a consistent and verifiable account of the many phenomena subsumed under the heading of 'learning'. Inevitably, our description of learning theory will be very sketchy, concentrating only on the most important and most relevant points, and leaving out many com-

FIGURE 42

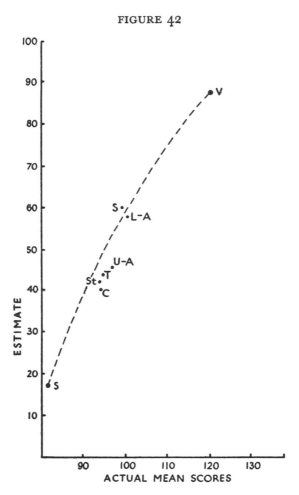

Stereotyped Estimates and Actual Mean Scores in Intelligence Tests of People living in Eight Austrian Counties

plications and reservations. The reader familiar with the literature will be able to amplify the account, or even to translate it into the language of other, rival theorists.

Learning theory sets itself the problem of accounting for the fact that behaviour is modified through experience. Historically, two main factors have been suggested by philosophers and others interested in such problems; these two factors have in turn suggested the names characteristic of the schools upholding the respective importance of either. One of these is the *hedonistic* school, stressing the importance of rewards and punishments; the other is the *associationist* school, stressing the importance of contiguity. Both notions are incorporated in modern learning theory, which may be said to have had its inception in the brilliant series of researches carried out in the first two decades of this century by Pavlov.

The general set-up of Pavlov's studies of conditioned responses is well known. A dog salivates when fed, or when shown food; it does not salivate to the sound of a bell. When a bell is rung just before feeding, however, it is found that after a few repetitions the bell itself causes saliva to flow, even though no food may be forthcoming. Thus a previously neutral stimulus, the bell, has become associated with the response previously elicited only by food; the animal has learned to respond to the bell, or, in more technical terms, it has become conditioned to the bell. It will be obvious that both hedonistic and associationistic factors are involved. If there had been no reward, or if the animal had been satiated, no learning would have taken place; similarly, if there had not been a number of repeated associations or pairings of bell and food, again there would have been no learning.

The process of rewarding the making of certain responses is known as *reinforcement*, and is based on the principle of *need-reduction*. An animal has certain periodically recurring needs for food, sexual stimulation, drink, and so forth; anything reducing the pressing urgency of these needs reinforces whatever activity may be going on at the time, thus making the occurrence of such activity at a later date more likely. If, following Skinner, we put a hungry rat into a box, empty except for a projecting lever, the rat will sooner or later press the lever. If such pressure is followed by the release of a pellet of food into the box, the animal's hunger will be reduced, and the reinforcement provided by the pellet will make it more likely for the animal to press the lever again. A number of repetitions of this kind will lead to the *learning* of this particular response.

Direct or primary reinforcement of this kind, however, is not the only kind. So-called *secondary* reinforcement is of the utmost importance as a mediating agent between response and primary reinforcement. As an example, we may again take the salivating dog, conditioned to the bell. If we now pair the bell with some other stimulus, say a red light, without ever giving the dog food after showing the red light, then the dog will in course of time become conditioned to the light, and salivate when the red light is switched on, even though neither food nor bell are provided.

As another example, take again the rat pressing the bar for its pellet of food. When the delivery of the food is accompanied by a special clicking sound, rats retain the habit of pressing the bar much longer under conditions when no food is forthcoming after the bar has been pressed, then do rats where no click acts as a secondarily reinforcing agent. Thus any feature in the primary reinforcing situation can in itself become a secondary reinforcing agent, and consequently the chain of reinforcement between response and primary reward can become very elongated indeed. This is an indispensable factor in any learning theory, as learning takes place only if reinforcement follows the stimulus-response conjunction within a very few seconds.

Stimulus-response connections (sometimes known as S-R bonds) correspond roughly to what are known to common sense as habits. And bearing in mind that the most immediate effect of an external stimulus is the excitation of a receptor organ (eye, ear, skin, etc.), and that a response is always mediated by an effector (arm, leg, vocal cords, etc.), we can see why Hull suggests that 'the process of habit formation consists of the physiological summation of a series of discrete increments, each increment resulting from a distinct receptor-effector conjunction closely associated with a reinforcing state of affairs'. The importance of both the hedonistic and the associationist principles will be obvious in this formulation.

Hull adds a warning, however. 'Habit strength cannot be determined by direct observation, since it exists as an organization as yet largely unknown, hidden within the complex structure of the nervous system. This means that the strength of a receptor-effector connection can be determined, i.e. can be observed and measured, only indirectly. There are two groups of such observable phenomena associated with habit: (1) the antecedent conditions which lead to habit formation, and (2) the behaviour which is the after-effect or consequence of the antecedent conditions persisting within

245

the body of the organism.' Quite generally, the work of psychologists in the field of learning has been concentrated on studying both the antecedent conditions of habit formation, and also the consequent behaviour of the organism.

It is the contention of this chapter that the concept of *attitude* corresponds in every detail to the concept of *habit* as discussed by Hull. More specifically, both concepts show the following characteristics: (1) Attitudes and habits are both *learned* receptor-effector connections. (2) Attitudes and habits are both *dispositions* to act which cannot be observed directly. (3) Attitudes and habits are *hypothetical constructs* requiring linking up with antecedent conditions and consequent behaviour for their measurement. (4) Attitudes and habits denote persisting states of the organism, resulting from reinforcement, which are a necessary but not a sufficient condition for the evocation of any particular type of action under investigation.

In spite of these points of agreement, common usage will not easily concede the synonymous usage of the two terms. In ordinary speech, the term *habit* usually refers to a well-worn mode of action, rather than to the hypothetical underlying state of the organism which gives rise to this action. We refer to a person's habit of scratching his head, meaning by that the observable fact that he frequently indulges in this mode of action, rather than the neurophysiological substratum determining his action. In order to avoid such semantic pitfalls, Hull has used the expression $_sH_R$ to refer to his conception of habit, using the initial letters of the terms *stimulus* and *response* linked together by the hypothetical construct *habit*. In this sense, *attitude* is merely a special kind of $_sH_R$, and in thus identifying the two we reap the inestimable advantage of being able to make use of the extensive knowledge gained in the field of learning theory to make predictions regarding the behaviour of attitudes.

One such prediction may be made on the basis of our knowledge of the phenomena of *generalization*. In our discussion of $_sH_R$, we have spoken of the setting up of receptor-effector connections as if the connections mediated by reinforcement were strictly confined to the receptor and effector processes actually involved. This is by no means so. A dog conditioned to one tone will also respond to other similar but not identical tones; it has become conditioned not to one specific stimulus but to a whole *class of stimuli*. A rat conditioned to produce a pellet of food by pressing a lever with its right paw will also respond by pressing with its left paw, or its head; what has become conditioned is not just one response but a whole *class of responses*. These facts are referred to as stimulus generalization and response generalization respectively. Without generalization of this kind learning would be almost impossible, as *exact* replicas of the conditioned stimulus hardly ever recur in this world, and as *exact* replicas of the conditioned response are hardly ever adequate to secure the reward. On the basis of this concept of generalization we may predict that an attitude origin- ally established in such a manner as to mediate one type of response will in time mediate many different types of response; the selection of the particular type of response appropriate to the occasion would then depend on factors still to be discussed.

There is considerable proof regarding the generalized nature of responses in the attitude field. We think of attitudes as determin- ing our actions and our words. There is little doubt that they also determine the way in which we perceive things, the way in which we learn and remember things, and the manner of our reasoning. Thus, it has been shown, for instance, that when groups of pro- and anti-Communist students are made to listen to a pro-Com- munist argument, the pro-Communist students learn and remem- ber the ideas contained in it much better than do the anti-Com- munist students. When the tables are turned, however, and both groups are made to listen to an anti-Communist argument, the anti-Communist students are superior in both learning and reten- tion. Similarly, when students were made to learn paired associates like Stalin-Devil, and were later asked to reproduce the second word on being given the first, recall and learning were again found to be congruent with measured attitude. Thus, what we learn and what we remember depends in part at least on our pre-existing attitudes towards the material with which we are presented.

The same is true of reasoning. It has often been shown, for instance, that subjects who are quite capable of obtaining the right solution when confronted with a syllogism expressed in an abstract form, such as—'No A's are B's, some C's are B's; is it logical to conclude from this statement that no C's are A's?'—will go wrong when confronted with a syllogism expressed in terms which are relevant to their attitudes and stereotypes. An example of such a sentence might be the following: 'A trustworthy man does not engage in deceitful acts. The bombing of Pearl Harbour by the Japanese was a deceitful act. Is it logical to conclude from these statements that no Japanese are trustworthy?' Such distortions of the reasoning process are so widespread and so strongly correlated with the strength of a person's attitude that several psychologists have used them as direct measures of such attitudes.

Perception also appears to be influenced by attitudes. Of the large literature on this subject we shall only quote one study reported by Postman and Schneider. These writers predicted that the personal values of their subjects, as measured by the Allport-Vernon Scale discussed in a previous chapter, would determine the speed with which they would be able to read words relevant to these values. In other words, a person high on the theoretical value should be able to read more quickly words relevant to this field than would a person with high scores in some other value area. Each of the six value areas was represented by six words, three of which were relatively easy, common words, whilst three were relatively infrequent, difficult words. The words used are given below in Table XXX:

TABLE XXX

Stimulus Words Classified by Value Area and Frequency of Occurence

	Theoretical	Economic	Value Area Political	Aesthetic	Religious	Social
Relatively *Frequent*	science knowledge truth	savings financial trade	leader citizen influence	orchestra artist music	faith religious spirit	society affection guest
Relatively *Infrequent*	conception logic analysis	assets commerce efficiency	politician dominant status	graceful literature poetry	confession blessing divine	kindness loving hospitable

These words were exhibited in random order to the subjects by means of a tachistoscope, which is an instrument permitting the presentation of stimuli for extremely short periods of time. The exact length of time required for each subject to recognize each word was determined, and the average of these times compared with each individual's position on the six value scales. The results showed, as expected, that recognition was quicker for words in a value area on which the subjects made high scores and slow for words in value areas on which the subjects made low scores. Thus,

248

the very speed of perception is determined by a person's values and attitudes.

There would be little point in citing more examples from the large experimental literature, or go into details of those mentioned. The fact which cannot be gainsaid is that attitudes become extensively generalized on the response side, and determine many, if not all, areas of psychological functioning. This, more than anything, illustrates the error of speaking about attitudes only in terms of 'words and actions'. The position is very much more complicated than that and a proper theory of attitudes must be able to account for these complications.

Having shown that the hypothesis of response generalization in the attitude field receives considerable experimental support, we must now return to a question already raised toward the beginning of this chapter. Granted that many different responses may serve to mediate an attitude, how shall we decide in any particular situation, on the probability of any particular manifestation, or even of no manifestation at all? Under what conditions shall we expect reaction to take the form of words, under what conditions the form of action? Clearly our account so far has been incomplete, and requires the addition of further concepts. These also are provided by Hull, and, like $_sH_R$, are given symbolical expression.

The first of the concepts is that of *strength of primary drive*, represented by the symbol D. The second concept is that of *reaction-evocation potentiality*, or, more briefly, *reaction potential*, represented by the symbol $_sE_R$. The drive concept is used as a common denominator of all primary motivations, whether due to food privation, water privation, thermal deviations from the optimum, tissue injury, the action of sex hormones, or other causes. Reaction potential is used to denote the probability of any given type of behaviour; it is determined by habit strength and drive conjointly according to the general formula:

$$_sE_R = {}_sH_R \times D$$

This distinction between *reaction potential* and *habit strength* is of the utmost importance for a proper understanding of the concept of attitude. In a sense, it is parallel to the distinction between learning and performance, which may be intuitively easier to understand. Learning refers to the modification which has taken place in a person's nervous system as a result of repeated exposure to a certain class of stimuli, such as French irregular verbs. Performance refers to a person's action in reciting, or writing down, what he has learned, or in using it in an appropriate context. The two concepts are clearly different; performance can be directly observed, learning has to be inferred from performance. Learning, by itself, does not produce performance; it merely constitutes the indispensable condition for successful performance. But in addition to learning, there must also be motivation; we do not recite irregular verbs at odd times, and without provocation, but wait until there is a special reason for doing so. Performance corresponds to Hull's concept of $_sE_R$, learning corresponds to $_sH_R$, and motivation corresponds to D. Behaviour, verbal or otherwise, depends both on the existence of those modifications of the nervous system which are produced by learning, and which are conceived to be the locus of habit by Hull, and on the presence of a drive. 'The state of an organism's needs plays an important role in the causal determination of which of the many habits possessed by an organism shall function at a given moment.'

This discussion may be made more concrete by reference to an experiment reported by Hull. Rats were taught to press a bar for food; the number of reinforcements varying from 5 to 90, thus giving rise to different degrees of $_sH_R$. Later the groups were subdivided and tested after from 3 to 22 hours of food privation, thus varying the strength of D. The actual test consisted in determining how many times the rats in the various groups would press the bar without receiving any pellets. Figure 43 shows that the number of reactions $(_sE_R)$ is a function of both D and $_sH_R$; the largest number of responses is given by the rats who had fasted the longest and who had had the largest number of training trials.*

We can now see how superficial is the view of those who decline to accept the evidence of attitude scales because they feel that actions are more important. To say that is to misconceive the whole problem. An attitude is a hypothetical construct, something that cannot be observed but only inferred. Such inference is always hazardous, and requires detailed analysis. If we wish to measure attitudes $(_sH_R)$, we can do so only indirectly by measuring some

* It may be of interest to those who feel that animal experiments and concepts like 'conditioning' derived from them, can have little relevance to human behaviour, that Stagner has succeeded in conditioning attitudes, and that these conditioned attitudes showed generalization.

form of overt response $(_R E_R)$ which is inevitably influenced by motivational conditions (D). An understanding of these is required before any useful kind of measurement can be undertaken, and the form of response chosen in any particular investigation depends on the motivating conditions obtaining at the time. One form of response is not *better* than another; it is merely *different*. It is difficult to argue from one set of responses to another, particularly when

FIGURE 43

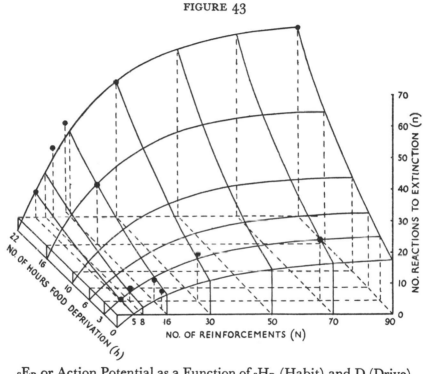

$_S E_R$ or Action Potential as a Function of $_S H_R$ (Habit) and D (Drive)

motivational conditions are changing, but we have shown in several chapters of this book that such predictions can be made successfully in terms of a suitable theoretical framework.

It will be clear from this discussion that if our interest lies in political action, the study of *attitudes* is not sufficient; we must also investigate the *drives* operating in any particular situation. It is only the combination of these two factors which will enable us to forecast what people will say or do in any given situation. Unfortunately, psychologists have concentrated almost entirely on technical problems of questionnaire construction and administration and have paid very little attention indeed to the question of drives. It must be admitted, of course, that experimentation in the motivational field is very much more complex and difficult than in almost any other, but, nevertheless, it may safely be surmised that until psychologists come to grips with the problem, much of their work will be of purely academic interest.

There are encouraging signs, however, that the importance of motivation in this field is being recognized and that experimental techniques are being worked out which should enable us to obtain a suitable body of factual information. One example may be quoted here to illustrate the type of work which may be done in this connection. The experiment in question was carried out by Sherif and is described in detail in his book, *Groups in Harmony and Tension*. Sherif took a group of twenty-four boys of average intelligence to a summer camp. These children were all close to twelve years old and came from lower middle class homes, and all of them were Protestants, as Sherif wished to exclude the operation of such factors as ethnic differences and differences in class, religion, education, age, sex, and so forth, and wanted instead to study the influence of newly created, experimentally controlled variables.

The experiment was carried out on a camp site consisting of about 125 acres of land, largely hills and timber, with a stream suitable for swimming and fishing running through it, and containing two bunk houses, an open mess hall, kitchen, infirmary, administration building, latrines, equipment sheds, and broad level areas for athletic events.

Three stages were planned:

'*Stage* 1 was planned as the period of informal groupings on the basis of personal inclinations and interests. All activities were camp-wide, offering maximum freedom for choice and "mixing up" of boys in various games and camp duties. Thus it became possible to single out budding friendship groups and, more or less, to equate the weights of such personal factors in the two experimental groups of Stage II.

Stage II was planned as the stage of formation of in-groups as similar as possible in number and composition of members. Each experimental group would participate separately in activities involving all the members of the group. Activities were chosen on the basis of their appeal value to the boys and their involvement of the whole group. Different activities afforded varied situations in which all members of a group could find opportunities to participate and "shine". All rewards given in this period were made on a group-unit basis, not to particular individuals.

Stage III was planned to study *intergroup relations* between the two experimental in-groups thus produced when these groups were brought into contact (1) in a series of competitive activities and situations and (2) in mildly frustrating situations so arranged that the actions of one group were frustrating to the other.'

Observations were carried out by participant observers whose functions were, of course, disguised from the children, and by other staff members, such as the official camp director, the activities director, the nurse, and Sherif himself, who appeared on the premises as a caretaker with the name of 'Mr. Mussee', a role which gave him freedom to be at crucial places at crucial times doing odd jobs without attracting the boys' attention.

After the boys had settled down (Stage I) they were split up into two groups, care being taken that these groups should be assembled on a purely artificial basis. Friendship pairs which had formed during the first period were broken up and the friends assigned to different groups. In this way, the artificially created groups had even less internal cohesion to begin with than they would have had on a chance basis. Very soon, members of the two groups gave names to their units, and the two groups became known as the Red Devils and the Bulldogs, respectively. The formation of these groups and the growth of internal structure within them essentially constituted the second stage. This formation of an 'in-group' sentiment proceeded extremely quickly and the two groups were firmly differentiated from each other after a few days.

The third stage involved bringing the two experimental groups into functional relationships which were competitive and mildly frustrating to one another. The frustrating situations were planned in such a way that on the whole they seemed to one group to have been caused by the other. This stage began with a competitive athletic contest, during which intergroup rivalry and hostility began to grow very rapidly indeed. Having set the process of group hostility formation going in this way, the experimenters then staged the first of a number of frustrating stiuations:

'On the evening of the Bulldogs' victory over the Red Devils in the athletic series and camp competition, both groups were asked to attend a party in the mess hall. Staff members not attached to either group openly expressed regrets that the boys were calling each other names and fighting. At this, members of the two in-groups came to the defence of their respective in-groups, placing all blame on the other group. The staff members reacted to this self-justification and blame of the out-groups by inviting both groups to a party to let "bygones be bygones". By careful timing and by indirectly interesting the Bulldogs in something else momentarily, the participant observers were able to see to it that the Red Devils got to the mess hall a few minutes before the Bulldogs. None of the subjects in either group suspected that this timing was deliberate.

The refreshments of ice cream and cake were on a table. Half of them had been battered, broken, or crushed to appear as though something had happened to them in transit; the other half remained whole and delectable. When the Red Devils arrived, they were told to serve themselves and to leave the Bulldogs their share. As we know, the Red Devils were the defeated group and had manifested considerable frustration and envy of the Bull Dogs for winning the highly valued knives.

Faced with the refreshments, half fresh and appetizing and half broken and crushed, the Red Devils, without any comment, picked up the good portion and carried it to their own table. At this point the Bulldogs arrived. Upon seeing the sorry-looking refreshments left for them and those the Red Devils had taken, they immediately protested by sulking and by remarks of hostility against the Red Devils ("Pigs", "Bums", and more objectionable terms). The Red Devils were at first rather complacent, justifying their actions in terms of "first come, first served", which became the standardized justification for all Red Devil members.'

This was only the first of several stage-managed frustrations the experimenters had planned, but it was so successful in causing hostility that the others had to be hastily abandoned. The meal described above was soon followed by fighting, at which table knives and saucers were thrown, until the staff intervened and stopped the fighting with considerable effort. In fact, the situation had become so ugly that it was decided to stop the third stage of the experiment immediately and to concentrate on breaking down the 'in-group' feeling of the Bulldogs and the Red Devils. This proved exceedingly difficult and a good deal of further fighting took place, and in spite of the efforts of camp leaders, the in-groups tended to persist until the camp broke up.

It would take us too long to describe in detail, as Sherif does, the growth of attitudes of members of one group to those of the other, the creation of stereotypes, and the interaction of these with the drive variables manipulated by the experimenter, as described above. The terrifying ease with which even a very slight manipulation of the drive variables produced hostility and intergroup tension between groups who had been extremely friendly to begin with, who spoke the same language, and who were not separated from each other by any ethnic, religious, or other factors, indicates the great promise which experimental studies in this field holds.

It does not require much imagination to see in this experiment a paradigm of the national and social struggles which rend our world, and it does not seem too far-fetched to suggest that a proper understanding of both the D and the $_sH_R$ variables concerned in creating the $_sE_R$ which so suddenly and catastrophically appeared in this experiment is an indispensable preliminary to political action superior to our present haphazard methods.

We have found in learning theory a firm theoretical foundation for the conception of attitudes; can we also look in the same field for an explanation of our concepts of tough-mindedness and extraversion? Before we can answer this point, we must make a distinction between two kinds of learning or conditioning. The reader may remember the two examples given early in this chapter —one of Pavlov's dog salivating to the sound of a bell, the other of Skinner's rat pressing a lever to obtain a pellet of food. While there are obvious similarities between these two types of neural modification through experience, we must note one important difference. In Pavlov's experiment, the salivation of the dog is in a sense coincidental; it does not in any way produce the food or aid in its production. In Skinner's experiment, however, the conditioned response (i.e. the pressing of the bar) is actually instrumental in producing the food. This difference has been recognized by psychologists who speak about classical conditioning (Pavlov) and instrumental conditioning (Skinner), or who alternately refer to the type of modification occurring in the Pavlov experiment as *conditioning*, that occurring in Skinner's experiment as *learning*. Let us

255

use the second type of nomenclature and ask ourselves what other differences there may be between learning and conditioning as so conceived.

In the first place, it will be noted that conditioning involves glands and the smooth muscles, i.e. those concerned with purely automatic activities, like breathing, heart beat, etc., while learning involves the skeletal muscles, i.e. those which mediate our voluntary actions. Conditioning, therefore, is concerned with *physiological* responses, learning with *behavioural* responses.

In the second place, the distinction corresponds roughly to that between the *central nervous system*, which is concerned with the transmission of impulses to the skeletal muscles, and the *autonomic nervous system*, which mediates responses of the glands and the smooth muscles, and is concerned with the expression of emotion.

The distinctions already made also correspond very roughly to the familar differentiation between *voluntary* and *involuntary* responses. The visceral and vascular responses mediated by the autonomic nervous system are beyond direct voluntary control, whereas practically all the skeletal responses are under voluntary control.

This distinction between conditioning of smooth muscles and glands, activated through the autonomic system, and learning mediated by skeletal muscles through the action of the central nervous system, has led Mowrer to suggest the following hypothesis:

'Under ordinary circumstances, the visceral and vascular responses occur in a smoothly automatic fashion, and serve what Cannon has called the "homeostatic", or physiological, equlibrium-restoring function. These same responses may, however, be made to occur, not only in response to actual physiological needs, but also in response to conditioned stimuli, or signals, of various kinds. And when the visceral and vascular responses occur on the latter basis, as *anticipatory* states, they *produce*, rather than eliminate, physiological disequilibrium and are consciously experienced as *emotion*. As such, they play enormously important motivational roles, roles so important to the survival of the organism that it is easily understood why the learning of these responses should be automatic, involuntary, distinct from the type of learning whereby ordinary habits are acquired. Biologically, it is clearly necessary that living organisms be equipped with a nervous system which will cause those skeletal responses to be fixated which reduce drives and give pleasure. But it is equally evident that living organisms must also be equipped with another nervous system which will cause emotional responses to be learned, not because they solve problems or give pleasure in any immediate sense, but because without such responses the organism would have slight chance of survival. There are grounds for believing that all emotions (including fear, anger, and the appetites) are basically painful (i.e. all have drive quality); and it is hard to see how they could be acquired by the same mechanism which fixes those responses (of the skeletal musculature) which are problem solving, drive reducing, pleasure giving. The latter are learned when a problem is resolved, ended; whereas it is often necessary that emotional responses become conditioned to signals which are associated with the *onset*, not the termination, of a problem.'

This is a very important distinction, which appears to be of considerable usefulness. Some types of learning are directly useful and produce results which are pleasant. We learn to ride a bicycle, play cricket, or make love, and the resulting pleasure 'stamps in' the actions which have produced this result. On the other hand, we are afraid when we see a bear in the wood, or hear bullets whining overhead, or find a bus bearing down on us. These reactions are unpleasant and are conditioned rather than learned; in spite of being unpleasant, however, they are exceedingly useful. As Mowrer puts it, learning is parallel to what Freud has called the *pleasure principle*, whereas conditioning is more closely related to the *reality principle*. 'In other words, living organisms require conditioned responses or emotions, not because it is pleasant to do so but because it is *realistic*.' It is certainly not pleasant to be afraid, for example, but it is very helpful from the standpoint of personal survival.

Mowrer develops this important distinction between learning and conditioning further by referring to child upbringing and education. As he points out, anthropologists tend to define 'culture' as accumulated and transmitted problem solutions. It is certainly true that some items of culture do in fact help us to solve problems; others, however, actually seem to make problems—problems of cleanliness, problems of conformity, problems of repression of sexual and aggressive impulses, and so forth. We must distinguish between problem solutions which are individually useful and which are learned, and problem solutions which are socially necessary

and which are conditioned. 'By and large, the solutions to individual problems involve the central nervous system and the
skeletal musculature, whereas the solutions to social problems involve the autonomic nervous system and the organs which mediate
emotional responses.' This differentiation is recognized in the
common-sense distinction between teaching and training. 'Teaching may be defined as a process whereby one individual helps
another learn to solve a problem more quickly or effectively than
would be likely on the basis of that individual's own unaided,
trial-and-error efforts. Here we are dealing with "items of culture"
which are individually helpful. Training, by contrast, may be
thought of as involving learning whose primary objective is social
rather than individual. In this connection one naturally thinks of
"items of culture" which are associated with such words as "morality", "character", "social responsibility", etc.'

The view presented here, in broad outline, gives us the following
picture. A child born into this world has a number of imperative
needs which require satisfaction. Similarly, society has certain
needs it must impress on the infant. The infant *learns* the methods
which most satisfy his needs and in most societies undergoes a
process of *teaching* in order to acquire the necessary skills. Society,
on the other hand, *conditions* him to act in conformity with its
precepts and he undergoes a process of *training* in order to become
socialized. The infant learns walking, the multiplication table, the
English language, and so forth; he becomes conditioned to use a
pot, and suppress the direct and immediate expression of his aggressive and sexual urges. While the division between learning and
conditioning in all these activities is probably nothing like as clear-
cut as Mowrer's writings would seem to suggest, nevertheless, there
is here a definite difference which it would be unreasonable to
overlook.

Now it will be clear to the reader that those attitudes which
combine to create our radical or our conservative ideology are
learned, using that term as defined above. We expect, therefore,
that Radical and Conservative attitudes will be formed essentially
in accordance with a definite system of rewards, i.e. in conformity
with the pleasure principle. We have already seen that, by and
large, this is so. There is a considerable correlation between social
class, status, and political alignment, and quite generally, individuals in our society tend to support parties from which they

expect definite benefits. In principle, therefore, the account of political behaviour in terms of $_sE_R$ as a multiplicate function of $_sH_R$ and D appears sufficient to account for our Radical and Conservative group of attitudes. In order to account for our tough-minded and tender-minded attitudes, however, we must have recourse to different kinds of analysis.

As our first step in this analysis, let us note that the speed with which socialization occurs and the success of the whole conditioning process must depend on two variables. The first is the *amount of conditioning* which society, in the form of parents, teachers, and so forth, inflicts on the individual; the other is the '*conditionability*' of the individual, i.e. the speed with which he will form the conditioned responses required. There is ample evidence to show that individuals differ considerably with respect both to the speed of acquisition of conditioned responses, and also the degree to which they are exposed to the conditioned processes. To take the latter aspect first, Allison Davis in America, Himmelweit in this country, and many other investigators also, have shown that there is a distinct tendency for middle-class children to be subjected to a considerably more prolonged and intensive conditioning process with respect to the suppression of directly aggressive and sexual modes of behaviour. Unless middle-class and working-class children differ considerably in their 'conditionability' we should, therefore, expect middle-class children to show a higher degree of 'socialization'. There is a good deal of evidence that this is true; we need only refer, for example, to the Kinsey report as evidence of very pronounced class differences in the sexual field.

Now socialization as a concept appears to be closely related to tender-mindedness. If the reader will glance back at the attitudes characterizing the two poles of the T-factor, he will notice that attitudes characterizing tough-mindedness are essentially concerned with immediate satisfaction of aggressive (war, persecution, hanging, flogging, etc.) and sexual (birth control, easier divorce, more abortion, etc.) impulses. Tender-minded attitudes, on the other hand, are concerned with ethical and religious ideas which act as barriers to such satisfactions and which, since time immemorial, have been part of the socialization process. On the basis, then, we should expect the 'under-socialized' working-class to be relatively tough-minded, the 'over-socialized' middle-class to be tender-minded. It will be remembered that this is precisely what in actual fact we do find. (It must be remembered, of course, that arguments involving very large groups, such as social classes, can be true only on the average. The reader will no doubt be able to adduce from his own experience many examples of working-class children whose upbringing contained far more 'socializing' influences than does the upbringing of the average middle-class children, and conversely there are undoubtedly many middle-class children whose parents do not behave in conformity with the norm of their group. Despite, however, many individual exceptions, the general rule is precisely in line with expectation on this hypothesis.)

We must next turn tó differences in 'conditionability', i.e. from the variable influence of society to the variable receptivity of the individual. Given an equal amount of socialization on the part of society, one would expect a person showing high conditionability, i.e. developing conditioned responses quickly and easily, to become 'over-socialized', while a person developing conditioned responses slowly and with difficulty, would tend to be 'under-socialized'. Pavlov was the first to notice the very marked differences with respect to conditionability which characterized his experimental animals, and similar findings have been made with respect to human beings.

Pavlov, on the basis of his psychiatric observations, formulated the hypothesis that conversion hysterics showed a preponderance of inhibitory over excitatory potential in the formation of conditioned reflexes, i.e. would form these only slowly and in a rather unstable manner. Conversely, he argued that, what we would now call 'anxiety neurotics' showed a considerable preponderance of excitatory over inhibitory potential and formed conditioned responses very quickly and in a very stable manner.

This hypothesis has received a good deal of factual support, notably by Welch and Kubis. These authors used the following method to establish conditioned reflexes. A list of 54 nonsense syllables, arranged in random order, was shown for six seconds each to the subject. One particular nonsense syllable 'KAX' was included several times in this series, and on every alternate representation of this syllable a loud buzzer was sounded. This buzzer produced a very strong psychogalvanic reflex. (This reflex consists in a lowering in the resistance of the skin of the body to the passage of an electric current. The reflex is very sensitive and can be measured very easily and with great accuracy.) After a while, the nonsense syllable by itself produced a fall in the electric resistance of the subject, even without the buzzer being sounded; in other words, the previously neutral stimulus, the nonsense syllable 'KAX', had become a conditioned stimulus and evoked the same response as the unconditioned stimulus, namely, the buzzer.

In one of their experiments, Welsh and Kubis found that a group of normal people needed 22 repetitions of the syllable—buzzer combination before the conditioned response was established. Neurotic patients suffering from anxiety only required 8 repetitions. Hysterics were found to be very difficult to condition altogether, and required at best many more repetitions than did the normal group.

In another experiment, Welsh and Kubis found no overlap at all in the number of repetitions required to establish conditioning between a group of neurotic patients showing considerable anxiety and another group of patients showing no anxiety whatever. These results, which have received confirmation by other writers, very strongly support Pavlov's hypothesis, and we may say, therefore, that conversion hysterics tend to condition only with great difficulty, whereas anxiety neurotics tend to condition very quickly and easily.

The most direct evidence on this point has been advanced by C. Franks (1954) from the Maudsley. He used a group of hysterics, a group of dysthymics (anxiety neurotics), and a group of normal people whose temperament would on the average be expected to be neither particularly extraverted nor particularly introverted. The conditioned response used was the blinking of the eyelid in response to a puff of air; the conditioned stimulus was a tone. After a few pairings of tone and air puff, the tone alone became capable of eliciting the eye wink. This process of conditioning was much speedier and more efficient in the dysthymic group than in the normal group, and it was slowest and least efficient in the hysteric group. The course of conditioning is shown in the first part of Figure 44; the second part of this Figure shows the course of the extinction of the phenomenon, i.e. the disappearance of the conditioned response when it is no longer reinforced. Here also dysthymics are seen to retain the conditioned response longer than normals, and normals longer than hysterics.

It will be remembered from an earlier chapter that the conversion hysteric is, as it were, the prototype of the *extravert*, whereas the anxiety neurotic is the prototype of the *introvert*. The generalization appears to be justified therefore that *introverts form quick and stable conditioned responses*, while *extraverts condition only slowly and with great difficulty*.

FIGURE 44

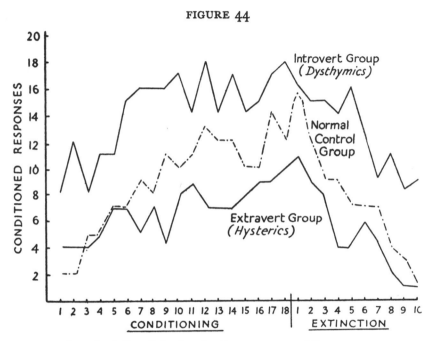

Speed of Conditioning in Extraverts and Introverts

If we put together these two propositions, namely, that conditioning lies at the basis of socialization, and that extraverts condition only with difficulty while introverts condition quickly and easily, it would seem to follow that if introverts and extraverts are subjected to the same degree of socialization pressure by society then introverts should become 'over-socialized' and extraverts 'under-socialized'.* And if, as was argued previously, socializa-

* The concepts of under-socialization and over-socialization, as defined here, may appear to some to bear some resemblance to two concepts of the Freudian hagiology namely, the *id* and the *super ego*. It is impossible to say whether this similarity is real or imagined as Freud's reification of mental mechanisms is a literary rather than a scientific device and does not provide any experimental method of proof or disproof.

tion may largely be equated with tender-mindedness, then we should expect extraverts to be tough-minded, introverts to be tender-minded. Again, it will be remembered that this is precisely what we have found to be true experimentally. Again, this is only a statistical truth in the sense that our deduction is verified on the average and that there may be individual exceptions. This is indeed inevitable, for the very simple reason that the pressure of socialization to which individuals are subjected differs from one individual to another, so that his own conditionability is not the only factor determining the outcome. It may be surmised that by combining knowledge of an individual's 'conditionability' and of the amount of pressure to which he has been subjected, we should be able to obtain a considerably better predictive accuracy than has been found so far by taking either of these two factors singly.

We may now enquire to what extent our data bear out this hypothesis. We have already shown the distinctly greater tendency towards aggression and dominance in Fascists and Communists, and in tough-minded people generally. This is precisely in line with the hypothesized under-socialization of these groups.

Regarding the socialization of the sex impulse, there is no direct evidence from experimental data, but the reader may recall the excesses which characterized the first years of existence of the U.S.S.R., and the constant immorality which was encouraged by the Hitlerian régime in Germany. Much has been written on the existence of similar sexual laxness in the Communist and Fascist parties in this country, but, as most of the reports are by former members of these parties or in any case by people whose interest is political rather than scientific, not too much stress can be laid on these suggestions.

One item of direct evidence in favour of our hypothesis comes from a paper by Dicks. This writer interviewed large numbers of German prisoners-of-war and rated them according to the degree of 'Fascist-mindedness' which they showed. Comparing the more Fascist-minded with the neutral and anti-Fascist groups, he concluded that in the former 'somatic conversions of a hysterical type predominated in the clinical picture'. In other words, the tendency for a correlation between hysteria and tough-mindedness, which we hypothesized, was found in this sample of German Nazis.

There would be little point in repeating all the other bits of evidence given in earlier chapters which fall into place in terms of this hypothesis. The reader will be able to carry out this task for himself and to form a judgment of the adequacy of the hypothesis. In essence, it seems to fulfil the main demands made of an hypothesis in the sense of accounting for the observed facts, and of suggesting new and hitherto undiscovered facts, the investigation of which could form the basis of a proof or disproof of the theory in question. It is to be hoped that further work along these lines will soon show to what extent our generalizations are supported by the facts, and to what extent they may require reformulation.

Chapter Nine

SUMMARY AND CONCLUSIONS

THROUGHOUT the eight chapters which comprise the bulk of this book an attempt has been made to keep the arguments fairly close to the facts, and accordingly the discussion has throughout been rather detailed. While this is necessary in order to give the reader an opportunity of examining the evidence for himself, it also has the unfortunate effect of somewhat blurring the main outlines of the argument. Accordingly, the present chapter has been added to recapitulate the main points made in the course of the discussion and to state, somewhat baldly, the main conclusions.

1. To begin with, it has been shown that social and political actions of all kinds are mediated through attitudes, and that consequently the study of the nature, development, and modification of attitudes is of fundamental importance to the development of a scientific psychology of politics.

2. Attitudes were shown to be very similar in many ways to habits. Attitudes and habits are both *learned* modifications of the central nervous system; both are *dispositions* to act which cannot be observed directly; both concepts are *hypothetical constructs* which require linking up with antecedent conditions and consequent behaviour for their measurement; and lastly, both denote *persisting states of the organism* which are a necessary, but not a sufficient condition for the evocation of any particular type of action.

3. Attitudes as so defined show a considerable degree of organization or structure. The fact that a person holds a particular attitude carries with it implications about other attitudes, and these implications can be given mathematical expression in the form of correlation coefficients. When such empirically determined cor-

265

relations are further analysed, it is found that they can all be regarded as being determined by two main principles or factors. One of these factors is the well known Radicalism-Conservatism continuum (R-factor). The other, which is quite independent of the first, was called Tough-minded versus Tender-minded (T-factor) in memory of a similar distinction made by William James in the philosophical field. In combination, these two factors, principles, or dimensions, appear sufficient to account for the great majority of observed relationships between social attitudes in this country, in the United States, in Sweden, Germany, and other countries having similar forms of social organization.

4. They also appear sufficient to account for the observed relationships between different political parties in this country. Thus, Fascists were found to be a tough-minded Conservative group, Communists a tough-minded Radical group. Conservatives and Socialists were found to be Conservative and Radical respectively on the R-factor, and intermediate with respect to the T-factor. Liberals were found to be the most tender-minded group and to be intermediate between Socialists and Conservatives with respect to the Radicalism-Conservatism variable. These relationships, which had been predicted from analysis of the interrelations between attitudes, were found in several independent studies and may therefore be regarded as firmly established. They indicate quite clearly that two dimensions are necessary in order to describe the positions of the main political groups active in this country at the moment.

5. Detailed experimental analysis disclosed that while the R-factor could truly be called a major dimension of social attitudes, the T-factor was of a different character altogether. It appeared essentially as a *projection* on to the field of social attitudes of certain fundamental personality traits, in the sense that a person's social attitude (Radical, Conservative, or intermediate) would seek expression in terms of the fundamental personality variables so closely connected with the T-factor.

6. Identification of these personality factors became our next task, and it was shown that there is a close relationship between Tough-mindedness and Extraversion on the one hand, and between Tender-mindedness and Introversion on the other. In view of the importance of this relationship, three separate experimental proofs were given, all of which verified this hypothesis.

7. While the relationship between Extraversion-Introversion

and Tough- and Tender-mindedness may therefore be considered a proven fact, nevertheless, it seemed likely that certain traits within the general grouping of traits denoted by the terms Extraversion and Introversion would be more characteristic than others of the Tough-minded and the Tender-minded respectively. The first trait or group of traits investigated in this connection was that of aggression and dominance, and it was shown that there was a distinct tendency for Tough-mindedness to be associated with both aggression and dominance. Certain more complex theories were considered, but as the experimental evidence did not favour them they had to be rejected. Among the theories so dealt with was the well-known 'scapegoat' theory.

8. Another set of traits possibly connected with Tough-mindedness is denoted by concepts such as rigidity, intolerance of ambiguity, narrow-mindedness, and mental concreteness. Some evidence was found that these traits do in fact tend to characterize tough-minded people in general, and Communists and Fascists in particular, but correlations were very much lower than they were in the case of aggression and dominance, and this hypothesis, therefore, is much less decisively proven than the former one.

9. In view of the fact that attitudes are acquired dispositions and resemble habits very closely, it was considered promising to investigate the application of modern learning theory to this field. By doing so it became possible to account for the fact that neither words nor actions can be counted upon invariably to reflect accurately a person's attitude. Learning theory draws an important distinction between that modification of the central nervous system which constitutes the essential basis of all learned behaviour, and performance, which is determined by a combination of this modification and a specific drive. Attitudes and habits correspond to these modifications of the central nervous system, the existence of which has to be inferred from actual behaviour; such behaviour, whether in terms of words or actions, requires in addition the action of a particular drive.

10. Within this general scheme, we must again differentiate two types of neural modification which account respectively for our R- and T-factors. These two types of modifications are called *learning* and *conditioning*. The term learning, in the narrower sense, applies to the modification of behaviour through the influence of reward and punishment and is concerned largely with the acquisi-

tion of voluntary responses and derives essentially from *hedonistic* theories of learning (pleasure principle). This type of learning appears to lie at the basis of attitudes in the Radicalism-Conservatism complex, as was shown by the close correspondence between such attitudes and social class and status.

11. Conditioning, on the other hand, applies to the modification of behaviour through the influence of association or contiguity, and is concerned largely with the acquisition of involuntary, emotional responses, and derives essentially from *associationist* theories of learning (reality principle). This type of conditioning appears to lie at the basis of attitudes in the tough- and tender-minded complex. Proof of this assertion was attempted in terms of the observed correlation between speed of conditioning and extra-version-introversion.

12. It should be noted that this connection between attitude measurement and learning theory, while supported by many facts, is nevertheless still at the speculative level, while the other conclusions summarized in this chapter have all received considerable direct proof to such an extent that they may be regarded as relatively well established. The interpretation of our results in terms of learning theory was included because it serves to bind together in a consistent scheme and to explain the major factual findings of our research. It was also hoped that the publication of such a theory, which could be supported or disproved by direct experimentation, might go some way towards directing research in this field into more profitable channels than the purely repetitive production of measuring scales which is so characteristic of its present state.

TECHNICAL NOTES

1. Detailed discussions of the definition of attitudes, sentiments, and other concepts relevant to the field are given by Allport (1929; 1935), French (1947), and Nelson (1939). Various definitions and discussions of points at issue are to be found in the papers by Bain (1930; 1936), Bernard (1930), Bertocci (1940), Bogardus (1925; 1931), Cattell (1940), Dewey (1922), Faris (1931), Horne (1936), Kempf (1935), Murray & Morgan (1945), Parks (1931), Pritchard (1932), Pyle (1928), Rice (1930), Sherif & Cantril (1945), Symonds (1927), Thomas & Znaniecki (1918), Thurstone (1929; 1931), Thurstone & Chave (1929), Titchener (1910), and Tuttle (1930); and the participants in the symposium mentioned in the text, i.e. Pear (1922), Rivers (1920; 1922), Shand (1914; 1922), and Tansley (1920; 1922). As an indication of the great variety of usage of the term 'attitude' we may quote a list given by Nelson (1939, p. 380) of twenty-three different ways in which the term has been defined or used.

(1) Organic drives.
(2) Purposes.
(3) Motives.
(4) A 'core of affect'.
(5) The emotional concomitants of action.
(6) Permanently felt dispositions.
(7) A special case of pre-disposition.
(8) Generalized conduct.
(9) A neural set. A Neuro-muscular set.
(10) A stabilized set.
(11) A state of readiness.
(12) A disposition of modifying arising experience.
(13) Verbal responses for or against a psychological object.
(14) Socially compelled behaviour of an enduring type.
(15) A response which is more obviously a function of disposition than of the immediate stimulus.
(16) The result of organization of experience.
(17) A directive or dynamic influence on the response to which related.
(18) A determiner of the direction of an activity.
(19) A guide for conduct. A point of reference for new experience.
(20) A trial response—substitute behaviour.
(21) A way of conceiving an object. A posture of consciousness.
(22) 'A sum total' of inclinations, feelings, notions, ideas, fears, prejudices, threats, and convictions about any specific topic.

(23) An integration of the specific responses into a general set.
This list will indicate more clearly than any argument why we have found it necessary in the text to stress the operational definition of attitude in terms of antecedent and consequent conditions.

2. The theory of intervening variables and hypothetical constructs in psychology is largely linked up with the writings of Hull (1943) and Tolman (1938). A very useful discussion of the nature of these concepts and the differences between them is given by MacCorquodale & Meehl (1948) who make references to various earlier writers, such as Benjamin (1937), Carnap (1936; 1937), Kaufmann (1944), Reichenbach (1938), Russell (1940), and others. Their main conclusion is that the practice of using the phrases 'intervening variable' and 'hypothetical construct' interchangeably may lead to fundamental confusion. They declare 'The distinction is between constructs which merely abstract the empirical relationships . . . and those constructs which are "hypothetical" (i.e. involve the supposition of entities or processes not among the observed). Concepts of the first sort seem to be identifiable by three characteristics. First, the statement of such a concept does not contain any words which are not reducible to the empirical laws. Second, the validity of the empirical laws is both necessary and sufficient for the "correctness" of the statements about the concept. Third, the quantitative expression of the concept can be obtained without mediate inference by suitable groupings of terms in the quantitative empirical laws. Concepts of the second sort do not fulfil any of these three conditions. Their formulation involves words not wholly reducible to the words in the empirical laws; the validity of the empirical laws is not a sufficient condition for the truth of the concept, inasmuch as it contains surplus meaning; and the quantitative form of the concept is not obtainable simply by grouping empirical terms and functions. We propose a linguistic convention in the interest of clarity: that the phrase *intervening variable* be restricted to concepts of the first kind, in harmony with Tolman's original definition; and that the phrase *hypothetical construct* be used for those of the second kind.' It will be clear to the reader that the concept of attitude, as used in this book, is a hypothetical construct rather than an intervening variable, as defined by these authors, and readers interested in the logical status of the concept may with advantage consult the detailed discussion of the differences between the concepts given by MacCorquodale & Meehl.

3. The most usual methods of deciding on a person's social status is by reference to his occupation. Several widely accepted scales are in existence in this country. The best known, perhaps, is the Registrar-General's Occupational Grading in terms of five classes:

> 'I. Upper and Middle Class.
> II. Intermediate.
> III. Skilled Workmen.
> IV. Intermediate.
> V. Unskilled Workmen.'

Also well known is the occupational code adopted by the Population Investigation Committee (the P.I.C.) code. The third is the Hall-Jones standard classification based on the Merseyside Survey. This classification makes use of seven categories, as follows:

Social Survey Code	Standard Classification
(a) Professional and Technical.	(1) Professional and High Administrative.
(b) Managerial and Executive.	(2) Managerial and Executive.
(c) Inspectional and Supervisory.	(3) Inspectional, Supervisory and other Non-Manual, higher grade.
(d) Clerical, higher.	(4) Inspectional, Supervisory and other Non-Manual, lower grade.
(e) Clerical, routine.	(5) Skilled Manual and routine grades of Non-Manual.
(f) Operative, skilled.	(6) Semi-skilled Manual.
(g) Operative, unskilled.	(7) Unskilled Manual.
(h) Other grades.	

(Hall & Jones, 1950, P. 33)

Comparison between these codes is made by Hall & Jones, who find considerable similarity. They also succeeded in showing, by asking various groups of people to grade a selected list of occupations in terms of social class, that there was considerable agreement not only between untrained subjects, but also between the mean ratings given by untrained subjects and their own classification.

That such a prestige rating is a good measure of social status is indicated in a paper by Cattell, who intercorrelated prestige ratings, average I.Q., average income, average number of years of education, and degree of birth restriction for 25 occupations, ranging from physician and banker at the one end to casual labourers, unskilled factory workers, and unemployed at the other. He found high correlations between the five criteria, i.e. those professions having the highest prestige rating also tended to have the highest I.Q., the highest income, the greatest amount of education, and the largest degree of birth restriction. The best index of all was found to be the prestige rating, closely followed by the I.Q.:

	1	2	3	4	5	Composite
(1) Prestige rating	—	·95	·92	·86	·83	·98
(2) I.Q.		—	·89	·86	·91	·97
(3) Income			—	·82	·81	·93
(4) Years of education				—	·82	·87
(5) Birth restriction					—	·84

Martin has shown that occupational grading, as indicated by the Hall-Jones index, is closely related to social class. Carrying out his research in two districts (Greenwich and Hertford) he found that 93 per cent of subjects in occupational grades one and two considered themselves middle-class, with only 4 per cent considering themselves working-class, and 3 per cent in the 'Don't Know' category. At the other extreme, those in occupational grades six and seven considered themselves as belonging to the working-class in 75 per cent of the cases, to the middle-class in 18 per cent only, with 7 per cent in the 'Don't Know' category. In grades three and four, percentages are 32 and 65 for working- and middle-class, respectively, whereas for category five the percentages are 67 and 30; in both cases 3 per cent fall into the 'Don't Know' category.

Martin also gives an interesting table 'which relates status and class to voting behaviour'. Status is expressed in terms of professional, salaried or manual, and the latter two groups are broken down in terms of whether the persons concerned consider themselves middle- or working-class. It will be seen from the table given below that salaried people considering themselves working-class voted Labour much more frequently than salaried people considering themselves middle-class. The same phenomenon is found among manual workers who considered themselves working- or middle-class respectively. These figures suggest that social class is a factor in voting behaviour which is, to some extent at least, independent of social status.

Social Class and Electoral Choice (1950)

		District	Lab. per cent	Lib. per cent	Con. per cent	D.V. per cent	N.S. per cent	N (=100) per cent
Professional	Middle	Greenwich	16	1	78	4	1	55
		Hertford	6	11	78	4	1	79
Salaried	Middle	Greenwich	22	6	62	4	6	77
		Hertford	8	14	70	3	5	132
Salaried	Working	Greenwich	44	6	44	6	–	54
		Hertford	18	15	48	17	2	54
Manual	Middle	Greenwich	58	3	32	5	2	59
		Hertford	41	12	29	13	5	52
Manual	Working	Greenwich	72	2	12	10	4	193
		Hertford	54	14	17	13	2	107

4. As the concept *correlation* is of fundamental importance in the type of work here discussed, a brief explanation may not be out of place. Biological phenomena often show a tendency to hang together or to be alike in certain ways; thus, people who are tall *tend* to be heavy, and people who do well on intelligence tests *tend* to do well in school and at University. It is important to give a mathematical expression to the degree of covariation that exists for any two variables. This expression is the coefficient of correlation. When there is no similarity or covariation at all, the correlation is zero; when there is complete identity or when the behaviour of one variable can be predicted with complete accuracy from the behaviour of the other, the correlation is 1·00. Most biological correlations lie between these two variables. Thus, the correlation between height and weight is about ·6, i.e. about equally far removed from perfect correspondence as from complete lack of correspondence. Height and intelligence only correlate about ·2, i.e. so little that no reasonable prediction of a person's intelligence can be made from his height, although there does exist a slight tendency for tall people to be more intelligent. The length of a person's right arm correlates with the length of his right leg about ·96, i.e. very near perfection; the length of his nose, however, shows almost zero correlation with his chest diameter. There are various types of correlations to suit different purposes; tetrachoric correlations, as mentioned in the text, are appropriate when continuous variables, like status and class, are dichotomized (upper

versus lower) for purposes of convenience. Correlations may be negative, as when possession of attribute A makes possession of attribute B less likely. Thus there exists a slight *negative* correlation ($-\cdot 20$) between intelligence and number of children in the family; the more intelligent children tend to come from less numerous families. While correlation implies a causal link, this link may be complex and indirect; because A and B are correlated, it does not follow that A has caused B, or that B has caused A. C may have caused both A and B, or there may be a whole chain of overlapping and interdependent causes.

5. An indication of the fact that the tetrachoric coefficient is not properly applicable to these data is given by the fact that although the correlation between attitude and class is higher than that between attitude and status, chi-squared calculated for both distributions with three degrees of freedom is higher for status (2204) than for class (1701). Similarly, both Pearson's contingency coefficient and Tschuprow's coefficient are higher for status ($\cdot 49$ and $\cdot 43$) than for class ($\cdot 45$ and $\cdot 39$). The most likely conclusion appears to be that the dependence of attitude on class and on status is approximately equal. Some calculations involving multiple correlations indicate that no better prediction is given by a combination of class and status than can be obtained from either alone.

6. Data on the relationship between voting and social class other than those quoted in the text are given in papers by Anderson & Davidson (1943), Benson & Wicoff (1944), Birch & Campbell (1950), Kerr (1944), Kitt & Gleicher (1950), and Linn (1949). Hayes (1939) presents an interesting study showing that the correlation between voting in the 1928 and 1932 presidential elections in America for 8,419 voters was only $\cdot 57$. Seventeen per cent of those studied changed party affiliation in these four years. This figure shows a very low degree of reliability for voting behaviour; as the data were obtained in America, however, they have not been used in our computations to correct for attenuation. It might also be surmised that reliability and consistency would be higher now than in the pre-Roosevelt era, when the main American parties were not related to status to anything like the same degree as they are now.

7. There is a considerable number of books and articles dealing with public opinion and attitude measurement and related topics such as market and consumer research. The best technical introduction is probably contained in McNemar's summary (1946). At a more elementary level is Gallup & Rae's book, *The Pulse of Democracy* (1940), while Cantril's *Gauging Public Opinion* (1944) contains a large amount of material. Other relevant books are the ones by Abrams (1951), Blankenship (1943; 1946), Chapin (1947), Chappell & Hooper (1944), Churchman *et al.* (1947), Jones (1950), Lydgate (1944), Robinson (1932), and Rogers (1949). Articles dealing with development and the general problems of opinion polling are those by Campbell (1946), Katz (1946), Lazarsfeld & Franzen (1945), Monachesi (1941), Radvanyi (1952), Stephan (1949), and Wilson (1947).

8.

Table

		20–29	30–49	50–64	65+	
		1	2	3	4	
Av. +	1	27	191	187	42	447
Av.	2	306	870	570	109	1855
Av. −	3	1350	2261	1129	248	4988
Very Poor	4	123	253	445	800	1621
		1806	3575	2331	1199	8911

9. The best brief introduction in this field is McNemar's article (1940), although for the practitioner, Yates's *Sampling Methods for Censuses and Surveys* (1949) is probably indispensable, or Deming's *Some Theories of Sampling* (1950). Other books and papers which give useful introductions, or discuss important points, are Bowley (1926; 1936), Cochran (1942; 1946), Cornfield (1942), Craig (1939), Hanna (1934), Hansen & Hurwitz (1943), Jensen (1926; 1928), Madow (1944), Mangus (1934), Neyman (1934; 1938), Schoenberg & Parten (1937), Stephan (1936; 1948), Sukhatme (1935), Woofter (1933), and Yates (1948). The papers by Haner & Meier (1951), Hochstim & Smith (1948), and Manheimer & Hyman (1949) may serve as a brief introduction to some experimental studies of the areas sampling and quota sampling methods, respectively.

10. Discussions of various advantages of the two-way, the multiple choice, and the open-end type of question are given by Campbell (1945), Cantril (1944), Gallup (1947), Hyman & Stember (1949), Kroeger (1947), Lazarsfeld (1944), and Payne (1951). Question wording and pretesting are discussed by Blankenship (1940; 1950), Cantril (1940), Crutchfield (1947), Gallup (1941), Jenkins (1941), Klare (1950), Payne (1949), and Rugg & Cantril (1942). The problem of bias is discussed by Kornhauser (1947) and Suchman (1947). The 'actuality' of a question is discussed by Hofstätter (1949; 1950; 1951) and Lazarsfeld & Robinson (1940). More specific problems are discussed by Field & Connelly (1942), Havighurst (1950), and Link (1943).

11. Problems of interviewing are dealt with in a symposium by Harris & Connelly (1948), by Cantril (1944), Gosnell & De Grazia (1942), Hofstätter (1949), Payne (1951), and many others. Various types of interviewer bias are discussed by Cahalan, Tamulonis & Verner (1947), Blankenship (1949), Fisher (1950), Stanton & Baker (1942), Stember & Hyman (1949), and Wyatt & Campbell (1950). The problem of non-respondents is discussed by Barnette (1950), Benson, Booman, & Clark (1951), Gaudet & Wilson (1940), Hilgard & Payne (1944), and Lundberg & Larsen (1949).

The quality of interviewers and the measurement of interviewing efficiency in an experimental study are dealt with by Benson (1941), Berdie (1943), Clarkson (1950), Crespi (1948), Guest (1947), Guest & Nuckols (1950), Heneman & Paterson (1949), Payne (1949), Hyman (1950), Shapiro & Eberhart (1947), Sheatsley (1950; 1951), Stewart & Flowerman (1951), Symonds & Dietrich (1941), and Williams (1942).

12. An excellent discussion of the 1948 pre-election polls is given in a book published by the Social Science Research Council (1949), and a detailed discussion of various factors involved is also given by the following writers: Bauer, Rieken & Bruner (1949), Blankenship (1948), Cahalan (1949), Cantril (1948), Chapin (1948), Deckinger (1948), Dodd (1948), Goldish (1948), Guest (1948), Gundlach (1948), Hausknecht (1948), Hyman (1949), Katz (1948; 1949), Likert (1948), Link (1948), McCarthy (1949), Meier (1949), Morgan (1948), Mosteller (1949), Parker (1948), Paterson (1948), and Peatman (1948).

13. The problem of reliability is taken up by the following writers: Janis, Fadner & Janowitz (1943), King (1944), Stock & Hochstim (1951), Wedell & Smith (1951), and Woodward & Franzen (1948).

The question of validity is discussed from various points of view by Churchman & Ackoff (1948), Connelly (1945), Crespi (1948), Dollard (1948), Eldersveld (1951), Fink & Lutz (1948), Gerberich (1947), Link & Freiberg (1942), Pace (1950), and Vaughn & Reynolds (1951).

14. The Bogardus Scale was originally published in 1925 with further contributions by the same author in 1928 and 1933. Of particular interest is the work of Adcock (1952) as it demonstrates the lack of uni-dimensionality of this scale. Other references of interest in connection with the Bogardus Scale are Freyre (1950), Guilford (1931), Hartley (1946), McCreary (1952), Meltzer (1939), Willems (1949), and Zeligs & Hendrickson (1933). A good summary of the main results and certain theoretical considerations of general psychological interest are given in a book by Sherif (1953).

15. Attitude scaling as a proper psychometric discipline originated with a brilliant series of papers by Thurstone (1927; 1928; 1929; 1931) and Thurstone & Chave (1929). In these he defined the notion of 'equal appearing interval' and attempted to measure a given person's attitude by the position of his median response on the scale. Likert (1932) and Likert et al. (1934) introduced the notion underlying the method of summated ratings, in which opinion statements are so arranged that answers to them can be assigned numerical values. The scale produce method used in the text of this chapter was originated by Eysenck & Crown (1949) in an attempt to combine the virtues of the equal appearing interval method and the method of summated ratings. This new method has been shown to be more reliable than the other two, and it might be made more reliable still by using an empirical weighting system rather than the fairly mechanical one illustrated in the text. Thus, weights could be chosen to maximize either reliability or validity and there appears to be little doubt that this method is more flexible than the other two. It will probably repay a more detailed study.

Guttman's contribution to the theory of uni-demensionality is contained in a series of papers (1944; 1947). In connection with these, reviews by Festinger (1947) and Eysenck (1951) might with advantage be consulted as well as the answers made by Guttman (1951). Discussions of various points in scale analysis will also be found in papers by Clark & Kriedt (1948), Ford (1950), and Jahn (1951), and Kriedt & Clark (1949).

Loevinger (1948) gives an extensive discussion of scale analysis and factor analysis, comparing both methods with her own technique of homogeneous tests, as outlined in a previous paper (1947). Her suggestions for the use of a coefficient of homogeneity does not appear to have been followed up sufficiently to make it possible to evaluate it on a concrete basis, but it should certainly be considered by anyone wishing to design a uni-dimensional or a homogeneous scale.

Of the very large number of papers dealing with scale construction, the following have been selected as representing the most worthwhile developments and comments: Attneave (1949), Ballin & Farnsworth (1941), Bittner & Rundquist (1950), Edwards (1952), Edwards & Kenney (1946), Edwards & Kilpatrick (1948), Farnsworth (1945), Ferguson (1941), Ojemann (1939), and Rundquist & Sletto (1930).

Finally, more general discussions will be found in papers by Edwards & Kilpatrick (1948), Ferguson (1939), and Schuman (1950).

16. The more important factorial studies of attitudes are summarized in *The Structure of Human Personality* (Eysenck, 1953). Among these worth consulting are those of Carlson (1934), Eysenck (1944, 1947), Ferguson (1939; 1941), Hatt (1948), Kulp & Davidson (1934), Sanai (1950), Stagner (1936), and Thurstone (1944). A brief discussion of some of these will be given in the next chapter.

17. The following scales for the measurement of factors R and T were constructed by Melvin (1954) on the basis of a large-scale factor analysis and item analysis of several hundred attitude statements. The scoring key is given after each of the items constituting the two scales. There are 16 items for the measurement of R and 32 items for the measurement of T; some items are used for measuring both dimensions. Some items in the scale are 'filler' items and are not scored at all.

As regards scoring, the R scale is always scored in the Radical direction. For items marked R+, agreement (+ or ++) is scored 1, and any other responses zero. For items marked R—, disagreement (— or ——) is scored 1, and any other responses zero.

The T scale is always scored in the tender-minded direction. For items marked T+, agreement (+ or ++) is scored 1, and any other responses zero. For items marked T—, disagreement (— or ——) is scored 1, and any other responses zero. The range of scores in the T scale is from 0 to 32; the range of scores on the R scale is from 0 to 16.

In order to establish the reliability of each scale, both the R and T scales have been divided into two parts of 8 and 16 items respectively. Items in part one have been given the subscript $_1$; items in part two have been given the subscript $_2$ (R_1 and R_2; T_1 and T_2).

In addition to R and T, an emphasis score (E score) is also derived. To obtain this score all ++ and —— endorsements are added together on all the items of the R and T scales. This score is indicative of the testee's 'tendency to certainty'.

The reliabilities (split-half corrected) of the R, T, and E scales have been established by Melvin, Coulter, and George. They vary somewhat from population to population but in a relatively unselected group lie between ·85 and ·95. No test-retest reliabilities are available but from experience with the old and less reliable scales, it appears likely that these would be in excess of the split-half reliabilities.

Factors R and T. Public Opinion Inventory

It is hoped you will be interested in this survey of public opinion. Below are given 60 statements which represent widely-held opinions on various social questions, selected from speeches, books, newspapers and other sources. They were chosen in such a way that most people are likely to agree with some, and to disagree with others.

After each statement, you are requested to record your personal opinion regarding it. You should use the following system of marking:

+ + if you strongly agree with the statement
+   if you agree on the whole
O   if you can't decide for or against, or if you think the question is worded in such a way that you can't give an answer
—   if you disagree on the whole
— — if you strongly disagree

Please answer frankly. Remember this is not a test; there are no 'right' or 'wrong' answers. The answer required is your own personal opinion. Be sure not to omit any questions. The questionnaire is anonymous, *so please do not sign your name.*

Do not consult any other person while you are giving your answers.

Opinion Statements		*Your Opinion*
1. The nation exists for the benefit of the individuals composing it, not the individuals for the benefit of the nation.		
2. Coloured people are innately inferior to white people.		
3. War is inherent in human nature.		
4. Ultimately, private property should be abolished and complete socialism introduced.	R_1+	
5. Persons with serious hereditary defects and diseases should be compulsorily sterilized.		
6. In the interests of peace, we must give up part of our national sovereignty.		
7. Production and trade should be free from government interference.	R_2-	
8. Divorce laws should be altered to make divorce easier.		T_1-
9. The so-called underdog deserves little sympathy or help from successful people.		T_2-
10. Crimes of violence should be punished by flogging.	R_1-	T_1-
11. The nationalization of the great industries is likely to lead to inefficiency, bureaucracy and stagnation.	R_1-	
12. Men and women have the right to find out whether they are sexually suited before marriage (e.g. by trial marriage.)	R_2+	T_1-
13. 'My country right or wrong' is a saying which expresses a fundamentally desirable attitude.	R_2-	

277

14. The average man can live a good enough life without religion. T_1-
15. It would be a mistake to have coloured people as foremen over whites.
16. People should realize that their greatest obligation is to their family.
17. There is no survival of any kind after death. T_1-
18. The death penalty is barbaric, and should be abolished R_2+ T_1+
19. There may be a few exceptions, but in general, Jews are pretty much alike. T_1-
20. The dropping of the first atom bomb on a Japanese city, killing thousands of innocent women and childdren, was morally wrong and incompatible with our kind of civilization. T_2+
21. Birth control, except when recommended by a doctor, should be made illegal. T_1+
22. People suffering from incurable diseases should have the choice of being put painlessly to death. T_1-
23. Sunday-observance is old-fashioned, and should cease to govern our behaviour.
24. Capitalism is immoral because it exploits the worker by failing to give him full value for his productive labour. R_2+
25. We should believe without question all that we are taught by the Church. R_1-
26. A person should be free to take his own life, if he wishes to do so, without any interference from society. T_2-
27. Free love between men and women should be encouraged as a means towards mental and physical health. R_1+ T_2-
28. Compulsory military training in peace-time is essential for the survival of this country. T_2-
29. Sex crimes such as rape and attacks on children, deserve more than mere imprisonment; such criminals ought to be flogged or worse. R_2-
30. A white lie is often a good thing. T_2-
31. The idea of God is an invention of the human mind. T_2-
32. It is wrong that men should be permitted greater sexual freedom than women by society.
33. The Church should attempt to increase its influence on the life of the nation. T_2+
34. Conscientious objectors are traitors to their country, and should be treated accordingly.
35. The laws against abortion should be abolished. T_2-
36. Most religious people are hypocrites. T_2-
37. Sex relations except in marriage are always wrong. R_2- T_2+
38. European refugees should be left to fend for themselves. T_1-

39. Only by going back to religion can civilization hope to survive.

40. It is wrong to punish a man if he helps another country because he prefers it to his own. R_1+

41. It is just as well that the struggle of life tends to weed out those who cannot stand the pace. T_1-

42. In taking part in any form of world organization, this country should make certain that none of its independence and power is lost. R_1-

43. Nowadays, more and more people are prying into matters which do not concern them. T_2-

44. All forms of discrimination against the coloured races, the Jews, etc., should be made illegal, and subject to heavy penalties.

45. It is right and proper that religious education in schools should be compulsory.

46. Jews are as valuable citizens as any other group. T_2+

47. Our treatment of criminals is too harsh; we should try to cure them, not punish them. R_1+ T_2+

48. The Church is the main bulwark opposing the evil trends in modern society. T_1+

49. There is no harm in travelling occasionally without a ticket, if you can get away with it. T_2-

50. The Japanese are by nature a cruel people.

51. Life is so short that a man is justified in enjoying himself as much as he can. T_1-

52. An occupation by a foreign power is better than war. R_2+ T_1+

53. Christ was divine, wholly or partly in a sense different from other men. T_2+

54. It would be best to keep coloured people in their own districts and schools, in order to prevent too much contact with whites.

55. Homosexuals are hardly better than criminals, and ought to be severely punished.

56. The universe was created by God. T_1+

57. Blood sports, like fox hunting for instance, are vicious and cruel, and should be forbidden. T_1+

58. The maintenance of internal order within the nation is more important than ensuring that there is complete freedom for all. T_2-

59. Every person should have complete faith in some supernatural power whose decisions he obeys without question.

60. The practical man is of more use to society than the thinker.

Personal details. It would be appreciated if you would fill in the following details:

61. Nationality ....

62. Male or Female ....

63. Age ....

64. Occupation (please give full details) ....
....

65. Father's Occupation (please give full details) ....
....

66. Age at which you finished your *full-time* education ....

67. Do you belong to any political party or to any organization, association, or group which is interested in political matters? If so, please give details (e.g. Liberal Party, Communist Party, Pacifist group, Anarchist group, etc.)
....
....

68. Assume that a General Election is to be held to-morrow. In your constituency you have a complete choice of all the political parties in this country. Which party would you prefer to vote for?
Any comments you may wish to make on this questionnaire would be very welcome.

18. Generalizations and conclusions in the text of this book are based largely on the sources quoted there, as well as on the work of Anderson (1938; 1948), Burgemeister (1940), Ferguson, Humphreys & Strong (1941), Fischer & Andrews (1947), Harris (1934), Hartmann (1934), McCarthy (1942), Peters (1942), Pintner (1933), Pintner & Forlano (1939), Rothney (1936), Sarbin & Berdie (1940), Schaefer (1936), Seashore (1947), Sisson & Sisson (1940), Smith (1949), Stone (1933), Traxler (1945), Tussing (1942), and Whiteley (1933; 1938).
The Strong Inventory is discussed in great detail in Strong's book *Vocational Interests of Men and Women*. This book gives a copy of the Interest Blank and also quotes the many hundreds of studies done in this field.

19. The reader may have noted a similarity of derivation between *attitudes* and *traits* and may wish to know just how the two are differentiated from each other. Both, it would appear, are hypothetical constructs regarding modifications of the nervous system, implying a disposition to act in certain ways, and both are measured in terms of observed precedent conditions and consequent behaviour.
There is little in the literature to guide us, and it may be surmised that the differences between attitudes and traits are less fundamental and far-reaching than they might appear at first sight. One possible distinguishing feature might be the fact that *attitudes usually refer to a specific group of people or things*, whereas traits refer to general aspects of behaviour. Thus, we might say that attitudes are traits having a specific referent, while traits are attitudes lacking a specific referent. Aggressiveness for example is a trait which will show itself in connection with any person or thing which thwarts or frustrates the person to whom we attribute this trait; he will slam the door, kick the dog, and beat his wife quite impartially. On the other hand, we speak about an *anti-Semitic attitude*

when this aggressiveness has found a specific referent, namely, the group of people known as Jews, or we talk about an *anti-Capitalist attitude* when aggressiveness has found another specific referent, namely, employers and 'rich people' in general.

This distinction links up with that between learning and conditioning made in Chapter Eight, and the reader who is interested in this point may find our discussion here easier to understand after reading that chapter. Briefly, it is suggested that traits are determined more strongly by inherited features of the central and autonomic nervous system (hence their generality) while attitudes are acquired in the course of the individual's life and represent learning modifications of the individual's nervous system (hence their specificity). A person can be aggressive or dominant or rigid in practically any environment whatsoever, but he would find it extremely difficult to be anti-Semitic in China, or anti-Capitalist among the Eskimos.

We do not, of course, wish to suggest that all traits are wholly innate and all attitudes wholly determined by environment. This would be a quite untenable view. It is suggested merely that the determination of traits in terms of heredity is much more strongly marked than is the determination of attitudes, and conversely that in the case of attitudes social learning plays a much more important part in our society than does inheritance. Some evidence for the influence of heredity on the determination of traits will be given later on in this chapter. The reader may also wish to consult the discussion of this point in *The Scientific Study of Personality*.

20. The reader may be interested in the detailed results of the factor analysis performed by E. George on the total group of subjects. Factor saturations for four factors are given in the Table below; these account for 53 per cent of the variance.

Test	Tender-mindedness	Radicalism	Neuroticism	Extraversion	h]
Theoretical Value	−·422	·324	−·220	−·284	·412
Economic Value	−·608	−·494	−·044	·079	·622
Aesthetic Value	·078	·361	·111	−·298	·238
Social Value	·179	·277	·153	·362	·263
Political Value	−·496	−·329	·026	·209	·339
Religious Value	·837	−·289	−·018	·147	·806
S (Social Shyness)	·244	·196	·526	−·515	·640
T (Introspectiveness)	·136	·265	·528	−·252	·431
D (Depression)	·050	−·037	·963	−·250	·494
C (Emotional Instability)	−·012	·087	·892	·003	·803
R (Rhathymia)	−·414	·115	−·196	·535	·509
Radicalism	−·099	·665	·046	−·039	·456
Tendermindedness	·800	−·091	·139	·170	·697
Emphasis	·098	·299	·057	·219	·150
Per Cent Variance	17·46	10·14	17·35	8·06	53·01

21. The main references for the technique of the Thematic Apperception

Test are papers by Kendig (1944), Morgan & Murray (1935), Murray (1937, 1938, 1943), Rapaport *et al.* (1946), and White (1944). Methods of interpretation are discussed by Harrison (1940, 1943), Rotter (1940, 1946), and Wyatt (1942, 1945). Data on reliability and validity of the Thematic Apperception Test are given by Balken & Masserman (1940), Bellak (1942, 1944), Combs (1946), Harrison (1943), Harrison & Rotter (1945), Masserman & Balken (1938, 1939), Slutz (1941), Tomkins (1942), White (1937), and many others. A detailed discussion of the tests is given by Bell (1948).

An important problem left unresolved by most current investigators is a question of whether T.A.T. stories really reveal fantasy behaviour of the subject or whether they can be used to reflect his actual behaviour. The problem is a very complex one which we cannot discuss here, but if the reader will turn to Chapter Eight, he will find a suggested solution to the rather similar problem of words and actions as indicators of attitudes.

22. Welsh assumes that the complexity-simplicity factor discovered by him is identical with, or at least similar to, the one discovered by Eysenck. In the text we have accepted this assumption, but it should be noted that direct proof of this identity would seem desirable. In Eysenck's experiment care was taken to eliminate extraneous sources of preference judgments which might result in the spurious appearance of a factor; this does not seem to have been done in the Welsh experiment. Thus, for instance, it will be noted that the figures used by Welsh differ in several dimensions. In the first place, there is the number of sides or number of lines; in the second place, there is the straight, ruled, or free-hand presentation of lines; in the third place, there is shading or absence of shading, in the fourth place, there are differences in the thickness of the lines. These four components are arbitrarily combined in various ways and no analysis is carried out to determine which is the crucial factor. In the Eysenck experiment with polygonal figures, no shading was involved, and all the sides were drawn by ruler, thus reducing the complexity of the elements involved.

It is unfortunate under the circumstances that no attempt was made by Barron and Welsh to obtain direct confirmation of their identification of the two factors. This might have thrown more light on the question under discussion. Much work needs to be done in this field before we can be quite certain of the exact conclusions warranted by the facts. In view of the obvious interest and importance of the subject, it is to be hoped that such experiments will soon be carried out to render our conclusions more certain.

23. A good summary of the literature of the frustration-aggression hypothesis is given by Himmelweit (1950). Other papers which may be used to introduce the reader to the rather complex techniques used are those of Adams (1940), Barker, Dembo, & Lewin (1941), Dollard, Doob, *et al.* (1939), Frederiksen (1942), Haggard & Freeman (1941), Jost (1941), Lewin, Lippit & White (1939) McClelland & Apicella (1945), Marquis (1943), Miller (1941), Rosenzweig (1941; 1943), Sargent (1948), Sears (1941), Seashore & Bavelas (1942), Sherman & Jost (1942), Wright (1942), and Zander (1944).

24. It is interesting to note that in spite of the wide usage of the term

rigidity, and in spite of the many attempts to measure this concept, there have been no attempts to show that rigidity tests intercorrelate in such a way as to substantiate the hypothesis that they all measure the same hypothetical trait. Recently Eriksen & Eisenstein (1953) and Goodstein (1953) have presented tables of correlations which suggest that it would be very dangerous indeed to accept this hypothesis. While correlations between rather similar tests do agree and are indeed found to correlate in the work of Coulter (1953) summarized in this book, most of the intercorrelations are insignificant and approach zero. The most likely conclusion, therefore, appears to be that we are dealing with several independent types of rigidity.

There is considerable danger that the concept of rigidity may fall into the same traps as the concept of perseveration, the history of which has been outlined in some detail by the writer in *The Structure of Human Personality* (1953). Here, also, the original hypothesis of an all-embracing general factor of perseveration was found to be misleading, and we now have several very much narrower factors which cover a limited field only, and are unrelated to each other. It appears a sad commentary on the inability of psychologists to learn from the mistakes of their predecessors that the errors of the perseveration research should be visited on rigidity research; one might have hoped that the lesson would have been learned once and for all that no traits should be hypothesized and 'measured' without adequate proof that these traits actually do exist as postulated and are measured by the tests constructed for that purpose.

25. Some of the best known studies indicating a slight positive correlation between intelligence and radicalism are those of Allport (1929), Harris, Remmers & Ellison (1932), Jones (1926), Moore & Garrison (1932), Murphy & Likert (1938), Symington (1935), Symonds (1925), and Vetter (1930). From the evidence adduced by some of these writers, particularly Murphy and Likert, it would appear that scholarship is a more important variable than intelligence, in the sense that Radical students tend to be more knowledgeable than Conservative students, matched for intelligence.

26. The interpretation of attitudes in terms of learning theory has received great impetus from the work of L. W. Doob (1947), whose definition of attitude may be of interest. According to him attitude is defined as '*an implicit, drive-producing response considered socially significant in the individual's society*'. Later on he slightly extends his definition to read as follows:
'An attitude is:
(1) 'an implicit response
(2) 'which is both (a) anticipatory and (b) mediating in reference to patterns of overt responses,
(3) 'which is evoked (a) by a variety of stimulus patterns (b) as a result of previous learning of gradients of generalization and discrimination,
(4) 'Which is itself cue-and drive-producing,
(5) 'and which is considered socially significant in the individual's society.'
While the writer would agree with Doob's general outlook, his own treatment is more in line with some criticisms brought forward by I. Chein (1948), who writes as follows: 'A second and more important inconsistency has to do with

the term in Doob's definition which asserts that an attitude is a response. Elsewhere, however, he writes that, "The individual . . . may not express his attitude in overt behaviour because its expression would be contrary to his general philosophy; *but his attitude persists*' (italics added). Now, by any ordinary usage of the word "response", a response occurs and is gone; it does not persist. In other words, if an attitude can persist, it cannot be a response. Dobb may, of course, have in mind a class of persistent responses, but such responses do not seem to belong in the stimulus-response formula and, hence, in behaviour theory. In all S-R psychologies one looks for a stimulus which immediately precedes the response, and to admit responses which keep going (perhaps for many years) is certainly to change the psychological significance of the stimulus term in the S-R formula.'

'Despite his definition of an attitude as a response, Doob often seems on the verge of thinking of an attitude as a habit or an established stimulus-response "bond". Thus he defines the strength of an attitude in terms of the strengths of the stimulus-response bonds in which it is involved. This would give meaning to Doob's statement that an attitude may persist, for, while the response may be momentary, the bond presumably persists. It may be more sensible, therefore, to think of an attitude as the *habit* rather than as a response.'

With this we are in full agreement and as will have been seen in our definition attitude is equated with habit rather than with response. Chein himself does not take this step but presents certain views of his own with which we cannot deal here. Both papers are well worth the reader's detailed study as the points at issue are vital for any theory of attitudes.

BIBLIOGRAPHY

This Bibliography is not meant to be in any sense complete; it merely indicates some of the main sources on which the writer has based himself.

Abrams, M. *Social surveys and social action*. London: Heinemann, 1951.

Adams, C. R. Individual differences in behaviour resulting from experimentally induced frustration. *J. Psychol.*, 1940, 10, 157–76.

Adcock, C. J. A factorial analysis of the Bogardus Scale. In: *The modification of international attitudes: a New Zealand study*. (Ed. J. R. McCreary) Wellington: Victoria Univ. Coll., Publications in Psychology, 1952, 2.

Allport, G. W. The composition of political attitudes. *Amer. J. Sociol.*, 1929, 35, 220–38.

Attitudes. In: *A Handbook of Social psychology*. (Ed. C. Murchison). Worcester: Clark Univ. Press, 1935.

, & Kramer, B. U., Some roots of prejudice. *J. Psychol.*, 1946, 22, 9–39.

, & Vernon, P. E., A study of values. Boston: Houghton Mifflin, 1931.

Anderson, R. G. Subjective ranking versus score ranking of interest values. *Personnel Psychol.*, 1948, 1, 349–55.

Technological aspects of counseling adult women. *J. appl. Psychol.*, 1938, 22, 455–69.

Anderson, D. & Davidson, P. E., *Ballots and the democratic class struggle; a study in the background of political education*. Stanford: Standford Univ. Press, 1943.

Asch, S. E. *Social psychology*. New York: Prentice-Hall, 1952.

Attneave, F. A method of graded dichotomies for the scaling of judgments. *Psychol. Rev.*, 1949, 56, 334–40.

Bain, R. Theory and measurement of attitudes. *Psychol. Bull.*, 1930, 27, 357.

285

Changed beliefs of college students. *J. abnorm. & soc. Psychol.*, 1936, 31, 1–11.

Balken, E. R., & Masserman, J. H. The language of phantasy: III. The language of the phantasies of patients with conversion hysteria, anxiety state, and obsessive-compulsive neuroses. *J. Psychol.*, 1940, 10, 75–86.

Ballin, M. R., & Farnsworth, P. R. A graphic rating method for determining the scale values of statements in measuring social attitudes. *J. soc. Psychol.*, 1941, 13, 323–27.

Barker, R., Dembo, T., & Lewin, K. Frustration and regression: an experiment with young children. *Univ. Iowa Stud. Child Welf.*, 1941, 18, No. 1.

Barnette, W. L., The non-respondent problem in questionnaire research. *J. appl. Psychol.*, 1950, 34, 397–98.

Barron, F. Personality style and perceptual choice. *J. Person.*, 1952, 20, 385,–401.

Complexity-simplicity as a personality dimension. *J. abnorm. soc. Psychol.*, 1953, 48, 163–72.

Some personality correlates of independence of judgment. *J. Person.*, 1953, 21, 287–97.

Barron, F., & Welsh, G. S. Artistic perception as a factor in personality style: its measurement by a figure-preference test. *J. Psychol.*, 1952, 33, 199–203.

Bauer, R. A., Rieken, H. W., & Bruner, J. S. An analysis of the stability of voting intentions: Massachusetts, 1948. *Int. J. Opin. Attit. Res.*, 1949, 3, 169–78.

Bell, J. E. *Projective techniques*. New York: Longmans, Green, 1948.

Bellak, L. An experimental investigation of projection. *Psychol. Bull.*, 1942, 39, 489.

The concept of projection: an experimental investigation and study of the concept. *Psychiatry*, 1944, 7, 353–70.

Benjamin, A. C., *An introduction to the philosophy of science. New York*: Macmillan, 1937.

Benson, E. G., & Wicoff, E. Voters pick their party. *Publ. Opin. Quart.*, 1944, 8, 164–74.

Benson, L. E. Studies in secret-ballot technique. *Publ. Opin. Quart.*, 1941, 5, 79–82.

Benson, S., Booman, W. P., & Clark, K. E. A study of interview refusals. *J. appl. Psychol.*, 1951, 35, 116–19.

Berdie, R. F. Psychological processes in the interview. *J. soc. Psychol.*, 1943, 18, 3–31.

Bernard, L. L. In: *Encyclopedia of the Social Sciences*. New York: Macmillan, 1930.

Bernberg, R. E. The direction of perception technique of attitude measurement. *Int. J. Opin. Attit. Res.*, 1951, 5, 397–406.

Bertocci, P. A. Sentiments and attitudes. *J. soc. Psychol.*, 1940, 11, 245–257.

Birch, A. H., & Campbell, P. Voting in behaviour in a Lancashire constituency. *Brit. J. Sociol.*, 1905, 1, 197–208.

Bird, C., Monachesi, E. D., & Burdick, H. Studies of group tensions: III. The effect of parental discouragement of play activities upon the attitudes of white children toward Negroes. *Child Dev.*, 1952, 23, 295–306.

Bittner, R. H., & Rundquist, E. A. The rank-comparison rating method. *J. appl. Psychol.*, 1950, 34, 171–77.

Blake, R. R., & Ramsey, G. V. *Perception. An approach to personality.* New York: Ronald Press, 1951.

Blankenship, A. B. The 'sample' study in opinion research. *Sociom.*, 1940, 3, 271–76.

Does the question form influence public opinion poll results? *J. appl. Psychol.*, 1940, 24, 27–30.

Consumer and opinion research: the questionnaire technique. New York: Harper, 1943.

How to conduct consumer and opinion research: the sampling survey in operation. New York: Harper, 1946.

What happened to the polls? *Int. J. Opin. Attit. Res.*, 1948, 2, 321–28.

A source of interviewer bias. *Int. J. Opin. Attit. Res.*, 1949, 3, 95–8.

Pre-testing a questionnaire for a public opinion poll. *Sociom.*, 1950, 3, 263–69.

Block, J., & Block, J. An investigation of the relationship between intolerance of ambiguity and ethnocentrism. *J. Person.*, 1951, 19, 303–11.

Bogardus, E. S. Social distance and its origins. *J. appl. Sociol.*, 1925, 9, 216–26.

Measuring social distance. *J. appl. Sociol.*, 1925, 9, 299–308.

Immigration and race attitudes. Boston: Heath, 1928.

Fundamentals of social psychology. New York: Appleton-Century, 1931.

A social distance scale. *Sociol. & Soc. Res.*, 1933, 17, 265–71.

Measuring changes in ethnic reactions. *Amer. Sociol. Rev.*, 1950, 15, 48–51.

Bowley, A. L. *Elements of statistics.* New York: Scribner, 1926.

Measurement of the precision attained in sampling. *Bull. Int. Stat. Inst.*, 1926, 22, Pt. 1, Appendix, 6–61.

The application of sampling to economic and sociological problems. *J. Amer. Stat. Assoc.*, 1936, 31, 474–80.

Brogden, H. E. The primary personal values measured by the Allport-

Vernon test, 'A Study of Values'. *Psychol. Mon.*, 1952, 66, No. 16.

Bruner, J. S., Postman, L., & McGinnies, E. Personal values as determinants of perceptual selection. *Amer. Psychol.*, 1947, 2, 285–286.

Burgemeister, B. B. The permanence of interests of women college students. *Arch. Psychol.*, 1940, No. 255, 59.

Cahalan, D. Implications to the social sciences of the 1948 mispredictions. *Int. J. Opin. Attit. Res.*, 1949, 3, 157–68.

—, Tamulonis, V., & Verner, H. W. Interviewer bias involved in certain types of opinion survey questions. *Int. J. Opin. Attit., Res.* 1947, 1, 63–77.

Campbell, A. A. Two problems in the use of the open question. *J. abnorm. soc. Psychol.*, 1945, 40, 340–43.

Measuring public attitudes: a summing up. *J. soc. Issues*, 1946, 2, 58–66.

The indirect assessment of social attitudes. *Psychol. Bull.* 1950, 47, 15–38.

Canon, W. B. *The wisdom of the body.* New York: W. W. Norton, 1932.

Cantril, H. Experiments in the wording of questions. *Pub. Opin. Quart.*, 1940, 4, 330–32.

Gauging public opinion. Princeton: Princeton Univ. Press, 1944.

The use of breakdowns. In: *Gauging public opinion.* (Ed. H. Cantril) Princeton: Princeton Univ. Press, 1944.

Polls and the 1948 U.S. Presidential Election; some problems it poses. *Int. J. Opin. Attit. Res.*, 1948, 2, 309–20.

—, & Allport, G. W. Recent applications of the study of values. *J. abnorm. soc. Psychol.*, 1933, 28, 259–73.

—, & Fried, E. The meaning of questions. In: *Gauging public opinion.* (Ed. H. Cantril) Princeton: Princeton Univ. Press, 1944.

—, & Sherif, M. *The psychology of ego-involvements.* London: 1947.

Carlson, M. B. Attitudes of undergraduate students. *J. soc. Psychol.*, 1934, 5, 202–12.

Carnap, R. Testability and meaning. Parts I–III. *Phil. Sci.*, 1936, 3, 419–71.

Testability and meaning. Part IV. *Phil. Sci.*, 1937, 4, 1–40.

Carter, L. F. The identification of 'racial' membership. *J. abnorm. soc. Psychol.*, 1948, 43, 279–86.

Cattell, R. B. Sentiment or attitude? *Char. & Pers.*, 1940, 9, 6–17.

The concept of social status. *J. soc. Psychol.*, 1942, 15, 293–308.

The ergic theory of attitude and sentiment measurement. *Educ. Psychol. Measmt.*, 1947, 7, 221–46.

BIBLIOGRAPHY

The discovery of ergic structure in man in terms of common attitudes. *J. abnorm. soc. Psychol.*, 1950, 45, 598–618.

, Heist, A. B., Heist, P. A., & Stewart, R. G. The objective measurement of dynamic traits. *Educ. Psychol. Measmt.*, 1950, 10, 224–48.

, Maxwell, E. F., Light, B. H., & Under, M. P. The objective measurement of attitudes. *Brit. J. Psychol. (Gen. Sect.)*, 1949, 40, 81–90.

Centers, R. *The psychology of social classes*. Princeton: Princeton Univ. Press, 1949.

Chapin, F. S. *Experimental designs in sociological research*. New York: Harper, 1947.

Factors related to errors of prediction by public opinion polls in the Presidential Election of 1948. *Int. J. Opin. Attit. Res.*, 1948, 2, 528–530.

Chappell, M. N., & Hooper, C. E. *Radio audience measurement*. New York: Stephen Days, 1944.

Chein, I. Behaviour theory and the behaviour of attitudes: some critical comments. *Psychol. Rev.*, 1948, 55, 175–88.

Churchman, C. W., Ackoff, R. L., & Wax, M. *Measurement of consumer interest*. Philadelphia: Univ. Pennsylvania Press, 1947.

The missing link—a post mortem. *Int. J. Opin. Attit. Res.*, 1948, 2, 489–93.

Clark, K. E., & Kriedt, P. H. An application of Guttman's new scaling techniques to an attitude questionnaire. *Educ. Psychol. Measmt.*, 1948, 8, 215–23.

Clarkson, E. P. The problem of honesty. *Int. J. Opin. Attit. Res.*, 1950, 4, 84–90.

Cochran, W. G. Sampling theory when the sampling units are of unequal sizes. *J. Amer. Statist. Ass.*, 1942, 37, 199–212.

Relative accuracy of systematic and stratified random samples for a certain class of populations. *Ann. Math. Stat.*, 1946, 17, 164–77.

Combs, A. W. The validity and reliability of interpretation from autobiography and Thematic Apperception Test. *J. clin. Psychol.*, 1946, 2, 240–47.

Connelly, G. M. Now let's look at the real problem: validity. *Pub. Opin. Quart.*, 1945, 9, 51–60.

Cooper, J. B. Attitudes and presumed knowledge. *J. soc. Psychol.*, 1951, 34, 97–110.

Corey, S. M. Professed attitudes and actual behaviour. *J. educ. Psychol.*, 1937, 28, 271–80.

Cornfield, J. On certain biases in samples of human population. *J. Amer. Stat. Ass.*, 1942, 37, 63–8.

Coulter, T. An experimental and statistical study of the relationship of prejudice and certain personality variables. *Ph.D. Thesis, Univ. London Lib.*, 1953.

Cowen, E. L. The influence of varying degrees of psychological stress on problem-solving rigidity. *J. abnorm. soc. Psychol.*, 1952, 47, 512–519.

, & Thompson, G. G. Problem-solving rigidity and personality structure. *J. abnorm. soc. Psychol.*, 1951, 46, 165–76.

Craig, A. T. On the mathematics of the representative method of sampling. *Ann. Math. Stat.*, 1939, 10, 26–34.

Crespi, L. P. Elections and poll validity. *Int. J. Opin. Attit. Res.*, 1948, 2, 481–88.

The interview effect in polling. *Pub. Opin. Quart.*, 1948, 12, 99–111.

Crutchfield, R. S. Variations in respondent's interpretations of an opinion-poll question. *Int. J. Opin. Attit. Res.*, 1947, 1, 1–12.

Davies, A. F. Prestige of occupations. *Brit. J. Sociol.*, 1952, 3, 134–47.

Deckinger, E. L. Why the pollsters failed. *Int. J. Opin. Attit. Res.*, 1948, 2, 585–91.

Deming, W. E. *Some theories of sampling.* New York: Wiley, 1950.

Dewey, J. *Human nature and conduct.* New York: Holt, 1922.

Dicks, H. V. German personality traits and Nazi ideology. In: *Propaganda in war and crisis.* (Ed. D. Lerner) New York: Steward, 1951.

Dodd, S. C. On predicting elections or other public behaviour. *Int. J. Opin. Attit. Res.*, 1948, 2, 494–502.

Dollard, J. Under what conditions do opinions predict behaviour? *Pub. Opin. Quart.*, 1948, 12, 623–32.

, Doob, L. W., *et al.*, *Frustration and aggression.* New Haven: Yale Univ. Press, 1939.

Doob, L. W. The behaviour of attitudes. *Psychol. Rev.*, 1937, 53, 135–156.

Public opinion and propaganda. London: Cresset Press, 1948.

The public presentation of polling results. In: *The pre-election polls of 1948. Report to the Committee on Analysis of Pre-Election Polls and Forecasts.* (Eds. F. Mosteller, *et al.*) New York: *Soc. Sci. Res. Co. Bull.*, 1949, 60, 29–53.

Duffy, E. A critical review of investigations employing the Allport-Vernon study of values and other tests of evaluative attitude. *Psychol. Bull.*, 1940, 37, 597–612.

, & Crissy, W. J. E. Evaluative attitudes as related to vocational interests and academic achievement. *J. abnorm. soc. Psychol.*, 1940, 35, 226–45.

Edwards, A. L. The scaling of stimuli by the method of successive intervals. *J. appl. Psychol.*, 1952, 36, 118–22.

, & Kenney, K. C. A comparison of the Thurstone and Likert techniques of attitude scale construction. *J. appl. Psychol.*, 1946, 30, 72–83.

, & Kilpatrick, F. P. Scale analysis and the measurement of social attitudes. *Psychomet.*, 1948, 13, 99–114.

, & Kilpatrick, F. P. A technique for the construction of attitude scales. *J. appl. Psychol.*, 1948, 32, 374–84.

Elsersveld, S. J. British polls and the 1950 General Election. *Pub. Opin., Quart.*, 1951, 15, 114–32.

Eriksen, C. W., & Eisenstein, D. Personality rigidity and the Rorschach. *J. Person.*, 1953. 21, 386–91.

Evans, R. I. Personal values as factors in anti-Semitism. *J. abnorm. soc. Psychol.*, 1952, 47, 749–56.

Eysenck, H. J. Some factors in the appreciation of poetry, and their relation to temperamental qualities. *Character & Pers.*, 1940, 9, 160–7.

The general factor in aesthetic judgments. *Brit. J. Psychol.*, 1940, 31, 94–102.

Personality factors and preference judgments. *Nature*, 1941, 148, 346.

The empirical determination of an aesthetic formula. *Psychol. Rev.*, 1941, 48, 83–92.

'Type'-factors in aesthetic judgments. *Brit. J. Psychol.*, 1941, 31, 262–70.

The experimental study of the 'Good Gestalt'—a new approach. *Psychol. Rev.*, 1942, 49, 344–64.

General social attitudes. *J. soc. Psychol.*, 1944. 19, 207–27.

Dimensions of Personality. London: Kegan Paul, 1947.

Primary social attitudes: 1 The organization and measurement of social attitudes. *Int. J. Opin. Attit. Res.*, 1947, 1, 49–84.

Social attitude and social class. *Brit. J. Sociol.*, 1950, 1, 56–66.

War and aggressiveness: a survey of social attitude studies. In: *The psychological factors of peace and war*. (Ed. T. H. Pear) London: Hutchinson, 1950.

Measurement and prediction. *Int. J. Opin. Attit. Res.*, 1951, 5, 95–102.

Primary social attitudes and the 'social insight' test. *Brit. J. Psychol.*, 1951, 40, 114–22.

Primary scoial attitudes as related to social class and political party. *Brit. J. Sociol.*, 1951, 2, 198–209.

The scientific study of personality. London: Routledge & Kegan Paul, 1952.

Primary social attitudes. II. A comparison of attitude patterns in England, Germany, and Sweden. *J. abnorm. soc. Psychol.*, 1953.

Social attitude research. In: *Current trends in British psychology,* (Ed. C. A. Mace & P. E. Vernon) London: Methuen, 1953.

The structure of human personality. London: Methuen, 1953.

Uses and abuses of psychology. London: Pelican, 1953.

, & Crown, S. National stereotypes: an experimental and methodological study. *Int. J. Opin. Attit. Res.,* 1948, 2, 1–14.

An experimental study in opinion-attitude methodology. *Int. J. Opin. Attit. Res.,* 1949, 3, 47–86.

Faris, E. The concept of social attitudes. In: *Social attitudes.* (Ed. K. Young) New York: Holt, 1931.

Farnsworth, P. R. Attitude scale construction and the method of equal appearing intervals. *J. Psychol.,* 1945, 20, 245–48.

Ferguson, L. W. Primary social attitudes. *J. Psychol.,* 1939, 8, 217–23.

The requirements of an adequate attitude scale. *Psychol. Bull.,* 1939, 37, 665–73.

A study of the Likert technique of attitude scale construction. *J. soc. Psychol.,* 1941, 13, 51–57.

The stability of the primary social attitudes. 1. Religionism and humanitarianism. *J. Psychol.,* 1941, 12, 283–88.

Personality Measurement. New York: McGraw-Vill, 1952.

, Humphreys, L. G., & Strong, F. W. A factorial analysis of interests and values. *J. educ. Psychol.,* 1941, 32, 197–204.

Festinger, L. The treatment of qualitative data by 'scale analysis'. *Psychol. Bull.,* 1947, 44, 149–61.

Field, H. H., & Connelly, G. M. Testing polls in official election booths. *Pub. Opin. Quart.,* 1942, 6, 610–16.

Fink, K., & Lutz, R. G. Fieldwork in the New Jersey election prediction. *Publ. Opin. Quart.,* 1948–9, 12, 724–26.

Fischer, R. P., & Andrews, A. L. A study of the effect of conformity to social expectancy on evaluative attitudes. *Educ. Psychol. Measmt.,* 1947, 7, 331–35.

Fisher, H. Interviewer bias in the recording operation. *Int. J. Opin. Attit. Res.,* 1950, 4, 391–411.

Fisher, J. The memory process and certain psychosocial attitudes, the special reference to the law of Prägnanz. I. Study of non-verbal content. *J. Person.,* 1951, 19, 406–20.

Fisher, S. An overview of trends in research dealing with personality rigidity. *J. Person.,* 1949, 17, 342–51.

Patterns of personality rigidity and some of their determinants. *Psychol. Mon.,* 1950, 64, 1–48.

Ford, R. N. A rapid scoring procedure for scaling attitude questions. *Pub. Opin. Quart.,* 1950, 14, 507–32.

Franks, C. An experimental study of conditioning as related to mental abnormality. *Ph.D. Thesis. Univ. London Lib., 1954.*

Frederiksen, N. The effects of frustration on negativistic behaviour of young children. *J. gen. Psychol.,* 1942, 61, 203–26.

French, V. V. The structure of sentiments. I. A restatement of the theory of sentiments. *J. Person.,* 1947, 15, 247–82.

The structure of sentiments. II. A preliminary study of sentiments. *J. Person.,* 1947, 16, 78–108.

The structure of sentiments. III. A study of philosophico-religious sentiments. *J. Person.,* 1947, 16, 209–44.

Frenkel-Brunswik, E. Psycho-analysis and personality reasearch. *J. abnorm. soc. Psychol.,* 1940, 35, 176–97.

A study of prejudice in children. *Hum. Rel.,* 1948, 1, 295–306.

Dynamic and cognitive categorization of qualitative material. I. General problems and the Thematic Apperception test. *J. Psychol.,* 1948, 25, 253–60.

Dynamic and cognitive categorization of qualitative material. II. Application to interviews with the ethnically prejudiced. *J. Psychol.,* 1948, 25, 261–77.

Distortion of reality in perception and in social outlook. *Amer. Psychol.,* 1949, 4, 253.

Intolerance of ambiguity as an emotional and perceptual personality variable. *J. Person.,* 1949, 18, 108–43.

Patterns of social and cognitive outlook in children and parents. *Amer. J. Orthopsychiat.,* 1951, 21, 543–58.

Personality theory and perception. In: *Perception—an approach to personality.* (Ed. R. R. Blake & G. V. Ramsey) New York: Ronald Press, 1951.

, & Sanford, R. N. Some personality factors in anti-Semitism. *J. Psychol.,* 1945, 20, 271–91.

Freyre, G. Reported in: *Tensions affecting international understanding.* (Ed. O. Klineberg) New York: *Soc. Sci. Res. Co. Bull.,* 1950, 62, 192–93.

Gallup, G. Question working in public opinion polls: comments on points raised by Mr. Stagner. *Sociom.,* 1941, 4, 259–68.

The quintamensional plan of question design. *Pub. Opin. Quart.,* 1947, 11, 385–93.

, & Rae, S. F. *The pulse of democracy.* New York: Simon & Schuster, 1940.

Gaudet, H. & Wilson, E. C. Who escapes the personal investigator? *J. appl. Psychol.,* 1940, 24, 773–77.

George, E. I. An experimental study of the relaton between personal values, social attitudes and personallty uaits. *Ph.D Thesis. Univ. London Lib.*, 1954.

Gerberich, J. B. A study of the consistency of informant responses to questions in a questionnaire. *J. educ. Psychol.*, 1947, 38, 299–306.

Goldish, S. The Minnesota Poll and the election. *Pub. Opin. Quart.*, 1948–9, 12, 722–24.

Goodstein, L. D. Intellectual rigidity and social attitudes. *J. abnorm. soc. Psychol.*, 1953, 48, 345–53.

Gordon, A. I. Frustration and aggression among Jewish university students: a survey at the University of Minnesota. *Jew. soc. Stud.*, 1943, 5, 27–42.

Goring, C. *The English Convict*. London: H.M.S.O., 1913.

Gosnell, H. F., & De Grazia, S. A critique of polling methods. *Pub. Opin. Quart.*, 1942, 6, 378–90.

Gough, H. G. Studies of social intolerance: I. Some psychological and sociological correlates of anti-Semitism. *J. soc. Psychol.*, 1951, 33, 237–46.

Studies of social intolerance: II. A personality scale for anti-Semitism. *J. soc. Psychol.*, 1951, 33, 247–55.

Studies of social intolerance: III. Relationship of the Pr scale to other variables. *J. soc. Psychol.*, 1951, 35, 257–62.

Studies of social intolerance: IV. Related social attitudes. *J. soc. Psychol.*, 1951, 33, 263–69.

, Harris, D. B., Martin, W. E., & Edwards, M. Children's ethnic attitudes. 1. Relationship to certain personality factors. *Child Dev.*, 1950, 20, 83–91.

Guest, L. A study of interviewer competence. *Int. J. Opin. Attit. Res.*, 1947, 1, 17–30.

Have these sources of polling error been fully explored? *Int. J. Opin. Attit. Res.*, 1948, 2, 507–9.

, & Nuckols, R. A laboratory experiment in recording in public opinion interviewing. *Int. J. Opin. Attit. Res.*, 1950, 4, 336–52.

Guilford, J. P. Racial preferences of a thousand American university students. *J. soc. Psychol.*, 1931, 2, 179–204.

Gundlach, R. H. There are hazards in predicting elections in critical times. *Int. J. Opin. Attit. Res.*, 1948, 2, 555–58.

Guttman, L. A basis for scaling qualitative data. *Amer. sociol. Rev.*, 1944, 9, 139–50.

Intensity and a zero point for attitude analysis. *Amer. sociol. Rev.*, 1947, 12, 56–7.

On Festinger's evaluation of scale analysis. *Psychol. Bull.*, 1947, 44, 451–65.

Suggestions for futher research in scale and intensity analysis of attitudes and opinions. *Int. J. Opin. Attit. Res.*, 1947, 1, 30–55.

The Cornell technique for scale and intensity analysis. *Educ. Psychol. Measmt.*, 1947, 7, 247–79.

Scale analysis, factor analysis, and Dr. Eysenck. *Int. J. Opin. Attit. Res.*, 1951, 5, 103–20.

, & Suchman, E. A. Intensity and a zero point for attitude analysis. *Amer. sociol. Rev.*, 1947, 12, 57–67.

Haggard, E. A., & Freeman, G. I. Reactions of children to experimentally induced frustration. *Psychol. Bull.*, 1941, 38, 581.

Hall, J., & Jones, D. C. Social grading of occupations. *J. Sociol.*, 1950, 1, 31–55.

Haner, C. F., & Meier, N. C. The adaptability of area-probability sampling to public opinion measurement. *Pub. Opin. Quart.*, 1951, 15, 335–52.

Hanna, H. S. Adequacy of the sample in budgetary studies. *J. Amer. Stat. Ass.*, 1934, 29 (Suppl.), 131–34.

Hansen, M. H., & Hurwitz, W. N. On the theory of sampling from finite populations. *Ann. Math. Stat.*, 1943, 14, 333–62.

Harding, J. Refusals as a source of bias. In: *Gauging public opinion.* (Ed. H. Cantril) Princeton: Princeton Univ. Press, 1944.

Harris, A. J., Remmers, H. H., & Ellison, C. G. The relation between liberal and conservative attitudes in college students, and other factors. *J. soc. Psychol.*, 1932, 3, 320–35.

Harris, D. Group differences in values within a university. *J. abnorm. soc. Psychol.*, 1934, 29, 95–102.

Harris, D. B., Gough, H. G., & Martin, W. E. Children's ethnic attitudes. II. Relationship to parental beliefs concerning child training. *Child Dev.*, 1950, 21, 169–81.

Harris, N., & Connelly, G. M. A symposium on interviewing problems. *Int. J. Opin. Atitt. Res.*, 1948, 2, 69–84.

Harrison, R. Studies in the use and validity of the Thematic Apperception test with mentally disordered patients. II. A quantitative validity study. *Char. & Person.*, 1940, 9, 122–33.

Studies in the use and validity of the Thematic Apperception test with mentally disordered patients. III. Validation by the method of 'blind' analysis. *Char. & Person.*, 1940, 9, 134–38.

The Thematic Apperception and Rorschach methods of personality investigation in clinical practice. *J. Psychol.*, 1943, 15, 49–74.

, & Rotter, J. B. A note on the reliability of the Thematic Apperception test. *J. abnorm. soc. Psychol.*, 1945, 40, 97–9.

Hartley, E. E. *Problems in prejudioo.* New York: King's Crown Press, 1946.

Hartmann, G. W. Sex differences in valuation of attitudes. *J. soc. Psychol.*, 1934, 5, 106–12.

The contradiction between the feeling-tone of political party names and public response to their platforms. *J. soc. Psychol.*, 1936, 7, 336–55.

Hatt, P. Class and ethnic attitudes. *Amer. Soc. Rev.*, 1948, 13, 36–43.

Hausknecht, G. Comment of five questions. *Int. J. Opin. Attit. Res.*, 1948, 2, 510–11.

Havighurst, R. J. Problems of sampling and interviewing in studies of old people. *J. Geront.*, 1950, 5, 158–67.

Hayes, S. P. The interrelations of political attitudes: IV. Political attitudes and party regularity. *J. soc. Psychol.*, 1939, 10, 503–22.

Helfant, K. Parents' attitudes *vs.* adolescent hostility in the determination of adolescent sociopolitical attitudes. *Psychol. Mon.*, 1952, 66, 1–23.

Heneman, H. G., & Paterson, D. G. Refusal rates and interviewer quality. *Int. J. Opin. Attit. Res.*, 1949, 3, 392–98.

Hilgard, E. R., & Payne, S. L. Those not at home: riddle for pollsters. *Pub. Opin. Quart.*, 1944 8, 254–61.

Himmelweit, H. T. Frustration and aggression. A review of recent experimental work. In: *The psychological factors of peace and war.* (Ed. T. H. Pear) London: Hutchinson, 1950.

Hochstim, J. R., & Smith, D. M. K. Area sampling or quota control?— Three sampling experiments. *Pub. Opin. Quart.*, 1948, 12, 73–80.

Hofstaetter, P. R. *Die Psychologie der öffentlichen Meinung.* Wien: Braumüller, 1949.

The actuality of questions. *Int. J. Opin. Attit. Res.*, 1950, 4, 16–26.

Importance and actuality. *Int. J. Opin. Attit. Res.*, 1951, 5, 31–52.

A factorial study of prejudice. *J. Person.*, 1952, 21, 228–39.

Horne, E. P. Socially significant attitude objects. *Bull. Purdue. Univ.*, 1936, 37, 117–26.

Hull, C. L. *Principles of behaviour.* New York: Appleton-Century, 1943.

Hyman, H. Interviewing and questionnaire design. In: *The pre-election polls of 1948. Report to the Committee on Analysis of Pre-Election Polls and Forecasts* (Ed. E. Mosteller, *et al.*) New York: *Soc. Sci. Res. Co. Bull.*, 1949, 60, 119–73.

Problems in the collection of opinion-research data. *Amer. J. Sociol.*, 1950, 55, 363–70.

, & Stember, H. Interviewer effects in the classification of responses. *Pub. Opin. Quart.*, Winter 1949, 669–82.

Jahn, J. A. Some further contributions to Guttman's theory of scale analysis. *Amer. sociol. Rev.*, 1951, 16, 233–39.

James, W. *Pragmatism.* New York: Longmans, Green, & Co., 1907.

Janis, I. L., Fadner, R. H., & Janowitz, M. The reliability of a content analysis technique. *Pub. Opin. Quart.*, 1943, 7, 293–396.

Jenkins, J. G. Characteristics of the question as determinants of dependability. *J. consult. Psychol.*, 1941, 5, 164–69.

Jensen, A. Report on the representative method in statistics. *Bull. Int. Stat. Inst.*, 1926, 22, 359–78.

The representative method in practice. *Bull. Int. Stat. Inst.*, 1926, 22, 381–439.

Purposive selection. *J. Roy. Stat. Soc.*, 1928, 91, 541–47.

Johnson, C. S. Measurement of racial attitudes. *Amer. Sociol. Soc. Papers*, 1931, 25, 150–53.

Jones, D. C. *Social surveys.* New York: Longmans, Green, 1950.

Jones, G. S. The opinions of college students. *J. appl. Psychol.*, 1926, 10, 427–36.

Jost, J. Some physiological changes during frustration. *Child Dev.*, 1941, 12, 9–15.

Kahn, L. A. The organization of attitudes toward the Negro as a function of education. *Psychol. Mon.*, 1951, 65, 39.

Katz, D. The measurement of intensity. In: *Gauging public opinion.* (Ed. H. Cantril) Princeton: Princeton Univ. Press, 1944.

The interpretation of survey findings. *J. soc. Issues*, 1946, 2, 33–44.

Polling methods and the 1948 polling failure. *Int. J. Opin. Attit. Res.*, 1948, 2, 469–80.

An analysis of the 1948 polling predictions. *J. appl. Psychol.*, 1949, 33, 15–28.

, & Cantril, H. An analysis of attitudes toward fascism and communism. *J. educ. soc. Psychol.*, 1940, 35, 356–66.

Katz, M. R. A hypothesis on anti-Negro prejudice. *Amer. J. Sociol.*, 1947, 53, 100–4.

Kauffman, F. *Methodology in the social sciences.* London: Oxford Univ. Press, 1944.

Kempf, E. J. Physiology of attitudes. *Med. Rec.*, 1935, 142, 403–6; 446–50.

Kendig, I. V. Projective techniques as a psychological tool in diagnosis. *J. clin. Psychopath. Psycother.*, 1944, 6, 101–10.

Kerr, W. A. A quantitative study of political behaviour, 1840–1940. *J. soc. Psychol.*, 1944, 19, 273–81.

King, M. B. Reliability of the idea-centred question in interview schedules. *Amer. sociol. Rev.*, 1944, 9, 57–64.

Kitt, A. S., & Gleicher, D. B. Determinants of voting behaviour. *Pub. Opin. Quart.*, 1950, 14, 393–412.

Klare, G. R. Understandability and indefinite answers to public opinion questions. *Int. J. Opin. Attit. Res.*, 1950, 4, 91–6.

Klein, G. S., & Schlesinger, H. J. Perceptual attitudes toward instability: I. Prediction of apparent movement experiences from Rorschach responses. *J. Person.*, 1951, 19, 289–302.

Klineberg, O. *Tensions affecting international understanding: a survey of research.* New York: Soc. Sci. Res. Co. Bull., 1950, 62, 227.

Kornhauser, A. The problem of bias in opinion research. *Int. J. Opin. Attit. Res.*, 1947, 1, 1–16.

Kounin, J. S. Experimental studies of rigidity: I. Measurement of rigidity in normal and feeble-minded persons. *J. Char. & Person.*, 1941, 9, 251–72.

Experimental studies of rigidity: II. Explanatory power of the concept of rigidity as applied to feeble-mindedness. *J. Char. & Person.*, 1941, 9, 273-82.

Kramer, B. M. Dimensions of prejudice. *J. Psychol.*, 1949, 27, 389–451.

Kriedt, P. H., & Clark, K. E. 'Item analysis' versus 'scale analysis'. *J. apl. Psychol.*, 1949, 33, 114–21.

Kroeger, H. J. The usefulness of the multiple-choice question. *Int. J. Opin. Attit. Res.*, 1947, 1, 102–5.

Krout, M. H., & Stagner, R. Personality development in radicals. *Sociomet.*, 1939, 2, 31–46.

Kulp, D. H., & Davidson, H. H. Sibling resemblance in social attitudes. *J. educ. Sociol.*, 1933, 7, 133–40.

The application of the Spearman tow-factor theory to social attitudes. *J. abnorm. soc., Psychol.*, 1934, 29, 269–75.

LaPiere, R. T. Attitudes *vs.* actions. *Social Forces*, 1934, 13, 230–7.

Type-rationalizations of group antipathy. *Social Forces*, 1936, 15, 232–7.

The sociological significance of measurable attitudes. *Amer. Sociol. Rev.*, 1938, 3, 175–82.

Lasswell, H. D. *Psychopathology and politics.* Chicago: Univ. Chicago Press, 1930.

Lazarsfeld, P. F. The controversy over detailed interviews—an offer for negotiation. *Pub. Opin. Quart.*, 1944, 8, 38–60.

, Berelson, B., & Gaudet, H. *The people's choice.* New York: Columbia Univ. Press, 1948.

, & Franzen, R. H. Prediction of political behaviour in America. *Amer. Soc. Rev.*, 1945, 10, 261–73.

, & Robinson, W. S. Some properties of the trichotomy 'Like, No

Opinion, Dislike' and their psychological interpretation. *Sociom.*, 1940, 3, 151–78.

Lerner, D. *Propaganda in war and crisis*. New York: Steward, 1951.

Levinson, D. J. An approach to the theory and measurement of ethnocentric ideology. *J. Psychol.*, 1949, 28, 19–39.

, & Sanford, R. N. A scale for the measurement of anti-Semitism. *J. Psychol.*, 1944, 17, 339–70.

Lewin, K., Lippit, R., & White, R. K. Patterns of aggressive behaviour in experimentally created social climates. *J. soc. Psychol.*, 1939, 10, 271–99.

Likert, R. A technique for the measurement of attitudes. *Arch. Psychol.*, 1932, 140, 55.

Public opinion polls: why did they fail? *Sci. Amer.*, 1948, 179, 7–11.

The polls: straw votes or scientific instruments. *Amer. Psychol.*, 1948, 3, 556–7.

, Roslov, S., & Murphy, G. A simple and reliable method of scoring the Thurstone scales. *J. soc. Psychol.*, 1934, 5, 228–38.

Lindzey, G. An experimental examination of the scapegoat theory of prejudice. *J. abnorm. soc. Psychol.*, 1950, 45, 296–309.

An experimental test of the validity of the Rosenzweig Picture-Frustration Study. *J. Person.*, 1950, 18, 315–20.

Thematic Apperception Test: Interpretive assumptions and related empirical evidence. *Psychol. Bull.*, 1952, 49, 1–25.

, & Riecken, H. W. Inducing frustration in adult subjects. *J. consult. Psychol.*, 1951, 15, 18–23.

, & Rogolsky, S. Prejudice and identification of minority group membership. *J. abnorm. soc. Psychol.*, 1950, 45, 37–53.

Link, H. C. An experiment in depth interviewing on the issue internationalism versus isolationism. *Pub. Opin. Quart.*, 1943, 7, 267–79.

Some milestones in public opinion research. *Int. J. Opin. Attit. Res.*, 1947, 1, 36–46.

What went wrong with the election polls? *Int. J. Opin. Attit. Res.*, 1948, 2, 503–6.

, & Freiberg, A. D. The problem of validity versus reliability in public opinion polls. *Pub. Opin. Quart.*, 1942, 6, 87–98.

Linn, E. L. The influence of liberalism and conservatism on voting behaviour. *Pub. Opin. Quart.*, 1949, 13, 299–309.

Loevinger, J. A systematic approach to the construction and evaluation of tests of ability. *Psychol. Mon.*, 1947, 61, 49.

The technic of homogeneous tests compared with some aspects of 'scale analysis' and factor analysis. *Psychol. Bull.*, 1948, 45, 507–529.

Luchins, A. S. Mechanization in problem-solving—the effect of Einstellung. *Psychol. Mon.*, 1942, 54, 95.

BIBLIOGRAPHY

Proposed methods of studying degrees of rigidity in behaviour. *J. Person.*, 1947, 15, 242–6.

Rigidity and ethnocentrism: a critique. *J. Person.*, 1949, 17, 449–66.

Personality and prejudice: a critique. *J. soc. Psychol.*, 1950, 32, 79–94.

Lundberg, G. A., & Larsen, O. N. Characteristics of hard-to-reach individuals in field surveys. *Pub. Opin. Quart.*, 1949, 13, 487–94.

Lurie, W. A. A study of Spranger's Value-Types by the method of factor analysis. *J. soc. Psychol.*, 1937, 8, 17–37.

Lydgate, W. A. *What our people think*. New York: Crowell, 1944.

McCarthy, P. J. Election predictions. In: *The pre-election polls of 1948. Report to the Committee on Analysis of Pre-Election Polls and Forecasts.* (Ed. F. Mosteller, *et al.*) New York: *Soc. Sci. Res. Co. Bull.*, 1949, 60, 15–28.

The cross-sections used in predicting the 1948 elections. In: *The pre-election polls of 1948. Report to the Committee on Analysis of Pre-Election Polls and Forecasts.* (Ed. F. Mosteller, *et al.*) New York: *Soc. Sci. Res. Co. Bull.*, 1949, 60, 81–118.

McCarthy, T. J. Personality tests of seminarians. *Stud. Psychol. Psychiat. Cathol. Univ. Amer.*, 1942, 5, 46.

McClelland, L. C., & Apicella, F. S. A functional classification of verbal reactions to experimentally induced failure. *J. abnorm. soc. Psychol.*, 1945, 40, 376–91.

McLeod, H. An experimental study of the inheritance of introversion-extraversion. *Ph.D. Thesis*, Univ. London, 1953.

MacCorquodale, K., & Meehl, P. E. On a distinction between hypothetical constructs and intervening variables. *Psychol. Rev.*, 1948, 55, 95–107.

McCreary, J. R. *The modification of international attitudes: a New Zealand study*. Wellington: *Victoria Univ. Publ. Psychol.*, 1952, 2.

McNemar, Q. Sampling in psychological research. *Psychol. Bull.*, 1940, 37, 331–65.

Opinion attitude methodology. *Psychol. Bull.*, 1946, 43, 289–374.

Madow, W., & Madow, L. On the theory of systematic sampling. *Ann. Math. Stat.*, 1944, 15, 1–24.

Maller, J. B., & Glaser, E. M. *Interest-values inventory*. New York: Bureau of Publications, Teachers Coll., Columbia Univ., 1939.

Mangus, A. R. Sampling in the field of rural relief. *J. Amer. Stat. Ass.*, 1934, 29, 410–15.

Manheimer, D., & Hyman, H. Interviewer performance in area sampling. *Pub. Opin. Quart.*, 1949, 13, 83–92.

Marks, E. S. The undecided voter. In: *The pre-election polls of 1948. Report to the Committee on Analysis of Pre-Election Polls and Forecasts.*

(Ed. F. Mosteller, *et al.*) New York: *Soc. Sci. Res. Co. Bull.*, 1949, 60, 263–89.

Marquis, D. P. A study of frustration of new-born infants. *J. exp. Psychol.*, 1943, 32, 123–38.

Martin, F. M. Social status and electoral choice in two constituencies. *Brit. J. Sociol.*, 1952, 3, 231–41.

Maslow, A. H. The authoritarian character and structure. *J. soc. Psychol.*, 1943, 18, 401–11.

Masserman, J. H., & Balken, E. R. The clinical application of phantasy studies. *J. Psychol.*, 1938, 6, 81–8.

The psychoanalytic and psychiatric significance of phantasy. I. *Psychoanal. Rev.*, 1939, 26, 243–79. II. *Psychoanal. Rev.*, 1939, 26, 535–49.

Meier, N. C. Polls and the 1948 election—in retrospect. *Int. J. Opin. Attit. Res.*, 1949, 3, 13–22.

Meltzer, H. Group differences in nationality and race preferences of children. *Sociom.*, 1939, 2, 86–105.

Melvin, D. An experimental and statistical study of two primary social attitudes. *Ph.D. Thesis, Univ. London Lib.*, 1955.

Miller, N. E. The frustration-aggression hypothesis. *Psychol. Rev.*, 1941, 48, 337–42.

, & Bugelski, R. Minor studies in aggression: the influence of frustrations imposed by the in-group on attitudes expressed toward out-groups. *J. Psychol.*, 1948, 25, 437–42.

Monachesi, E. D. An evaluation of recent major efforts at prediction. *Amer. sociol. Rev.*, 1941, 6, 478–86.

Montague, M. F. Some psychodynamic factors in race prejudice. *J. soc. Psychol.*, 1949, 30, 175–87.

Moore, G., & Garrison, R. C. A comparative study of social and political attitudes of college students. *J. abnorm. soc. Psychol.*, 1932, 27, 195–208.

Morgan, R. Last-minute changes in voting intention. *Pub. Opin. Quart.*, 1948, 12, 470–80.

Morgan, C. D., & Murray, H. A. A method for investigating phantasies. The Thematic Apperception Test. *Arch. Neurol., Psychiat. Chic.*, 1935, 34, 289–306.

Morse, N., & Allport, F. H. Anit-Semitism: a study of the causal factors and other associated variables. *Amer. Psychol.*, 1949, 4, 261.

Mosteller, F. The reliability of interviewers' ratings. In: *Gauging Public Opinion.* (Ed. H. Cantril) Princeton: Princeton Univ. Press, 1944.

Measuring the error. In: *The pre-election polls of 1948. Report to the Committee on Analysis of Pre-Election Polls and Forecasts.* (Ed. F. Mosteller, *et al.*) New York: *Soc. Sci. Res. Co. Bull.*, 1949, 60, 54–80.

BIBLIOGRAPHY

Mosteller, F., & Cantril, H. The use and value of a battery of questions In: *Gauging Public Opinion.* (Ed. H. Cantril) Princeton: Princeton Univ. Press, 1944.

Mosteller, F., & McCarthy, P. J. Estimating population proportions. *Pub. Opin. Quart.*, 1942, 6, 452–8.

Mosteller, F., Hyman, H., McCarthy, P. J., Marks, E. S., & Truman, D. B. *The pre-election polls of 1948. Report to the Committee on Analysis of Pre-Election Polls and Forecasts.* New York: Soc. Sci. Res. Co. Bull., 1949, 60, 396.

Mowrer, O. H. *Learning theory and personality dynamics.* New York: Ronald Press, 1950.

Murphy, G., & Likert, R. *Public opinion and the individual.* New York: Harper, 1938.

Murray, H. A. Techniques for a systematic investigation of fantasy. *J. Psychol.*, 1937, 3, 115–43.

Explorations in personality. New York: Oxford Univ. Press, 1938.

Manual for the Thematic Apperception Test blank. Cambridge: Harvard Univ. Press, 1943.

, & Morgan, C. D. A clinical study of sentiments: I. *Genet. Psychol. Mon.*, 1945, 32, 3–149. II. *Genet. Psychol. Mon.*, 1945, 32, 153–311.

Mussen, P. H., & Wyszynski, A. B. Personality and political participation. *Hum. Relat.*, 1952, 5, 65–82.

Nelson, E. Attitudes: 1. Their nature and development. *J. Gen. Psychol.*, 1939, 21, 367–99.

Neumann, G. B. A study of international attitudes of high school students. *Teach. Coll. Contrib. Educ.*, 1927, No. 239.

Newcomb, T. M. *Personality and social change.* New York: Dryden Press, 1943.

Newcomb, T. M., & Svehla, G. Intra-family relationships in attitude. *Sociomet.*, 1937, 1, 180–205.

Neyman, J. On two different aspects of the representative method; the method of stratified sampling and the method of purposive selection. *J. Roy. Stat. Soc.*, 1934, 97, 558–606.

Contribution to the theory of sampling human populations. *J. Amer. Stat. Ass.*, 1938, 33, 101–16.

Nystrom, G. H. The measurement of Filipino attitudes toward America by the use of the Thurstone technique. *J. soc. Psychol.*, 1933, 4, 249–52.

O'Connor, P. Ethnocentrism, intolerance of ambiguity and abstract reasoning ability. *J. abnorm. soc. Psychol.*, 1952, 47, 526–30.

Ojemann, R. H. A revised method for the measurement of attitude. *Univ. Ia. Stud. Child Welf.*, 1939, 17, 5–18.

Pace, C. R. Opinion and action: a study in validity of attitude measurement. *Educ. Psychol. Measmt.*, 1950, 10, 411–19.

Parker, C. E. Polling problems in state primary elections. *Pub. Opin. Quart.*, 1948–9, 12, 728–31.

Parks, R. E. Human nature, attitudes ,and the mores. In: *Social attitudes.* (Ed. K. Young) New York: Holt, 1931.

Paterson, D. G. Note on the constant error in the Gallup Presidential Election Poll. *Int. J. Opin. Attit. Res.*, 1948, 2, 559–60.

Payne, S. L. Interviewer memory faults. *Pub. Opin. Quart.*, 1949–50, 13, 684–5.

Case study in question complexity. *Pub. Opin. Quart.*, 1949–1950, 13, 653–8.

The art of asking questions. Princeton: Princeton Univ. Press, 1951.

Peak, H. Observations on the characteristics and distribution of German Nazis. *Psychol. Mon.*, 1945, 59, No. 6.

Pear, T. H. The relations of complex and sentiment, IV. *Brit. J. Psychol.*, 1922, 13, 130–40.

(Ed.) *Psychological factors of peace and war.* London: Hutchinson, 1950.

Peatman, J. G. D.K.'s for Truman. *Int. J. Opin. Attit. Res.*, 1948, 2, 537–42.

Peters, R. A study of the intercorrelations of personality traits. *Cath. Univ. Amer. Stud. Psychol. Psychiat.*, 1942, 5, 7.

Pintner, R. A comparison of interests, abilities, and attitudes. *J. abnorm. soc. Psychol.*, 1933, 27, 351–7.

, & Forlano, G. Dominant interests and personality characteristics. *J. gen. Psychol.*, 1939, 21, 251–60.

Porter, G. Student opinions on war. *Ph.D. Thesis, Univ. Chicago Lib.*, 1926.

Postman, L., Bruner, J. S., ; McGinnies, E. Personal values as selective factors in perception. *J. abnorm. soc. Psychol.*, 1948, 43, 142–54.

, & Schneider, B. H. Personal values, visual recognition, and recall. *Psychol. Rev.*, 1951, 18, 271–84.

Preston, M. G., & Kahn, L. A. The prejudice of out-groups. *Int. J. Opin. Attit. Res.*, 1949, 3, 214–28.

Pritchard, E. E. Nature of kinship extension. *Man*, 1932, 7.

Prothro, E. T. Ethnocentrism and anti-negro attitudes in the deep South. *J. abnorm. soc. Psychol.*, 1952, 47, 105–8.

Pyle, W. H. *The psychology of learning.* Baltimore: Warwick & York, 1928.

Radvanyi, L. Ten years of sample surveying in Mexico. *Int. J. Opin. Attit. Res.*, 1951–2, 5, 491–510.

BIBLIOGRAPHY

Rapaport, D., Gill, M., & Schafer, R. *Diagnostic psychological testing.* *Vol. II.* Chicago: Year Book Pubs., 1946.

Reichard, S. Rorschach study of the prejudiced personality. *Amer. J. Orthopsychiat.*, 1948, 18, 280–6.

Reichenbach, H. *Experience and prediction.* Chicago: Univ. Chicago Press, 1938.

Rice, S. A. *Statistics in social studies.* Philadelphia: Univ. Penn. Press, 1930.

Rivers, W. H. R. *Instinct and the unconscious.* Cambridge: Cambridge Univ. Press, 1920.

The relations of complex and sentiment. 1. *Brit. J. Psychol.*, 1922, 13, 107–12.

Robinson, C. *Straw votes.* New York: Columbia Univ. Press, 1932

Robinson, D., & Rohde, S. Two experiments with an anti-Semitism poll. *J. abnorm. soc. Psychol.*, 1946, 41, 136–44.

Rogers, L. *The pollsters; public opinion, politics and democratic leadership.* New York: Knopf, 1949.

Rokeach, M. Generalized mental rigidity as a factor in ethnocentrism. *J. abnorm. soc. Psychol.*, 1948, 43, 259–78.

Rigidity and ethnocentrism: a rejoinder. *J. Person.*, 1949, 17, 467–474.

The effect of perception time upon rigidity and concreteness of thinking. *J. exp. Psychol.*, 1950, 40, 206–16.

A method for studying individual differences in 'narrow-mindedness'. *J. Person.*, 1951, 20, 219–33.

'Narrow-mindedness' and personality. *J. Person.*, 1951, 20, 234–51.

Prejudice, concreteness of thinking and reification of thinking. *J. abnorm. soc. Psychol.*, 1951, 46, 85–91.

Toward the scientific evaluation of social attitudes and ideologies. *J. Psychol.*, 1951, 31, 97–104.

Attitude as a determinant of distortions in recall. *J. abnorm. soc. Psychol.*, 1952, 47, 482–88.

Rosenblith, J. F. A replication of 'some roots of prejudice'. *J. abnorm. soc. Psychol.*, 1949, 44, 470–89.

Rosenzweig, S. Need-persistive and ego-defensive reaction to frustration as demonstrated by an experiment on repression. *Psychol. Rev.*, 1941, 48, 347–9.

An experimental study of repression, with special reference to need-persistive and ego-defensive reactions to frustration. *J. exp. Psychol.*, 1943, 32, 64–74.

Rothney, J. W. M. Evaluative attitudes and academic success. *J. educ. Psychol.*, 1936, 27, 292–8.

Rotter, J. B. Studies in the use and validity of the Thematic Apperception Test with mentally disordered patients. I. Method of analysis and clinical problems. *Char. & Person.*, 1940, 9, 18–34.

Thematic Apperception Tests: suggestions for administration and interpretation. *J. Person.*, 1946, 15, 70–92.

Rugg, D. 'Trained' *vs.* 'untrained' interviewers. In: *Gauging public opinion.* (Ed. H. Cantril) Princeton: Princeton Univ. Press, 1944.

How representative are 'representative samples'? In: *Gauging public opinion.* (Ed. H. Cantril) Princeton: Princeton Univ. Press, 1944.

, & Cantril, H. The wording of questions. In: *Gauging public opinion.* (Ed. H. Cantril) Princeton: Princeton Univ. Press, 1944.

The wording of questions in public opinion polls. *J. abnorm. soc. Psychol.*, 1942, 37, 469–95.

Rundquist, E. A., & Sletto, R. F. *Personality in the depression; a study in the measurement of attitudes.* Minnesota: Univ. Minn. Press, 1930.

Russell, B. *Inquiry into meaning and truth.* New York: Norton, 1940.

Saenger, E., & Proshansky, H. Projective techniques in the service of attitude research. *J. Person.*, 1950, Symposium No. 2, 23–34.

Sanai, M. An experimental study of politico-economic attitudes. *Int. J. Opin. Attit. Res.*, 1950, 4, 563–77.

Sanford, F. H. Authoritarianism and leadership. Philadelphia: Stephenson, 1950.

Sarbin, T. R., & Berdie, R. F. Relation of measured interests to the Allport-Vernon study of values. *J. appl. Psychol.*, 1940, 24, 287–296.

Sargent, S. S. Reaction to frustration. A critique and hypothesis. *Psychol., Rev.*, 1948, 55, 108–15.

Sarnoff, I. Identification with the aggressor: some personality correlates of anti-Semitism among Jews. *J. Person.*, 1951, 20, 199–218.

Schaefer, B. R. The validity and utility of the Allport-Vernon study of values test. *J. abnorm. soc. Psychol.*, 1936, 30, 419–22.

Schanck, R. L. A study of a community and its groups and institutions conceived of as behaviour of individuals. *Psychol. Mon.*, 1932, 43, No. 2, 1–133.

Schoenberg, E. H., & Parten, M. Methods and problems of sampling presented by the Urban Study of Consumer Purchases. *J. Amer. Stat.*, 1937, 32, 311–22.

Schuman, E. A. A logic of scale construction. *Educ. Psychol. Measmt.*, 1950, 10, 79–93.

Scodel, A., & Mussen, P. Social perceptions of authoritarians and non-authoritarians. *J. abnorm. soc. Psychol.*, 1953, 48, 181–4.

Sears, R. Non-aggressive reactions to frustration. *Psychol. Rev.*, 1941, 48, 343–6.

Seashore, H. G. Validation of the study of values for two vocational groups at the college level. *Educ. Psychol. Measmt.*, 1947, 7, 757–64.
, & Bavelas, A. A study of frustration in children. *J. Genet. Psychol.*, 1942, 61, 279–314.

Seltzer, C. C. Phenotype patterns of racial reference and outstanding personality traits. *J. Genet. Psychol.*, 1948, 72, 221–45.

Shand, A. F. *The Foundations of Character.* London: Macmillan, 1914.
The relations of complex and sentiment. III. *Brit. J. Psychol.*, 1922, 13, 123–9.

Shapiro, M. B. Some correlates of opinions on the upbringing of children. *Brit. J. Psychol. (Gen. Sect.)*, 1952, 43, 141–9.

Shapiro, S., & Eberhart, J. C. Interviewer differences in an intensive interview survey. *Int. J. Opin. Attit. Res.*, 1947, 1, 1–17.

Sheatsley, P. B. An analysis of interviewer characteristics and their relationship to performance. *Int. J. Opin. Attit. Res.*, 1950, 4, 473–98.
An analysis of interviewer characteristics and their relationship to performance. Part II. *Int. J. Opin. Attit. Res.*, 1951, 5, 79–94.
An analysis of interviewer characteristics and their relationship to performance: Part III. *Int. J. Opin. Attit. Res.*, 1951, 5, 191–220.

Sherif, M., & Cantril, H. The psychology of 'attitudes'. Part I. *Psychol. Rev.*, 1945, 52, 295–319.

Sherif, M., & Sherif, C. W. *Groups in harmony and tension.* New York: Harper, 1953.

Sherman, M., & Jost, H. Frustration reactions of normal and neurotic persons. *J. Psychol.*, 1942, 13, 3–19.

Sims, V. M. Factors influencing attitude toward the T.V.A. *J. abnorm. soc. Psychol.*, 1938, 33, 34–56.
, & Patrick, J. R. Attitude toward the Negro of Northern and Southern college students. *J. soc. Psychol.*, 1936, 7, 192–203.

Sisson, E. P., & Sisson, B. Introversion and the asthetic attitude. *J. Gen. Psychol.*, 1940, 22, 203–8.

Slutz, M. The unique contribution of the Thematic Apperception Test to developmental study. *Psychol. Bull.*, 1941, 38, 704. (Abstract).

Smith, M. B. Personal values as determinants of a political attitude. *J. Psychol.*, 1949, 28, 477–86.

Spranger, E. *Types of men.* (Trans. 5th German ed. of Lebensformen by P. J. W. Pigors.) Halle: Niemeyer, 1928.

Stagner, R. Fascist attitudes: an exploratory study. *J. soc. Psychol.*, 1936, 7, 306–19.
Fascist attitudes: their determining conditions. *J. soc. Psychol.*, 1936, 7, 438–54.
Correlational analysis of nationalistic opinions. *J. soc. Psychol.*, 1940, 12, 197–212.

Some factors related to attitude toward war, 1938. *J. soc. Psychol.*, *S.P.S.S.I. Bull.*, 1942, 16, 131–42.

Studies of aggressive social attitudes. 1. Measurement and inter-relation of selected attitudes. *J. soc. Psychol.*, 1944, 20, 109–120.

Studies of aggressive social attitudes. II. Changes from peace to war. *J. soc. Psychol.*, 1944, 20, 121–8.

Studies of aggressive social attitudes. III. The role of personal and family scores. *J. soc. Psychol.*, 1944, 20, 129–40.

The conditioning technique applied to a public opinion problem. *J. soc. Psychol.*, 1949, 29, 103–11.

, & Drought, N. Measuring children's attitudes toward their parents. *J. educ. Psychol.*, 1935, 26, 169–76.

, & Katzoff, E. T. Fascist attitudes: a factor analysis of item correlations. *J. soc. Psychol.*, 1942, 16, 3–9.

, & Krout, M. H. Correlational analysis of personality development and structure. *J. abnorm. soc. Psychol.*, 1940, 35, 339–55.

, & Osgood, C. E. An experimental analysis of a nationalistic frame of reference. *J. soc. Psychol.*, *S.P.S.S.I. Bull.*, 1941, 14, 389–401.

Stanton, F., & Baker, K. H. Interviewer-bias and the recall of incompletely learned materials. *Sociom.*, 1942, 5, 123–34.

Stember, H., & Hyman, H. Interviewer effects in the classification of responses. *Pub. Opin. Quart.*, 1949–50, 13, 669–82.

Stephan, F. F. Practical problems of sampling procedure. *Amer. Soc. Rev.*, 1936, 1, 569–80.

History of the uses of modern sampling procedures. *J. Amer. Stat. Ass.*, 1948, 43, 12–39.

Development of election forecasting by polling methods. In: *The pre-election polls of 1948; report to the Committee on Analysis of Pre-Election Polls and Forecasts.* (Ed. F. Mosteller, *et al.*) New York: *Soc. Sci. Res. Co. Bull.*, 1949, 60, 8–14.

Stewart, N., & Flowerman, S. H. An investigation of two different methods for evaluation of interviewer job performance. *Personnel Psychol.*, 1951, 4, 161–70.

Stock, J. S. Some general principles of sampling. In: *Gauging public opinion.* (Ed. H. Cantril) Princeton: Princeton Univ. Press, 1944.

, & Hochstim, J. R. A method of measuring interview variability. *Pub. Opin. Quart.*, 1951, 15, 322–34.

Stone, C. L. The personality factor in vocational guidance. *J. abnorm. soc. Psychol.*, 1933, 28, 274–5.

Stouffer, S. A. An experimental comparison of statistical and case history methods of attitude research. *Ph.D. Thesis*, Univ. Chicago Lib., 1930.

, et al. *Measurement and prediction. Studies in social psychology in World War II, Vol. 4.* Princeton: Princeton Univ. Press, 1950.

, & Macrae, D. Evidence pertaining to last-minute swing to Truman. In: *The pre-election polls of 1948; report to the Committee on Analysis of Pre-Election Polls and Forecasts.* (Ed. F. Mosteller, *et al.*) New York: *Soc. Sci. Res. Co. Bull.*, 1949, 60, 251–62.

Strong, E. K. *Vocational interests of men and women.* Stanford: Stanford Univ. Press, 1948.

Suchman, E. A. A solution to the problem of question 'bias'. *Pub. Opin. Quart.*, 1947, 11 445–55.

Sukhatme, P. V. Contribution to the theory of the representative method. *Roy. Stat. Soc. Suppl.*, 1935, 2, 253–68.

Super, D. A. *Appraising vocational fitness.* New York: Harper, 1949.

Symington, T. A. Religious liberals and conservatives. *Teach. Coll. Contrib. Educ.*, 1935, No. 640.

Symonds, P. M. A social attitudes questionnaire. *J. educ. Psychol.*, 1925, 16, 316–22.

What is an attitude? *Psychol. Bull.*, 1927, 24, 200–1.

, & Dietrich, D. H. The effect of variations in the time interval between an interview and its recording. *J. abnorm. soc. Psychol.*, 1941, 36, 593–8.

Tansley, A. G. *The new psychology and its relation to life.* New York: Dodd, Mead, 1920.

The relations of complex and sentiment. II. *Brit. J. Psychol.*, 1922, 13, 113–22.

Telford, C. W. An experimental study of some factors influencing the social attitudes of college students. *J. soc. Psychol.*, 1934, 5, 421–8.

Thomas, W. I., & Znaniecki, F. *The Polish peasant in Europe and America. Vol. I.* Boston: Badger, 1918.

Thouless, R. H. The tendency to certainty in religious beliefs. *Brit. J. Psychol.*, 1935, 26, 16–31.

Thurstone, L. L. A law of comparative judgment. *Psychol. Rev.*, 1927, 34, 273–86.

The method of paired comparisons for social values. *J. abnorm. soc. Psychol.*, 1927, 21, 384–400.

Attitudes can be measured. *Amer. J. Sociol.*, 1928, 33, 529–54.

The measurement of opinion. *J. abnorm. soc. Psychol.*, 1928, 22, 415–430.

Theory of attitude measurement. *Psychol. Rev.*, 1929, 36, 222–41.

The measurement of social attitudes. *J. abnorm. soc. Psychol.*, 1931, 26, 249–69.

A factorial study of perception. Chicago: Univ. Chicago Press, 1944.

BIBLIOGRAPHY

In: *A history of psychology in autobiography. Vol. IV.* (Ed. E. G. Boring, et al.) Worcester: Clark Univ. Press, 1952.

—, & Chave, E. J. *The measurement of attitude.* Chicago: Univ. Chicago Press, 1929.

Titchener, E. B. *A text-book of psychology.* New York: Macmillan, 1910.

Tolman, E. C. The determiners of behaviour at a choice point. *Psychol. Rev.*, 1938, 45, 1–41.

Tomkins, S. S. Limits of material obtainable in the single case study by daily administration of the Thematic Apperception Test. *Psychol. Bull.*, 1942, 39, 490.

Traxler, A. E. The correlation between two tests of academic aptitude. *Sch. & Soc.*, 1945, 61, 383–4.

Truman, D. B. Political behaviour and voting. In: *The pre-election polls of 1948. Report to the Committee on Analysis of Pre-Election Polls and Forecasts.* (Ed. F. Mosteller, et al.) New York: *Soc. Sci. Res. Co. Bull.*, 1949, 60, 225–50.

Turnbull, W. Secret versus non-secret ballots. In: *Gauging public opinion.* (Ed. H. Cantril) Princeton: Princeton Univ. Press, 1944.

Tussing, L. An investigation of the possibilities of measuring personality traits with the Strong Vocational Interest Blank. *Educ. & Psychol. Measmt.*, 1942, 2, 59–74.

Tuttle, H. S. Habit and attitude. *J. educ. Psychol.*, 1930, 21, 418–28.

van Dusen, A. C. Wimberley, E., & Mosier, C. I., Standardization of a values inventory. *J. educ. Psychol.*, 1939, 30, 53–62.

Vaughn, C. L., & Reynolds, W. A. Reliability of personal interview data. *J. appl. Psychol.*, 1951, 35, 61–3.

Vernon, P. E., & Allport, G. W. A test for personal values. *J. abnorm. soc. Psychol.*, 1931, 26, 231–48.

Vetter, G. B. The measurement of social and political attitudes and the related personality factors. *J. abnorm. soc. Psychol.*, 1930, 25, 149–189.

Wedell, C., & Smith, K. U. Consistency of interview methods in appraisal of attitudes. *J. appl. Psychol.*, 1951, 35, 392–6.

Welch L., & Kubis, J. The effect of anxiety on the conditioning rate and stability of the P.G.R. *J. Psychol.*, 1947, 23, 83–91.

— Conditioned P.G.R. (psychogalvanic response) in states of pathological anxiety. *J. nerv. ment. Dis.*, 1947, 105, 372–81.

Werner, H. Abnormal and subnormal rigidity. *J. abnorm. soc. Psychol.*, 1946, 41, 15–24.

Weschler, I. R., & Bernberg, R. E. Indirect methods of attitude measurement. *Pub. Opin. Quart.*, *Spring*, 1951, 209–138.

White, R. W. Prediction of hypnotic suggestibility from a knowledge of subjects' attitudes. *J. Psychol.*, 1937, 3, 265–77.

The interpretation of imaginative productions. In: *Personality and the behaviour disorders, Vol. I*. (Ed. J. Mc. V. Hunt) New York: Ronald Press, 1944.

Whiteley, P. L. A study of the Allport-Vernon test for personal values. *J. abnorm. soc. Psychol.*, 1933, 28, 6–13.

The constancy of personal values. *J. abnorm. soc. Psychol.*, 1938, 35, 405–8.

Wilks, S. S. Objectives and limitations. In: *The pre-election polls of 1948. Report to the Committee on Analysis of Pre-Election Polls and Forecasts*. (Ed. F. Mosteller, *et al.*) New York: *Soc. Sci. Res. Co. Bull.*, 1949, 60, 1–7.

Willems, E. Racial attitudes in Brazil. *Amer. J. Sociol.*, 1949, 54, 402–408.

Williams, D. Basic instructions for interviewers. *Pub. Opin. Quart.*, 1942, 6, 634–41.

Williams, F. Information as a determinant of opinion. In: *Gauging public opinion.* (Ed. H. Cantril) Princeton: Princeton Univ. Press, 1947.

, & Mosteller, F. Education and economic status as determinants of opinion. In: *Gauging public opinion.* (Ed. H. Cantril) Princeton: Princeton Univ. Press, 1944.

Wilson, E. C. The measurement of public opinion. *Ann. Amer. Acad. Polit. Sci.*, 1947, 250, 121–9.

Woodward, J. L., & Franzen, R. A study of coding reliability. *Pub. Opin. Quart.*, 1948, 12, 253–7.

Woofter, T. J. Common errors in sampling. *Soc. Forces*, 1933, 11, 521–525.

Wright, M. E. Constructiveness of play as affected by group organization and frustration. *Char. & Person.*, 1942, 11, 40–9.

Wyatt, D. F., & Campbell, D. T. A study of interviewer bias as related to interviewers' expectations and own opinions. *Int. J. Opin. Attit. Res.*, 1950, 4, 77–83.

Wyatt, F. Formal aspects of the Thematic Apperception Test. *Psychol. Bull.*, 1942, 39, 491.

Advances in the techniques of the Thematic Apperception Test. *Psychol. Bull.*, 1945, 42, 532.

Yates, F. Systematic Sampling. *Roy. Soc. Phil. Trans.*, 1948, A. 241, 345–77.

Sampling methods for censuses and surveys. London: Griffin, 1949.

Zander, A. F. A study of experimental frustration. *Psychol. Mon.*, 1944, 56, 3, 38.

Zauradski, B. Limitations of the scapegoat theory of prejudice. *J. abnorm. soc. Psychol.*, 1948, 43, 127–41.

Zeleny, L. D. Selection of the unprejudiced. *Sociomet.*, 1947, 10, 396–401.

Zeligs, R., & Hendrickson, G. Racial attitudes of 200 sixth-grade children. *Sociol. & soc. Res.*, 1933–4, 18, 26–36.

INDEX

Abrams, M., 273
Accuracy of Sampling, 49
Ackoff, R. L., 273
Actuality, 52
Adams, C. R., 282
Adcock, C. J., 275
Adorno, T. W., 147
Aesthetic preferences, 181
A.F. of L., 51
Age, 22, 27, 126
Aggression, 149, 199, 203
Allport, G. W., 4, 12, 161, 269, 283
American Institute of Public Opinion, 57, 59, 61
Anderson, D., 273
Anderson, R. G., 280
Andrews, A. L., 280
Anti-Semitism, 81, 89, 148
Anxiety, 175
Apicella, F. S., 282
Area Sampling, 42, 44
Artificial insemination, 53
Asch, S., 4, 185, 189
Associationism, 244
Atom bomb, 36
Attitudes, 12, 17, 31, 112, 247, 265
Attitude inventory, 122
Attitude scales, 98
Attneave, F., 276
Authoritarianism, 111, 149, 153, 193, 202
Autokinetic phenomenon, 105, 186, 225

Bain, A., 10
Bain, R., 269
Baker, K. H., 274
Balken, E. R., 282
Ballin, M. R., 276
Barker, R., 282
Barnette, W. L., 274

Baron, F., 4, 182, 184, 189
Bauer, R. A., 275
Bavelas, A., 282
Beeton, Mrs., 38
Bell, J. E., 282
Bellak, L., 282
Benjamin, A. C., 270
Benson, E. G., 273
Benson, S., 274
Berdie, R. F., 274, 280
Bernard, L. L., 269
Bertocci, P. A., 269
Bias, 55, 66
Birch, A. H., 273
Bittner, R. H., 276
Blankenship, A. B., 273, 274, 275
Block, J., 225
Bogardus, E. S., 82, 269
Booman, W. P., 274
Bowley, A. L., 274
British Institute of Public Opinion, 16, 31, 42, 44, 53, 76
Brogden, H. E., 163
Bruner, J. S., 275
Bulldogs, 253
Bunche, R., 156
Burgemeister, B. B., 280

Cahalan, D., 274, 275
Campbell, A. A., 273, 274
Campbell, D. T., 274
Campbell, P., 273
Cantril, H., 51, 54, 58, 59, 62, 67, 269, 273, 274, 275
Cardinal measurement, 98
Carlson, M. B., 276
Carnap, R., 270
Cattell, R. B., 4, 115, 269, 271
Census, 38

Centers, R., 16, 20, 22, 24, 27, 28, 139
Chapin, F. S., 273, 275
Chappell, M. N., 273
Chave, E. J., 269, 275
Cheating, 104
Chein, I., 283
Child rearing, 192
Churchman, C. W., 273, 275
C.I.O., 5
Clark, K. E., 274, 275
Clarkson, E. P., 274
Class, social, 14, 19, 134
Cochran, W. G., 274
Combs, A. W., 282
Commercial television, 53
Communist, 3, 104, 137, 152, 180, 202, 221
Complex, 12
Complexity factor, 182, 189
Concreteness of thinking, 227
Conditioning, 244, 255, 262
Connelly, G. M., 274, 275
Conscientious objectors, 104
Conservatism, 14, 85, 112, 126, 128, 137, 148, 170, 178, 179
Consistency, coefficient of, 72
Conventionalism, 149
Coolidge, C., 156
Corey, S. M., 104
Cornfield, J., 274
Corporal punishment, 34
Correlation coefficient, 18, 114
Cosine law, 115
Coulter, T., 4, 140, 152, 179, 202, 224, 276, 283
Cowen, E. L., 230
Craig, A. T., 274
Crespi, L. P., 274, 275
Crissy, W. J. E., 162, 168
Crown, S., 4, 81, 275
Crutchfield, R. S., 274

Davidson, H. H., 191, 276
Davidson, P. E., 273
Davis, A., 259
Death penalty, 34
Deckinger, E. L., 275
De Grazia, S., 274
Dembo, T., 282
Deming, W. E., 274
Democratic party, 23, 25, 40, 75
Denier, 108
Depression, 177

Dewey, J., 269
Dicks, H. V., 263
Dietrich, D. H., 274
Division of opinion, 49
Divorce, 36
Dodd, S. C., 275
Dog-Cat Test, 223
Dollard, J., 215, 275, 282
Dominance, 203
Doob, L. W., 282, 283
Drives, 251
Duffy, E., 162, 168
Durant, H., 4
Dysthymia, 262

Eberhart, J. C., 274
Eddison, T., 156
Education, 20, 26, 28, 126
Edwards, A. L., 276
Eisenstein, D., 283
Eldersveld, S. J., 275
Ellison, C. G., 283
Engels, F., 15
Eriksen, C. W., 283
Ethnocentrism, 85, 148, 184, 192, 220
Extraversion, 174, 177, 196
Eysenck, H. J., 81, 148, 184, 275, 276, 284

Factor analysis, 94
Fadner, R. H., 275
Faris, E., 269
Farnsworth, P. R., 276
Fascism scale, 157
Fascist, 3, 137, 152, 180, 202, 221
Ferguson, L. W., 145, 148, 156, 170, 276, 280
Festinger, L., 4, 275
Field, H. H., 274
Fillibuster, 51
Fink, K., 275
Fischer, R. P., 280
Fisher, S., 274
Flogging, 34
Flowerman, S. H., 274
Ford, R. N., 275
Forlano, G., 280
Flugel, J., 4, 5
Fortune, 51, 54
Franklin, B., 156
Franks, C., 262
Franzen, R. H., 273, 275
Freeman, G. I., 282

French, V. V., 269
Frenkel-Brunswik, E., 4, 147, 192, 195, 221, 231, 233
Force scale, 158
Frederiksen, N., 282
Freiberg, A. D., 275
Freyre, G., 275
Frustration-aggression hypothesis, 215

Gallup, G., 273, 274
Garrison, R. C., 283
Gaudet, H., 274
Gauge, 108
Gallup, G., 40, 54, 76, 79
Gallup poll, 40, 42
Galton, F., 240
George, E. I., 4, 175, 177, 276, 281
Gerberich, J. B., 275
Gill, M., 282
Gill, S., 52
Gleicher, D. B., 273
Goldish, S., 275
Goodstein, L. D., 283
Goring, C., 240
Gosnell, H. F., 274
Gough, H. C., 192, 195, 231
Gross, O., 174
Guest, L., 274, 275
Guilford, J. P., 176, 275
Gundlach, R. H., 275
Guttman, L., 275

Habit, 242, 246
Haggard, E. A., 282
Hall, J., 271
Haner, C. F., 274
Hanna, H. S., 274
Hansen, M. H., 274
Harding, J., 69
Harris, A. J., 283
Harris, D., 280
Harris, D. B., 192
Harris, N., 274
Harrison, R., 282
Hartley, E. L., 240, 275
Hartmann, G. W., 241, 280
Hartshorne, H., 105
Hatt, P., 276
Hauskrecht, G., 275
Havighurst, R. J., 274
Hayes, S. P., 273
Hedonism, 244
Helfant, K., 191

Heneman, H. G., 274
Height, measurement of, 80
Hendrickson, G., 275
Hildebrand, H. P., 177
Hilgard, E. R., 274
Himmelweit, H. T., 259, 282
Hochstim, J. R., 274, 275
Hofstaetter, P. F., 52, 242, 274
Homeostasis, 256
Hooper, C. E., 273
Hoover, H., 40, 156
Horne, E. P., 269
Hull, C. L., 13, 245, 270
Humanitarianism, 146
Humphreys, L. G., 280
Hurwitz, W. N., 274
Hyman, H., 274, 275
Hysteria, 175, 182, 262

Idealism, 165
Ideology, 113
Impulsiveness, 182
Independence of judgment, 190
Instability, 177
Intelligence, 209, 221, 235
Interests, 166
Intervening variables, 13
Interviewing, 65
Intolerance of ambiguity, 210, 221, 224
Introspectiveness, 177
Introversion, 174

Jahn, J. A., 275
James, W., 119, 130, 170, 199
Janis, I. L., 275
Janowitz, M., 275
Jenkins, J. G., 274
Jensen, A., 274
Johnson, C. S., 102
Jones, D. C., 271, 273
Jones, G. S., 283
Jost, H., 282
Jung, C. G., 171

Katz, D., 68, 273
Katz, M. R., 275
Kaufmann, F., 270
Kempf, E. J., 269
Kendig, I. V., 282
Kenney, K. C., 276
Kerr, W. A., 273
Kilpatrick, F. P., 276
King, M. B., 275

INDEX

Kinsey, A. C., 260
Kitt, A. S., 273
Klare, G. R., 274
Koestler, A., 132
Kornhauser, A., 274
Kriedt, P. H., 275
Krout, M. H., 191
Kroeger, H. J., 274
Kubis, J., 261
Kulp, D. H., 276

LaPiere, R. T., 239
Larsen, O. N., 274
Lasswell, H. D., 191
Lazarsfeld, P. F., 29, 74, 273, 274
Leadership, 153
Learning theory, 243
Levinson, E. J., 4, 147
Lewin, K., 282
Liberalism, 111, 126, 137, 179
Likert, R., 4, 102, 274, 283
Lindzey, G., 179, 215
Link, H. C., 274, 275
Linn, E. L., 273
Lippitt, R., 282
Lippmann, W., 240
Literary Digest, 39, 46
Loevinger, J., 276
Luchins, A. S., 219
Lundberg, G. A., 274
Lurie, W. A., 162
Lutz, R. G., 275
Lydgate, W. A., 273

Madow, W., 274
Majority influence, 188
Mangus, A. R., 274
Manheimer, D., 274
Maps Test, 220
Marquis, D. P., 282
Martin, F. M., 192, 271
Marx, K., 15
Masserman, J. H., 282
May, M. A., 105
McCarthy, T. J., 275, 280
McClelland, L. C., 282
MacCorquodale, K., 270
McCreary, J. R., 275
McDougall, W., 10, 11, 12, 110, 215
McKinnon, D, W. 4
McLeod, H., 196
McNemar, Q., 79, 273, 274
Meehl, P. E., 4, 270

Meier, N. C., 274, 275
Meltzer, H., 275
Melvin, D., 4, 132, 140, 152, 276
Metallic Metals Act, 52
Miller, N. E., 282
M.M.P.I., 231
Monachesi, E. D., 273
Moore, G., 283
Morgan, C. D., 269, 282
Morgan, R., 275
Mosteller, F., 73, 75, 76, 275
Mowrer, O. H., 4, 256
Multiple choice questions, 50
Murphy, G., 283
Murray, H. A., 269, 282

Nationalization, 35
National Opinion Research Centre, 68
Nelson, E., 269
Negro prejudice, 102
Neumann, G. B., 104
Neuroticism, 177, 235
Newcomb, T. M., 4, 191
Neyman, J., 274
Nuckols, R., 274
Nylon stockings, 108
Nystrom, G. H., 103

Office of Public Opinion Research, 55,
    57, 69
Ojemann, R. H., 276
Open end questions, 50
Opinion, 111
Ordinal measurement, 98

Pace, C. R., 275
Pacifist, 104
Parker, C. E., 275
Parks, R. E., 269
Parten, M., 274
Paterson, D. G., 274, 275
Patrick, J. R., 102
Pavlov, I. P., 244, 255
Payne, S. L., 57, 58, 274
Pear, T. H., 269
Peatman, J. G., 275
Perception, 248
Persistence forecasting, 76
Personalization, 58
Peters, R., 280
Picture Frustration Test, 216, 231
Pintner, R., 280
Politcal predisposition, 30

INDEX

Politics, 7
Porter, G., 104
Postman, L., 248
Presidential Election, 29, 39, 76
Principle of certainty, 120
Pritchard, E. E., 269
Profit, 51
Projectivity, 149
Psychology, types of, 9
Psychopathy, 175
Punitiveness, 201
Pyle, W. H., 269

Question wording, 50
Quota sampling, 42

Radicalism, 14, 85, 128, 170, 178, 193
Radvanyi, L., 273
Rae, S. F., 273
Random sampling, 41
Rapaport, D., 282
Rapport, 67
Realpolitik, 120
Red Devils, 253
Reference axes, 117
Refusals in interviewing, 69
Reichenbach, H., 270
Reification of thinking, 227
Reinforcement, 244
Reliability, 71, 92
Religion, 21, 29, 30, 33
Religionism, 146
Remembering, 247
Remmers, H. H., 283
Reproducability, 96
Republican Party, 23, 25, 29, 40, 43, 75
Reynolds, W. A., 74, 275
Rhathymia, 176
Rice, S. A., 269
Rieken, H. W., 275
Rigidity, 182, 210, 218
Rigidity scale, 222
Rivers, W. H. R., 269
Robinson, C., 273
Robinson, W. S., 274
Rogers, L., 273
Rokeach, M., 4, 219, 227
Roosevelt, E., 156
Roosevelt, F. D., 40, 46
Roosevelt, T., 156
Roper, E., 56
Rorschach Test, 230
Rosenzweig, S., 201, 282

Rothney, J. W. M., 280
Rotter, J. B., 282
Rugg, D., 60, 274
Rundquist, E. A., 276
Russell, B., 270

Sampling, 38, 39, 77
Sampling error, 47
Sanai, M., 276
Sanford, F. H., 153, 200
Sanford, N., 4, 147
Sarbin, T. R., 280
Sargent, S. S., 282
Scale of values, 231
Scalogram, 96
Scalogram analysis, 94
Scapegoat theory, 215
Schaefer, B. R., 280
Schafer, R., 282
Schanck, R. L., 239
Schneider, B. H., 248
Schoenberg, E. H., 274
Schuman, E. A., 276
Sears, R., 282
Seashore, H. G., 242, 280
Secret polling, 65
Sentiment, 10
Sex, 126
Sex hygiene, 32
Shand, A. F., 10, 269
Shapiro, M. B., 4, 193
Shapiro, S., 274
Sheatsley, P. B., 274
Sheerness, 118
Sherif, M., 105, 185, 252, 269, 275
Sherman, M., 282
Sims, V. M., 102, 103
Sisson, E. P., 280
Skinner, B. F., 244, 255
Sletto, R. F., 276
Slutz, M., 282
Smith, A., 10
Smith, D. M. K., 274
Smith, K. U., 275
Smith, M. B., 280
Sociability, 177
Social distance, 82, 240
Social Science Research Council, 275
Socialism, 126, 137, 179
Socialization, 259
Spencer, H., 10
Split Ballot technique, 54
Spranger, E., 159

Stability, coefficient of, 72
Stagner, R., 156, 191, 199, 276
Stanton, F., 274
Status, 14, 19
Stember, H., 274
Stephan, F. F., 273, 274
Stereotypes, 57, 239
Stewart, N., 274
Stock, J. S., 275
Stout, G. F., 10
Stratification, 15, 27
Stratified sampling, 41
Stone, C. L., 280
Strong, E. K., 166, 167, 280
Strong, F. W., 280
Study of values, 161
Submissiveness, 184
Suchman, E. A., 274
Sukhatme, P. V., 274
Sunday observance, 33
Super, D. A., 169
Superstition, 149
Svehla, G., 191
Symington, T. A., 283
Symonds, P. M., 269, 274, 283

Tamulonis, V., 274
Tansley, A. G., 269
Telford, C. W., 104
Thematic Apperception Test, 179, 202, 216
Thomas, W. I., 269
Thompson, G. G., 230
Thouless, R. H., 120
Thurstone, L. L., 3, 4, 167, 269, 275, 276
T.V.A., 103
Tender-mindedness, 119, 130, 170, 178, 190, 193
Titchener, E. B., 269
Tolman, E. C., 270
Tomkins, S. S., 282
Tough-mindedness, 119, 130, 170, 178, 180, 190, 199, 218, 230
Trait, 171
Traxler, A. E., 280

Truman, H. S., 156
Turnbull, W., 66
Tussing, L., 280
Tuttle, H. S., 269
Twin Studies, 197
Two way questions, 50
Type, 171

Unidimensionality, 96

Validity, 71, 92, 100
Values, 159
Van Dusen, A. L., 168
Vaughn, C. L., 74, 275
Verner, H. W., 274
Vernon, P. E., 161
Vetter, G. B., 283
Voting behaviour, 15

War, 35
Washington, George, 156
Water Jar Test, 219
Wax, M., 273, 275
Wedell, C., 275
Welch, L., 261
Welsh, G. S., 182, 282
White, R. K., 282
White, R. W., 282
Whiteley, P. L., 280
Wicoff, E., 273
Willems, E., 275
Williams, D., 274
Wilson, E. C., 273, 274
Woodward, J. L., 275
Woofter, T. J., 274
Wright, M. E., 282
Wyatt, D. F., 274
Wyatt, F., 282

Yates, F., 274

Zander, A. F., 282
Zeligs, R., 275
Znaniecki, F., 269